S0-AUQ-136

Netscape Communicator: A Jumpstart Tutorial

LIMITED WARRANTY AND DISCLAIMER OF LIABILITY

THIS PRODUCT MAY BE USED ON A SINGLE PC ONLY. THE LICENSE DOES NOT PERMIT THE USE ON A NETWORK (OF ANY KIND). YOU FURTHER AGREE THAT THIS LICENSE GRANTS PERMISSION TO USE THE PRODUCTS CONTAINED HEREIN, BUT DOES NOT GIVE YOU RIGHT OF OWNERSHIP TO ANY OF THE CONTENT OR PRODUCT CONTAINED ON THIS CD. USE OF THIRD PARTY SOFTWARE CONTAINED ON THIS CD IS LIMITED TO AND SUBJECT TO LICENSING TERMS FOR THE RESPECTIVE PRODUCTS. USE, DUPLICA-TION OR DISCLOSURE BY THE UNITED STATES GOVERNMENT OR ITS AGENCIES ARE LIMITED BY FAR 52.227-7013 OR FAR 52.227-19, AS APPROPRIATE.

CHARLES RIVER MEDIA, INC. ("CRM") AND/OR ANYONE WHO HAS BEEN INVOLVED IN THE WRITING, CREATION OR PRODUCTION OF THE ACCOMPANYING CODE ("THE SOFTWARE"), OR THE THIRD PARTY PRODUCTS CONTAINED ON THIS CD, CANNOT AND DO NOT WARRANT THE PERFORMANCE OR RESULTS THAT MAY BE OBTAINED BY USING THE SOFTWARE. THE AUTHOR AND PUBLISHER HAVE USED THEIR BEST EF-FORTS TO ENSURE THE ACCURACY AND FUNCTIONALITY OF THE TEXTUAL MATERIAL AND PROGRAMS CONTAINED HEREIN; HOWEVER, WE MAKE NO WARRANTY OF ANY KIND, EXPRESSED OR IMPLIED, REGARDING THE PERFORMANCE OF THESE PRO-GRAMS.THE SOFTWARE IS SOLD "AS IS " WITHOUT WARRANTY (EXCEPT FOR DEFECTIVE MATERIALS USED IN MANUFACTURING THE DISK OR DUE TO FAULTY WORKMANSHIP); THE SOLE REMEDY IN THE EVENT OF A DEFECT IS EXPRESSLY LIMITED TO REPLACE-MENT OF THE DISK, AND ONLY AT THE DISCRETION OF CRM.

THE AUTHOR, THE PUBLISHER, DEVELOPERS OF THIRD PARTY SOFTWARE, AND ANY-ONE INVOLVED IN THE PRODUCTION AND MANUFACTURING OF THIS WORK SHALL NOT BE LIABLE FOR DAMAGES OF ANY KIND ARISING OUT OF THE USE OF(OR THE IN-ABILITY TO USE) THE PROGRAMS, SOURCE CODE, OR TEXTUAL MATERIAL CONTAINED IN THIS PUBLICATION. THIS INCLUDES , BUT IS NOT LIMITED TO, LOSS OF REVENUE OR PROFIT, OR OTHER INCIDENTAL OR CONSEQUENTIAL DAMAGES ARISING OUT OF THE USE OF THE PRODUCT.

THE USE OF "IMPLIED WARRANTY" AND CERTAIN "EXCLUSIONS" VARY FROM STATE TO STATE, AND MAY NOT APPLY TO THE PURCHASER OF THIS PRODUCT.

Netscape Communicator: A Jumpstart Tutorial

Elisabeth Parker

CHARLES RIVER MEDIA, INC.
Rockland, Massachusetts

Copyright © 1997 by CHARLES RIVER MEDIA, INC.
All rights reserved.

No part of this publication may be reproduced in any way, stored in a retrieval system of any type , or transmitted by any means or media, electronic or mechanical including, but not limited to, photocopy, recording, or scanning, without *prior written permission* from the publisher.

Executive Editor: Jenifer L. Niles
Interior Design/Comp: Publishers' Design and Production Services, Inc.
Cover Design: Marshall Henrichs
Printer: InterCity Press, Rockland, MA

CHARLES RIVER MEDIA, Inc.
P.O. Box 417, 403 VFW Drive
Rockland, MA 02370
781-871-4184
781-871-4376(FAX)
chrivmedia@aol.com
http://www.charlesriver.com

This book is printed on acid-free paper

Netscape screen shots *Copyright 1996 Netscape Communications Corp. Used with permission. All Rights Reserved. This electronic file or page may not be reprinted or copied without the express written permission of Netscape.*

Netscape Communications Corporation has not authorized, sponsored, or endorsed, or approved this publication and is not responsible for its content. Netscape and the Netscape Communications Corporate Logos, are trademarks and trade names of Netscape Communications Corporation. All other product names and/or logos are trademarks of their respective owners.

All brand names and product names mentioned are trademarks or service marks of their respective companies. Any omission or misuse (of any kind) of service marks or trademarks should not be regarded as intent to infringe on the property of others. The publisher recognizes and respects all marks used by companies, manufacturers, and developers as a means to distinguish their products.

Netscape Communicator: A Jumpstart Tutorial
by Elisabeth Parker
   ISBN 1-886801-64-9
   Printed in the United States of America

97 98 99 00 7 6 5 4 3 2 1 First Printing

CHARLES RIVER MEDIA titles are available for site license or bulk purchase by institutions, user groups, corporations, etc. For additional information, please contact the Special Sales Department at 781-871-4184.

DEDICATION

To San Francisco, my fabulous new home.

Contents

Acknowledgments

I would like to thank the following people for helping me out with this book:

Dave Mercer wrote the chapters on Composer, Netscape Conference, and using Netscape's server products. He owns and operates AFC Computer Services, an Internet/Intranet programming and Web site development company based in Spring Valley, CA. He still owns his first computer, a Commodore 64. Dave also writes articles for ComputorEdge, San Diego's home grown computer magazine. You can visit Dave's Web site at http://www.afc-net.com/ or email him at mercer@afcnet.com.

Peter Dyke (http:// www.compuvar.com) and Bruce MacFarland contributed their expertise and gave us lots of helpful hints

Rich Grace and Puddy kept me company.

Jenifer Niles, my editor, kept things moving along.

Suzanne Anthony and the other people at Netscape sent a steady supply of preview CDs and updates so we could get the server chapters done.

Dave Fugate is my fabulous agent.

Thanks, every one!

Introduction

Congratulations on getting Netscape Communicator. Whether you use the Internet for business or fun, Communicator makes your time in cyberspace more productive and enjoyable. And while everyone loves cruising the Web with Netscape's popular Navigator browser, there's a whole lot more to Communicator than that. Think of it as an entire system that puts the information you need at your fingertips and lets you communicate effectively with others. Sure, you can have lots of fun with Communicator. But it's also a valuable business tool that helps you work better.

With Communicator, home users and business users can do the following:

- Browse the Web and enjoy exciting cutting-edge Web page content.
- Download useful shareware and explore other Internet resources.
- Send and receive HTML-formatted email messages with live content (and regular emails too)
- Create basic Web pages even if you're a complete beginner
- Participate in public news groups and office discussion groups focused on just about any topic.
- Teleconference with voice and data communications via the Internet
- Subscribe to automatically updating channels with Netcaster
- Schedule meetings and use of office resources with your colleagues with Netscape Calendar (Communicator Pro version only)
- and more!

If you're new to the Internet, dive in! Communicator makes every thing easy. Meanwhile, if you're experienced, you'll be excited about all the things you can do with Communicator.

What's in this Book?

Communicator's user-friendly design goes along way towards making your online experiences more productive and enjoyable. However, we could all use a little help with setting up the program and making the most of its capabilities. Whether you purchased Communicator for your home computer, found it installed on your computer at work one day, or got Communicator from your Internet service provider (Earthlink at http://www.earthlink.com/ provides its customers with Communicator), The *Netscape Communicator Jumpstart Tutorial* can get you up and running.

The book is organized so you can explore Communicator at your own pace – or quickly learn about specific features as the need arises. Step-by-step instructions with illustrations make installing, customizing, and using Communicator a painless process. I also understand that everyone uses their computers in different ways. Whether you use Communicator at home, in the office, or on the road, I've done my best to address your needs.

The *Netscape Communicator Jumpstart Tutorial* covers everything from getting and installing Communicator to the basics of setting up Netscape server products on an Intranet so you and your coworkers can use Communicator's Calendar enterprise scheduling tools, set up in-house discussion groups, distribute custom versions of Communicator that are tailored to your organization's users and needs, and automate processes so that maintaining your Intranet server doesn't take every minute of your day.

This book covers the following:

- **Chapter 1. The Internet and Intranets:** Briefly covers the difference between the Internet and office Intranets, what they have to offer, and how they evolved.
- **Chapter 2. Netscape Communicator at a Glance:** Introduces you to what you can do with Communicator – such as browse Web pages, view multimedia and other files with plug-ins, send email, subscribe to channels, and more.
- **Chapter 3. Setting Up Communicator:** Gets you started by telling you how to get Communicator and how to install it with the Set up wizard.
- **Chapter 4. Test Driving Navigator:** Takes you for a quick ride so you can familiarize yourself with Navigator's features. Navigator, Netscape's popular browser, is now an important part of Communicator.
- **Chapter 5. Setting Preferences:** As you become more familiar with Communicator, you can tailor it to your needs. You also need to enter

your Mail and News preferences so you can send and receive email and participate in news and discussion groups.

- **Chapter 6. Receiving Channels with Netcaster:** Server push is the hottest new thing on the Internet. With Netcaster, you don't browse the Web looking for information. You subscribe to channels and the information comes to you.

- **Chapter 7. Working with Plug-ins:** Plug-ins make the Web more fun and functional. With the right plug-ins, you run applications and launch files straight from your Web browser. You can view live video broadcasts, collaborate on projects with coworkers, explore virtual reality worlds, and more.

- **Chapter 8. Marking Your Itinerary with Bookmarks:** If you like a Web site and want to visit again, bookmark it! This chapter explains how Navigator's Bookmarks feature helps you maintain and organize lists of useful and interesting places to go.

- **Chapter 9. Finding Resources:** Sure, the "Information Superhighway" has lots to offer. But where's the road map? Search engines can help. This chapter explains how to use search engines and points you towards some places of interest.

- **Chapter 10. Managing Communications with the Message Center:** You'd be surprised at how fast email and news and discussion group messages can pile up. Fortunately, the Message Center helps you keep everything organized and manage it all

- **Chapter 11. Emailing With Messenger:** Every body loves email. This chapter tells you how to send, receive, organize, format, and attach files to your email messages in Messenger, Communicator's email component.

- **Chapter 12. Participating in News and Discussion Groups:** Think of news and discussion groups as a community bulletin board studded with a lively jumble of messages. You can ask questions, help out with answers, and participate in lively discussions on a variety of topics. News and discussion groups also help coworkers who hardly ever get to see each other get to know one another and communicate more effectively.

- **Chapter 13. Email, News, and More for People On the Go:** You can also download email, news and discussion groups, channels, and Calendar information, then view and work with everything offline. Working offline is useful for people who travel a lot or who don't have a dedicated Internet connection.

- **Chapter 14. Keeping Track of Contacts with Your Address Book:** Who can remember hundreds of email addresses? Not me. That's why Communicator comes with an Address Book. Think of it as your electronic rolodex.
- **Chapter 15. Setting Up for Conference Calls:** Yes – believe it or not, you can actually make a phone call over the Internet. But first you have to set up Netscape Conference, Communicator's teleconferencing component.
- **Chapter 16. Using Netscape Conference:** Once Conference is ready to go, you can start having online conference meetings ... or long telephone conversations with your friends from far away! You can also exchange files, share images and other data on the whiteboard, and more.
- **Chapter 17. Creating HTML Documents with Composer:** Not only does Communicator turn you into a savvy cyberspace denizen, it also turns you into a Web master. Whether you want to finally use that free Web folder space your Internet service provider offers its customers, or need to churn out daily updates at work for your Intranet Web site, Composer makes it easy.
- **Chapter 18. Security Features and Doing Business Online:** Sure, the Web lets you download all kinds of neat stuff and order from online catalogues. But is it safe? What about computer viruses and credit fraud? Fortunately Communicator has lots of security features so you can do business online and transfer data without worries.
- **Chapter 19. Customizing Communicator for Your Network:** Do you have an Intranet server at work? You can create customized copies of Communicator tailored to your organization's needs and integrate Communicator with Netscape server products.
- **Chapter 20. Setting Up News Groups with Collabra:** Netscape's Collabra server helps you make the most of in-house discussion groups. Sure, running a server is a complicated undertaking. But this chapter can get you started.
- **Chapter 21. Enterprise Scheduling with Calendar:** As you probably know, scheduling meetings in an office is one of the more aggravating things in life. Calendar can help you and your colleagues work together and plan more effectively by keeping track of people and office resources. This chapter tells you how to use Calendar and gets you up and running with Netscape's Calendar server.

To make your life easier, I've even included an appendix with a glossary and index so you can look things up when you get stuck.

Helpful Icons

The *Netscape Communicator Jumpstart Tutorial* uses helpful icons throughout the book to highlight information that you might find important. While reading, keep an eye out for the following:

Offers a helpful hint or neat little trick you can use.

Lets you know when you might run into trouble

Points out useful information.

The Internet Keeps Changing

The Internet changes constantly—and so do Internet applications like Communicator. Some organizations and individuals change their home pages every day. This makes the Internet dynamic and vital but it can also prove a little inconvenient. New sites keep cropping up all the time, while others move to new locations or discontinue publication.

I have done my best to point you towards the latest resources and information. However, you may find that some of the Web sites displayed in the book illustrations don't look the same any more. You may also discover that some changes have been made to Communicator since the time of this writing.

Email Me or Visit My Home Page!

With the previous caveat in mind, please feel free to email me or visit my home page if you want to ask questions, make suggestions, pass along information, offer feed back, or (hopefully!) shower me with praise.

My email address is eparker@byteit.com and my Web site is located at http://www.byteit.com/. I also plan on maintaining a Web page devoted to questions and updates, so drop by some time!

About the Author

Elisabeth A. Parker is a technology writer and consultant specializing in Web site design and development. Recent books include "Home Page Improvement" (IDG Books), "Build a Web Site in a Day" (Ventana), "Netscape Communicator: A Jumpstart Tutorial" (Charles River Media), and "Internet Explorer: A Jumpstart Tutorial". In her past lives, Elisabeth graduated with a B.A. in English from Boston College; taught American Literature and Creative Writing to high school students; published *The Fine Print*, a bimonthly magazine focused on Boston's arts, music, and political scene for three years; and freelanced her graphic design, production, writing, and editing abilities to anyone who would pay her. Elisabeth now lives in San Francisco, CA with her fiance, Rich Grace, and Puddy the big, fat cat. For more information, or just for grins, visit her home page at `http://www.byteit.com/`.

The Internet and Intranets

Before we get into Netscape Communicator, let's talk about the Internet (or the net, as people call it for short) and Intranets. Going online puts the world at your fingertips. You can send electronic mail (email) to friends, family, and business associates around the globe; find resources on every topic from apples to zebras; exchange information about educational, business, technical, and recreational topics; get the latest news on practically any subject; play games; download software upgrades and useful shareware applications and utilities; share information with coworkers and others across networks; and collaborate on projects. All for the low cost of a local phone call and the monthly fee for maintaining your Internet account.

Doing all these neat things used to mean figuring out a confusing array of Internet applications. Sending and receiving email requires an email program. Uploading and downloading files requires an FTP client. Viewing Web pages requires a Web browser. And so on. Now, Netscape Communicator gives you everything you need in a single, easy-to-use software package. If you're in a hurry, you can skip this chapter for now. But come back later, because the following overview helps you make the most of Netscape Communicator by explaining how the Internet and Intranets work.

This chapter covers the following:

- How the Internet works
- About Intranets
- What you can do via the Internet or Intranets
- Getting on the Internet

How the Internet Works

You keep hearing about how the Internet is a network of file servers and telephone lines linked across the world. But that sounds impossible. How does it work? Fortunately, you don't have to be a computer guru to grasp the basic concept. Remember the game "telephone" from your kindergarten days? Everyone sits in a circle holding pairs of paper cups linked with strings. The first person whispers a message into the paper cup, the next person passes the message along, and so on. The last person in the circle repeats the message—which generally winds up hilariously garbled and everyone laughs

The Internet works along the same lines, as shown in Figure 1-1, except that the messages come out intact at the other end (most of the time!). When you send email or a message requesting information—which is basically what you do when you enter a URL (`http://www.website.com/`)—it goes from your computer to your modem. Your data transfers via the modem, through the telephone line, and to your Internet service provider's (ISP) file server. The file server processes your message, figures out where to send it, and passes the data along its telephone lines to the nearest file server. Your message continues going from file server to file server until it reaches its destination.

FILE SERVERS AND TELEPHONE LINES

File servers are giant computers that can quickly store and process huge amounts of information—called data, in computer parlance. They have connections to high-speed telephone lines that transmit the data to other file servers. File servers also can serve as *gateways* to the Internet because they contain the necessary software and routing information required for handling email, serving up Web pages and newsgroups, and so son. Most of us have neither the money, equipment, nor the knowledge required to run our own file server so that we can use the Internet. That's why we pay ISPs monthly fees to access *their* file servers. They, in turn, connect to the Internet's *backbone*. The backbone is a network of servers that function similarly to telephone switchboards and route all the data. They are run by the government and academic, scientific, and for-profit organizations.

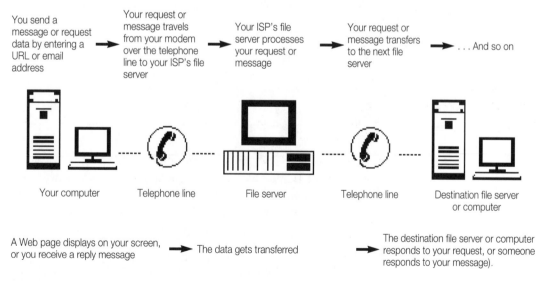

FIGURE   *The Internet (or an office network) is a system of personal computers (clients), file servers, and telephone lines.*
1.1

Who's in Charge of the Internet?

Good question. If only someone knew! Think of the Internet as the last frontier—a dynamic, chaotic outpost where people do (almost) whatever they want. Fortunately for us, the net abounds with academics, computer scientists, business people (including the people at Netscape Communications Corporation), and others who set standards, create Internet applications, generate searchable databases, and perform other services that make the net easier for the rest of us to use.

For a long time, the Internet was used and funded by mostly military, government, and academic organizations. Now, entrepreneurs and corporations sense profit potential and are taking up the slack—in some ways, a good thing considering military, government, and educational spending cuts over the past few years.

Listed below are a few of the organizations that contribute to Internet development, set standards, and provide support.

- **InterNIC** (http://nc.internic.net/) InterNIC keeps track of domain names, Internet addresses, URLs, and other vital domain-related information. If you want to register a domain name for yourself or your organization, you can do it here—and check InterNIC's database to see whether the name is already taken. A domain name is the name of an organization's or individual's server. The name becomes part of the organization's URLs and email addresses. For example, netscape.com.
- **European Laboratory for Particle Physics (CERN)** (http://www.cern.ch/) Development of the World Wide Web began at this research facility.
- **World Wide Web Consortium** (http://www.w3.org) This group of organizations sets standards, publishes a journal, and hosts conferences. The Massachusetts Institute of Technology's Laboratory for Computer Science hosts its Web site.
- **National Center for Supercomputing Applications (NCSA)** (http://www.cgi.ncsa/ioic/edu/indices/Discover/introduceNCSA.html) NCSA developed Mosaic, the first Web browser, and continues to provide resources and information related to the Web.
- **Internet Architecture Board (IAB)** (http://www.los-nettos.net/iab/) The IAB, an international organization, has monthly

teleconference meetings to discuss Internet issues and to encourage consensus. The meeting minutes are published on the site.

These sites—only a few of which are listed here—are primarily targeted to the academic and technical communities. But they do also have lots of resources and information concerning the Internet. In addition, corporations that develop computer and Internet products such as Netscape Communications Corporation (`http://home.netscape.com/`), Microsoft (`http://www.microsoft.com/`), Apple (`http://www.apple.com/`) can give you a sense of the latest goings-on in cyberspace and what new technology you'll have to run out and buy tomorrow.

CLIENT OR SERVER?

You've probably heard the words "client-server" used in relation to the Internet and Internet applications. That sounds highly technical, but all it really refers to is the relationship between computers on the Internet or on networks. When a computer (and the person using it) requests data or services (such as routing outgoing email) from the server, it acts as a *client*. That's why Web browsers, email programs, FTP applications, news readers, and other types of applications that you use to access and use the Internet are called *client applications*. Most of us use our computer and Internet applications as clients. When a computer serves up data and processes requests, it acts as a *server*. File servers are set up so that many users can connect and make requests at once.

WHAT IS A URL?

By now, you probably wonder how email messages, requests for data, and responses to requests know where to go. This brings us to URLs. When you send a letter to someone's house or office by U.S. mail (or "snail mail," as net enthusiasts like to call it), the post office knows where it goes because (you hope!) you scrawled the correct address on the envelope. File servers are just like people's offices and houses that way—each has its own address on the Internet, and many organizations and individuals may "live" at the address. Only with Web sites, the "address" is the domain—for example, `website.com`. We call Internet addresses "Uniform Resource Locators," or URLs for short (by the way, you pronounce "URL" as "you are ell" not "earl!"). A typical URL looks like the one below:

```
http://www.charlesriver.com/
```

What a URL Tells You

Newsgroups, FTP, and Gopher sites all use URLs. But let's talk about URLs in terms of browsing the Web, since that's probably what you're used to. When cruising the net, you are actually requesting data by entering URLs. To the naked human eye, URLs look like the incoherent ravings of a techno-alien. But the Internet-savvy person you'll soon become knows that this nonsensical line of gibberish reveals important information. For example, the `http://www.charlesriver.com/` URL points to the welcoming page of Charles River Media's Web site, as shown in Figure 1-2. The welcoming page in any Web site is also called the index document. When a document name contains the word "index," the browser knows to look automatically for it when you enter a URL with no specific document name.

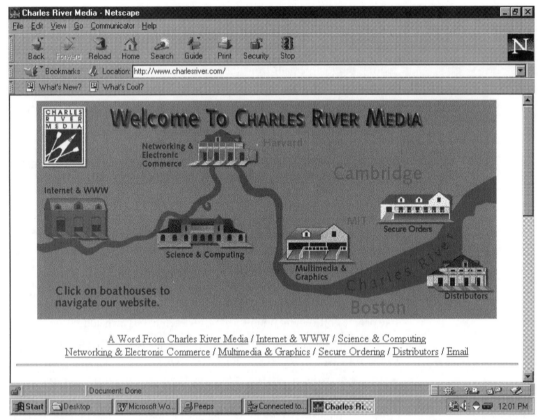

FIGURE 1.2 *The* `http://www.charlesriver.com/` *URL points to the welcoming page of Charles River Media's Web site.*

Let's dissect Charles River Media's Web site address and find out what it tells us.

http://www.charlesriver.com/

Protocol: *Protocols* are standard formats that tell computers and peripherals (such as modems and printers) how to talk with each other. They determine how data are viewed, handled, and transferred. The first letters, http, tell us the type of Internet site and what protocol it uses. Because "http" stands for "Hyper Text Transfer Protocol," which is used for Web pages, we know that the URL points to a Web page. We'll talk more about protocols, and the World Wide Web later in this chapter.

http://**www**.charlesriver.com/

Server type: There are all different kinds of servers. The next part of the URL tells us what kind of file server hosts the content you've requested. Because "www" stands for "World Wide Web," we can tell that this is a Web server.

http://www.**charlesriver**.com/

Server name: The name of the server is "charlesriver"—short for Charles River Media, the publisher of the Web site (and this book). The full domain name for this organization and server is **charlesriver.com.**

http://www.charlesriver.**com**/

Organization type: We can also tell that the server is dedicated to business purposes because the domain name suffix – "com" stands for commercial. For more explanation about domain names and domain name suffixes, see the following "What's in a Domain Name" section.

http://www.charlesriver.com/**toc/commtoc.htm**

Directory and file name: If you follow some links page that Charles River Media created for this book, as shown in Figure 1-3, you'll notice that the URL gets longer. That's because file server administrators and Web site developers organize and store information in *directories* (another word for "folders"), just like you do on your own computer. The URL shown above tells you that the "Netscape Communicator: A Jumpstart Tutorial" Web page document is named "comm-toc.htm" and is stored in the "toc" directory. Once you start exploring the Internet, you'll notice that some URLs point to files that are stored in the subdirectory of a subdirectory and so on—which makes for incredibly long URLs.

Of course, these rules don't always hold true. For example, you would think that Netscape Communications Corporation's URL would be `http://www.netscape.com/`, but instead it's `http://home.netscape.com`. URLs still seem confusing, don't worry. Back when you had to use separate client applications to access different types of information on the Internet, the URL information determined what program you should launch. Thanks to Netscape Communicator—an all-in-one application, you don't really have to think about it.

URLs and email addresses consist of numeric, text, and special characters. Sometimes words are separated by dashes or underscores, but they NEVER have any spaces in them!

NOTE

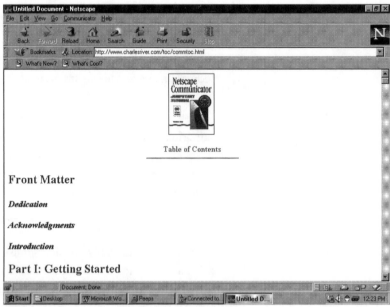

FIGURE   *You can also tell where a Web page is located on the server. The URL for this*
1.3   *page (as displayed in the browser location window) tells you that this page is named "commtoc.htm" and that it is stored in the "toc" directory.*

WHAT'S IN A DOMAIN NAME?

A domain name is a server's or group of servers' address on the Internet. In general, having a domain name (which gives you a custom email and Web site address) implies that you or your organization maintains a server with a direct connection to the Internet, but this is not always the case. Anyone can file a domain name for a Web site with InterNIC registration services—even if you actually connect to the Internet through an ISP's server. In most cases, your ISP will give you a form to fill out and will handle the process for you. InterNIC keeps track of file server domains and Internet addresses and charges $50 per year for having a domain name. Unless you have a particular reason for wanting a domain name—for example, I use `byteit.com` as my domain name so that if I move or change ISPs people can still email me and find my web site—you don't need to worry about it. For more information, visit InterNIC's Web site at `http://nc.internic.net/`.

As a general rule, the domain name also tells you what type of organization runs the file server or site by the domain name suffix. Common file server name suffixes are as follows:

> **.edu:** Indicates a school, college, university, or other educational institution.
>
> **.org:** Indicates a nonprofit organization or a miscellaneous enterprise.
>
> **.com:** Indicates a commercial organization or business
>
> **.net:** Indicates an Internet service provider (ISP) or other organization whose activities relate to networks.
>
> **.gov:** Indicates a government organization
>
> **.mil:** Indicates a military organization
>
> **.int:** Indicates an international organization.
>
> **country abbreviations:** Some servers also use country abbreviations, such as `.nl` for the Netherlands or UK for the United Kingdom of Great Britain, as domain name suffixes.

In addition, plans are in the works for additional domain name suffixes to denote other types of organizations and activities, such as `.rec` for "recreational."

Common Internet Protocols

Protocols are standard formats that tell computers how to handle and transfer data. Many protocols exist in the computer world. But these are the ones you'll come across most often during your excursions into the Internet.

HTTP: Hyper Text Transfer Protocol (for Web servers that serve up Web pages)

FTP: File Transfer Protocol (for FTP servers that enable users to upload and download files—now you can upload and download via the Web and HTTP as well)

GOPHER: Gopher (Gopher servers use an early protocol that enabled searching for and viewing text documents)

SMTP: Standard Mail Transfer Protocol (for mail servers that enable sending and receiving email)

POP3: Post Office Protocol 3 (also for mail servers that enable sending and receiving email)

NNTP: Network News Transfer Protocol (for news servers that host newsgroups, which allow people to download, read, and post messages to the server for others to view)

UUCP: Unix to Unix Protocol (an older protocol that is also for news servers that host newsgroups, which allow people to download, read, and post messages to the server for others to view).

PPP: Point to Point Protocol (tells your modem to connect you to the Internet; you need a PPP or SLIP account)

SLIP: Serial Line Interface Protocol (an older protocol that tells your modem to connect you to the Internet—now most people use PPP)

TCP/IP: Transmission Control Protocol/Internet Protocol (a popular Internet and networking protocol that tells file servers and computers how to transfer data back and forth)

Open Transport: A TCP/IP-based protocol for the Power Macintosh

About Intranets

You have probably come across the buzzword "Intranet" and wondered what that means. Meanwhile, you might already be using one every day at work. An Intranet is a closed office network that uses Internet protocols and applications for distributing and sharing files within an organization. Intranets work like smaller closed versions of the Internet and often let you connect to the Internet, too. Like the Internet, Intranets have servers, but instead of being connected to the outer world via telephone lines, only authorized users within the network (like your coworkers) can access the server.

If you have more than one computer in your office, then you probably have some familiarity with networking. Networking technologies help people do day-to-day things like exchange files between one computer and another, and share printers, scanners, and other peripheral devices. On a primitive level of networking, you have the mainframe. With mainframe systems, all data—such as word processing documents and database information—are stored on a server. When people need to create, view, or edit files, they log on to their terminal and access the file from the server. Offices whose more sophisticated needs require employees to use personal computers often use *groupware* products like Lotus Notes, Microsoft Exchange, and now, Netscape Communicator. Groupware facilitates office communications, and enables coworkers to easily access data and collaborate on projects via the server. With groupware, everyone wins. You get many of the advantages of mainframe systems without giving up the advantages of working with your favorite applications on a PC. Meanwhile, administrators can still set *access levels* to determine who gets to see what—so you don't have to worry about rival coworkers viewing your personnel files.

The first groupware applications took a step in the right direction, but complications immediately arose. Groupware programs work best when everyone uses the same operating system and applications. Yet many organizations have people working on a variety of platforms, such as Windows 95, Windows 3.1x, Macintosh, OS-2, and UNIX systems. And what happens when the Windows 3.1x-using Head of Sales needs to make some quick text edits to the presentation or brochure that the Macintosh-using Marketing Department is working on? Alas, often the same thing that happened before the advent of groupware: People can't open each other's files and wind up wasting time with printouts and futile attempts to convert and reformat files.

INTRANET ADVANTAGES

Suddenly, everyone started noticing the World Wide Web and other Internet technologies. People on the Internet have been communicating and exchanging files across platforms for years. Now, Web browsers like Netscape Communicator make it possible to access virtually any type of data and launch most types of Internet applications from user-friendly Web pages.

With today's tools, practically any type of file can be formatted for viewing on the Web. Internet protocols make it easy for organizations to send messages, display data, exchange files, and set up different types of computers so they can talk to each other. Internet technologies can also be used securely. After all, Internet server administrators have to deal with the same issues as organizational network administrators: preventing unauthorized access to applications and data, setting up passwords and access levels, and keeping the system from crashing.

Intranets offer administrators and users the following advantages:

- **Ease of Use:** Compared with other types of networking, Intranets require less effort for the administrator to set up and maintain. Users can work more productively when accessing network services becomes as simple as launching Netscape Communicator and clicking on buttons and links.
- **Remote Access:** Many offices have a number of telecommuters, consultants, sales people who frequently go on the road, and people who take work home with them. Intranet setups make it easy for authorized users to access data and communicate regularly with coworkers.
- **Information and Resource Management:** Intranet server tools, like the ones that come with Netscape Suite Spot, make it easy to keep track of people's schedules and use of resources, such as conference rooms, equipment, printers, and network services. In addition, Web page updates and link checking can be automated, and files across the network can be cataloged and made searchable. This way, the Human Resources Director can come in Friday evening after a big meeting and quickly find the department managers' employee performance reports.
- **Security:** Like any kind of network, Intranets can be made secure to prevent unauthorized access to data. Administrators can also set up levels of restricted access, so users can get information they need without accidentally viewing confidential files.

WHERE NETSCAPE COMMUNICATOR FITS IN

When we think of Netscape, most of us think of the Web browser. But there's more to Netscape Communicator than that. As Chapter 2 explains more fully, Netscape Communicator is a suite of applications that you can use for practically anything you could possibly want to do on the Internet.

Netscape Communicator is a great tool for home users, but it is also ideal for groupware purposes.

With Netscape Communicator's server software (discussed more fully in chapters 19–21), administrators can set up a server that combines high-end groupware capabilities with user-friendly Internet technologies. Suddenly, it becomes amazingly easy to view and publish company announcements and updates as Web pages, discuss ongoing projects and issues via office newsgroups, hold meetings online with real-time conferencing tools, track schedules, upload and download files, and exchange email messages. The following sections will talk about what you can do via the Internet and Intranets in greater detail.

What You Can Do via the Internet or Intranets

This part of the chapter takes a quick tour of all the neat stuff you can do with Netscape Communicator via the Internet or Intranets. I'll save all the gory details and how to's for the following chapters. You can browse the Web, send and receive email, participate in newsgroups, upload and download files, have conference meetings online with either voice or data communications, collaborate on projects and trade schedules, transact business securely online, and more. None of these capabilities are new—people have been doing these things on the Internet for years. But it used to require downloading a bewildering array of obscure shareware applications. Now, thanks to Netscape Communicator, you can fully utilize the Internet's potential with a single application. Pretty amazing, huh?

BROWSE WEB PAGES

The World Wide Web is the technical innovation that launched a thousand net surfers. Before the Web existed, the Internet was difficult to use and only file server directories and plain text documents could be displayed. The Web's snazzy graphics and multimedia handling capabilities revolutionized the Internet. All of the sudden, exploring the Internet and downloading files became as simple as pointing and clicking on hypertext links, and nontechnical folks started going online. And by the way, Web pages aren't just easy to *look* at. They're simple and inexpensive to create and manage. You can tell people about your last vacation (like the Web page shown in Figure 1-4) or make the latest sales figures for your company's product available to your coworkers. Netscape Communicator makes it easy for you to find, view, and publish information.

What's HyperText?

Hypertext has added new dimension to the Internet. Web pages are ordinary text documents—like the ones you type in your word processor-formatted with Hyper Text Markup Language (HTML). HTML provides a set of codes that tell Web browsers like Netscape how to display text and graphics. By entering HTML codes, the "Webmaster" (a person who generates Web pages) can also create hypertext links. You can click on the hypertext links to quickly jump from place to place because they point directly to other URLs.

Hypertext makes the Internet appealing and user-friendly, and it's a powerful tool for locating and publishing resources. You can quickly search for topics and experience content immediately instead of waiting for files to download. Hypertext is so easy to use or incorporate into existing software applications that even those of you with little computer experience can find information or publish simple documents on the Web or on office networks.

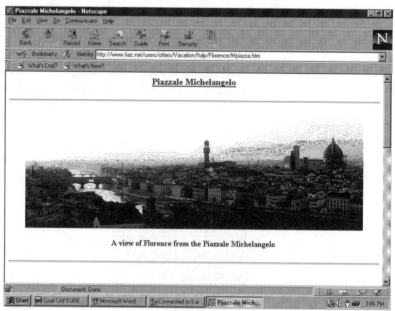

FIGURE *See some great photos from Melanie and Jamie's Trip to Italy*
1.4 (http://www.tiac.net/users/otters/Vacation/Italy/)
. . . Netscape Communicator makes viewing and creating Web pages easy.

What's a Web Browser?

Web browser applications like Netscape Navigator (Netscape Communicator's Web browsing component) let you view hypertext Web pages and click on hypertext links to jump to other Web pages. With Netscape Navigator, Web pages can even act as an interface for viewing and working with other types of Internet content. For example, clicking on the link to an email address launches Netscape Messenger (or your current email program), so I can send an email message to the specified email address, as shown in Figure 1-5. Similarly, clicking on the link to a newsgroup launches Collabra, Netscape Communicator's news reader application.

SEND AND RECEIVE EMAIL

Everyone loves email. You can look busy at work while writing letters to your friends. Oops. I mean, you can communicate with business associates and coworkers quickly and efficiently, without ever printing anything out or getting put on hold. And no matter where they live, email generally costs less than a postage stamp! But seriously, email gives you an efficient way to cir-

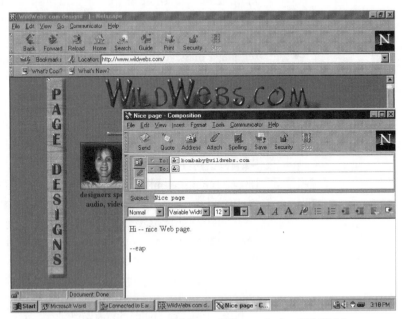

FIGURE *When you click on the email link on a Web page (such as WildWebs' at*
1.5   `http://www.wildwebs.com/`), *Netscape Messenger launches so I can send an email message.*

The First Web Browser

The National Center for Supercomputing Applications (NCSA) at the University of Illinois introduced Mosaic—the first browser capable of displaying hypertext—in 1992. Back then, display capabilities were limited. You could view plain, unformatted text and graphics, and that was about it. Meanwhile, Marc Andreessen, the main programmer for the Mosaic project, moved on to found Netscape Communications, Inc. The Netscape browser immediately gained popularity, and its capabilities grew by leaps and bounds. Today's Web browsers can display all kinds of sophisticated layouts and cutting-edge content.

So what happened to Mosaic? It's still around, lots of people use it, and it's free. But in terms of innovations, Mosaic lags far behind Netscape Communicator. The NCSA Web site (`http://www.ncsa. uiuc.edu/Indices/WebTech/`) is well worth checking out, though. You'll find a wealth of Web-related information and resources.

---

culate memos, plan events, provide customer support, and distribute timely information. For those of you who are busy or out of the office a lot, email lets you respond to messages during calmer moments.

With Netscape Messenger, you can enter the address of the person you're sending a message to, your return address, a subject line, and your text, as shown in Figure 1-6. You then send your letter. You can also send mail from your browser, which is often more convenient. We will discuss email and Netscape Messenger further in Chapters 10 and 11.

PARTICIPATE IN NEWSGROUPS

Imagine an office bulletin board cluttered with a lively jumble of announcements and messages. That may give you some idea of how newsgroups work. To access newsgroups, you need a news reader application—or Collabra (the news reader component of Netscape Communicator)—and access to a server that provides newsgroups (most ISPs do). You can subscribe to newsgroups whose topics interest you, read postings, make announcements, ask questions, send replies, and participate in discussions.

Newsgroups can help you network, keep up with the latest developments in your field, or discuss various topics with people who have similar interests. Whether you specialize in administrative support or zoology, there's proba-

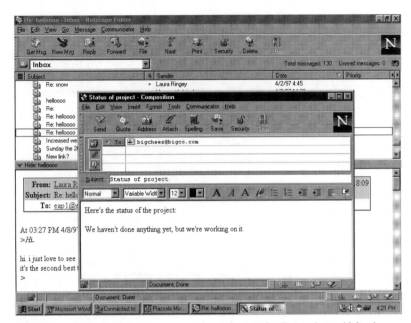

FIGURE *With Netscape Messenger you send email to people all over the world for the cost*
1.6 *of a local phone call.*

bly a newsgroup out there for you. You can even share a few jokes via humor-related newsgroups, such as `zipnews.living.humor` (shown in Figure 1-7). In addition, Collabra server software makes it easy for organizations to start in-house Intranet newsgroups so coworkers can discuss projects and exchange information about business-related topics. We'll talk more about getting news in Chapters 10 and 12.

UPLOAD AND DOWNLOAD FILES

Netscape Communicator also makes it easy to *upload* and *download* files. In the old days, you needed a special *File Transfer Protocol* (FTP) program to upload Web page material to your server, or to download shareware, images, games, and other files to your computer. This sounds kind of neat, except that FTP programs are harder to use than Web browsers, and FTP programs had no search capabilities. Unless you had an FTP address (URL) and the location of the file, finding things on the Internet was next to impossible.

Now, the World Wide Web makes locating and downloading files easy. With a Web browser like Navigator, all you need to do is click on a link. Up-

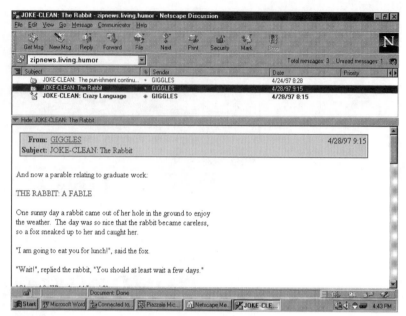

FIGURE *Netscape Collabra lets you access newsgroups.*
1.7

loading files to your Web page directory, or another directory on your server is also easy. We'll discuss uploading files further in Chapter 17.

By the way, Web servers also allow users to upload and download files, but many individuals and organizations still use FTP servers. Because of this, you'll still run into the word "FTP" during your travels on the Internet. But never fear. You can access FTP sites with Netscape Navigator—they just don't look as nice as Web sites do.

NOTE

Downloading versus Uploading: When you transfer files to your computer from a server, it's called "downloading." When you transfer files from your computer to a file server via the Internet, it's called "uploading." When you download shareware, keep using it, and don't pay the programmer, it's called "freeloading."

NOTE

Steal These Files!

After reading about uploading and downloading files, you're probably wondering, "Why would someone let me steal their stuff?" They do it for fun, altruism, profit—or possibly all the above. For example, some record labels offer audio and video files to promote their artists. Software companies—Like Netscape Communications Corp.—often offer products from the Web because it makes it easier for users to try and buy them. Or they can provide their customers with easy access to upgrades and bug fixes.

The Internet also offers an excellent way to distribute software, documents, clip art, multimedia, games, and more. When files are distributed for use by members of an organization, you need to enter a name and password to access them. When individuals or organizations want to distribute files for use by the general public, they set up an "anonymous ftp folder" so people can access the files without a password.

HOLD ONLINE CONFERENCE MEETINGS

Sometimes, communicating via email, newsgroups, and Web pages isn't enough. Only a telephone call will do. Now, thanks to Netscape Conference, you can talk with people via the Internet. Simply enter an email or direct IP address (if you know it), and click the Dial button, as shown in Figure 1-8. If the other person's online and has Netscape Conference set up, they'll receive your call and you can start talking. In addition, Netscape Conference lets you and your friends or colleagues view Web pages together, exchange files, jot down notes, and even share a white board. Sure, there are other technologies around that let you do these things—people have been having real-time text conversations via Internet Relay Chat (IRC) for years. But Conference makes it so easy. For more details on how Netscape Conference works, read Chapters 15 and 16.

COLLABORATE ON PROJECTS AND TRACK SCHEDULES

Have you ever needed to print out a 1,000-page document only to find that everyone else in the office needs the printer, too? Or tried to schedule a meeting for a project that involves people from different departments and had difficulty finding a time when everyone can attend? Netscape Calendar helps you avoid these problems. If your office Intranet uses Netscape's Calendar

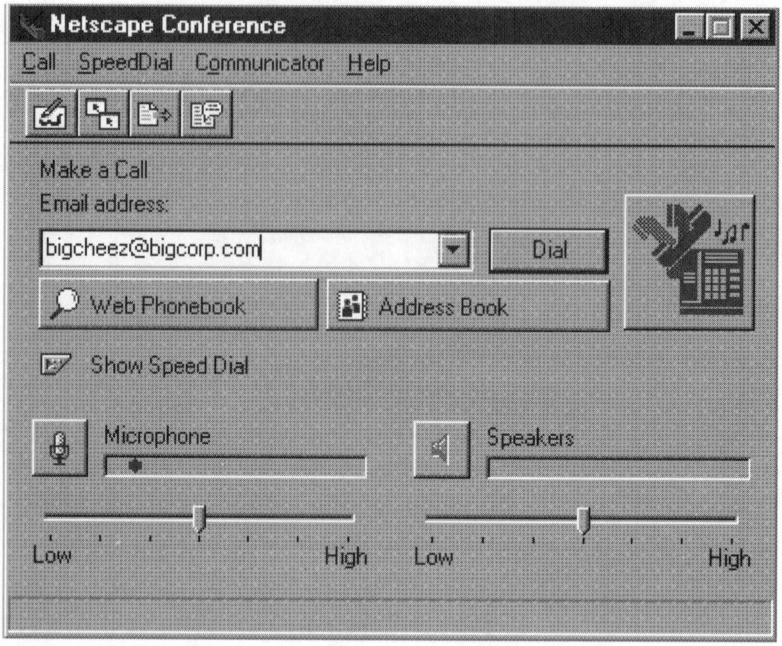

FIGURE *Have telephone conversations online with Netscape Conference.*
1.8

Server, Calendar helps you keep track of your coworkers' schedules, when network resources are available, and more. How does this work? Everyone on the network uses Netscape Calendar, as shown in Figure 1-9, and enters information about upcoming and ongoing projects and meetings—such as related times and dates, what office and server resources they'll be using, and who else is involved in the project or meeting. The next time you have a meeting or a big printing job coming up, you can log on to the Calendar server, find out what everyone else is doing and when, and reserve time accordingly.

TRANSACT BUSINESS SECURELY ONLINE

As security technologies become more sophisticated, more and more people are doing business online. Nowadays, you can use the Web to check stock quotes, order office supplies and software, subscribe to publications and information services, manage bank accounts, check on the status of shipments,

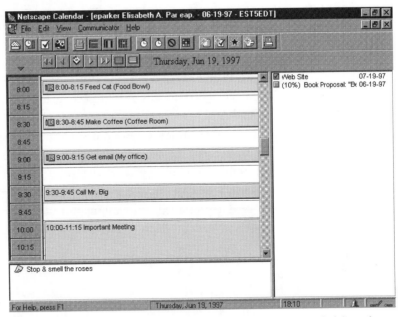

FIGURE *Netscape Calendar helps Intranet users keep track of people's schedules and*
1.9 *office resources.*

and more. In addition, you can have confidential discussions on private
newsgroups and send private email. Netscape Communicator's security features makes it reasonably safe to transfer your credit card numbers and other
confidential information over the Web. In addition, Netscape Communicator and its server components help network administrators ensure that communications via office networks stays private. Chapter 18 covers security
features in greater detail.

AND MORE!

There's far more to the Internet and Netscape Communicator than a single
chapter can possibly discuss. You can access files from the server at work
even when you're away from work, do research, shop, plan trips, download
shareware and software updates, play games, communicate with people
around the globe, and more. Chapter 2 talks about how Netscape Communicator brings all of this to you in greater detail.

Getting on the Internet

Most of us can't afford to buy a file server and have to dial into somebody else's. Some of you lucky ones out there can access a file server at work or school for free. The rest of us have to find a local Internet service provider (ISP) and pay to use its file server. Fortunately, this generally doesn't cost much. There are lots of startup companies that offer competitive services and rates.

Finding an ISP can seem overwhelming—especially if you don't know much about the net. You can expect to pay around $19.00 to $29.00 per month (but think of what you'll save on telephone bills once you start using email!), plus a startup fee. In return, the ISP will give you all the software you need to get started, technical support, advice, and access to resources on its server. Most providers even give you space to put up your own Web page at no extra charge.

TIP

If you access the Internet through work, ask your network administrator for tips on using Communicator more productively. He or she might be able to help.

When choosing an Internet provider, look for the following features:

- PPP: You need to have a PPP account to use Communicator. PPP stands for Point to Point Protocol.
- Flat rate: Many Internet providers offer flat rates—for example, $20 per month for anywhere between 20 and 40 hours of access per month. You might spend a lot of time exploring and trying to find your way around at first. The flat rate will let you relax instead of worrying about the huge bills you might rack up at an hourly rate. You'll be surprised at how quickly the hours fly by.
- Local dial-up: Make sure that your Internet provider has file servers within your local dialing area. Otherwise, you'll wind paying long-distance telephone charges. If you travel frequently, then consider an Internet provider with many points of presence so that you can generally reach one of its servers with a local phone call.
- Starter kit: Your Internet provider should offer a "starter kit"—a suite of basic Internet applications and detailed instructions on how to install and use them. This suite probably won't include Netscape Communicator, but you can always purchase Communicator later.
- Technical support: Make sure that your Internet provider offers technical support. We all need it at one time or another.

Get referrals: Do you have any friends on the net? If so, find out what Internet providers they use.

For lists of Internet service providers in your area, try Meckler Media's The List at `http://thelist.iworld.com/`.

How the Internet Came to Be

In 1969, the University of California at Los Angeles (UCLA) and the Defense Advanced Research Projects Agency (DARPA) launched ARPANET, the grandmother of the Internet. The network facilitated research by connecting four universities' computers—UCLA, University of Utah, University of California at Santa Barbara, and Stanford Research Institute.

Other organizations saw the advantages of linking up and got together with the National Science Foundation and started NSFNet, which later connected with ARPANET. As for the military—who originally began experimenting with an Internet prototype as a means for communication in case of nuclear war—they didn't want everyone poking around in their files. So they created their own network, MILNET.

In the mid-1970s, computers began catching people's interest. But would-be enthusiasts faced a major obstacles. Personal computers didn't exist yet. Back then, computers looked like those enormous machines that appear in *Star Trek* reruns and only large organizations could afford them.

Fortunately, a few experimental programs—including the famous Xerox PARC Foundation in Palo Alto, California—offered access to the young hackers. Meanwhile, corporations like General Electric began renting time on their computers during off-hours to offset computer maintenance costs. Some of these arrangements evolved into today's online services, like CompuServe (now called CSi). As technology expanded, so did the Internet. High-speed telephone lines, more powerful and less expensive computers, and user-friendly software now make the Internet accessible to many of us.

2

Netscape Communicator at a Glance

Netscape Communicator isn't just an application: It's a whole bunch of applications. With Communicator, you can take advantage of everything the Internet has to offer and do lots of things, such as browse the Web, send and receive email, join newsgroup discussions, create and upload Web pages, conference with people online, and have news and other content delivered to your virtual doorstep with server push delivery. In addition, if your network administrator at work uses Netscape server products with Netscape Communicator, you can communicate and collaborate with coworkers more easily. This sounds like an overwhelming amount of stuff, but never fear. Communicator's user-friendly *interface* makes everything as simple as pointing and clicking.

What's an "Interface?"

I keep mentioning Netscape Communicator's user-friendly "interface," which isn't very user-friendly of me. "Interface" refers to how you communicate with your computer. If you can (fairly) easily figure out what to do with an application just by looking at the screen, then you're looking at a "user-friendly interface."

This chapter gives you an overview of what Netscape Communicator has to offer, and introduces you to the following:

- Communicator Standard versus Pro
- Navigator, the Web browser
- Messenger, the email application
- Collabra, the news reader
- Composer, the Web page authoring tool
- Conference, for Internet telephone calls
- Netcaster, for receiving Internet broadcasts
- Calendar, for enterprise scheduling and resource management
- IBM Host On-Demand, for accessing remote servers via Telnet

---

Communicator Standard versus Pro

If you've visited Netscape's Web site (http://home.netscape.com), you may have noticed that Communicator comes in two flavors: the Standard version and the Pro version. The Standard version of Communicator costs

$49 and is for people who want to use it at home, or in an office that has not set up an Intranet. The Pro version of Communicator costs $79 and works hand in glove with Netscape Intranet server tools like Collabra and Calendar to automate office communications and scheduling.

Navigator, the Web Browser

Naturally, Netscape Navigator, the popular Web browser, is a central part of Communicator. You can use Navigator to explore the Web, view Web pages posted on your company's Intranet, and access other network services and Internet resources. By selecting links, toolbar buttons, and menu items, you can launch Communicator's other components so you can participate in online discussion groups, send and receive email, upload and download files on FTP servers, check out online broadcasts (the Netcaster section in this chapter talks more about this), and more.

Even without Communicator's other applications, Navigator is well worth having in itself. Its support for impressive page displays, multimedia, Java, and JavaScript make Web browsing an interactive, content-rich experience. Take Netscape's Web page demonstration, as shown in Figure 2-1, as an example of how Web pages viewed with Navigator can be both fun and useful. The fictitious company, Royal Airways, gives you everything you need to plan a business trip or vacation. Click on the buttons to display information about each option. To choose an option—such as the destination city and type of hotel—select the appropriate icon and drag it onto the baggage cart. Voila! It turns into a suitcase. When you're finished clicking on options, the Web site tallies up the total cost of your trip for you. If this were a real company's Web site, you would also be able to book reservations and pay for your trip online.

When you launch Communicator, the Navigator component automatically appears. Chapters 4 through 9 cover Navigator in greater detail.

EASY ACCESS TO OTHER COMMUNICATOR COMPONENTS

Do you want to check your email or jump to a newsgroup and check the postings while browsing the Web? It's as easy as pointing and clicking. If you click on a link to a newsgroup or discussion group, Communicator launches Collabra. If you click on an email link, Communicator launches Messenger

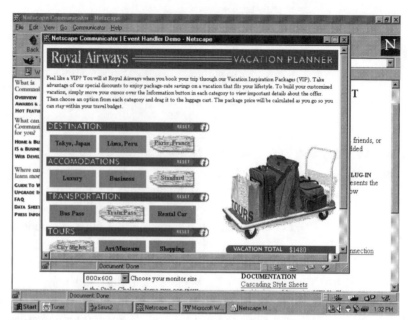

FIGURE *Netscape's Royal Airways demonstration site shows how Navigator's support for*
2.1 *dynamic Web pages makes the Web more exciting and functional (to see it, visit*
Netscape's home page at `http://home.netscape.com/`*).*

and a blank email message window appears. You can also access Netscape Communicator's various components from the component bar (shown on the bottom right of the application window in Figure 2-1). Communicator even lets you edit your Web page on the fly. To change something while viewing your page, simply click on the Composer icon.

You can display the component bar as a larger palette so you can see it better by selecting **Show Component Bar** *from the Communicator menu.*

TIP

Toolbar buttons are as follows:

Navigator: Launches Navigator, Communicator's Web browser component.

Mailbox: Launches Messenger so you can compose, send, and receive email.

>   **Discussion Groups:** Launches the Message Center so you can select a
>   news server (on the Internet or an organizational Intranet) and join
>   in newsgroup discussions.
>
>   **Composer:** Launches Composer so you can create and edit Web pages.

Chapter 4 talks about Navigator's main window and the toolbars in greater detail.

FILE TRANSFER PROTOCOL (FTP) AND GOPHER

Don't overlook FTP and Gopher sites just because they don't look as snazzy as Web pages. FTP and Gopher sites have been around for a long time, offer lots of resources, and are still an important part of the net. As Chapter 1 mentions, FTP stands for File Transfer Protocol. It's an older technology for uploading and downloading files to and from servers. Many people still use it because FTP has many advantages (Chapter 17 talks more about FTP). As for Gopher, the University of Minnesota developed it several years ago. Since this was one of the few publicly available technologies for viewing text and searching for data online at the time, it quickly became popular. Many Gopher sites remain active and contain lots of fun and useful information. Although Navigator can't give FTP and Gopher sites a makeover, it *can* make getting acquainted with them easier for you.

For more about Gopher sites, visit Life on the Internet's Gopher Page at `http://www.screen.com/start/guide/gopher.html`.

TIP

Messenger, the Email Application

Netscape Messenger isn't just an email program. Think of it as more like a kit for communicating with others in more sophisticated ways and keeping your correspondence organized. Messenger comes with a built-in address book, spell check, and other editing features. When sending mail to other Communicator users, you can jazz up your emails with fancy text formatting, graphics, multimedia, and functional links to material on the Intranet or Internet, like Netscape's demonstration message shown in Figure 2-2. You can even set up special mail filters to sort email by sender or subject line as your messages download so you don't even have to sort all of your messages

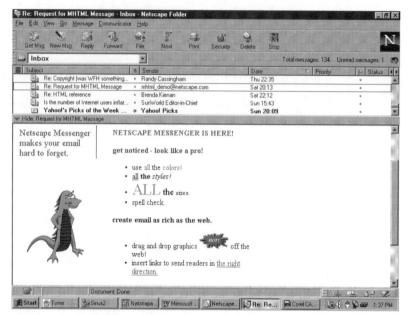

FIGURE **2.2** *Netscape Messenger helps you send email messages with graphics and live content.*

yourself. To launch Messenger, click on the Mailbox component bar icon on the bottom right of the Communicator window. Chapters 10 and 11 tell you about using the Message Center and Messenger to send, receive, and compose email messages.

Messenger and Collabra Protocols

While we're talking about email and newsgroups with Messenger and Collabra, let's talk about protocols again (for more on protocols, see Chapter 1). Sure, you can do great things with Communicator via office Intranets. But the people at Netscape haven't forgotten about individual users. You'll find that Netscape's news and email programs support all of the protocols currently used by most client applications, including:

Post Office Protocol 3 (POP3): This is a common protocol for handling email messages.

Standard Mail Transmission Protocol (SMTP): This is another common protocol for handling email messages.

Internet Message Access Protocol 4 (IMAP4): Increasing numbers of ISPs and server administrators support this protocol so you can store your email in directories on the server.

Lightweight Directory Access Protocol (LDAP): This protocol enables you to search directories through your browser to find files and information.

Network News Transfer Protocol (NNTP): Collabra supports NNTP so you can access standard newsgroups on the Internet as well as discussion forums on an office Intranet.

The News Reader, the New Sender

With the Netscape Message Center, as shown in Figure 2-3, and Messenger you can subscribe to in-house discussion groups and Internet newsgroups, read people's postings, and put your own two cents in. Communicator supports NNTP news server-generated newsgroups, Netscape Collabra server discussion groups, and fully threaded news reading. The hierarchical display makes it easy for you to see where conversational news threads begin. You

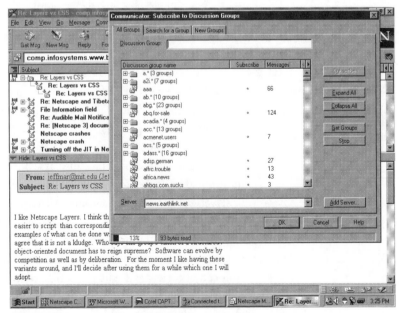

FIGURE   *Netscape Communicator's Message Center and Collabra make it easy to locate*
2.3   *news servers and participate in news and discussion groups.*

can also sort, list, and organize newsgroup messages the same way as you do with your email in Netscape Messenger. In fact, since email and news both involve composing, sending, and receiving messages, the email and news reading components share the same interface. This means you can learn how to use them a lot faster.

Internet newsgroups focus on all different kinds of topics, relating to business, hobbies, academic research, and more. In addition, if your office's network administrator uses Netscape's Collabra server software, you and your coworkers can also set up in-house discussion groups to talk about projects, ask questions about company-related topics, and more. To access newsgroups, click the Message Center component bar icon on the bottom right of the Communicator window. Chapters 10 and 12 cover the Message Center and participating in newsgroup more fully.

What's "Threaded News Reading?"

Think of news threads as conversations. One person posts an announcement, asks a question, or expresses an opinion and others respond. Every time someone makes an announcement or starts a new conversation, a new thread begins. You can also post messages with embedded multimedia files, attached documents, and live URLs.

Composer, the Web Page Authoring Tool

Communicator doesn't just let you *view* Web pages. The Composer component, as shown in Figure 2-4 (with Margaret Weigel's home page at `http://www.tiac.net/users/regrets/`), also helps you create and edit them. No, Composer isn't the best tool for developing high-end Web sites with frames and other fancy displays. But it does make it easy to generate and make changes to simple HTML documents and upload them to your server. For someone who wants a slick, simple tool for quickly formatting, editing, and updating pages, Composer is ideal. If you're in charge of posting updates and announcements for your department on your company's Intranet or Internet Web site, Composer helps you do it in a snap.

You can also view and edit pages that contain Java Applets, JavaScript, and plug-in elements. To launch Composer, click on the Composer toolbar icon at the bottom right of the Communicator window. Chapter 17 tell you more about how Composer can help you with your Web site.

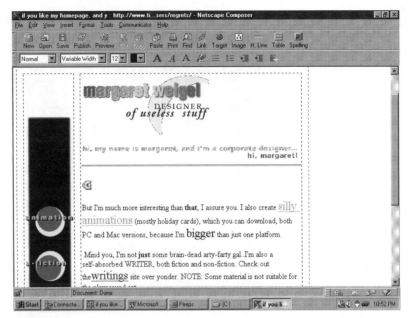

FIGURE *Creating, editing, and uploading simple HTML documents is a breeze with*
2.4 *Netscape Composer.*

Conference, for Internet Telephone Calls

By now you might be saying, "Well, the Internet's great and wonderful, and all, but sometimes I'd rather just make a phone call and talk with a human for a change." Guess what? Now you can. With Netscape Conference, as shown in Figure 2-5, you can dial up an email address. If the person you want to talk to is on online too and also has Communicator with Netscape Conference, then the two of you can talk. Just think of the savings on long distance phone bills (though I'm sure the phone company will figure out a way around it!). In addition, Conference also has other features to make it easier to communicate and collaborate on projects, such as a shared whiteboard and an application for exchanging files.

Conference comes with the following components:

Telephone Dialer: Enter an email or IP address to place a phone call. The dialer also has an address book to help you keep track of your contacts.
Conference Text Chat: You can also type notes in the Text Chat window.

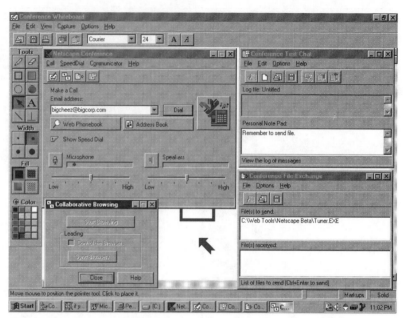

FIGURE *Netscape Conference gives you just about everything you need to have a*
2.5 *telephone meeting online.*

Whiteboard: The Whiteboard makes it easier to discuss visual elements
in projects. You can take a picture of what's on your screen or use an
existing image, then import it to the white board so the two of you
can look at it. You can also select graphics, pen, pointer, and text
tools as aids to your discussions.

Collaborative Browsing: If the topic of your meeting involves viewing
Web sites, you can use the Collaborative Browsing feature so that
both of you are "on the same page," so to speak.

Conference File Exchange: If you need to exchange database information, word processing documents, presentations, images, and other
types of files, Conference File Exchange makes it easy.

You can launch Conference by selecting the Conference option from the
Communicator menu. Chapters 15 and 16 discuss Netscape Conference in
greater detail.

Netcaster, for Receiving Internet Broadcasts

So are you impressed with Communicator? You haven't even checked out Netcaster yet. With Netcaster, you can subscribe to Internet or Intranet broadcast channels that download data in the background while you're doing something else. You'll find content that's similar to what you see on the Web—only without the inconvenience of waiting for pages to download. Broadcast channels can deliver virtually any kind of data such as computer-related news and resources from the CNET Channel (CNET), as shown in Figure 2-6, to more complex services like document sharing and Internet chat (and of course, you'll find plenty of games . . . but don't tell your boss!). When used on an Intranet, Netcaster also makes it easier for server administrators to distribute company news, software updates, and other data to everyone in the company. Finally, Netcaster is integrated with Castanet's popular Marimba Tuner—a cutting-edge application for receiving Internet broadcasts. To find out more about Internet broadcasts, read the "Tuning in to Internet Broadcasts" section in Chapter 6.

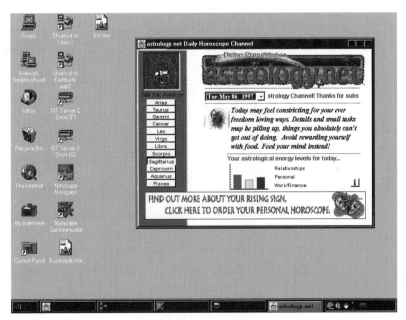

FIGURE **2.6** *Netcaster and Marimba Tuner download Internet broadcasts—such as CNET's computer-related news and resources—automatically.*

Calendar, for Enterprise Scheduling and Resource Management

If you have Communicator Pro installed on an Intranet with Calendar Server, then you're in luck. Netscape Calendar, as shown in Figure 2-7, makes it easy to schedule meetings, track projects, and let everybody know who's doing what and when. Calendar works a lot like a personal information manager (PIM) application. When you have an appointment, meeting, or deadline, you enter it in the appropriate date and time slot. Your coworkers all do the same thing. In addition, the network administrator also designates office resources, like conference rooms, photocopiers, and printers, so that people can indicate when these resources will be in use. Everyone's entries are updated and integrated across the server so you can quickly find out things like when your presentation is due, who's going to an upcoming conference, and when the conference room will be in use. Doesn't that sound neat? Networking professionals call this type of technology *enterprise scheduling*. For more about using Calendar and setting up a Calendar server for your Intranet, see Chapter 21.

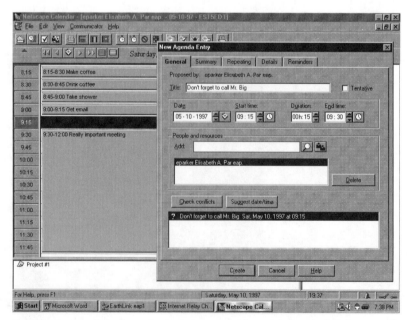

FIGURE **2.7** *Netscape Calendar makes it easy to meet with coworkers and schedule time with office resources.*

IBM Host On-Demand, for Accessing Remote Servers via Telnet

The Web provides an easy way to display and exchange information. But sometimes you might need access to non-Web data on your company's server. When you're on the road and need documents, spreadsheets, and other files from your computer at work, IBM Host On-Demand might be able to help. If your network has Telnet capabilities, you can dial into your server, access your computer, and get your files.

"How convenient," you might say, "Why couldn't I do this before?" Actually, you could. Telnet is one of the oldest Internet technologies, and all Windows computers come with HyperTerminal—a Telnet application. Now that the glamorous Web gets all the attention, nobody talks about basic stuff like Telnet anymore. This is a shame because Telnet can still be useful in some situations. For example, researchers can Telnet to various library catalogues around the world to see if the texts they need are available. And you can also download files straight from your computer at work if it is networked to the server and the server administrator sets it up for you.

However, newcomers to the Internet aren't accustomed to Telnet applications and text-based Telnet sites. Since most people are used to accessing content through the Web rather than via Telnet, they might find it easier to use IBM Host On-Demand—a Java application that is integrated with Communicator.

If you're a network administrator with users clamoring for a way to get their files and work when they're away from the office, consider giving them Telnet access . IBM Host On-Demand supports most commonly used server products, including IBM, Lotus, Novell, Netscape, and Microsoft.

Basically, Telnet works similarly to other Internet technologies. Someone sets up a Telnet server, and you enter a URL to access the server. The Telnet program works in *emulation* mode to display information and the files stored on the remote computer. Some servers are open to the public, others require you to enter a name and password, and most of them restrict access to certain directories. Ask you server administrator if Telnet is available on your Intranet and get the server telephone number and server port number (if you don't know the server port number, stick with the default 23 entry).

To get an idea of how this works, let's try the Environmental Protection Agency's Telnet site:

Select the IBM Host On-Demand option from the Communicator menu.

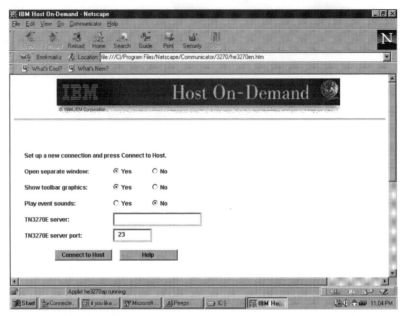

FIGURE **2.8**   *If your office has Telnet capabilities, you can access your computer files from remote locations with IBM Host On-Demand.*

When the application appears, as shown in Figure 2-8, enter the following URL:

```
epaibm.rtpnc.epa.gov
```

TIP

If you have Communicator set up to launch a Telnet application (Chapter 5 talks about this in greater detail), you can also Telnet by clicking on i"nks to Telnet sites, or by entering a URL in Navigator's location window. Telnet URLs are preceded by "telnet:" instead of "http://" because it's a different type of protocol. For example, to get to the EPA's Telnet site via Navigator, you would enter: `telnet:epaibm.rtpnc.epa.gov`.

Click the **Connect to Host** button. A really scary-looking **Java Security** dialog box appears, as shown in Figure 2-9, but don't worry about it. Just click the **Grant** button to continue (Chapter 18 discusses security in more detail).

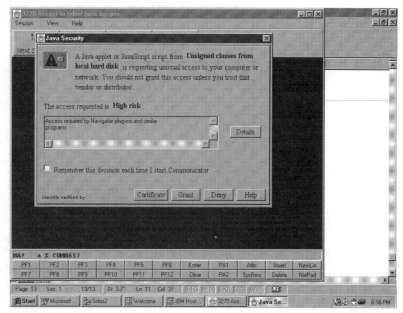

FIGURE *Ignore this scary-looking security message and click the **Grant** button.*
2.9

When the Telnet Client window appears, wait for the information to download, as shown in Figure 2-10.

Remember that this isn't the Web—Telnet sites are all text. To move to a different page, you have to enter a number (here, your only option is 6—the rest of the site is closed to public access!). Telnet sites generally have clearly written instructions so you can find your way around.

To exit, click the **Close** button.

IBM Host On-Demand's client window displays the following:

Menu Bar: Displays menu items.

Next Session: Toggles between Telnet sites that you have logged on to (IBM Host On-Demand lets you log on to two sites simultaneously).

Copy Session: Logs on to the current site in a second window (this can be useful if you're worried about getting lost and not being able to find the main page!)

Debug: Displays a text file of all communications between the server and client application, and everything that has happened during the ses-

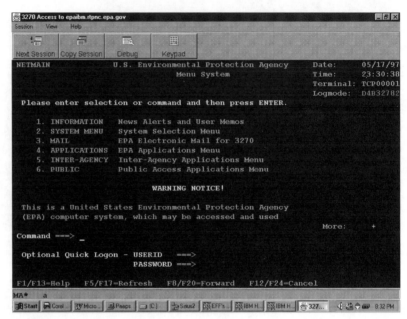

FIGURE
2.10
Voila! You're logged on to the server.

sion. This feature can be especially helpful to systems administrators who need to figure out why something went wrong.

Toggle Keypad: Toggles between displaying and hiding the Key pad.

Session Display Window: Displays the Telnet site.

Keypad: Supports common Telnet keyboard functions.

Operator Information Area (OIA): Displays status and error messages so you can see what's happening with your connection.

TIP

Need some help? Select the Index option from the Help menu, and a handy-dandy Web page appears. And if you click on the "Understanding the Operator Information Area" link, you'll find out what all those baffling status and error messages mean!

The Web is a much easier way to find information than Telnet. Then again, there's a lot more to Telnet than a bunch of text. You can find sites with news, lively bulletin board communities, and more. For lists of interesting Telnet sites, visit EFF's Extended Guide to the Internet at `http://www.eff.org/papers/eegtti/eeg_96.html` and George-town's Libraries, Catalogs, and Databases page `http://www.george-town.edu/labyrinth/library/library_catalogues.html`.

If you get seriously into Telnet, then consider learning how to use HyperTerminal (Windows users can find it in their Accessories folder) or NCSA Telnet (Macintosh users can download this freeware application from `ftp://ftp.ncsa.uiuc.edu/Mac/Telnet/Telnet2.6/Telnet2.6UserGuide`*). IBM Host On-Demand only supports sites that comply with the TN3270 protocol. Many sites do, but there are still some servers using older protocols, and you wouldn't want to miss out on anything!*

3 Getting and Setting Up Communicator

N ow that we've talked about the Internet and Netscape Communicator's features, let's get up and running. Whether you purchased Communicator in a box, or downloaded it from Netscape Communications Corporation's Web site, you'll find it quick and easy to install. This chapter tells you what you need in order to run Netscape, where to get it, how to download it, and how to install it. In addition, we'll digress a bit and talk about decompression utilities, like WinZip and StuffIt Expander. You'll need these if you ever plan on downloading anything from the Internet.

This chapter covers the following:

- System requirements
- Getting Communicator
- Installing Communicator
- Getting decompression utilities

System Requirements

Netscape Communicator has a lot of features, which can make it somewhat demanding on your computer's resources. Before jumping into Communicator, make sure your computer meets its system requirements and that you have the following:

- An up-to-date processor: PC 486 or Macintosh 06800 processor or higher. Ideally, you should have a Pentium or PowerPC processor, but you can still run Communicator on older systems. Also, Communicator runs best on systems with 100 MHz (Megahertz) processor speeds and faster.
- A recent operating system: Ideally, you should have Windows 95 or Macintosh System 7.5 or higher. These operating systems come with TCP/IP software and are more Internet-ready than the older ones. However, you can definitely get by with Windows 3.1x and higher (make sure you have the Win32s patch, though), or Macintosh system 7.0 and higher.

Netscape Communicator is also available for users of other operating systems, including OS/2, various versions of UNIX, Digital Alpha, and more. However, this book is for Windows and Macintosh users.

- A PPP/SLIP account: Get a full-Internet access PPP or SLIP Internet connection. As mentioned in Chapter 1, PPP and SLIP are protocols that enable you to access the World Wide Web. Most Internet service providers (ISPs) now offer this type of access and start you off with a disk full of all the software you need to get you up and running. You will probably have to get Communicator on your own, however.

- TCP software: As I mentioned in Chapter 1, TCP is a protocol that helps your computer, your modem, and the server communicate with each other and transfer data. Windows 95 and Macintosh System 7.5 and higher come with TCP/IP software built in. If you have Windows 3.1x, your ISP starter kit will probably come with Trumpet Winsock, a $25 TCP/IP shareware package. Macintosh users running system 7.0 and higher (but haven't upgraded to system 7.5) can purchase MacTCP from a Macintosh dealer.

- Adequate Random Access Memory (RAM): You need at least 8 MB of memory, and 16 MB would be ideal. Please note that Virtual Memory applications won't work with many of the more graphics-intensive Netscape plug-ins like QuickTime VR or Shockwave (Chapter 7 talks more about plug-ins). "Memory" is actually a shortened term for Random Access Memory (RAM). The more RAM you have, the more your computer can handle doing at once (such as browsing the Web, checking email, and maintaining your connection to your ISP's server).

- Sufficient disk space: To comfortably accommodate Communicator, a host of plug-ins, your email, and so on, you should have about 40 MB of free disk space on your hard drive.

- Modem: You need a speedy modem that can transmit data at a rate of at least 28.8 Kilobits per second (Kbps). 33.6 and 56 Kbps modems are also becoming cheaper and more popular.

If your network administrator has already installed Netscape Communicator on your computer at work, then you don't have to worry about all of this (except making sure you have enough disk space). If you're trying to persuade your boss to give you Internet access, then the above list might be helpful. But you should also probably give your boss a list about how the Internet and Netscape Communicator would help you do your *work*!

You can never Be too rich, too thin, or have too much RAM or disk space on your computer. Because Communicator has so many components, it can make heavy demands on your system's resources.

Getting Communicator

There are many ways to get Netscape Communicator. The easiest way is to go to work one day and find it installed on your system. Or your Internet service provider might give you a copy with your account. But most of us have to find and purchase Communicator ourselves. Fortunately, Communicator doesn't cost very much and getting a copy couldn't be easier. The standard version of Communicator (without features that can only be used via office Intranets anyway) costs only $49, and the Pro version costs a mere $79. You can either go to your nearest computer store and buy Communicator in a box, or you can use your old Web browser to download the latest version of Communicator via the Web. Netscape Communications Corporation lets you try out Communicator for 90 days. You can then visit the General Store section of Netscape's Web site and purchase Communicator with a credit card.

Do you need an Internet account and a copy of Netscape Communicator? Kill two birds with one stone and sign up with an Internet service provider that provides the latest version of Netscape. Earthlink (`http://www.earthlink.net/`*) is one of several companies that does this, and they have local dial-ups all over the country.*

To get Communicator via the Web, do the following (the illustrations for these sections display my old version of Navigator):

Netscape's Website changes frequently and may not appear exactly as shown in the following figures.

1. Launch your old Web browser and go to Netscape's home page at `http://home.netscape.com/`, as shown in Figure 3-1.
2. Select the version of Communicator you want (Standard or Pro with or without popular plug-ins) from the pulldown list beneath the **Get the Latest Netscape Software** heading shown in Figure 3-1.
3. Click the **Try It** button (when you're ready to purchase Communicator, you can visit again and do the same thing, only you would click the **Buy It** button).

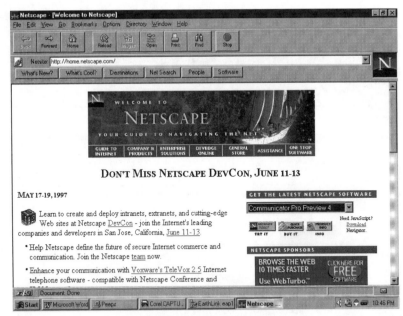

FIGURE *Visit Netscape's welcoming page at* http://home.netscape.com, *and*
3.1 *select the Communicator product you wish to download from the* **Get the Latest**
*Netscape Software** *pulldown list, then click the* **Try It** *button.*

4. When the Download Netscape Communicator Software page appears,
scroll down until you reach the form shown in Figure 3-2. The form
prompts you for the following options:

5. At the **Desired Product** prompt, select either Netscape Communicator Standard or Netscape Communicator Pro from the pulldown list.

*You can also choose the All Components plus Plug-ins versions of Communica-
tor Standard and Communicator Pro. The components and plug-ins don't cost
extra and can save you a lot of time in downloading them later. But they take up
more disk space and make Communicator take longer to download now. Unfortunately, this download only takes care of Netscape's proprietary plug-ins. To
find out how to get other plug-ins, see Chapter 7.*

6. At the **Operating System** prompt, select your computer's operating
system from the pull-down list.

7. From the **Desired Language** pulldown list, select English (or whatever
language you wish — Netscape supports many languages).

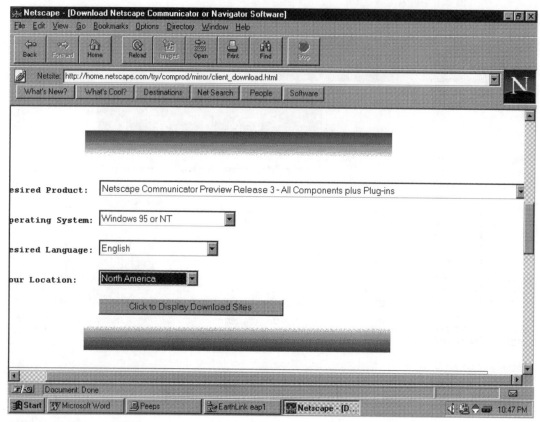

8. From the **Your Location** pulldown list, select the continent where you are (this directs you to the nearest servers).

9. Click the **Click** to **Display Download Sites** button.

10. When the list of download sites appears, as in Figure 3-3, click one of them to download Communicator. If the server is busy, try another link.

Now you can take a break, pour yourself some coffee and read the newspaper. Netscape Communicator takes an hour (or longer!) to download.

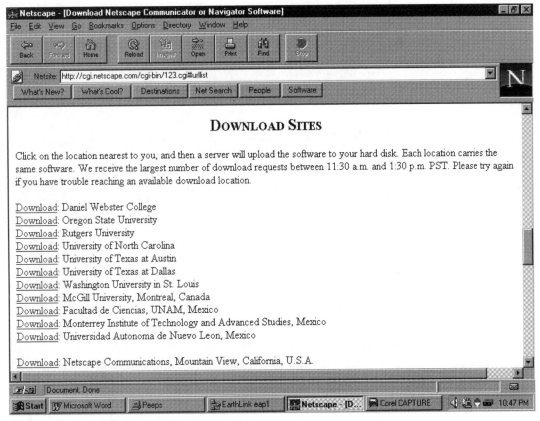

FIGURE   *Click on a download site link.*
3.3

If you use a Macintosh, don't do anything on your computer while downloading Communicator. Macintosh computers don't have multithreading capabilities — they can't download your file properly and let you do other things at the same time.

CAUTION

Depending on what browser you currently use, the Communicator installer will either automatically download to a folder specified in the browser preferences, or a Save dialog box appears so you can browse for the folder you wish to save the installer to.

NOTE

> ### *Try a Beta Preview*
>
> Rats! Did you do all this and get an error message announcing that the software you requested isn't available for your operating system? Don't be discouraged. Development for non-Windows 95 and NT operating system versions of software often lag a little behind, but your version will be available soon.
>
> If you're feeling adventurous, see if there's a preview *beta* version of Communicator available for your operating system. Betas are what computer people call experimental versions of upcoming products. Netscape's preview betas generally work fine, but have a few glitches and features that aren't enabled yet. You can use betas free of charge for a limited period of time (and keep downloading the latest ones) until the real version is available for your operating system.
>
> Why does Netscape let you try out unfinished software? They want feedback from users about what works and doesn't work, and they also want people to get excited about the final product. You can find preview beta software by going through the same process as you go through to access the "real" thing, only you should select the item on the list that indicates a preview version.

Installing Communicator

Once you get Communicator, you can install the program. Whether you downloaded the program from the Internet or purchased the box version, setup procedures should work similarly. However, if you downloaded it, you'll launch the installer from the folder you downloaded the file to; whereas, if you purchased Communicator in a store, you would launch the installer from the CD-ROM. The following section goes through the basic steps of setting up Communicator. Depending on which version you have and which operating system you use, the setup routine may vary. But never fear. The installer program makes everything easy.

To set up Netscape Communicator, do the following:

1. Launch the Communicator setup program by clicking on the installer icon.

TIP

*If you're confused about something in the setup routine, never fear. You can cancel setup at any time by clicking the **Cancel** button.*

2. When the **Setup** screen appears and displays the **Setup Type** dialog box, as shown in Figure 3-5, choose the **Typical** radio button, then

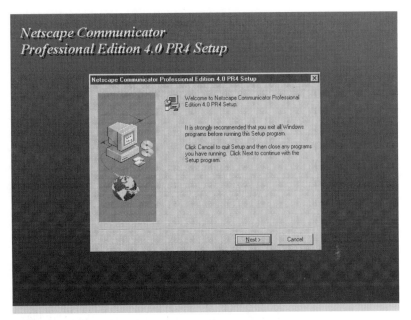

FIGURE   *Setup dialog box, choose next to continue setup.*
3.4

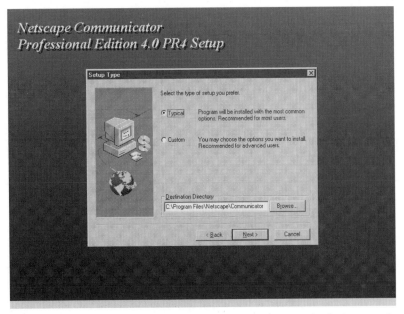

FIGURE   *When the **Setup Type** dialog box appears, choose the **Typical** radio button and*
3.5   *click Next.*

click the **Next** button. (You can also click the **Browse** button to display a window with the folders on your computer if you want to install Communicator in a different destination folder.)

NOTE

Some people call them "folders," some people call them "directories," but both words mean the same thing: the places where you put your files.

TIP

*If you know a little about Communicator and need to save a little disk space, try the **Custom** radio button. This lets you install some components and not others. However, if you choose a custom set up, be aware that some features described in this book may not be available to you.*

3. When the **Select a Program Folder** dialog box appears, as shown in Figure 3-6, choose a program folder for Communicator. This makes Communicator application icons appear in program groups and as items on the **Start** menu so you can find them quickly. Either keep Communicator's default setting (it will create its own program folder) or select an existing program folder from the list. Click the **Next** button to move on.

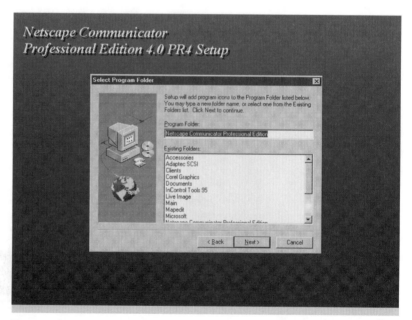

FIGURE *Choose a program folder for Communicator, then click the **Next** button.*
3.6

*Macintosh users won't see this dialog box because Macs don't have program groups. But you can still make Communicator easy to find by creating an alias. To create an alias, select the application icon, then select **Make Alias** from the **File** menu. When the alias icon appears, move it to your desktop. You can also add it to your Apple menu by moving the alias to the **Apple Menu Items** folder inside the **System** folder.*

4. When the **Start Copying Files** dialog box appears, as shown in Figure 3-7, confirm your settings. The setup type and the list of components to be installed appears in the scrolling window. Click the **Back** button to make changes or click the **Install** button to begin copying files and installing Communicator.

5. The **Setup** dialog box shown in Figure 3-8 appears to tell you the status of setup and to let you cancel setup by clicking the **Cancel** button.

6. When setup is finished, the dialog box shown in Figure 3-9 appears and asks you if you want to view the README file now. Click **Yes.**

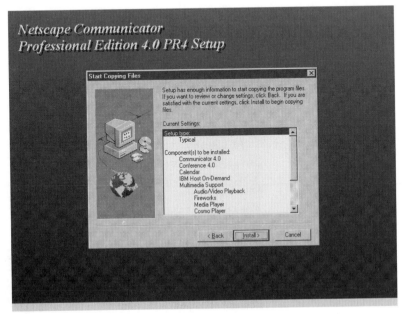

FIGURE *Click Install to start copying your files.*
3.7

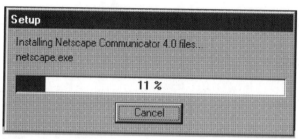

FIGURE *Setup dialog box.*
3.8

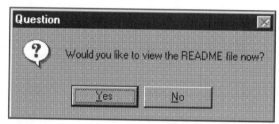

FIGURE *Click Yes to view the README file.*
3.9

What's a README File?

The README file is a plain text document that provides more information about an application. Most programs come with one. If you double click on the README file icon, it will display plain, unformatted text in a system text editor program like NotePad (Windows) or SimpleText (Macintosh). Sometimes the README file provides additional information about using the product, and sometimes it is a *licensing agreement.* The agreement outlines the rules and conditions of using the software. To close out of the README file, click on the **Close** box, or select the **Close** command from the **File** menu.

7. When the **Information** dialog box shown in Figure 3-10 appears, tells you that the Setup is complete, click **OK**.
8. You have to restart your computer before Communicator will work. When the **Restarting** dialog box appears, as shown in Figure 3-11, you can choose to restart your computer now or restart it later. Click the OK button.

FIGURE *Click OK to exit setup.*
3.10

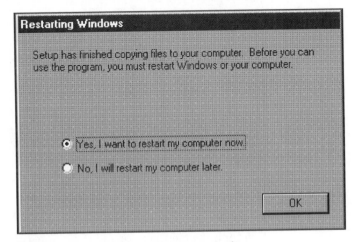

FIGURE *Choose to restart your computer now or later.*
3.11

Congratulations! Once you restart your computer, you'll be ready to launch Communicator.

Getting Decompression Utilities

You might find this digression annoying now, but you'll forgive me later on. Presentations, CAD drawings, collections of images, utilities, shareware, and software updates are often larger than 2 MB (Megabytes). Large files can take interminable amounts of time to download.

To make large files or groups of files smaller and more manageable, their creators compress them into archives. You can then download the files and decompress the archive so you can use the files inside. The most popular compression programs are WinZip (Windows) and StuffIt (Macintosh).

WinZip, by Nico Mak Computing, Inc., creates "zipped" files with the .ZIP file name extension. StuffIt, a shareware utility by Aladdin Systems, creates "stuffed" file archives with the .HQX, .SEA, .CPT, .SIT, and .BIN file name extensions. To open these file formats, you either need a copy of StuffIt, or the freeware StuffIt Expander. StuffIt Expander can open compressed files, but it cannot compress files.

How Do I Register and Figure out How to Use Shareware?

Since you're about to download shareware, let's take a moment. You'll come across lots of shareware during your travels on the net. Shareware works on a try-before-you-buy honor system. You can use the application without paying for it, and if you like the application, you're supposed to send a check to the author or pay online with a credit card. Shareware programmers seem to be getting more savvy these days, though. Many programs stop working after a certain number of days.

WINZIP

WinZip is the most popular and easy-to-use compression and decompression utility for Windows 3.1x and Windows 95 users. You can get an evaluation copy from the WinZip Web site at http://www.winzip.com/. If you like WinZip (and you probably will), please send Nico Mak Computing a check for $29 so the nice programmers don't starve. You can also pay online. Also, remember that Windows 3.1x users need the *16-bit* version of WinZip and Windows 95 and NT users need the *32-bit* version. The newer types of Windows operating systems are 32-bit.

TIP

Windows users can also decompress StuffIt files. Go to Aladdin Systems' Web site at http://www.aladdinsys.com/ *and get UnStuff for Windows.*

STUFFIT EXPANDER

StuffIt Expander is a freeware program from Aladdin Systems. It expands Macintosh-formatted compressed archives with file extensions ending in .SEA, .SIT, .HQX, .BIN, .BINHEX, and .CPT. In order to compress files, you'll need to purchase StuffIt in a computer store near you.

TIP

Macintosh users can decompress ZIP files with UnZip for Macintosh. You can get it at SOFTSware at `ftp://ftp.ino.com/inohd/ftp/software/uz201.sea.Hqx.`

You can get StuffIt Expander in two ways:

1. World Wide Web: Go to Aladdin Systems' home page (`http://www.aladdinsys.com/`) and download StuffIt Expander by clicking on the link. You can also find information about StuffIt and other Aladdin Systems products on this site. There's one problem, though. You won't be able to decompress StuffIt Expander unless you already have a binary file or BinHex decoder! And if you had one, you wouldn't need StuffIt Expander. But never fear . . . you can send away for StuffIt Expander by email!

2. Email: Most email programs, like Eudora, automatically decode binary files. This is probably the easiest way to get StuffIt Expander if you don't already have it. Send email request to: `mthomas@macatawa.org`. In the body of your email, request StuffIt Expander. Your copy of Expander will arrive within the next 48 hours as an email attachment. Or, send email to: `info@aladdinsystems.com`. In the subject line, type "getexpander". Leave the body of the message empty.

NOTE

If you decide to have StuffIt Expander emailed to you as an attachment, please note that attachments sometimes take a few minutes to transfer.

Creating a User Profile

Some offices can't provide everyone with a direct connection to the Internet. In many cases, the network administrator sets up a designated computer for Internet access that is shared by groups of coworkers. Fortunately, Netscape Communicator Pro makes it easy for you (or your network administrator) to create user profiles. This enables users to have individual mail boxes, subscribed news and discussion groups, address books, bookmarks, and preferences even though they all share the same Netscape Communicator Pro application. User profiles can also be useful at home if two or more family members share the same computer, or if you want to create separate profiles for personal and business Internet use.

NOTE

If you use Netscape Communicator Pro, you must create a user profile, even if you're the only user.

Don't complain about that obnoxious coworker to your friends via email! User profiles do not have password protection and your coworkers can access your information, though hopefully they'll respect your privacy.

To create a user profile, do the following:

1. Select the Programs folder from the Start menu, select the Netscape Communicator Professional Edition folder, then select the Profile Manager icon.
2. When the Profile Manager window appears, as shown in Figure 3-12, click the New button (any existing user profiles also appear on the list).
3. When the New User Setup dialog box appears, read the instructions and click the Next button.
4. When the New Profile Setup dialog box appears, enter your full name and your email address in the appropriate text fields, then click the Next button.
5. When the second New Profile Setup dialog box appears, enter a Profile Name (the name that appears on the Profile Manager list) in the

FIGURE *Profile Manager window.*
3.12

appropriate text field. You can also specify a directory path for where you want to store your profile folder (which contains your preferences, address book, messages, etc.), though I recommend sticking with the default path name (which is usually C:\Program Files\Netscape\Users\your-user-name\ unless your network administrator has created a different one). Click the Next button.

6. When the Mail and Discussion Groups Setup dialog box appears, enter your name, email address and the name of your outgoing mail server in the appropriate text fields (if you don't know, ask your Internet service provider or network administrator). Click the Next button.

7. When the second Mail and Discussion Groups Setup dialog box appears, enter your mail server user name (the first part of your email address before the @ sign) and the name of the incoming mail server in the appropriate text fields, and indicate your mail server type by clicking the POP3 or IMAP radio button (if you don't know this information, ask your Internet service provider or network administrator).

8. When the third second Mail and Discussion Groups Setup dialog box appears, enter the name of your news server and the port number. If your organization uses a secure server, click the Secure check box (if you have regular dial up access through an ISP, you probably would not select the Secure check box). If you don't know this information, ask you Internet service provider or network administrator. Most servers use Port 119.

9. Click the Finish button.

That's all there is to it! The next time you launch Communicator, the Profile Manager appears. You can then open your personalized version of Communicator by selecting your user profile from the list and double-clicking on it.

CHAPTER 4

Test Driving Navigator

Now that we've spent three chapters talking about the Internet, Communicator's features, and getting set up, let's take Navigator for a test drive. Navigator has been a popular stand-alone Web browser for the past few years and is now integrated with Communicator. What's so great about Navigator, as opposed to the many other Web browsers out there? Anyone who has surfed the Web and seen all the pages that say "This page looks better with Netscape Navigator" knows the answer to that. With Navigator, you never have to miss out on cutting-edge Web pages. In addition, Navigator is integrated with Communicator's other components so you can access other Internet services like email and newsgroups by simply clicking on a link or component bar icon. This chapter gets you started with the basics—like how to use the toolbars, menus, and status bars—so you can get started.

This chapter covers the following:

- Launching Navigator
- Using Navigator's toolbars
- Understanding status indicators
- Following links
- Exploring Web page content
- Electronic forms and email links
- Dynamic content (Java, JavaScript, ActiveX)
- File downloads
- Multimedia
- Virtual reality

This chapter also briefly explains how hypertext links work.

Launching Navigator

Launching Navigator is as easy as double-clicking on the Navigator icon. For Windows 95 users, the installation routine automatically creates a Navigator shortcut on your desktop as well as a folder with Communicator component icons on your **Start** menu. For Windows 3.1x users, the installation routine automatically creates a Communicator program group from which you can launch Navigator and other components. Macintosh users can make a Navigator alias (Chapter 2 tells you how) and put it in their Apple menu or on the desktop. To launch Navigator, double-click on the Navigator icon on your desktop or program group, or select it from the Start menu (Windows 95 only).

VIEWING NAVIGATOR'S MAIN WINDOW

When you launch Navigator, the Navigator Main Window appears as shown in Figure 4-1. The people at Netscape constructed their Web browser so that it would be simple for you to use. However, there's a lot of stuff here and all these little icons can seem overwhelming at first. But never fear. Once you familiarize yourself with its look and feel, a quick glance can tell you everything from what options you have, to the status of a page or file you're downloading.

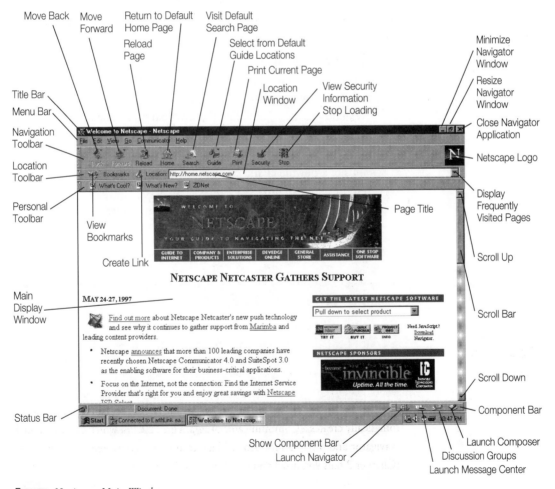

FIGURE *Navigator Main Window.*
4.1

Navigator's main window has the following elements:

Title Bar: The blue bar with white text at the top of the screen displays the title of the current Web page.

Menu bar: Displays a row of items from which you can pull down menus with lists of commands and options (some of which are not available as clickable icons).

Navigation Toolbar: Displays icons for frequent tasks performed while navigating the Web, such as moving backwards and forwards and printing pages.

Location Toolbar: Provides options for visiting sites on the Web and displays the current page URL in the **Location** window.

Personal Toolbar: You can customize this toolbar and add your favorite Web sites to it (Chapter 8 tells you how).

Main Display Window: Displays Internet content, such as Web pages and FTP directories.

Scroll Bar: Enables you to move up and down on the current page. You can do this by either sliding the scroll bar button up and down, or by clicking on the up and down arrows.

Status Bar: Provides information about the current page, such as the status of a download and whether the page is secure (Chapter 18 talks more about security).

Component Bar: Makes accessing other Communicator components as easy as pointing and clicking.

The following sections discuss these page elements in greater detail.

Using Key Combinations

You can use key combinations instead of pulling down file menus or clicking toolbar buttons all the time. To use key combinations, hold down the **Control** or **Alt** key (Windows) or **Command** (Macintosh) key while pressing down a letter or number at the same time. Whenever you can use key combinations, I'll enter them in parentheses so you know what they are as CTRL+... or ALT+... (Windows) and CMD+... (Macintosh). You can also easily find out what the key combinations for different commands are for yourself. All you have to do is pull down your menu lists and look at the items. When available, the keyboard command appears next to the appropriate menu list item.

LAUNCHING COMMUNICATOR COMPONENTS

Sure, exploring the World Wide Web is fun and informative. But chances are you need to get other things done—such as check your email or the latest postings from your department's discussion group. No problem. You can quickly access other Communicator components via the Communicator menu or the component bar, located at the bottom right of the Navigator main window. The component bar always displays at the bottom right of the current window, regardless of which Communicator application you are using. In addition, icons for each Communicator component appear as individual items in your Communicator **Start Menu** folder (Windows 95), **Program Group** (Windows 95 and 3.1x), and **Program** folder (Macintosh).

Do you find the icons on the Communicator component bar difficult to see? You can display the bar as a larger, floating palette (as shown in Figure 4-2) by selecting the **Show Component Bar** option from the Communicator menu or by clicking the **Show Component Bar** button to the left of the bar. To *dock* the component bar (return it to its original position), click the **Close** button.

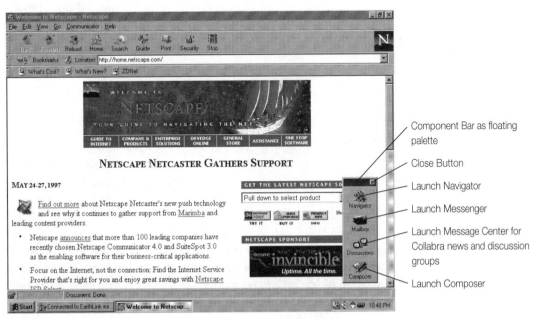

Component Bar as floating palette

Close Button

Launch Navigator

Launch Messenger

Launch Message Center for Collabra news and discussion groups

Launch Composer

FIGURE *You can display the Communicator component bar as a floating palette.*
4.2

The **Component bar** provides the following options:

Navigator: Click to launch or display the Navigator window (you can also select **Navigator** from the Communicator menu or use the CTRL+1 or CMD+1 key combination).

Mailbox: Click to launch or display Netscape Messenger so you can send, receive, and compose email messages (you can also select **Messenger Mailbox** from the Communicator menu or use the CTRL+2 or CMD+2 key combination).

CAUTION

Before sending email and participating in news and discussion groups, you need to enter your mail and news server settings. I'll cover those topics in detail Chapter 5.

Discussions: Click to display the message center for accessing news and discussion groups (you can also select Collabra Discussion Groups from the Communicator menu or use the CTRL+3 or CMD+3 key combination).

Composer: Click to launch or display Composer so you can create and upload Web pages (you can also select **Page Composer** from the Communicator menu or use the CTRL+4 or CMD+4 key combination).

But what about all those other Communicator components discussed in Chapter 2? Don't worry. They don't appear as icons on the component bar, but you can still easily select them from the Communicator menu:

Conference: Launches the Conference component (or use the CTRL+5 or CMD+5 key combination). For more about Netscape Conference, read Chapters 15 and 16.

Calendar: Launches Netscape Calendar component (or use the CTRL+6 or CMD+6 key combination). This enterprise scheduling feature is only available for Communicator Pro users. For more about Calendar, read Chapter 21.

IBM Host On-Demand: Launches Communicator's Java Telnet component for accessing files stored on remote servers (or use the CTRL+5 or CMD+5 key combination). For more about IBM Host On-Demand, see Chapter 2.

Netcaster: Launches Netcaster so you can tune into Internet broadcasts (or use the CTRL+5 or CMD+5 key combination). For more about Netcaster, see Chapter 6.

TIP

Can't remember what all the icons and other screen elements do? No problem! Communicator Tooltips (Windows) and Balloon Help (Macintosh) remind you when your cursor passes over interface elements. To see what I'm talking about, move your cursor over a toolbar icon, leave it there for a second (but don't press your mouse key down), and see what happens.

Using Navigator's Toolbars

THE NAVIGATION TOOLBAR

The easiest way to start exploring the Web is by using the Navigation toolbar. Netscape starts you off with lots of great places to go and makes it as easy as pointing and clicking on the little toolbar icons. You can visit Netscape's home page, move back, forward, stop loading pages when you change your mind, and more.

The Navigation toolbar offers the following options:

Hide Navigation Toolbar: Click the bar on the left (it has a downward arrow and turns blue when your cursor passes over it) to hide the Navigation toolbar. To display it again, click the tab that appears beneath the other toolbars, or select **Show Navigation Toolbar** from the **View** menu.

Back: Returns you to the last Web site you visited (you can also use the ALT+left arrow key combination). When there are no previous pages to return to, this icon is disabled.

Forward: If you have moved backwards, this button moves you forward again (you can also use the ALT+right arrow key combination).

Reload: Reloads a fresh copy of the current Web page, instead of a copy from your Cache folder. The contents of recently visited sites get saved in your cache file so they don't take as long to view the next time you visit them (you can also use the CTRL+R or CMD+R key combination).

Home: Returns you to the default home page. This is the page that you land on when launching Navigator. Unless you, your Internet service provider (ISP), or network administration changes the default, the default home page is Netscape's page at `http://home.netscape.com/`. We'll talk more about changing your default page in Chapter 5.

TIP

Network administrators can also use Netscape's Administration Kit to distribute customized versions of Communicator that have their organization's home page set as the default home page. For more about using Netscape server tools for managing Intranets, read Chapters 19 through 21.

Search: Jumps you to a search engine on Netscape's Web site so you can search for information by key word. For more about using search engines, read Chapter 9.

Guide: Displays a pulldown menu with useful and fun places to visit on the Internet. You can select an item to jump to a page. Guide items include Netscape's "What's New" and "What's Cool" for a guide to interesting, useful, and cutting-edge sites. Who knows? These sites may even offer inspiration for features you can add to your personal or organizational Web site!

Print: Prints content from the current page.

Security: Displays security information for the current page so you can decide whether you feel safe submitting a credit card number or other confidential information to a Web site. For more about Communicator's security features,,see Chapter 18.

Stop: Cancels downloading the file you requested, or the Web page whose URL you just entered (you can also hit the ESC key). This option is useful when you come across those Web pages that take forever to appear! Or when you change your mind about downloading a file.

Try clicking on some of the links on Netscape's home page (or the current default home page) or from the Guide list. See? Exploring the Web is easy. The section in this chapter on following links explains how this works in greater detail.

TIP

Do you have a small computer monitor? You can save "screen real estate" by hiding your toolbars and using key combinations or selecting menu items instead. All of the toolbar items have corresponding menu items. To hide your toolbars, click on the vertical bars (they have a tiny arrow and turn blue when you pass your cursor over them). To display them again, simply click on the little tabs that appear beneath the Menu bar, or select the **Show** *toolbar commands from the* **View** *menu.*

THE LOCATION AND PERSONAL TOOLBARS

Once you've found some places to go on the Web, the Location and personal toolbars become highly useful. They make it possible for you to navigate the Web by entering URLs in the **Location** window, save URLs for places you plan on visiting again by placing them in your **Bookmarks** folder, and even adding items to your personal toolbar for easy access.

The Location toolbar has the following elements:

Hide Location Toolbar: Click the bar on the left (it has a downward arrow and turns blue when your cursor passes over it) to hide the Navigation toolbar. To display it again, click the tab that appears beneath the other toolbars, or select **Show Navigation Toolbar** from the **View** menu.

Bookmarks: Displays items from your **Bookmarks** folder, as shown in Figure 4-3. If this is the first time you've used Netscape, your Bookmarks list may be empty—but it won't be for long. Your systems administrator or ISP may have even created a list for you. For more on adding, editing, and organizing bookmarks, see Chapter 8. You can also display your bookmarks by selecting **Bookmarks** from the Communicator menu.

Make Link: Drag the icon into your bookmarks, an email, or newsgroup message that you're composing with Messenger, or a Web page that you're editing to create a link to the current page displayed in Navigator.

Location Window: Enter a URL and hit the **Enter** key to jump to a Web site. Click on the little downward arrow to the right of the Location window to display a list of some Web pages you've been visiting a lot lately. You can jump to a Web page by selecting an item from the list.

The personal toolbar lets you add your favorite URLs to it for easy access. Netscape has already placed several items on the toolbar for you, and you can add more if you wish.

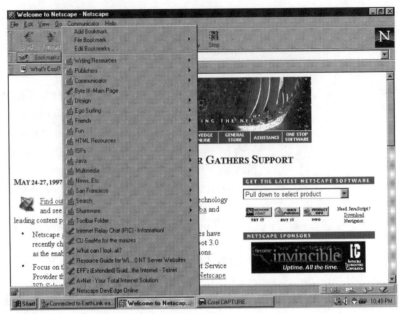

FIGURE *Bookmarks menu displayed.*
4.3

To add a URL and Netscape page icon to the personal toolbar, do the following:

Go to the Web page you want to put on the list by entering the URL in the **Location** window.

Click on the **Bookmarks** icon and select the **File Bookmark** option.

Select the **Toolbar Folder** item from the list (this may be the *only* item on the list if you're a new Navigator user) and release the mouse.

The item now appears on the personal toolbar so you can visit the page by simply clicking on the icon. We'll talk more about editing and reorganizing bookmark folders in Chapter 8. If you have little use for creating a personal toolbar, hide it by clicking on the vertical bar to the left. To display the personal toolbar, click the tab that appears beneath the other toolbars, or select **Show Navigation Toolbar** from the **View** menu.

Understanding Status Indicators

Status indicators tell you what's going on with your Internet connection. When jumping to a new Web site or downloading a file, look at the bottom border of the Navigator window. This is the status bar, and it gives you two types of information:

> **Security status information:** The little lock in the lower left corner of the Navigator window tells you whether the Web page you're visiting is secure. If the lock is fastened, that means that the site is secure and you can feel reasonably safe about submitting credit card information to an online merchant. Most of the time, the lock will appear as un-fastened, since only Web sites that deal with confidential information require security. If you double-click on the lock icon, a document information window appears with more details. Chapter 18 tells you more about Communicator's security features.

> **Download status information:** The rest of the status bar gives you information about what's going on with your download, such as whether it has successfully connected to the requested server and what percentage of the content has been downloaded so far.

Remember that even when you're just visiting a Web page, you're actually downloading data! Navigator requests page content from a server, then displays it for you.

In addition, the Netscape logo at the upper right corner of the Navigator screen is also a status indicator. It displays animated shooting stars while data is transferring. If you click on it, you land on Netscape's home page.

Following Links

Now that we've taken a look at Navigator's window, and perhaps explored the default home page and Guide locations for a while, let's try venturing out from the nest. How do you travel around the Web? Just follow the hypertext links. As you recall from Chapter 1, hypertext links let you jump around from place to place. You'll know when you're looking at a hypertext link because it usually looks different from surrounding elements on the page.

Web pages often use the following types of links :

Text links: Underlined words that appear in a distinctive color from the rest of the text. The linked text is also usually underlined.

Graphical links: Images can also be linked. How can you tell the difference between an ordinary image and a linked image? It's usually intuitive. Graphical links look like they're supposed to take you somewhere.

Image maps: Image maps are larger, more complex graphics. You can click on different parts of an image map to access different pages.

Pulldown lists: Some Web sites display pulldown lists with options that you can select to find different types of information.

Links aren't complicated at all. All you have to do is click on them, and you'll be exploring the Web in no time!

How Do Hypertext Links Work?

Links display on your screen as highlighted text or images. But if you learn a little HTML and view a Web page's source code by selecting the **View Source** command from the **View** menu, you may notice that linked text and images has lots of gobbledy-gook surrounding it—including something that looks like a URL (by the way, if you want to try this, I recommend starting off with very short pages or else the source code gets confusing!).

For example, if you created a home page and wanted to let your visitors jump to Netscape's Web site, you would probably enter text that would appear as follows:

Check out <u>Netscape's Home Page!</u>

When your visitors click on the highlighted, underlined text, they'll land on Netscape's home page. This works so simply that we hardly need to think about it. However, there's a little more to links than meets the eye.

The text for this line in the HTML source document (which is what you see when you view source code) doesn't look as simple as the text shown above. It reads as follows:

```
<P ALIGN="LEFT">Check out <A
HREF="http://home.netscape.com/">Netscape's Home
Page</A>!</P>
```

The `<P ALIGN="LEFT">` HTML formatting tag tells Navigator to display the text as default paragraph text that aligns to the left. The `<A HREF= ....>` Anchor tag tells Navigator to point the following text (or it could be an image) to Netscape's URL. We call this an Anchor tag because it anchors a Web page element to a specified location. The `</A>` and `</P>` tags tell Navigator to close the anchored entry and to end the default paragraph formatting.

So much for my little introduction to how HTML works for now. Chapter 17 talks more about Web pages and creating them with Composer.

Exploring Web Page Content

Let's face it. No matter how useful Communicator's other components are, many of you will probably use Navigator a lot. The Web's ease of use, and impressive search, text, and graphics display, and file transfer capabilities make it an ideal medium for researching, publishing, and distributing information. Whether you use the Web for business or fun, Navigator can help you communicate better and find whatever you're looking for.

Although few things are more satisfying than curling up with a good book, newspaper, or magazine, nothing beats the Web for providing a wealth of information at your fingertips—any time of the day or night. Whether you need the perfect quote for a research paper or presentation (Try "Bartlett's Familiar Quotations" at `http://www.columbia.edu/acis/bartleby/bartlett`) or stock market updates (Try "StockMaster" at `http//www.ai.mit.edu/stocks.html`), you can find it on the Web.

In addition, the Web is becoming increasingly interactive. Not only can you find an article with desperately needed information that you couldn't find anywhere else—the article may include a live demonstration of the concepts it discusses and include a link to the magazine that published the article so you can subscribe on the spot! Navigator has always been on the cutting edge and supports the latest display and interactive capabilities on the Web so you don't miss out on anything.

DISPLAY AND GRAPHICS FEATURES

Thanks to Navigator's advanced design and display features, Web page developers create exciting layouts that make information easier to find, demonstrate instructions and procedures, and add visual impact. Navigator supports frames, colored and patterned backgrounds, tables, style sheets, and other cutting-edge design elements so you can view attractively designed pages like the one shown in Figure 4-4. If you've been using a less advanced browser, the Web will look like a whole different place from now on! Plus you will no longer have to skip sites because they look better with a browser that you don't have (Navigator supports most content created for Internet Explorer, too!).

Believe it or not, HTML documents don't really include images. Image files are stored separately in a directory on the file server. The markup tags tell Navigator where to place the image, and point to the image file.

NOTE

The Web can display two types of images:

.GIFs (**Graphic Interchange Format**): The .GIF file format is generally used for simple illustrations. GIF files can also be made transparent (the image background color is eliminated so it appears to float against the Web page's background) and assembled into simple animations.

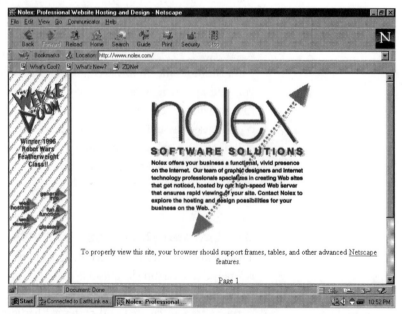

FIGURE *With Navigator, you can view cutting-edge home pages with attractive, well-*
4.4 *organized layouts like Nolex Software Solutions' home page*
(http://www.nolex.com/)

.JPEGs (Joint Photographic Experts Group): The Joint Photographic Experts Group, an international standards organization, created this file format so photo-quality images could be displayed on the Web. Because of the DOS file naming conventions (i.e., picture1.jpg), .JPEG files often have the .JPG file name suffix.

Both .GIF and .JPEG files compress to small files so they don't take too long to download and display on Web pages.

Alphabet Soup

With all these .GIFs, .JPEGs, and other file types I keep talking about, this chapter is starting to look like alphabet soup! Who cares about all these file types? Well, Navigator does. Before it can load Web pages or any other types of files, it needs to know what the file types are. Communicator is able to do this because Web site developers name their files with the appropriate file name extensions. File name extensions identify what type of data is contained in the file. For example, a .GIF file would be named something like "image.gif".

You should be aware of the fact that file formats with four-letter suffixes like .JPEG and .MPEG often have alternative three-letter suffixes like .JPG and .MPG. This isn't because technical people want to torment you with acronyms. It's because of DOS file-naming conventions.

Back in the old days, most people used computers that ran an operating system called DOS. With DOS, file names could only have up to eight letters and were followed with a three-letter file name extension. For example, word processing documents generally ended with the .doc file name extension, as in "letter.doc". Many of us have computers that can handle long file names, so we can use names like "letter to my mean old boss.doc". However, there are lots of Windows 3.1x users out there—and they still use DOS file naming conventions.

Electronic Forms and Email Links

ONLINE FORMS

Whether you're signing an innocuous online guest book like the one shown in Figure 4-5, or ordering office supplies with a credit card, Navigator can handle them. A quick glance at the status bar even tells you whether the Web site is secure so you can decide whether you want to fill in the form.

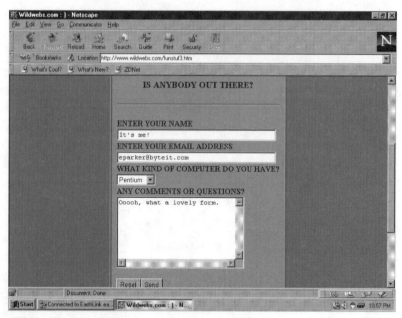

FIGURE *Navigator supports forms, and tells you whether they're secure.*
4.5

Since Navigator supports standard security technologies, you can submit confidential information securely and privately.

Many Web designers invite people to sign their guest books because they're curious about who's visiting the site and want some feedback. Since no credit cards are involved in situations like this, you don't have to worry about security (unless you're a highly secretive person!). If you've never filled out an online form before, go ahead! It's easy. Simply enter your information in the text boxes following the prompts. Some forms also let you select options from pulldown lists or rows of check boxes or radio buttons. When you're finished, click the **Submit** button.

EMAIL LINKS

A more simple way for people to get feedback on their Web sites is to create email links, and you'll frequently come across them. When you click on an email link, a new message window appears with the Web site contact person's email address so you can compose and send a message to that person.

Dynamic Content

Navigator can handle dynamic Web pages that use programming and scripting languages like Java, JavaScript, and Active X for greater interactivity and usefulness. When Sun Microsystems introduced the Java programming language and Netscape built Java support into Navigator version 2.0, it revolutionized the Web. For the first time, developers could build applications into their Web pages without using special server applications (Java programs that load from Web pages are called Java applets). This means that even people who don't run their own servers and have ISPs hosting their pages can add powerful capabilities to their sites. However, Java is still a complex programming language that takes time to master (although nowadays, you can find software that helps nonprogrammers work with Java). Netscape later introduced JavaScript—a lightweight scripting language that lacks many of Java's capabilities but is more accessible for nontechnical folks. Now, Navigator even supports ActiveX, a programming technology introduced by Microsoft.

Would you like to add some Java applets, JavaScript scripts, or ActiveX controls to Web pages that you've created? Visit EarthWeb's Gamelan page at `http://www.gamelan.com/`*. They have lots of resources and shareware related to these new technologies.*

Yikes! Do all these programming languages sound complicated? They are, but let the programmers worry about it. All you need to know is that Java, JavaScript, and ActiveX technologies help Web site developers create more exciting Web pages. The Vacation Planner Demo page, shown in Figure 4-6, shows how a JavaScript-enabled Web page can help make planning a vacation simple and fun. You can select options and drag them towards the baggage cart. As the cart becomes loaded with suitcases, each option is added to your vacation total. If this were a real company Web site, there would also be links to information about the destinations, hotels, transportation, and tours, and you could order your tickets on line. For more information and examples of dynamic content at work, visit Netscape's Communicator page at `http://home.netscape.com/inf/comprod/products/communicator/index.html`.

If you're involved with your company or department's Web site (on the Internet or Intranet), you can add powerful capabilities to your Web site with JavaScript. You don't even need to be a programmer—Netscape is coming out with a prod-

uct called Visual JavaScript that helps nonprogrammers build JavaScript scripts into Web pages. In addition, if you use Netscape Server products, you probably have a component called LiveWire. LiveWire can help you integrate your Web site with your database. For more information, visit Netscape's home page at `http://home.netscape.com/.`

Java, JavaScript, and ActiveX are demanding on your computer's resources. In addition, for the time being, Windows 3.1x and Macintosh computers don't handle dynamic page content as well as many of us would like. For security reasons, you also may not want to randomly download Java applets, JavaScript scripts, and ActiveX controls to your computer—although most of them are perfectly safe. Fortunately, you can disable Java and JavaScript via your Preferences menus (Chapter 5). In addition, Navigator's security features (Chapter 18) help you deal with potentially risky content. Once you understand how these features work, you won't have to worry!

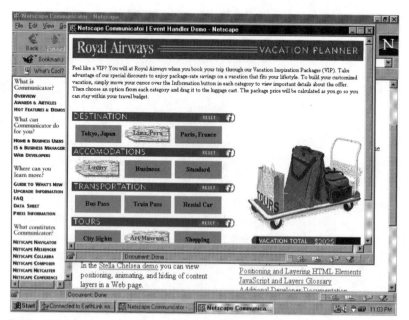

FIGURE   *Navigator supports Web pages with dynamic content.*
4.6

File Downloads

Before we get into multimedia, let's talk about downloading files. Whenever you request a Web page by clicking on a link, selecting a toolbar item or bookmark, or entering the URL in the location window, you download files. This includes page elements that load with the HTML document, including text, graphics, and dynamic content.

In many cases, links don't lead to other Web pages. Instead, you click on them to download other types of files, including shareware, large documents (such as software documentation), images, and multimedia files. You can then install the shareware later, and view the images or multimedia files with separate applications or plug-ins.

DOWNLOADING FILES VIA LINKS

When you click on a link to download a file that you don't have a plug-in for (I'll get to that in a minute), the **Save As...** dialog box appears, as shown in Figure 4-7. You can then browse for a folder to save the file to, and click the **Save** button. A dialog box then appears to tell you the status of the download. If you change your mind, you can click the **Cancel** button.

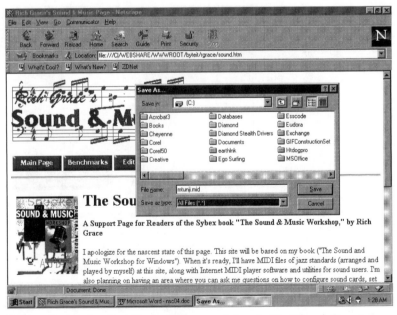

FIGURE *You can download files by clicking on a link to the file. When the Save As...*
4.7 *dialog box appears, you can choose a folder to save your file to.*

DOWNLOADING FILES WITH PLUG-INS

If you have a plug-in that handles the type of file you want to download, Navigator launches the plug-in and loads the file in a separate window. For example, I clicked on a link to a MIDI music file and Live Update's Crescendo MIDI plug-in played it back in a separate window, as shown in Figure 4-8. This way, you can view the file immediately and don't have to activate the plug-in and open the file yourself.

But what's a plug-in? Plug-ins are applications, created by third parties, that are designed to work with Navigator. They expand Navigator's capabilities by enabling it to handle file types that aren't native to the browser. For example, Navigator is not a movie player application. But if someone has an Apple QuickTime movie on his or her home page, that person can play back the movie straight from the Web with the QuickTime plug-in. Chapter 7 gives you the details on getting and installing plug-ins for popular file types on the Web.

We may live to regret the Web's multimedia capabilities. How can we escape boring company meetings and presentations if the network administrator can make the video and audio recordings available on the server?

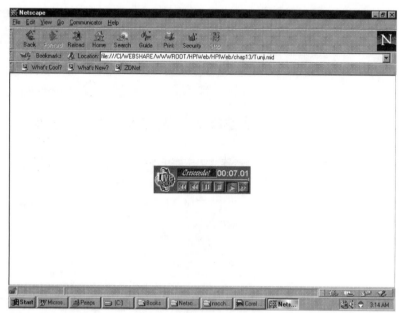

FIGURE *If you have a plug-in that handles the type of file you're downloading,*
4.8 *Navigator launches the file in a separate window.*

DOWNLOADING EMBEDDED FILES

Some Web designers *embed* files—especially audio, video, and Shockwave movies—in their Web pages. Like images, embedded files (and the player application when relevant) appear directly in the Web page itself. For example, Rich Grace's home page at `http://www.byteit.com/rgrace/` features an embedded MIDI music sample that plays back with Live Update's Crescendo music player. The Crescendo music player plug-in appears as a page element rather than launching in a separate window, as shown in Figure 4-9. Embedded files download to your cache folder (Chapter 5 tells you about your cache folder) but Navigator does not display an option for saving the file to a folder of your choice.

What happens when you encounter a file and don't have the right plug-in? Navigator displays an error message. Fortunately, Netscape has an entire plug-ins page and plug-ins are easy to download and install. Chapter 6 talks about plug-ins in greater detail.

FIGURE   *Embedded file played back with a plug-in.*
4.9

DOWNLOADING FILES WITHOUT LINKS

You can save images and embedded files to your computer even if the Web page designer does not provide a link. I'll tell you how, as long as you promise not to use any files on your Web page or for any purpose other than personal enjoyment without getting the creator's permission first. After all, copyright and trademark laws do exist. You can generally request permission by sending an email—most people include email links on their Web pages.

To save an image or embedded file to your computer, do the following:

Click on the page element you want to download with your right mouse button (Windows) or click on the page element and hold down your mouse key (Macintosh).

When the pop-up menu appears, as shown in Figure 4-10, select the **Save As...** command.

When the **Save As...** dialog box appears, select a folder and save the file.

You can also save page background images the same way. Just click anywhere on the page (except on an image or link) and follow the steps above.

FIGURE *Page element pop-up menu.*
4.10

Multimedia

Imagine visiting a few prospective homes that you're thinking of buying, and exploring the interiors . . . from your real estate agent's "Virtual Realty" site. Or being able to view an interactive, multimedia portfolio before hiring an independent contractor or employee? Or a student being able to hear Martin Luther King's "I Have a Dream" speech, instead of just reading about it in a dreary textbook. Thanks to Navigator's plug-in capabilities, multimedia can make the Web come alive.

AUDIO

What do Geffen Records (`http://www.geffen.com/`) and the National Coalition for the Homeless (`http://www.nch.art.net/`) have in common? Although the two organizations differ considerably, both use audio to add a sense of immediacy to their material. Audio on the Web offers record companies a fun, economical way to promote their artists' releases. Or, in the National Coalition for the Homeless' case, it can give voice to serious matters of public concern.

You can hear a wide variety of historical speeches (`http://www.webcorp.-com/sounds/index.htm`), catch the latest news broadcasts (`http://www.realaudio.com/contentp/abc.html`), or browse through Sun Site's eclectic collections of sounds (`http://sunsite.unc.edu/pub/multimedia/sun-sounds/`)—including animal noises, presidential speeches, TV commercials, and more.

Navigator has built-in support for the following audio file formats:

.AU: A standard sound file format developed by Sun Microsystems.
.AIFF: Associated with the discontinued (but once popular) Amiga computer by Commodore.
.SND: Generated by Creative Labs' SoundBlaster audio products.

Navigator also supports audio files that are served up from Netscape Live-Media servers with its Multimedia Player. However, other sound file formats have gained popularity on the Web and require plug-ins for playing them back.

Listed below are some other audio file types that you'll probably run into while exploring the Web:

.WAV: The standard Microsoft Windows audio format.

.MPEG: Generally used when combining audio with video. Due to older DOS file name conventions, .MPEG files are also sometimes referred to as .MPG, .MPE, and . MP2. .MIDI sound file formats are also used frequently on the Web, and increasing numbers of developers have started using Progressive Network's Real Audio (RA) sound file format as well. These file types require plug-ins before you can play them back. Chapter 7 covers file types and plug-ins in greater detail.

VIDEO

Large file sizes and slow modems used to make serving up video on the Web a tricky proposition. Well, it still is, but recent innovations in compression techniques and improved connection speeds have opened up more possibilities. It only took me five minutes to download the short, black and white QuickTime movie shown in Figure 4-11. You can view it yourself at http://www.wildwebs.com/.

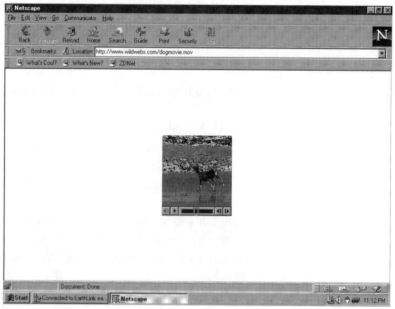

FIGURE Quick Time movie viewed with Navigator and the Quick Time Plug-in.
4.11

The following types of movies are common on the Web:

.AVI Movies: Microsoft created this popular video format to work with its movie viewer for Windows.

QuickTime Movies: QuickTime became a favorite when Apple started including the QuickTime player with all of its Macintosh machines. Later on, Apple made QuickTime available for Windows users, too.

.MPEG Movies: The MPEG (Motion Pictures Expert Group) file format is widely used for creating movies because it enables small file sizes without sacrificing quality.

Also, you also shouldn't miss the many Shockwave (.DCR) movies out there. Shockwave is a plug-in for viewing cutting-edge animations, games, and movies created in Macromedia's Director program. Chapter 7 talks about file formats and plug-ins in greater detail.

TIP

Are you worried about accidentally downloading files that may crash your system? You can disable downloads of active Web page content via Navigator's Preferences. For more information, see Chapter 6.

Virtual Reality

When people say that Virtual Reality Markup Language (VRML) adds a new dimension to the Web, they mean it literally. If you have ever seen a CD-ROM computer game like Bröderbund and Cyan's Myst or Virgin Interactive and Trilobyte's 7th Guest, or played a video arcade game with high-end graphics, then you already have an idea of what to expect. Virtual Reality worlds and scenes are three-dimensional. You can use your mouse to creep through a castle's corridors, pilot a plane, or help build an object.

VRML also has the potential for more than just fun and games. For example, an architecture firm could invite prospective clients to take virtual tours of the buildings they've designed. Navigator comes with Live 3D, a built-in application for viewing virtual reality worlds. Although some types of virtual reality may special plug-ins (Chapter 7 talks more about plug-ins), Live 3D does support standard VRML. To start exploring virtual worlds, visit Netscape's Live 3D demonstration page, as shown in Figure 4-12. Here, you can test Live 3D, view demonstrations, and follow links.

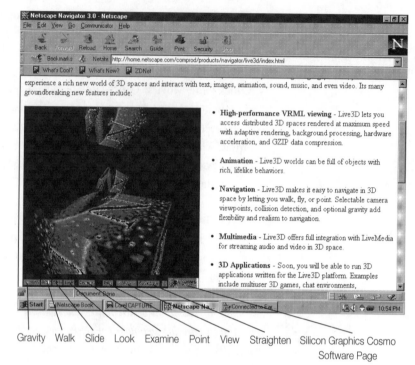

Gravity Walk Slide Look Examine Point View Straighten Silicon Graphics Cosmo
Software Page

FIGURE *You can start exploring virtual worlds from Netscape's Live3D page at*
4.12 http://home.netscape.com/comprod/products/communic
ator/multimedia/live3d/index.html

EXPLORING VIRTUAL REALITY WORLDS

Finding your way around virtual reality (VR) worlds is much easier than you think. When you land on a Web page with three-dimensional content, a the picture and a simple toolbar appear. You can start exploring by clicking anywhere on the scene, holding down your mouse key, and slowly rolling your mouse from one direction to the other. See how the view changes? For more control over how you move through VR worlds, you can use the toolbar buttons.

The toolbar offers the following options:

Gravity: Toggles gravity on and off. When the gravity is off, you can fly above the ground in the scene.

Walk: Move backwards, forwards, right, or left by dragging the mouse in the appropriate direction. To move and turn simultaneously, drag your mouse diagonally.

Slide: Move up, down, backwards, forwards, right, or left above the ground (to fly higher, you need to turn the Gravity off).

Look: Displays the scene around you while you stand still, so you can see everything without having to move.

Point: Move straight towards a specified object in the scene.

Straighten: Resets the view so you're standing at ground level and looking straight ahead.

View: Jumps you to the next viewpoint in the VR world. To display a list of view points, click the **View** button with your right mouse button.

Cosmo Software: Jumps you to Silicon Graphics' Cosmo Software page. Silicon graphics helped develop Live3D and has more information about it.

There are other types of VRML viewers out there—as I talk about in Chapter 7—but they all work similarly.

CHAPTER

5

Setting Communicator Preferences

Before we go any further, you may need to set your Communicator Preferences. If you use Communicator on an Intranet at work, then your network administrator may have already entered all of the Preferences settings for you. But the rest of us have to do it ourselves. Preferences are default settings that tell an application how to process information, perform tasks, and display menus, toolbars, and other features. Once default settings are entered or edited, Communicator remembers them so you don't have to enter them every time you launch the application or do frequently performed tasks.

The people at Netscape have entered most of the default settings you need in order for the program to work. However, Communicator still needs some information from you—such as your email address and the location of your mail and news servers—before you can use many of its features. As you get accustomed to Communicator, you can also use the Preferences menu to tailor Communicator to your needs and even empty your cache folder when Navigator gets a little sluggish.

This chapter explains Preferences settings for the following:

- Appearance (Fonts and Colors)
- Navigator (Languages and Applications)
- Mail and Groups (Identity, Messages, Mail Server, Groups Server, Directory)
- Composer and Publishing
- Offline (Discussion Groups)
- Advanced (Cache, Proxies, Disk Space)

If you're in charge of setting up Communicator for coworkers across an office Intranet, you can use the Netscape Administration Kit (NAK) to create installation packages with customized preferences settings. For more information, see Chapter 19.

Displaying the Preferences Window

This may seem like a lot of settings, but the people at Netscape make it easy for you. You can find everything from a single window. To view and edit your preferences, all you have to do is select the **Preferences** option from the **Edit** menu in Navigator's main window. When the **Preferences** window displays, as shown in Figure 5-1, you can choose options. The **Preferences Cat-**

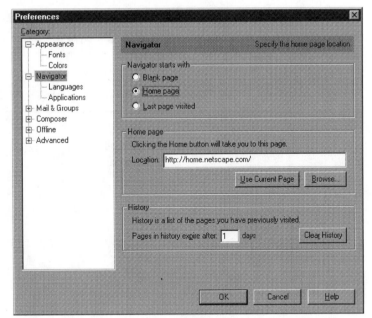

FIGURE   *Communicator Preferences window with Navigator item selected.*
5.1

egory list appears on the left. When items appear with a + sign next to them, you can click the + sign to display additional categories. The options on the right side of the window correspond to the currently selected **Category** list item on the left.

If you get confused while setting your preferences, never fear. Just click the handy **Help** *button in the lower right-hand corner for a quick explanation of your options.*

TIP

When you finish changing your preferences, click the **OK** *button in the Preferences window!*

CAUTION

Appearance

The **Appearance** window, as shown in Figure 5-2, provides options for launching Communicator components on startup, as well as how toolbars appear. The default is to automatically launch Navigator when you double-click on the **Communicator** icon. This makes sense, since you can easily get

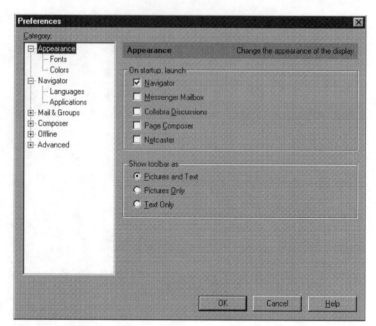

FIGURE *Appearance Preferences window.*
5.2

to all of Navigator's components. But you can also choose to launch other components, like Messenger, Collabra Discussions (newsgroups), Page Composer, and Netcaster simultaneously, if you wish. For an overview of Communicator's various components, see Chapter 2.

In addition, you can also choose how you want to display Communicator's toolbars by selecting a radio button for one of the following options:

- **Pictures and Text:** Displays toolbars with both the graphical icons and explanatory text. This is the default selection.
- **Pictures Only:** Displays toolbars with only the pictures (not a good idea for a beginner!).
- **Text Only:** If you have a small computer monitor and need a little more room, text-only toolbar buttons can save you space.

The Appearance category also has a couple of sub-categories for **Fonts** and **Colors** (which I cover in the following sections). If you do not see these options, then click on the + button next to the **Appearances** item on the **Category** list.

FONTS

You can choose default font settings for displaying text on Web pages from the **Fonts** window, shown in Figure 5-3. The default fonts are set to 12 point Times Roman and 10 point Courier—which are easy-to-read, conservative type faces. However, you may prefer a different font or wish to have fonts display larger so you don't have to squint at the computer screen.

You can change settings for the following options:

- **For the Encoding:** The default is Western because we use the Western European style alphabet. Unless you'd like Web pages to appear in Cyrillic, Greek, or Japanese letters, don't change this!
- **Variable Width Font:** This refers to the typeface used to display regular body text. Type-faces like Times Roman (the default) are easiest on the eyes, which is why books, newspapers, and magazines are usually set in variations of these type-faces. But if you prefer to read Web pages in a different font, you can select a new font from the pull-down list.

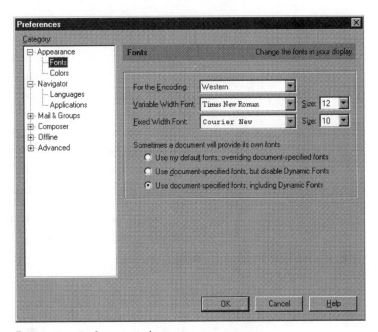

FIGURE   *Font Preferences window.*
5.3

- **Size:** The default Variable Width Font size is 12 point. However, if you have trouble reading text on Web pages, you may prefer a slightly larger font, such as 14 point. You can select a new default size from the pulldown list.
- **Fixed Width Font:** This refers to the secondary type face—sometimes used to differentiate long quotes or technical instructions and command lines. Unlike regular body text on the Web, fixed width fonts also preserve spacing attributes on Web pages. Until the Netscape people made Navigator capable of displaying tables, Web designers often used fixed width fonts for tables and column lists. Now it is not commonly used. The default fixed width font is Courier, but you can change it by picking a new font from the pulldown list.
- **Size:** The default Fixed Width Font size is 10 point. However, as mentioned earlier, you may prefer a slightly larger size, such as 12 point. Select a new default size from the pulldown list.

Web sites are getting much fancier these days, and Web page designers often specify fonts in their pages. You can tell Navigator how to handle these types of Web pages by selecting an option from the following radio buttons:

- **Use my default fonts, overriding document-specified fonts:** I do not recommend this option, since designers work hard on making their pages look a certain way, and their pages would appear less attractive.
- **Use document-specified fonts, but disable Dynamic Fonts:** Pages formatted with Dynamic Fonts look great, but designers have to use JavaScript—a scripting language—in order to do this. If you don't want little programs downloading to your computer, but would still like to enjoy people's page layouts intact most of the time, select this option.
- **Use document-specified fonts, including Dynamic Fonts:** To enjoy the Web and type-faces in their full splendor, choose this option.

In most cases, I recommend sticking with the default settings created during installation rather than changing any of the options in this window.

COLORS

The Preferences Colors window, as shown in Figure 5-4, offers options for changing page display colors. In Navigator, Web pages default to displaying black text with blue unvisited links, purple visited links, and a gray background. However, most Web page designers set up pages to display custom colors and patterned backgrounds. I really see no reason to change the **Colors** settings, but maybe I'm missing something, so I'll explain the available choices anyway.

- **Text:** This is the default color in which Web page text appears. To change the default text color, deselect the **Use Windows colors** checkbox below, then click the color box to the right. When the color palette appears, select a color and click OK.
- **Background:** This is the default color the Web page's background appears in (if we were talking about printed pages, this would be the paper color). To change the default background color, deselect the **Use Windows colors** checkbox below, then click the color box to the right. When the color palette appears, select a color and click OK.
- **Use Windows colors:** If you don't want to change the text and background colors, leave this checkbox selected.
- **Unvisited Links:** Links change color after you click on them (or *visit* them). This is the color that links appear in before you've clicked on

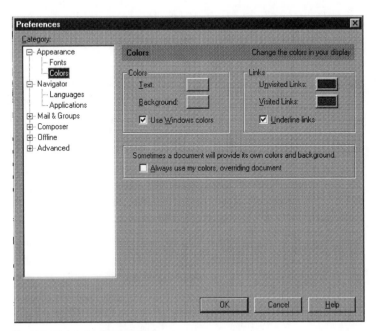

FIGURE *Colors Preferences window.*
5.4

them. To change the default unvisited color, deselect the **Use Windows colors** checkbox below, then click the color box to the right. When the color palette appears, select a color and click OK.

- **Visited Links:** This is the color that links appear in after you've already clicked on them. To change the default visited link color, deselect the **Use Windows colors** checkbox below, then click the color box to the right. When the color palette appears, select a color and click OK.
- **Always use my colors, overriding document:** Web developers usually design pages with custom background, text, and link colors. You can choose to display Web pages in your default colors instead, by selecting the checkbox. But I don't recommend doing this.
- **Underline links:** Linked text appears underlined when this checkbox is selected

TIP

Not everyone who designs Web pages is particularly good at it! Sometimes the color combinations people use make their pages difficult to read. If the information on their page is really important to you, then go to the **Colors Preferences** *and click the* Always use my colors, overriding document *checkbox. You can change it back when you're done reading the page.*

Navigator

The **Navigator** window, as shown in Figure 5-5, lets you specify what Web page you want to load when you launch the application. You can even specify your favorite home page as Navigator's default, and tell Navigator how to handle your page history.

The Navigator window offers the following options:

- **Navigator starts with:** Choose which page you want to display when you first launch Navigator by selecting a radio button. You can choose to display a blank page, a default home page, or the last page you visited. Unless you change this setting, Navigator loads Netscape's home page (unless your ISP or server administrator has configured it to load a company home page instead!).
- **Home Page:** If you select the **Home Page** radio button above, you can enter a URL in the text box to load a page of your choice every time you launch Navigator. You can also click the **Use Current Page** button

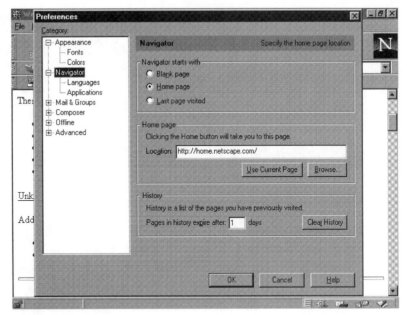

FIGURE *Navigator Preferences window.*
5.5

to enter the URL of the current page in the text box, or if you're connected to a network, you can click the **Browse** button to display a page on your organization's server.

- **History:** Have you done a lot of exploring lately? Navigator maintains a history list of the URLs that you've visited recently. You can tell Navigator how long to keep URLs in your **History** list by entering a number of days in the text box.

*You can also delete your history list by clicking the **Clear History** button. This can often pep up Navigator when it gets sluggish, and also keeps your supervisor from seeing how much browsing you've done lately!*

TIP

LANGUAGES

Some servers are set up to run multiple Web sites in different languages. Navigator can tell these servers which language you speak so you don't wind up with Web pages written in some language you don't understand (though

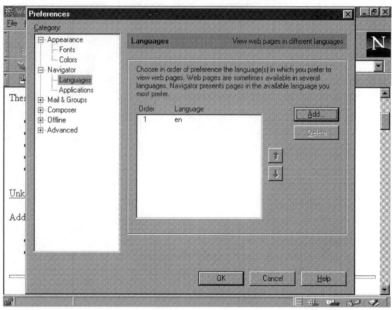

FIGURE *Languages Preferences window.*
5.6

it's sometimes fun to do that!). The **Languages** window, shown in Figure 5-6, lets you create a list of languages that you can read in order of preference. That way, if a server has nothing in your primary language, it can jump you to a set of pages written in the next language on your list.

Your primary language (or, at least your server administrator's primary language) should already appear on the list. When you download Communicator from Netscape's Web site, the form asks what language you prefer (see Chapter 3).

To add new languages to the list, do the following:

1. Open the **Languages** window by selecting **Languages** from the category list on the left (if you don't see it, click the + sign next to the Navigator list item).

2. When the **Languages** window appears, click the **Add** button on the right.

3. When the **Add Languages** dialog box appears, as shown in Figure 5-7, select a language from the list, then click **OK**.

Repeat the second and third steps to add more languages.

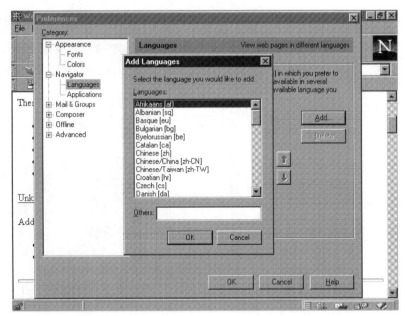

FIGURE   *Add Languages dialog box.*
5.7

To raise a language to a higher priority, select it and click the up arrow to move it up on the list. To make a language lower priority, select it and click the down arrow to move it down the list.

APPLICATIONS

You can tell Navigator how to handle files that you encounter on the Web or download as email attachments through the **Applications Preferences** window, as shown in Figure 5-8. If the **Applications** item doesn't appear on the **Category** list, click the little + sign next to the Navigator item. You see, Navigator does many things, but it can't open every single type of file that exists on the Internet by itself. That's why we have plug-ins and helper applications. These applications are integrated with Navigator so that different file types—such as audio and video—can launch directly in the browser window. In most cases, plug-ins configure themselves to work with Navigator automatically when you install them. But in case you need to edit your plug-in preferences, you can edit file types that appear on the list, and add new ones. Chapter 7 tells you how to work with plug-ins and helper applications in detail.

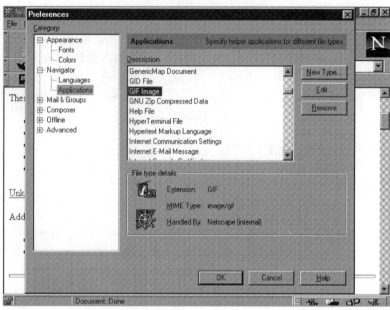

FIGURE *Applications Preferences window.*
5.8

Mail and Groups

As with Navigator, you can change the appearance settings for your email and newsgroup messages. Chapters 10 to 13 talk about email and newsgroups in greater detail. Although these settings aren't critical to how your email and newsgroups work, changing these settings can help make your messages easier to view, sort through, and read. The **Mail & Groups** window, as shown in Figure 5-9, offers the following options:

- **Style:** When people send you messages and you reply, you can include quoted text from their messages. This makes it easier to respond to specific points. You can choose a font option, such as **Italic** or **Bold**, from the pulldown list so you can tell quoted text apart from new text more easily.
- **Size:** You can also specify a size for quoted text from the pulldown menu.
- **Color:** You can also specify a color for quoted text from the pulldown menu.

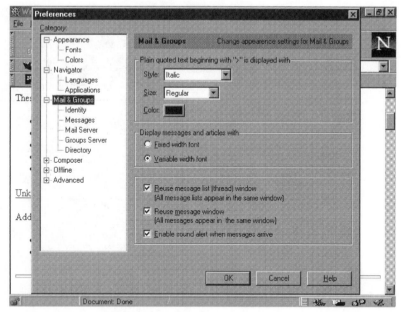

FIGURE *Mail & Groups Preferences window.*
5.9

- **Display messages and articles with:** Select the **Fixed width font** or the **Variable width font** radio button to choose what type of text you wish to display messages and articles with. Variable width fonts are easier to read, so you should leave this button selected.

- **Reuse message list (thread) window:** Select this checkbox to load discussion and newsgroup message lists from a new group into the current message center window instead of launching a new window (Chapters 10 and 12 talks about news and discussion groups in greater detail).

- **Reuse message window:** Select this checkbox to load messages into the same window, instead of opening new windows for each one.

- **Enable sound alert when messages arrive:** Select this checkbox to make the message center play a sound when you receive new messages.

IDENTITY

Before you can send and receive email and newsgroup messages, you have to enter items in the **Identity Preferences** window, as shown in Figure 5-10.

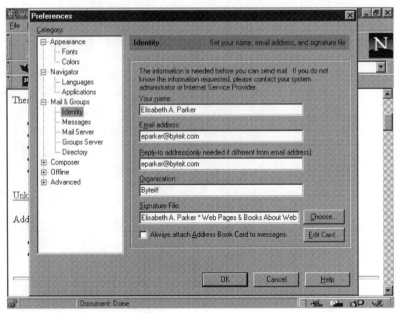

FIGURE *Identity Preferences window.*
5.10

The identity preferences include important information such as your name and your email address, so that people can reply to your messages.

The **Identity Preferences** window prompts you for the following:

- **Your name:** Enter your name in the text field. Or you can enter a nickname or the department you work for.
- **Email address:** Enter your email address. If you don't know it, your ISP or network administrator can tell you. In most cases, email addresses consist of a user name and a domain separated by an @ sign, as in user@company.com.
- **Reply-to address:** When you send email messages and people reply to you by using their email program's **Reply** command, this is the address that the reply messages get sent to. In most cases, it isn't necessary to fill in this text box. However, if you have multiple email accounts and prefer to have replies sent to a different address, you should enter the address in this text field.

*If you need to send personal email from work, but want the person to reply to your home email address, you can go to the **Identity** preferences and change the **Reply to** address information. Just remember to change it back!*

- **Organization:** Enter the name of your company or organization in this text field. If you're using Communicator for non-work purposes, you can leave this blank.
- **Signature File:** You can add a signature to your outgoing email messages. To add a signature line, enter it in the text field (it can be longer than the text field). You can include any information you want in your signature file. Most people enter their name, company, email address, and Web site address here. You can also add a favorite quotation.

*If your signature line has a lot of text in it, or you want to add some carriage returns between lines, you can also use a text file as your signature. Simply create a plain text file with a text editor like Note Pad (Windows) or Simple Text (Macintosh). These applications come with your computer. When you're finished typing, save the file and add the three letter .TXT extension (such as "signfile.txt"). When you return to the **Identity Preferences** window, click the **Choose** button. When the **Signature File** dialog box appears, browse for your signature file, select it and click **OK**. The signature file will be appended to your outgoing messages.*

- **Always attach Address Book Card to messages:** Check this box to attach your **Address Book Card** to outgoing messages. Think of this as your business card in cyberspace. When exchanging email messages with other Communicator users, you can attach a card with your name, address, telephone number, and other contact information. The message recipient can then add your address book card to their address book for easy reference.

Before you check off this option, think about whether you really want everyone you exchange email with to have your address and telephone number!

- To create your address book card, do the following:
- Click the **Edit Card** button.
- When the **Name** window appears, as shown in Figure 5-11, enter your first name, last name, organization, job title, email address, nickname, and additional notes. Click the **Contact** tab.

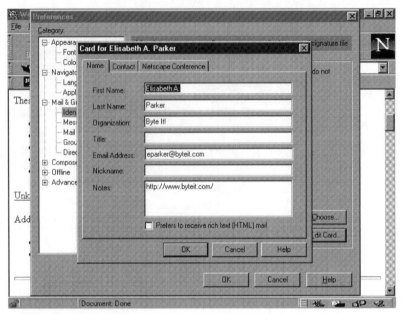

FIGURE *To create an address book card, enter your information in the **Name** window.*
5.11

- When the **Contact** window appears, as shown in Figure 5-12, enter your snail mail (non-Internet) address along with your telephone and fax numbers. Click the **Netscape Conference** tab.
- When the **Netscape Conference** window appears, as shown in Figure 5-13, select a server for looking up people's email addresses. You may have a Netscape Conference server at work. If not, you can choose one of the public Internet directories from the pulldown list. Netscape conference lets you call people via the Internet by entering their email address. Chapters 15 and 16 tells you more about it.

MESSAGES

The **Messages Preferences** window, as shown in Figure 5-14, offers options for handling outgoing email messages and news postings. You can specify how messages are sent, whether you want copies of outgoing messages to be sent to another address, and whether you want to quote received messages when sending replies. The options that most people use are automatically configured during the installation of Communicator. However, you may want to make some changes depending on your needs.

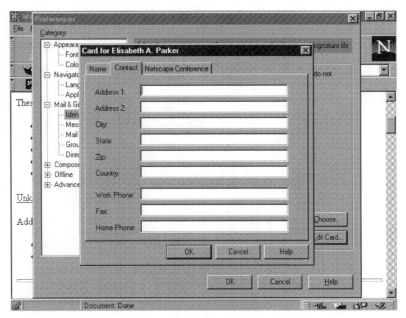

FIGURE *Enter your contact information in the **Contact** window.*
5.12

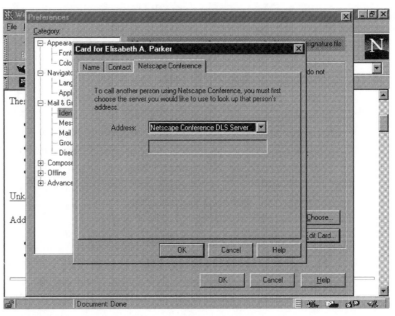

FIGURE *Choose a search directory from the Netscape **Conference** window so you can*
5.13 *search for people's email addresses when you need to call them.*

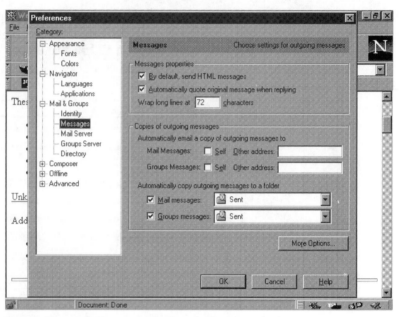

FIGURE *Messages Preferences window.*
5.14

The **Messages Preferences** window lets you edit the following settings:

- **Messages properties:** To automatically format messages in HTML (with text formatting like colors and headlines and automatic creation of working links for any email addresses or URLs mentioned in your messages), select the **By default send HTML messages** checkbox. To automatically copy the text of received messages into your reply messages (so you can respond to them point by point), select the **Automatically quote original message when replying** checkbox. Messenger also automatically wraps your text so you don't have to enter carriage returns. You can enter a number for how many characters per line in the **Wrap long lines at __ characters** number field.

If you select the By default send HTML messages *option, people without HTML capable email and news clients may not be able to read your email messages and news and discussion group postings.*

- **Copies of outgoing messages:** If you like to keep track of the messages you send, you can have copies of all outgoing messages automatically sent to yourself and/or to a different email address. This can also be useful in business situations where your supervisor needs copies of emails sent to clients, customers, and coworkers (don't forget to change the preferences if you need to send personal email!). To automatically send copies of email messages, select the **Self** checkbox to send them to yourself, or enter another email address in the **Other address** text field following the **Mail Messages** item. The **Groups Messages** item offers the same options for news and discussion groups postings.

*Automatically copying outgoing messages can be useful if you have multiple email addresses and like to keep track of everything you send. But you don't really need to send messages to yourself. You can conserve Internet and network resources by having your outgoing messages copied to the **Sent** folder instead.*

- **Automatically copy outgoing messages to a folder:** It's a good idea to save copies of the email, news, and discussion group messages you send for future reference. To save copies of outgoing messages, select the **Mail messages** and **Groups messages** checkboxes. You can also select a folder to save the messages from the pull-down lists. The Messages Preferences window defaults to saving email and groups messages to the Sent folder.
- **More options:** Click the **More Options** button to display the **More Messages Preferences** dialog box, as shown in Figure 5-15. These preferences offer additional options for formatting your email messages. I recommend that you keep the default settings. I find that they generally work regardless of what email client the recipient has.

MAIL SERVER

In order to send and receive email messages, you need to first enter your mail server settings, as shown in figure 5-16. Your ISP's or network's mail server routes your outgoing mail and stores your incoming mail until you tell **Messenger** to download it for you. If you don't know what to enter for these settings, ask your ISP or network administrator. In some cases, you may find that they have already filled in the information for you (ISPs and network administrators can do this with the Netscape Administration kit discussed in Chapter 19).

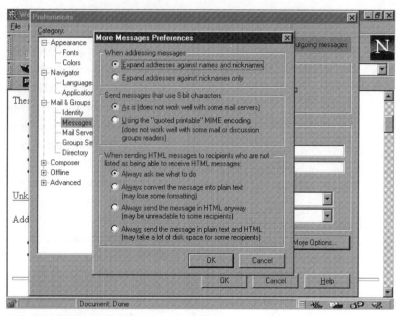

FIGURE *More Messages Preferences dialog box.*
5.15

The **Mail Server Preferences** window prompts you for the following:

- **Mail server user name:** Enter your account user name here (this should be the first part of your email address before the @sign).
- **Outgoing mail (SMTP) server:** Enter the name of your Internet service provider or company's outgoing mail server.
- **Incoming mail server:** Enter the name of the server that handles incoming mail.

NOTE

In most cases, the outgoing and incoming mail servers have the same name.

- **Mail server type:** Select a **Mail server type** radio button. Most people have POP3 accounts, for which messages and folders are stored locally on your computer. If you access your account through an Internet service provider, you probably have a POP3 account. IMAP accounts store all email messages on the server rather than on your hard drive. You can ask your ISP or network administrator what type of server you have.

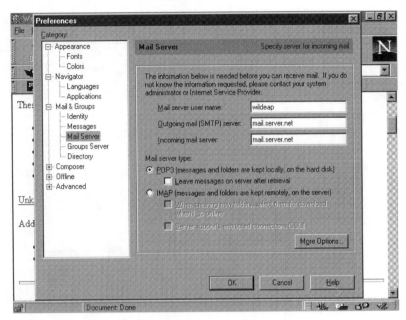

FIGURE   *Mail Server Preferences window.*
5.16

If you go on the road and access your email from someone else's computer but also need to save your messages for when you get back, select the **Leave messages on server after retrieval** *checkbox. This option keeps copies of messages on the server so you can download them to your computer when you get back. Just don't forget to uncheck the checkbox later, or the network administrator might get mad.*

- More Options: Click the **More Options** button to display the **More Mail Server Preferences** dialog box shown in Figure 5-17. Here you can select a new local directory for storing your messages if you prefer a different folder than the one Communicator sets up for you, and enter an IMAP mail directory when applicable. You can also tell Messenger to check for your mail at specified intervals and have it remember your password after you enter it the first time. In most cases, you'll be fine if you stick with Communicator's default settings.

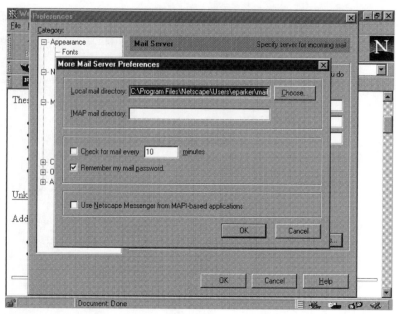

FIGURE   *More Mail Server Preferences dialog box.*

5.17

GROUPS SERVER

In order to download and post news and discussion group messages, you need to first enter your **Groups Server** settings, as shown in Figure 5-18. Your ISP's or network's news server stores newsgroups and routes your postings. If you don't know what to enter for these settings, ask your ISP or network administrator. In some cases, you may find that they have already filled in the information for you (ISPs and network administrators can do this with the Netscape Administration kit discussed in Chapter 19).

The Groups Server Preferences window prompts you for the following:

- **Discussion groups (news) server:** Enter the name of your news server here.
- **Port:** If you connect to the Internet through a proxy server (for more about proxy servers, see Chapter 19), enter the port number here (in many cases, the number is 80). If your office uses a secure server, select the **Secure** checkbox.
- **Discussion group (news) folder:** If you want to download news messages to a different folder than the one Communicator has set up for you, click the **Choose** button to select a new folder.

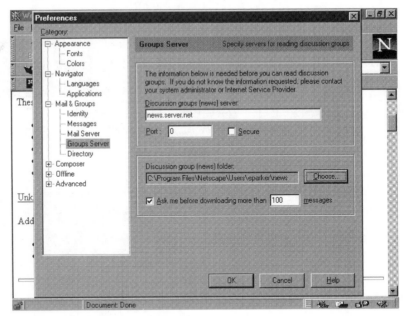

FIGURE   *Groups Server Preferences window.*
5.18

- **Ask me before downloading more than ___ messages:** Select the checkbox and enter a number if you want to limit downloads to a certain number of messages at a time.

DIRECTORY

The **Directory Preferences** window, shown in Figure 5-19, contains a list of directories where you can enter people's first and last names so you can send email messages and make conference calls. When you click on your address book's **Search** button and enter the name, the address book goes to these directories and does the searching for you. Communicator comes with a list of email directories on the Internet. Chapter 14 talks more about how the address book and directory searches work.

When you request a search, the address book visits the first directory on the list. If it doesn't find a match, it moves on to the next directory on the list, and so on. You can change the order of items on the list by selecting an item and clicking the up or down arrow.

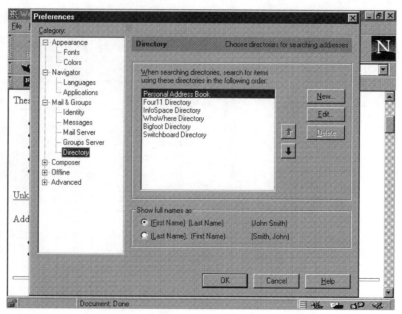

FIGURE *Directory Preferences window.*
5.19

To add a new directory (such as one that's available on your company's server), do the following:

1. Click the **New** button.
2. When the **Directory Server Property** dialog box appears, as shown in Figure 5-20, enter the **Description** (name), **LDAP Server** URL, and other information.
3. Click **OK** to return to the Directory Preferences window.

Now you might be wondering what an LDAP server is. LDAP stands for Lightweight Directory Access Protocol. LDAP servers are used for creating directories that you can search with Messenger's address book search features. Like Web pages, LDAP directories have a URL and can be accessed via the Internet or closed Intranets.

Composer

Composer makes it easy for you to create Web pages and upload them to your ISP's server or the server on your network (for more about generating Web pages and uploading them, see Chapter 17). The **Composer Prefer-**

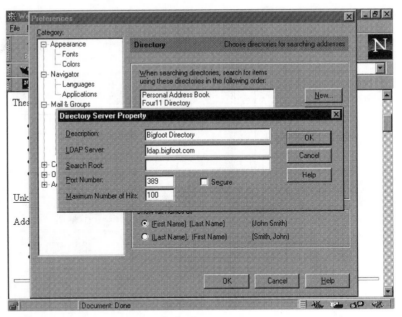

FIGURE *Directory Server Property dialog box.*
5.20

ences window, shown in Figure 5-21, lets you set general preferences for generating Web pages. Here you can enter basic information and specify external editors for HTML source code and for images.

You can set the following options in the **Composer Preferences** window:

- **Author Name:** Enter your name here. This automatically generates *comments* in the pages you create that identify you as the author. Comments are used in HTML documents to include information that does not get displayed on the page.
- **Automatically save page every ___ minutes:** Select the checkbox and enter a number of minutes to automatically save your work at specified intervals.
- **External Editors:** If you sometimes need to work with a different HTML editor, you can make it more integrated with Composer. Click the **Choose** button to the right of the **HTML Source** text field and browse for your HTML editor's application file when the **Choose an HTML editor** dialog box appears and click **OK**. You can also choose your favorite graphics program for working with images. Click the **Choose** button to the right of the **Images** text field and browse for

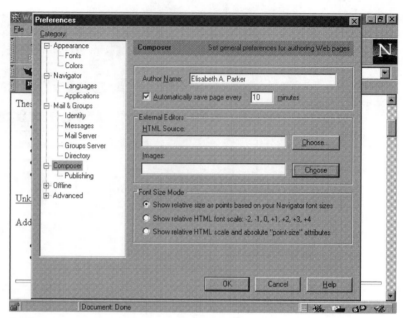

FIGURE *Composer Preferences window.*
5.21

your image program. You can then edit images straight from Composer.

- **Font Size Mode:** Select a radio button to determine how you want to view your fonts. I recommend keeping the default selection, **Show relative size as points based on your Navigator font sizes.**

Publishing

In order to upload your Web pages to the server, you need to enter your settings in the **Publishing** window, shown in Figure 5-22. Here, you can tell Composer where to find your directory on the server and how to handle links and images while creating pages so they'll work correctly after you upload them. Composer works best when posting pages to a server on a local network, but you can also use it to work with pages on a remote server.

The **Publishing** window has the following options:

- **Maintain links:** Your server probably doesn't have the same directory structure as you have on your computer (on servers, folders are called directories). This can affect whether links to documents within your

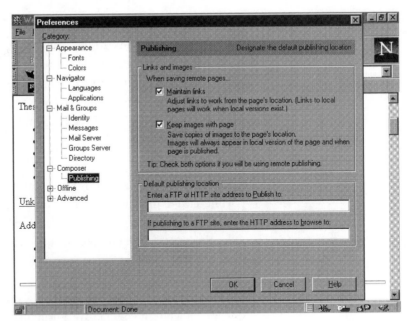

FIGURE   *Publishing Preferences window.*
5.22

Web folder work or not. Click the **Maintain links** checkbox to enable Composer to automatically set up the links.

- **Keep images with page:** As with links, if the directory you keep your Web pages and images in is set up differently than the one on the server, your images may not display after uploading. To avoid this, click the **Keep images with page** checkbox.

*You must select the **Maintain links** and **Keep images with page** checkboxes In order to use Composer for publishing Web pages to a server. Chapter 17 explain this in greater detail.*

CAUTION

- **Enter a FTP or HTTP site address to Publish to:** Enter your Web folder's FTP or HTTP site address. If you don't know it, ask your Internet service provider or network administrator. In most cases, this location is different from the URL that people enter to visit your page.
- **If publishing to a FTP site, enter the HTTP address to browse to:** This is the URL that people enter in their browser location window to visit your page.

Offline

The title for the **Offline Preferences** window, as shown in figure 5-23, is a bit confusing. It really should be called something like "Connection Mode." Some people have dedicated lines and are connected to the Internet all the time. Most of us—in the workplace and at home—dial up the server when we need to access the Internet and otherwise aren't connected to it. This effects how Communicator launches and downloads information from the server.

Select a radio button to choose one of the following options:

- **Online Work Mode:** This is for people whose computers are always connected to the Internet. When you launch Communicator, the default startup application (usually Navigator) immediately starts downloading material from the server. For example, Navigator immediately tries to find the default start page or Messenger tries to send and receive messages.
- **Offline Work Mode:** If you have to dial up the server to get access to the Internet, or if you do have a dedicated line but don't want Communicator to download stuff all the time, select this option. Offline

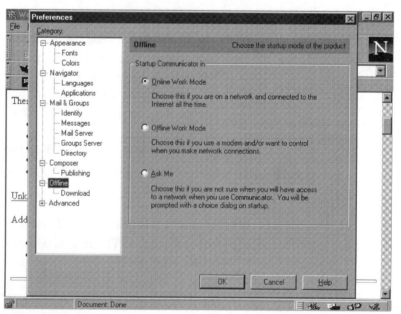

FIGURE *Offline Preferences window.*
5.23

Work Mode lets you review email and news messages, view channel content, and other material that has already been downloaded to your computer without making demands on the server. You can send and receive email messages and newsgroup postings, download channel content, and request Web page content—Communicator's components just won't do it automatically just because you launched them.

- **Ask Me:** Select this option if you want to display a dialog box with the above two choices when you launch Communicator.

DOWNLOAD

News and discussion groups can be fun and informative. But they can often involve downloading huge numbers of files. This can take forever. The **Download Preferences** window, shown in Figure 5-24, helps limit the number of messages that download from the news server while still keeping yourself up to date.

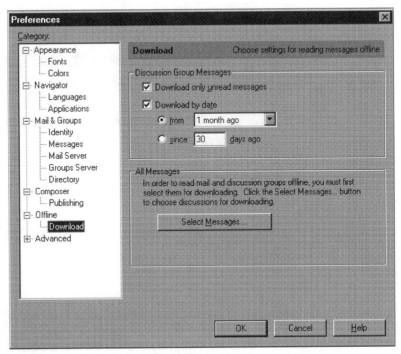

FIGURE *Download Preferences window.*
5.24

You can choose from the following options.

- **Download only unread messages:** Downloads only postings that you haven't read yet instead of downloading all of the postings every time you access the newsgroups' server.
- **Download by date:** You can also choose to download only recent messages to specify a number of months or weeks, select the from radio button and choose the number of months from the pulldown list. To specify a number of days, click the **since** radio button and enter a number of days.
- **Select Messages:** If you prefer to quickly download news and discussion group messages, then log off and read them offline, you can select groups that you want to download automatically when you launch the Message Center. To select newsgroups for automatic downloading, click the **Select Messages** button. When the **Discussion Groups** dialog box appears, as shown in Figure 5-25, select the newsgroups you want and click **OK.**

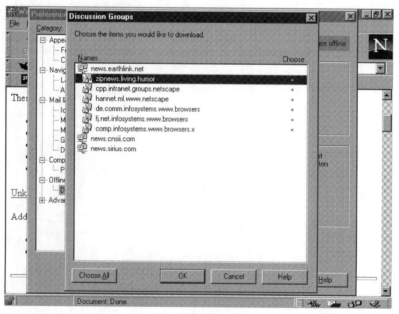

FIGURE *Discussion Groups dialog box.*
5.25

Advanced

Active Web page content, like Java applets, make the Web more exciting and functional. But it also makes extra demands on your computer and can cause security risks if you access active pages from your company's network. You (or your network administrator) can decide whether you want Navigator to be able to download active content by selecting options from the **Advanced Preferences** window, as shown in Figure 5-26.

You can enable or disable the following options:

- **Automatically load images:** Most Web pages have images these days, so it isn't a good idea to disable images.
- **Enable Java:** Java is a *client side* technology, which means applets load and run in your browser, instead of on the server. You can choose whether to allow Java applets.
- **Enable JavaScript:** Like Java applets, JavaScript pages load and run in your browser, thereby putting demands on your computer rather than the host server. To disable JavaScript, deselect the checkbox.

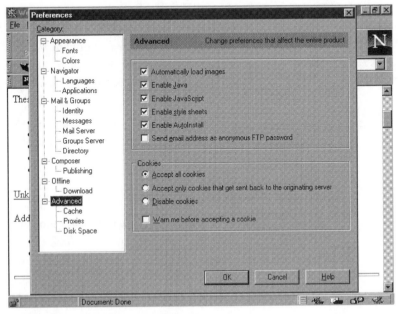

FIGURE   *Advanced Preferences window.*
5.26

- **Enable style sheets:** Netscape Style sheets enable Web page designers to have more control over their page layouts and how fonts appear. This form of dynamic page content is activated by JavaScript.
- **Enable AutoInstall:** If your network administrator plans on distributing automatic software updates to users over the network, then they'll probably have this option selected.

*You may be able to take advantage of the **AutoInstall** option on your computer at home. Netcaster and Marimba make it possible for software vendors (like the people you bought your last fax software or computer game from) to automatically update customers' software via channels. For more information about channels, see Chapter 6.*

- **Send email address as anonymous FTP password:** Some organizations offer public access to their FTP sites, but still want to know who you are. This process is known as *anonymous FTP* because instead of entering a user name and password to access the server, you enter "anonymous" for your user name and your email address as the password. Select this setting if you want to automatically send your email address as the anonymous FTP password. I don't recommend choosing this option, unless you only need to access anonymous FTP sites.
- **Cookies:** Some Web sites generate custom pages for you based on information you enter in an online form, or on the pages you visit on their site. How does this happen? The server generates a little data file called a *cookie* and stores it on your computer to help it "remember" you. This data file is basically harmless, but some people don't like the idea of it. You can choose whether to accept cookies and ask Navigator to warn you before accepting a cookie by selecting an option.

CACHE

When you need to keep something easily accessible, you keep it in your briefcase, purse, or backpack. When computers need to keep something easily accessible, the store it in a cache folder. Communicator's cache is a folder that stores Web page data on your computer so it doesn't take as much time for them to download when you revisit them. To download a "fresh" page, you can click Navigator's **Reload** button. The **Cache Preferences** window, as shown in Figure 5-27 lets you enter settings for your cache folder so Navigator can properly handle your Web page content.

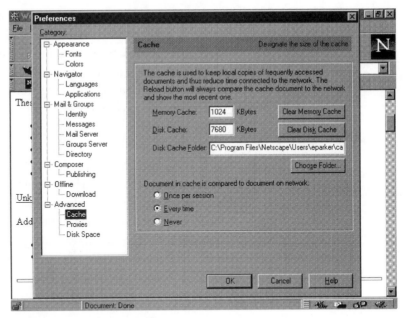

FIGURE *Cache Preferences window.*
5.27

You can enter or edit the following settings (if you're not sure about your settings, the default settings generally work just fine):

- **Memory Cache:** Reserves a specified amount of RAM (Random Access Memory) for Communicator while the application is running. The default is 1024 KB, the minimum amount of available memory Communicator needs to remember all the tasks it must perform.
- **Clear Memory Cache:** You can select this button to clear Communicator's memory cache. This can sometimes help when Navigator and other components start running sluggishly.
- **Disk Cache:** Navigator defaults to keeping 7680 KB worth of information available in its disk cache. This includes a history of recent Internet sites you've visited, along with text, images, and other files. When you return to a site you've visited during the same session, you'll notice that the page doesn't take as long to load the second time around. This is because Navigator loads the information straight from your disk cache rather than from the server. Depending on your needs,

you can enter a higher setting for your disk cache (if you enter a lower setting, Java applets and plug-ins may not load correctly).

- **Clear Disk Cache:** Click this button to clear the disk cache. This can sometimes help when Navigator and other components start running sluggishly or otherwise misbehaving. You'll lose your history list, but your bookmarks, preferences, and other vital information stay intact.

- **Disk Cache Folder:** Communicator sets up a disk cache folder for you during installation. If you prefer to store it in another location, click the **Choose Folder** button and browse for a folder.

- **Document in cache is compared to document on network:** You can decide how often Navigator detects whether a page has been updated since the last time you visited and downloads the new page. You can choose **Once per session** (every time you launch Navigator), **Every time** (every time you visit a page), or **Never** (this enables faster downloads, but you never get an updated copy of the page unless you hit the **Reload** button).

PROXIES

Proxy servers handle Internet connections protected by firewalls (server security software) and determine how individual connections interact with external servers. Firewalls protect networks containing confidential data from outsiders. Since only corporations and other organizations generally need firewalls, you only have to worry about proxies if you use Communicator at work. In most cases, your network administrator enters the proxy settings for you.

The Proxies window, as shown in Figure 5-28 has the following options:

- **Direct Connection to the Internet:** Select this radio button if you dial up your server directly (i.e., you do *not* connect to the Internet through a firewall and proxy server).

- **Manual proxy configuration:** Click the **View** button to edit your proxy configuration—a text file that looks like total gibberish unless you know something about proxy servers.

- **Automatic proxy configuration:** Network administrators can create a proxy file configuration document, keep it on the server, and link your proxy preferences to it. If so, the location of the proxy configuration document appears in the text field to the right.

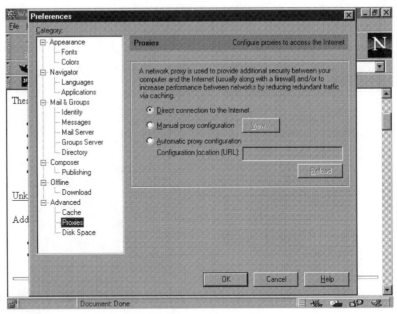

FIGURE   *Proxies Preferences window.*
5.28

DISK SPACE

You'll be surprised at how many email and newsgroup messages you accumulate over the course of time. You can determine the amount of disk space that get taken up by your email and newsgroup messages through the **Disk Space Preferences** window, as shown in Figure 5-29. Here, you can set limits for the size of messages (which aren't large themselves, but which often come with large attachments).

The **Disk Space Preferences** window offers the following options:

- **All Messages:** You can choose not to download messages larger than a specified size and to automatically compact (compress) your message folders when it will save you a specified amount of disk space.
- **Discussion Group Messages Only:** You can also decide when to clean out your discussion and newsgroup folders by choosing only to keep messages that have been delivered within a specified number of days, or to keep a specified number of the most recently arrived messages. You can also choose to only keep unread messages.

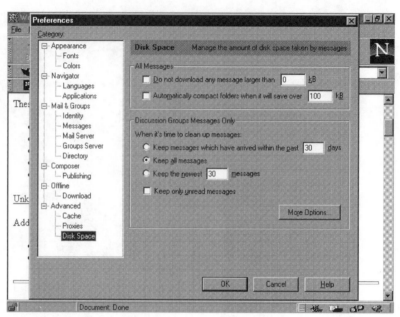

FIGURE *Disk Space Preferences window.*
5.29

6 Receiving Channels with Netcaster

The Internet has lots of great information and resources. But what if you don't have time to browse the Web every time you need something? No problem. Communicator's Netcaster delivers site content to your virtual doorstep. It's like having your newspaper dropped off at your house instead of having to go to the news stand and buy it. How does this work? You subscribe to channels—special types of servers that can handle frequently updated data—and then tell Netcaster how often to give you updates. Netcaster then visits your channels' servers and downloads new information automatically while you're doing something else. You can then launch your channels any time you want and you don't have to wait for them to download. Because the information gets "pushed" to you, instead of your having to get it, people call this kind of automated downloading *server push*.

What do channels look like and what do you use them for? Channels are Web pages that get delivered to your computer automatically so you don't have to go out and look for them. For example, the CNET Channel, as shown in Figure 6-1, keeps you up to date with developments in the computer industry. Channels have many uses, such as facilitating communica-

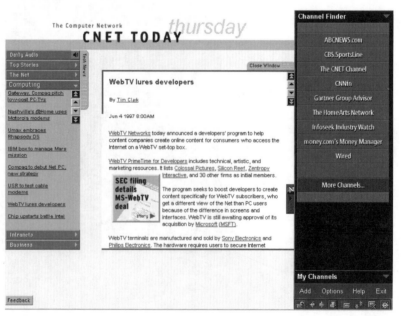

FIGURE *CNET Channel.*
6.1

tions, automatically distributing and updating Java software over networks, and playing computer games. In addition, Netcaster is integrated with Marimba's popular Castanet Tuner application, so you can download both Netcaster and Marimba channels (for more about Marimba, visit its home page at http://www.marimba.com/.).

TIP

If you're a network administrator, you can set up your server to distribute information and deploy Java applications over your Intranet more efficiently. To find out how, visit Netscape (http://home.netscape.com/) or Marimba (http://www.marimba.com/) and look into their server products.

This chapter covers the following:

- Getting started with Netcaster
- Working with Netcaster on your desktop
- Choosing Netcaster options
- Finding and subscribing to channels
- Getting help

Getting Started with Netcaster

Using Netcaster is easy. Select the **Netcaster** option from the **Communicator** menu, and the Netcaster window launches. When the **Java Security** dialog box shown in Figure 6-2 appears, click the **Grant** button. If you don't want to see this dialog box again, click the **Remember this decision each time I start Communicator** checkbox. This dialog box looks rather scary. But all it means is that accessing channels means downloading material to your computer that has not been *digitally signed*. Many channels use Java and JavaScript to update pages dynamically (Netcaster itself is a Java applet).

NOTE

The term dynamic Web pages *refers to Web pages that are enhanced with a little programming (such as Java, JavaScript, and CGI scripts) to either make them more responsive to users or to gather data from the server and automatically update Web page material. This saves Web page content providers the extra work involved in having to format Web page material over and over again every time they want to offer new material. You'll find that most channels are formatted as dynamic Java and JavaScript-enabled Web pages.*

FIGURE *Java security dialog box.*
6.2

A digital signature verifies that the applets you're about to load are safe. The only problem is most developers—even big software companies—haven't started software certificates yet (we'll talk about digital signatures and certificates in Chapter 18). Which means that—although protecting your system protected from downloads that may harm your computer is a good thing—you could also miss out on a lot.

Netcaster consists of the following components:

- **The Netcaster window:** Displays channels and other Netcaster options. The Netcaster window *docks* to the right side of your computer screen. This means that it stays in that particular spot and becomes part of your computer's interface—similar to the Windows 95 task bar and Start menu.

- **Webtop:** Channel content displays next to the Netcaster window when it loads. Some channels appear as regular Web pages in a separate window and some load as Web-tops. Webtops attach themselves to your computer's desktop and fill the entire screen. You cannot use any of the icons on your desktop while you have a Webtop running (don't worry—the Netcaster toolbar buttons offer options so you can get your desktop back!).

- **Channel Finder:** The people at Netscape get you started with the **Channel Finder**—a list of channels with interesting and useful content. To load a channel and check it out, just double-click one of the buttons.
- **More Channels:** Netscape also provides a frequently updated list of more channels to explore. To view the **More Channels** page, double-click the **More Channels** button.
- **Netcaster selector tab:** Click to hide the Netcaster window when it gets on your nerves. To display the Netcaster window again, click on the tab again (it stays around, on the side of your computer screen).
- **My Channels:** Click to display a list of the channels you subscribe to (you may not have anything on this list yet).

In addition, Netcaster provides a row of toolbar buttons.

- **Security status:** Tells you whether the site is secure.
- **Previous:** Goes to the previous page on your Webtop.
- **Next:** Goes to the next page on your Webtop.
- **Print:** Prints the content contained in the current Webtop.
- **Show/Hide Webtop:** Switches back and forth between displaying and hiding the Webtop.
- **Send Webtop forward and back:** Switches back and forth between moving the Webtop forward where you can see it and moving it backwards so you can work with your other applications.
- **Close Webtop:** Closes the current Webtop.
- **Open a new window in Navigator:** Launches a blank Navigator window.

Working with Netcaster on Your Desktop

By now, you might be getting the feeling that Netcaster takes over your computer screen. Unfortunately, that's true, because it becomes part of your desktop environment. When Netcaster is running, the Netcaster window displays even when you work with other applications, and the currently selected Webtop anchors itself to your desktop—which means that you have to access your other current applications in a whole new way. This can make Netcaster annoying to work with at first, but once you get the hang of it, Netcaster also offers many conveniences.

Netcaster works best when you have it running all the time. But for many of us, using Netcaster in offline mode is a better option. For more details, see the "Downloading and Receiving Channels Online" and "Downloading and Receiving Channels Offline" sections later in this chapter.

Listed below are some hints to help you work more efficiently with Netcaster:

- **Hide the Netcaster window:** To hide the Netcaster window, click the **Selector** tab. The **Netcaster Selector** tab still appears on your desktop, but the Netcaster window disappears.

- **Displaying the Netcaster window:** To display the Netcaster window again when you want to access your channels, click the **Netcaster Selector** tab.

- **Exiting Netcaster:** If you're short on system resources (such as RAM, disk space, and processor speed) and don't have a permanent connection to the Internet or a network, then there's no reason to run Netcaster all the time. You can close the Netcaster application by clicking the **Exit** item on the Netcaster window's menu bar and launch Netcaster when you're online and want to download channels. For more about working with Netcaster offline, see the "Downloading and Receiving Channels Online" and "Downloading Channels Offline" sections later in this chapter.

- **Closing Webtops:** To close the current Webtop or channel display, click the **Close Webtop** toolbar icon in the Netcaster window.

- **Displaying currently open application windows:** Click the **Forward/Back** toolbar icon in the Netcaster window to send the Webtop back so your application window displays. To display the Webtop again, click the **Forward/Back** toolbar icon again. Windows 95 users can also display currently open application windows by selecting them from the task bar. Macintosh users can also display currently open applications windows by selecting them from the **Recent Applications** or **Recent Documents** folders in the Apple menu.

- **Launching other applications with Netcaster running:** Windows 95 users can launch another application from the **Start** menu. Windows 3.1x users can launch other applications from their program groups by sending the Webtop back with the **Forward/Back** toolbar icon in the Netcaster window to display their default program groups. Macintosh users can select an application from the Apple menu (Chapter 3 tells you how to make an alias and add it to your Apple menu). Windows 95 and Macintosh users can also select shortcuts or aliases from the desktop by closing the current Webtop and hiding the Netcaster window.

- **Launching Communicator applications with Netcaster running:** Click the **Navigator** toolbar button in the Netcaster window to open a new window in Navigator. You can then select other Communicator applications from Navigator.

For now, I feel that working with Netcaster in offline mode works out better for most users. To find out how to do this, see the "Downloading and Receiving Netcaster Channels" section later in this chapter.

Choosing Netcaster Options

Netcaster also provides you with options so you can add, delete, and edit channels; adjust Netcaster window and Webtop layout settings; specify a default channel; and choose security options. Netcaster's options work similarly to the Communicator preferences we talked about in Chapter 5. But fortunately, there are fewer settings to worry about and we won't need to devote the entire chapter to Netcaster's options!

To view your Netcaster options, click **Options** on the **Menu** bar. When the **Options** window appears, as shown in Figure 6-3, you can enter settings for your channels, Netcaster's layout, and security by clicking the **Channels**, **Layout**, and **Security** tabs.

To save changes, click the **OK** button. Or you can cancel your changes at any time by clicking the **Cancel** button. To close the options window, click the **Close** box in the upper right corner of the **Options** window. You can also click the **Help** button for more information about available options.

WORKING WITH YOUR CHANNELS LIST THROUGH THE CHANNELS OPTIONS WINDOW

The **Channels Options** window enables you to make adjustments to your channels list. The "Finding Subscribing to Channels" section in this chapter tells you more about adding channels to your list. When you select **Options** from the menu bar, the Options window appears first. You can also adjust other Netcaster settings by clicking the **Layout** and **Security** tabs. Here, you can add, delete, and update channels, and edit channel properties.

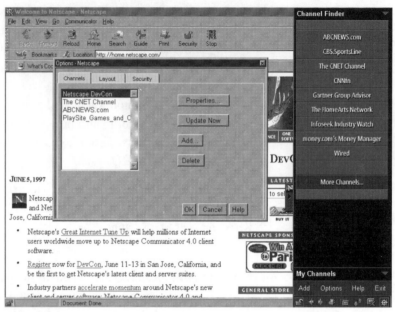

FIGURE *Netcaster Channels Options window.*
6.3

You can do the following through the **Channels Options** window:

- **Select a channel from your list:** The scrolling list on the left side of the **Channels Options** window displays a list of the channels you currently subscribe to (if you haven't added any channels yet, go to the "Finding and Subscribing to Channels" section in this chapter to create your list).

- **Display channel properties:** To display and edit channel properties, select a channel from the scrolling lists and click the **Properties** button. The "Adding Channels in the Channels Properties Window" section explains channels properties in greater detail.

- **Update a channel:** If you want to update channel information right now, select a channel from the list and click the **Update Now** button.

- **Adding a channel to your list:** To add a channel to your list, click the **Add** button to display a blank **Channels Properties** window. The "Adding Channels in the Channels Properties Window" section explains this in greater detail. You can also display the **Channels Properties** window to add channels to your list by clicking the **Add** item on Netcaster's menu bar.

- **Delete a channel from your list:** To delete a channel from your list, select the channel, then click the **Delete** button.

When you're finished selecting options, click the **OK** button. If you get stuck and don't have this book with you, click the **Help** button.

ADJUSTING NETCASTER'S LAYOUT THROUGH THE LAYOUT OPTIONS WINDOW

You can also adjust how Netcaster appears on your computer screen and create a default channel to display automatically when you launch Netcaster. To adjust your layout options, click on the **Options** window's **Layout** tab. When the **Layout Options** window appears, as shown in Figure 6-4, you can change your settings.

You can do the following through the Layout Options window:

- **Change Netcaster's layout:** When you launch Netcaster, the Netcaster window displays on the right side and the Webtop (channel content) displays on the left side. You can switch the Netcaster window and Web top positions around by selecting the **Left side of the screen op-**

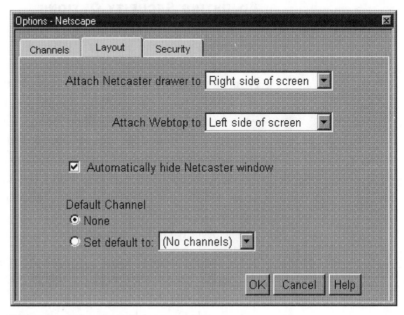

FIGURE *Netcaster Layout Options window.*
6.4

tion from the **Attach Netcaster draw to pulldown list**, and selecting the **Right side of the screen option** from the **Attach Webtop to pull-down list**.

- **Hide the Netcaster window:** The Netcaster application is a Java applet that loads from a Web page. When you launch Netcaster by selecting the **Netcaster** option from the Communicator menu from within another Communicator component, a Web page launches in a separate window. Since having a lot of Navigator Web page windows open on your computer screen at once can get confusing, you can choose to always hide the Netcaster window by selecting the **Automatically hide Netcaster window** checkbox.

- **Set a default channel:** You can set up a default channel that loads automatically when you launch Netcaster. Select the **Set default to:** radio button and select a channel from the pulldown list.

- **Choose not to have a default channel:** If you prefer to choose which channel to load first when launching Netcaster, select the **None** radio button.

When you're finished selecting options, click **OK**.

ADJUSTING SECURITY OPTIONS

You can also adjust Netcaster's security settings in the Security Options window, shown in Figure 6-5. As with Web pages (channels are Web pages that download to your computer automatically), some channels give you cookies. As mentioned earlier, cookies are little data files that enable the server to remember who you are and assemble custom pages for you. For more on cookies, see Chapter 18. For now, these settings apply to Castanet channels. Castanet is a cutting-edge, free channel receiver application by Marimba. Netcaster is integrated with Castanet so you can receive both Netcaster and Marimba channels. For more information about Marimba's Castanet application and channels created with Marimba server products, go to `http://www.marimba.com/`.

The **Security Options** window offers the following options:

- **Accept Castanet cookies:** Leave the checkbox selected to receive Castanet channels with cookies or disable the checkbox by clicking it to remove the check mark.

- **Enable Castanet logging:** Some channels create *log files* based on the links you follow most frequently on that channel. Log files are created

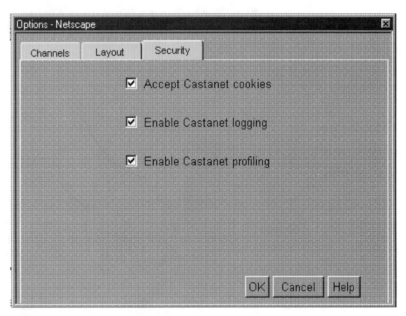

FIGURE   *Netcaster Security Options window.*
6.5

and saved to your computer. The channel server uses this information to determine the topics that interest you the most and to make it easier for you to find those topics the next time you select that channel. To enable Castanet logging, leave the checkbox selected. To disable Castanet logging, click the checkbox to deselect it.

- **Enable Castanet profiling:** Some channels include forms that generate a user *profile*. This works similarly to log files. You fill in items in the form to prompt you for your name, what topics interest you, the area you live in, and other information that enables the server to generate custom pages for you based on your interests. The channel server then saves a user profile file to your hard drive so it can "remember" your information. To enable Castanet profiling, leave the checkbox selected. To disable Castanet profiling, click the checkbox to deselect it.

Click the **OK** button to save your settings. Castanet logging and profiling are types of cookies and future versions of Netscape Communicator and Netcaster may enable more types of cookies, which will be added to this list.

If you disable the **Accept Castanet cookies** checkbox, then you won't be able to receive logs, profiles, or other cookies offered by Castanet channels.

Finding and Subscribing to Channels

Netcaster's integration with Communicator makes it easy to find and subscribe to channels. You can add channels to your Channels list straight from the Netcaster **Channel Finder**, from the Web, and through the **Channels Properties** window. When you subscribe to channels, they get added to your channels list, shown in Figure 6-12 in the "Downloading and Receiving Channels Online" and "Downloading and Receiving Channels Offline" sections later in this chapter. To display your list of subscribed channels, click the **My Channels** option in the Netcaster window.

ADDING CHANNELS FROM NETCASTER'S CHANNEL FINDER

The easiest way to subscribe to channels is to select them from the **Channel Finder** in the Netcaster window. The **Channel Finder** comes with a list of useful channels. To subscribe to a channel on the **Channel Finder** list, do the following:

1. Click an item on the list.
2. Wait for the channel to load (channels take a few minutes to load the first time).
3. When the channel Webtop appears, as shown in Figure 6-6 (here, I selected the CNET Channel), click the **Add Channel** button on the upper corner of the channel page Webtop.
4. When you download channels by selecting them from the **Channel Finder** list, you may notice that a logo, channel name, and **Add Channel** button display below the list item. You can also click the **Add Channel** button to add the currently displayed channel to your list.

You can jump to topics of interest the same way as you would on a regular Web page—by clicking on links. Netscape also constantly adds more channels to its list. Although these channels can't be added to the list in the Netcaster window, these updates are easy to find.

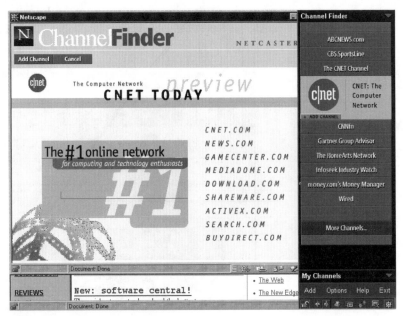

FIGURE
6.6   *Netcaster's Channel finder provides a list of interesting channels. You can download channels like the CNET Channel, which offers lots of useful computer-related resources, by clicking on list items. CNET also has a regular Web page located at* http://www.cnet.com/. *When you select an item from the channel finder, the channel's logo and an* **Add Channel** *button appear below the list item.*

To check out the latest additions to Netscape's channels list, do the following:

1. Click the **More Channels...** button on the **Channel Finder** list.
2. When the **ChannelFinder** page appears, as shown in Figure 6-7, you can select items from the page by clicking on the **Add Channel** button underneath the list item.
3. Wait for the channel to download and appear on your Webtop.

Netcaster automatically adds the channel to your list.

ADDING CHANNELS FROM WEB PAGES

You can also add channels to your list while browsing the Web with Navigator. When you click on a link to a channel, Netcaster launches and adds the channel to your **My Channels** list automatically. Marimba's home page at

FIGURE **6.7** *Click the More Channels... item on the Channel Finder list to display Netscape's Channel Finder page with the latest available channels.*

`http://www.marimba.com/` (shown in Figure 6-8) offers links to a lively assortment of Marimba channels—including daily horoscopes, games, chat groups on business-related and other topics, Java applications like the Corel Office Suite, and more—which you can access through Netcaster.

ADDING CHANNELS IN THE CHANNELS PROPERTIES WINDOW

You can also add channels and Web pages to your **My Channels** list manually in the **Channel Properties** window. Yes, you can also tell Netcaster to automatically download content from the Web pages that you visit most frequently. This is useful when you want to browse information offline, as discussed later in this chapter.

To add channels to your **My Channels** list manually from the **Channels Properties** window, do the following:

1. Click the **Add** option on the Netcaster window menu bar (you can also add items from the **Options** window discussed in the "Working

FIGURE **6.8** *Marimba's home page has lots of links to interesting Castanet channels that you can access through Netcaster.*

with your Channels List through the Channels Options Window" section by clicking the **Add** button).

2. When the **Channel Properties General** window displays, as shown in Figure 6-9, enter the name of the channel in the **Name** text field and enter the URL in the **Location** text field. If you have a permanent Internet connection, you can also tell Netcaster to update the channel at specified intervals by leaving the **Update this channel or site every:** checkbox selected and selecting a number of hours from the pulldown list. If you prefer to work with Netcaster offline, deselect the checkbox.

3. Click the **Display** tab. When the **Channel Properties Display** window appears, as shown in Figure 6-10, you can choose whether to display channels as a **Default Window** (a regular Web page) or a **Webtop Window** (a window that anchors to your desktop and fills your Computer screen) by selecting the appropriate radio button.

4. Click the Cache tab. When the **Channel Properties Cache** window appears, as shown in Figure 6-11, enter a number following the **Download** prompt to determine how many levels deep in the Web site

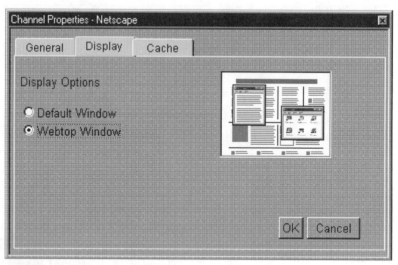

FIGURE *General Channel Properties window.*
6.9

FIGURE *Display Channel Properties window.*
6.10

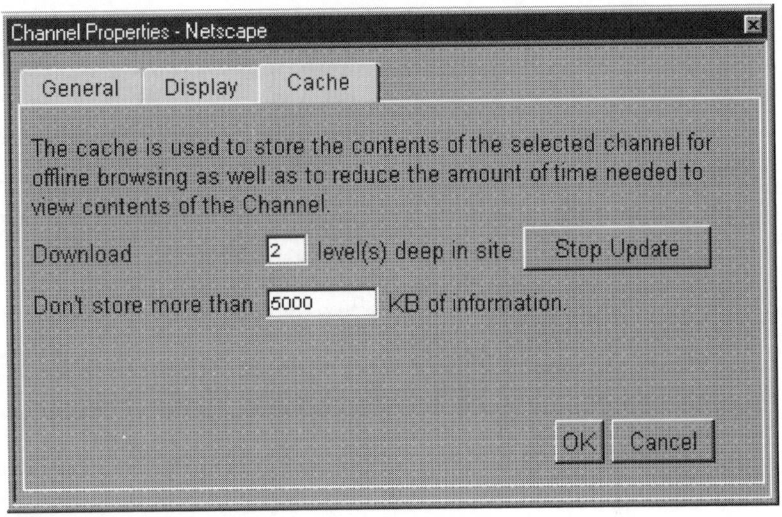

FIGURE *Cache Channel Properties window.*
6.11

should be downloaded. Levels deep refers to the number of directory and sub directory levels in a Web site. Web site directories often run two or three levels deep. You should enter at least a value of 2 or 3 to ensure that Web site links to site material work when you view it offline. You can also specify a maximum amount of data, as measured in Kilobytes (KB) to download from the channel by entering a number following the **Don't store more than** prompt. The default setting is 6000 KB, or about six floppy disks worth.

Click **OK** to save your changes, or click **Cancel** if you change your mind.

DOWNLOADING AND RECEIVING SUBSCRIBED CHANNELS

Once you've subscribed to your channels, you can easily download and view content to the Webtop. All you have to do is select the channel of your choice from the **My Channels** list. The **My Channels** list appears similarly to the one shown in Figure 6-12. Channels that have been specified as Webtops in the **Display Channel Properties** window have square Webtop indicator next to the channel name. When the channel is currently active, the Webtop indica-

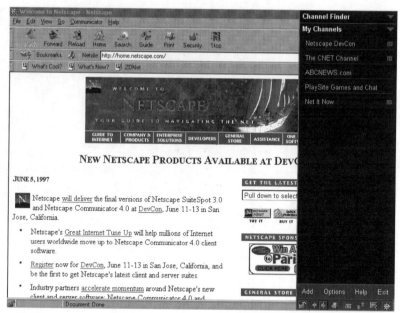

FIGURE *Netcaster window with My Channels list displayed*
6.12

tor glows. To view your **My Channels** list, click the **My Channels** option above the Netcaster window's menu bar. To return to the **Channel Finder** list, click the **Channel Finder** option above the **My Channels** list.

Netcaster stores downloaded channel content in your *cache folder*. As Chapter 5 explains in greater detail, the cache temporarily stores downloaded Web pages and channels. With Navigator, this helps you return to recently visited pages more quickly because it accesses content from your computer instead of having to download everything all over again. However, with Navigator, you still have to be online to access pages in your cache. If you are not connected to the Internet and enter a URL in Navigator's location window, nothing happens.

Netcaster, on the other hand, stores Web pages and channels in your cache in a way that lets you access content that you've subscribed to even when you're offline. The application handles channel delivery differently depending on whether you have a permanent connection to the Internet and whether you're working in online or offline mode (as discussed in the offline preferences section in Chapter 5). You can work with Netcaster in the following ways:

- **Online mode with a permanent Internet connection:** If you have a dedicated connection to the Internet or an Intranet, leave Netcaster running all the time, and have Communicator set up to work in online mode, you can tell Netcaster to download channel updates automatically. When you select a channel, the latest update displays on the Webtop from the cache. You can also update channels manually.
- **Online mode with a dial-up Internet connection:** If, like most of us, you don't have a dedicated line to the Internet, then automatic downloads won't work. You'll need to download channels manually when you dial up your ISP's server. When you launch Netcaster and select a channel, Netcaster starts downloading pages.
- **Offline mode:** Once you've downloaded channels, you can log off and view them offline.

The following sections tell you more about working with Netcaster online and offline.

Downloading and Receiving Channels Online

Whether you use Netcaster online or offline, you still have to download channels and Web pages at some point in order to receive them. You can either download channels manually or tell Netcaster to download channels at specified intervals. But the nice thing about Netcaster is that, unlike downloading Web pages in Navigator, it works in the background so you can do other things while you wait. If the Netcaster window gets in your way while you're trying to get your work done, you can click on the **Netcaster Selector** tab to hide it.

Updating Channels Manually

Whether or not you have Netcaster set up for automatic updates, you can also download channels manually. If you do not have a permanent connection to the Internet or a network, then you *have* to download channels manually.

To download channels manually, do the following:

1. Launch Netcaster from a Communicator application by selecting Netcaster from the Communicator menu.

2. When the Netcaster window appears, click the **My Channels** option just above the menu bar.

3. When the **My Channels** list displays, click the channel you want to update with the right mouse key (Windows) or click the channel while holding down the option key (Macintosh).

4. When the pop-up menu appears, as shown in Figure 6-13, select the **Start Update** option.

You can also display the **Channels Options** window, select a channel from the list, and click the **Update Now** button. The **Channels Options** window is shown in Figure 6-3 earlier in this chapter. After downloading your channels, you can view them online or offline.

Updating Channels Automatically

If you have a dedicated connection to the Internet, you can also specify automatic updates for your channels in the **Channel Properties** window. The channel properties default to updating your channels and Web pages every twelve hours. In order for your automatic downloads to work, you must have

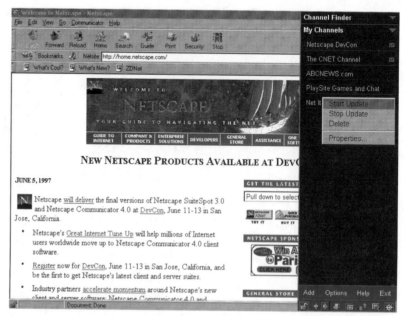

FIGURE *To update channels with new material, choose Start Update from the pop-up*
6.13 *menu.*

Netcaster running all the time. You can also enter other default settings for each channel in the **Channel Properties** window, as explained in the previous "Adding Channels in the Channels Properties Window" section.

To specify automatic download times for the channels on your list, do the following:

1. Click the **Options** item on the Netcaster window's menu bar.
2. When the **Channel Options** window appears (as discussed in the "Working with your Channels List through the Channels Options Window" section and shown in Figure 6-3 earlier in this chapter), select an item from your **Channels** list, and click the **Properties** button.
3. When the **Channels Properties** window appears, as shown in Figure 6-9 in the previous section, select the **Update this channel or site every:** checkbox, then specify a number of hours from the pulldown list.
4. Click **OK** to save your changes.

You can also access your channels properties from the **My Channels** list by right-clicking (Windows) or option-clicking (Macintosh) a channel and selecting the **Properties** option from the pop-up menu.

If you plan on using Netcaster in online mode for automated downloading, remember to set your Communicator Offline preferences to Online Work Mode, as explained earlier in this chapter.

CAUTION

Downloading and Receiving Channels Offline

Netcaster is an exciting innovation, but it makes considerable demands on your computer system's resources. In addition, it also only downloads channel updates automatically if you have a dedicated Internet or Intranet connection. Hopefully, future versions of Communicator and Netcaster will enable you to tell Netcaster to dial up your ISP and download channels at specified intervals. But for now, if you don't have a dedicated connection, feel that your computer isn't sufficiently up to speed to keep Netcaster running all the time, or simply find Netcaster annoying, you can use Netcaster offline.

Using Netcaster offline means that you launch the Netcaster application when you're online and want to use it, download your channels manually, disconnect from the Internet, and view content from your channels at your leisure. If you frequently visit certain Web sites, Netcaster can save you a lot of browsing and download time since everything gets downloaded at once instead of one page at a time. This also enables you to catch up on your Web reading when you cannot get onto the Internet.

When you view Web pages offline, links to HTML documents outside of the Web site will not work.

To work with Netcaster offline, do the following:

1. Launch Netcaster from a Communicator application by selecting **Netcaster** from the Communicator menu.
2. Update your channels as described in the previous "Updating Channels Manually" section (you can click the **Netcaster Selector** tab to hide the Netcaster window so you can get your other work done).
3. When you're finished with updating your channels, disconnect from your Internet connection by opening Navigator and selecting **Go Offline** from the **File** menu.

The updated material will display when you receive channels by selecting an item from the **My Channels** list. You can either view your channels now,

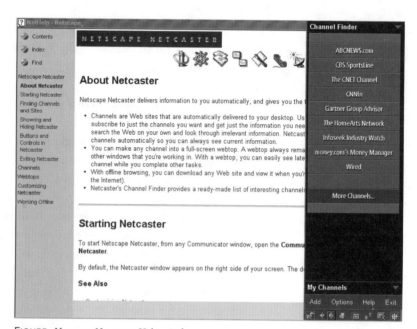

FIGURE *Netscape Netcaster Help window*
6.14

or exit Netcaster and view them later. When you select the **Go Offline** item from Navigator's **File** menu, a dialog box appears to ask whether Communicator should download your email and newsgroup messages for you before you disconnect (Chapter 13 talks about working with email and newsgroups offline in greater detail). Unfortunately, this dialog box doesn't offer options for downloading channels. Hopefully, Netscape will fix this in future versions of Communicator.

Getting Help

If you ever get stuck, never fear. Help is just a mouse click away. Click the **Help** item on the Netcaster window menu bar to display the Netscape Netcaster help window, as shown in Figure 6-14. You can select items from the frame on the left, view and index and table of contents, or search for your topic by keyword.

CHAPTER 7

Working with Plug-Ins

I magine touring a few houses or condominiums you're thinking of buying and exploring the interior and the neighborhood . . . from your real estate agent's "virtual Realty" site. Or a student being able to hear Martin Luther King's "I Have a Dream" speech instead of just reading about it in a dreary textbook. Plug-ins expand Navigator's capabilities and make the Internet more useful, informative, and fun. Plug-ins make it possible to communicate in new and exciting ways. With plug-ins, you can view portable documents, check out live online video and radio broadcasts, and launch a variety of files that Navigator doesn't directly support.

This chapter covers the following:

- What are plug-ins?
- Finding plug-ins
- Downloading and installing plug-ins

What Are Plug-Ins?

Plug-ins are third-party applications that launch files not supported by standard Web browsers. Originally developed to work with Netscape Communications' Navigator browser, plug-ins now also work with Microsoft's Internet Explorer.

Let's say you've just created a file with one of your usual applications and you want to put it on your Web page. But how would visitors to your page be able to view the file? Smart software developers create plug-ins that go with their applications. That way, people can put whatever they want on their Web pages and tell visitors where to get the right plug-in to view it.

The browser's *applications program interface* (API) makes it easy for developers to develop smoothly integrated applets (small applications) that launch files directly from the Web. If you already have plug-ins installed for a previous version of Navigator, they will also work with the new version of Navigator that comes with Communicator.

Applications program interface (API) refers to how an application accesses the operating system, other programs, and utilities.

TIP

Finding Plug-Ins

Plug-ins aren't always easy to find. But you don't need to worry about them unless you come across a Web page that requires you to have one in order to view the content. You can find plug-ins from the following sources:

- **Serendipity:** If you land on a Web page that requires a plug-in, it will usually provide a link.

- **Your software company:** The company that develops the applications you use may also have Web page plug-ins that go with your programs. For example, Microsoft has Word, PowerPoint, and Excel viewers so you can put your documents, presentations, and spreadsheets on the Web.
- **Netscape plug-ins page:** To get updates on the latest available browser plug-ins, go to Netscape's plug-ins page at http://home.netscape.com/comprod/products/navigator/version_2.0/plugins/ as shown in Figure 7-1. Plug-ins are organized into categories, including 3D and Animation, Business Utilities, Audio and Video, Image Viewers, and Presentations.

Navigator also comes with its own plug-ins. Live 3D for 3D worlds (as discussed in Chapter 4), and Media Player for real-time streaming audio and video broadcast. Once you find the plug-ins, getting them is easy. Most companies offer them free so you can view content that their customers have created and put on the Web. You'll also find plenty of instructions for installing and using the plug-ins and some fun samples to come back and

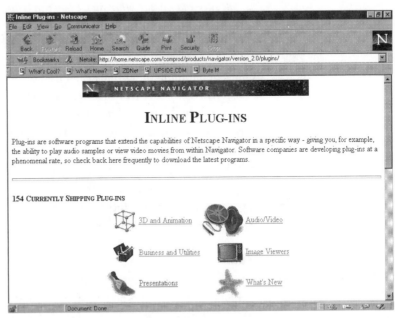

FIGURE *You can find just the plug-in you need from Netscape's plug-ins page at*
7.1 http://home.netscape.com/comprod/products/navigator/version_2.0/plugins/.

check out once you get the plug-ins set up. Of course, purveyors of plug-ins generally want to know who you are and ask you to fill out a form before you can start downloading.

Not all plug-ins are free! Most vendors do offer them free of charge, but some are offered on a try-before-you buy shareware basis.

PLUG-INS WE CAN'T DO WITHOUT

The Web abounds with more plug-ins than I could possibly include in this book. Chances are the companies who develop the applications you use at work every day have developed plug-ins so you and your coworkers can share files via the Internet and Intranets. If you need a plug-in for a specific purpose, there's probably one available. Meanwhile, there are a few applications that are so popular among Web content developers that you absolutely need the corresponding plug-ins, otherwise you'll miss a lot of neat stuff.

To start exploring with your new plug-ins, start from the pages where you got the plug-ins. Adobe (Acrobat Reader), Apple (QuickTime), Progressive Networks (RealAudio), LiveUpdate (Crescendo), and Macromedia (Shockwave) all offer sample files and links to other sites so you can cruise the Web in style.

Acrobat Reader for Online Publications

With the Acrobat Reader plug-in by Adobe Systems, you can view and print online publications or download and read them later. We call these Portable Document Format (PDF) files because you can distribute them over networks and the Internet. If you have the Acrobat Reader plug-in, you can view PDF files, no matter what kind of computer or application originally generated them. Publishing portable documents requires a software program called Acrobat. But viewing them only requires the freeware Acrobat Reader plug-in. You can download it from Adobe's home page at `http://www.adobe.com/`, then view files like the one shown in Figure 7-2. The Acrobat Reader is available for Windows and Macintosh users.

RealPlayer

Internet radio has recently emerged as a dynamic new communications medium, and now video broadcasting is following on its heels. You can listen to real-time audio and video broadcasts with news, music, interviews, speeches from conferences, and more from around the world online with the Progressive Networks' RealPlayer plug-in shown in Figure 7-3. It's easy, fun,

FIGURE *With the Acrobat reader, you can view and print out brochures and forms that*
7.2 *people formatted into PDF files for distribution on the Web—like this tax form*
from the California Franchise Tax Board at http://www.ftb.ca.gov/.

FIGURE *With RealAudio, you can watch and listen to audio and video Internet*
7.3 *broadcasts.*

and exciting. And believe it or not, it *does* work on a regular 28.8 Kbps modem (the Progressive Networks people even claim it works on the slower 14.4 Kbps modems). But first you need a sound card (many computers come with them built in) the RealPlayer plug-in. You can download it from `http://www.realaudio.com/`. The RealPlayer is freeware, but if you get serious about real-time streaming audio and video, you should purchase the $29.99 RealPlayer Plus. The RealPlayer is available for Windows and Macintosh users.

What's Real-Time Streaming?

Face it. Audio and video on the Web seems really neat—until the downloads take so long that it doesn't seem worth it. Audio and video files are huge. If you wanted to listen to a half-hour live audio or video newscast, you wouldn't have enough space on your hard drive to handle it, even if you could download the file!

Real time streaming allows video and audio to "stream" from the site, to your browser, and into your cache—which automatically gets emptied when it's full. When you download real-time streaming audio or video, you don't have to wait for the entire file to download before you listen to it— the file starts playing immediately—just as if you turned on the television or radio.

QuickTime with QuickTime VR

Multimedia enthusiasts have been downloading movies from the net and playing them back with Apple Computer's QuickTime video player for years. Now you can view them online with Apple's QuickTime plug-in. But wait before you start making popcorn—understand that you won't have much time to eat it. Most movies on the net are short clips. A full-length feature would take up more disk space than most of us have on our hard drives.

In addition, you can get QuickTime bundled with QuickTime VR—a cool viewer for exploring QuickTime virtual reality worlds. For example, the Carlsbad Web site at `http://www.in-carlsbad.com/`, lets you "walk through" houses that are for sale and various scenes around Carlsbad, California. By the way, QuickTime VR is different than regular VR, so even though Netscape comes with the Live3D Virtual Reality plug-in, you should still download the version of QuickTime that comes with QuickTime VR.

FIGURE   *You can listen to MIDI music with the Crescendo plug-in.*
7.4

You can get the QuickTime plug-in from Apple's QuickTime video page at
`http://www.quicktime.apple.com/`. QuickTime is available for Windows and Macintosh users; QuickTime VR is available for Windows 95 and Macintosh users.

I have noticed that QuickTime VR only works when your monitor is set to 24-bit or 32-bit mode.

CAUTION

Crescendo

LiveUpdate's Crescendo MIDI music player plug-in, shown in Figure 7-4, launches high-quality MIDI-formatted music files for Web-surfing music. The LiveUpdate Web site also has lots of fun MIDI files you can listen to. Crescendo comes in the freeware version and the higher-end Pro version. You can get the Crescendo from the LiveUpdate Web site at `http://www.liveupdate.com/`. Crescendo is available for Windows and Macintosh users.

Shockwave Flash

You may have downloaded movies from the Web before. But you've never seen anything like this. Macromedia Inc.'s innovative Director software has impressive animation capabilities. While artists use Director to create all kinds of animated and interactive works, including movies, games, slide shows, and cartoons with audio, all Director-generated files are called "movies." In addition, Shockwave lets you view files created with other cutting-edge Macromedia products like Freehand, Flash, and Authorware. Unlike the other plug-ins we've looked at so far, Shockwave does not have an interface per se. Instead, it enables content created for viewing with Shockwave Flash and embedded in a Web page to launch in your browser, as shown in Figure 7-5. To get the latest and greatest version of Shockwave Flash with all the bells and whistles, check out Macromedia's home page at `http://www.macromedia.com/`. Shockwave Flash is available for Windows and Macintosh users.

FIGURE 7.5 *Shockwave movie launching in Navigator (this is part of my Virtual Kitty site at* `http://www.byteit.com/puddy/`).

Ping Live

Portable Network Graphics (.PNG) by Siegel & Gale, is an up-and-coming image format that may replace .GIF images in the future. .PNG image files have the advantages of smaller file sizes, higher image quality, and speedier downloads. If you want to see what .PNG files are like, get the plug-in from the Siegel & Gale Web site at `http://www.siegelgale.com/`.

Real Space

Although Netscape has its own Virtual Reality viewer, you should check out Live Picture's RealSpace VR plug-in. It offers impressive display capabilities and allows you to fully enjoy VR spaces created by artists who use Live Picture's imaging and VRML rendering products. You can get the plug-in and get a good start on your virtual journey by visiting `http://www.livepicture.com/`.

Downloading and Installing Plug-Ins

Downloading and installing plug-ins is easy. Simply go to the site where the plug-in you want is located, download the correct plug-in for your computer, and follow the installation instructions. The installation instructions are generally either posted on the plug-in's Web page, or in a plain-text read-me file that comes with the plug-in installation file.

To set up your files, all you have to do is follow the Setup Wizard's instructions and respond to its prompts. Some of plug-in Setup Wizards even ask you if you want to install plug-ins for Netscape or Internet Explorer.

However, you'll find it easier to successfully download and install plug-ins if you keep the following tips in mind:

- **Get your decompression utility:** Plug-ins are sometimes served up as compressed files, otherwise they would take too long to download. To extract files, you either need WinZip (Windows) or StuffIt Expander (Macintosh). For more information on obtaining a decompression utility, go to Chapter 3.
- **Create a special folder for downloads:** This helps you remember where your installer files are for plug-ins and other applications that you download from the Internet. Also, before you download a plug-in installation file, you should create and name a special folder for it.

Since most installer file names are completely incomprehensible, you might not remember which file is which.

- **Get the correct plug-in:** Most plug-in home pages offer Windows 95, Windows NT, Windows 3.1x, and Macintosh versions. Make sure you get the right one.

- **Follow the Web site instructions:** Plug-in Web sites generally have easy to understand instructions for downloading, installing, and using plug-ins. Take a little time to read them.

- **Read Me!:** Most downloadable files come with a text file called "Read Me." Here, you'll find important information about installing and using the software, as well as your license agreement.

- **Make sure you install your plug-ins to the correct folder or directory:** The Setup Wizard usually finds the correct plug-in folder automatically. But this might not happen if you have other browsers or a previous version of Navigator installed on your system. Plug-ins should be installed in Communicator's plug-ins folder. Unless you told the Communicator Setup Wizard to install it somewhere else, the directory path to where your plug-ins should go is:

```
C:\Program files\Netscape\Communicator\program\plugins\
```

Also, plug-ins sometimes conflict with each other and can drag down your computer's performance. Does this mean you should avoid plug-ins? Heck no! Plug-ins usually work great and make the Internet a more exciting and interactive place. Just don't go to Netscape's plug-ins page and start downloading *everything*—wait until you come across some compelling content, and if you need a plug-in, go get it. The plug-ins that I mentioned in the previous section should get you off to a fine start.

CONFIGURING FILE TYPES

Plug-ins work just fine most of the time. But sometimes something goes wrong. When this happens, you might want to check your applications preferences. The **Applications Preferences** window, shown in Figure 7-6, tells Navigator about different file types and which applications or plug-ins are supposed to handle each file type. In most cases, the plug-in Setup Wizard configures the applications preferences for you, so you will rarely ever have to bother with this. However, it can't hurt to know a little about how this works.

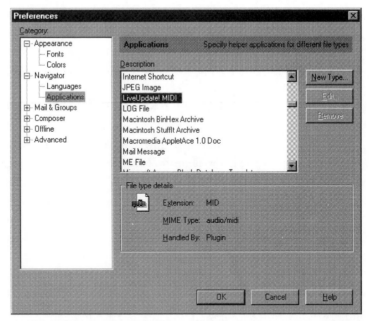

FIGURE
7.6 *The **Applications Preferences** window consists of a scrolling list of registered file types (file types that your computer knows about) and a **File type details** box that displays information about the selected file type. Here, I have **Live Update! MIDI** selected.*

The File type details consist of the following information:

1. **Extension:** Displays what file name extensions the selected file type uses (LiveUpdate MIDI generally has the .MIDI or .MID file name extension).

2. **MIME:** The MIME (Multipurpose Internet Mail Extensions) gives Netscape more detailed information about the file type. For example, a .MIDI file is a type of audio file, and the MIME type is audio/MIDI. Most types of files have universally recognized MIME types.

3. **Handled With:** Tells Navigator what plug-in or application to launch when it encounters the selected file type. LiveUpdate! and standard .MIDI files are handled with LiveUpdate's Crescendo plug-in.

4. **New Type:** Click on this button to set up a new file type.

5. **Remove:** Removes the selected file type.

6. **Edit:** Brings up the **Edit** screen for the selected file type.

In general, when a plug-in doesn't work properly, it's either because Navigator can't find the plug-in, or because there is more than one application or plug-in assigned to the same file type.

SETTING UP NEW FILE TYPES AND EDITING FILE TYPES

You can also configure new file type settings and edit existing ones, provided you know all the necessary information. Once again, in most cases, Navigator and the plug-in Setup Wizards do all this for you so you will probably never have to do this.

To configure a new file type, click the **New** button in the application window. When the **New Type** dialog box displays, as shown in Figure 7-7, enter the following information:

- **Description of type:** Enter the generic file type—for example, "Midi File."
- **File extension:** Enter the file name extension associated with the new file type. If there are multiple possible file name extensions, separate them by commas, as in: MIDI, MID.

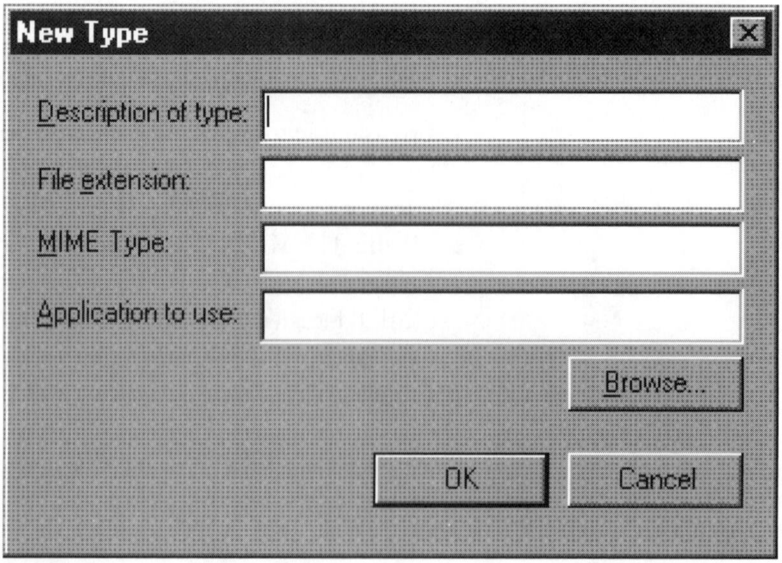

FIGURE *New Type dialog box*
7.7

- **MIME Type:** Once again, most files have an associated MIME type. If you don't know the MIME type for the file type in question, look through the read me files or associated documentation on the Web site.
- **Application to use:** Click the **Browse** button to search for the executable file for the application you want to handle content that fits the new file type.

Once you set up a new file type, click **OK**. When you return to the **Applications Preferences** window, the new file type appears on the scrolling list. You can also enter additional information or make changes by selecting the file type and clicking the **Edit** button.

When the **Edit Type** dialog box appears, you can enter the following information:

- **Save to disk:** Select the **Save to Disk** radio button if you prefer that the Web page content that matches this file type be launched separately rather than immediately and from within Navigator.
- **Application:** Select this radio button if you want content that matches this file type to be opened straight from Navigator. The application path in the text field should already lead to the correct application, but if you've moved the program, click the **Browse** button to locate it.
- **Ask me before opening downloaded files of this type:** You can tell Navigator to display a warning dialog box before launching content that matches the currently selected file type.

When you're finished making your changes, click **OK**.

8 Marking Your Itinerary with Bookmarks

Navigator's Bookmarks feature lets you mark your itinerary as you travel the Internet. You can create a hot list of links to places with useful information, news, software, multimedia, and other content that you want instant access to. Bookmarks save your place while you're surfing Web pages the same way that bookmarks save your place while turning a book's pages. When you drop by Web sites that you would like to return to, you can add to your collection of links. As your list grows longer, you can sort, arrange, and make notes to your entries for easier navigating.

This chapter covers the following:

- Viewing your Bookmark list
- Adding Bookmarks to your list
- Organizing and editing Bookmarks
- Bookmarks as HTML documents
- Importing and exporting Bookmark files
- Maintaining multiple Bookmark lists

Viewing Your Bookmarks List

There are two ways to view your bookmarks list. You can select the **Bookmarks** menu from Navigator's main window to add and file items as you go along. Or you can display the **Bookmarks** window by selecting the **Bookmarks** menu's **Edit Bookmarks** option so you can edit, organize, and customize your list through the **Bookmarks** window. If you installed Communicator over an old version of Navigator and stick with the folder or directory location defaults during the setup routine, you'll also notice that your old bookmark list stays intact.

FROM THE BOOKMARKS MENU

You can display your **Bookmarks** menu, as shown in Figure 8-1, by clicking the **Bookmarks** icon on the **Location** toolbar. If you haven't had a chance to add any bookmarks yet, that's OK. Communicator comes with an interesting selection of bookmarks. The **Bookmarks** menu displays your list of entries, along with commands for adding, filing, and editing bookmarks. From here, you can select items from your list to jump to the Internet. You can also add bookmarks by selecting the **Add** command, add bookmarks into designated folders by selecting the **File** command, or display the Bookmarks window by selecting the **Edit** command. In addition, you'll find a **Toolbar**

FIGURE *Click the Bookmarks icon on the Location toolbar to display the Bookmarks*
8.1   *menu.*

folder. This folder contains the items that appear on your personal toolbar. For now, Netscape has included the What's New and What's Cool sites for you. You can also add your own items to the personal toolbar, as I explain later in this chapter.

FROM THE BOOKMARKS WINDOW

You can display the **Bookmarks** window, as shown in Figure 8-2, by selecting the **Edit** command from the **Bookmarks** menu. Viewing the Bookmarks window is similar to browsing through folders or directories in the Windows 95 Explorer, Windows 3.1x File Manager, or Macintosh Finder. From here, you can edit bookmark properties, create folders, maintain multiple bookmark lists, and organize and sort bookmarks alphabetically by name, URL, creation date, or last visit date.

The **Bookmarks** window consists of the following elements:

- **Title bar:** Displays the name of your Bookmarks list HTML document (such as bookmarks.htm)—this can be useful if you maintain

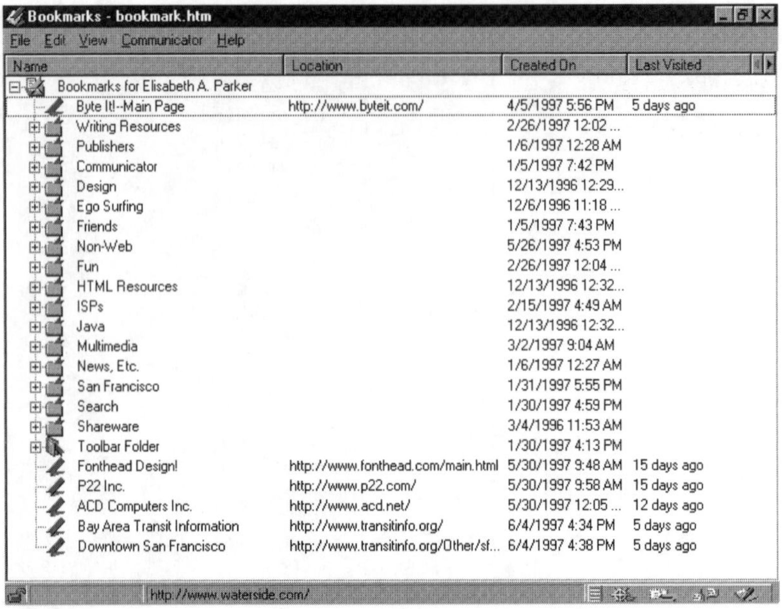

FIGURE **8.2** *The Bookmarks window offers numerous options for organizing and customizing your lists.*

multiple bookmarks lists. I explain this in greater detail later in the chapter.

- **Menu bar:** Displays menu items.
- **Columns:** Displays information about bookmark list items by column, including the **Name** (Web page title), **Location** (URL), **Created On** (creation date), and **Last Visited** (date last visited).
- **Folders:** You can create folders so you can organize your bookmarks by category.
- **Bookmarks:** Unless you sort bookmarks into folders, they appear as list items in the Bookmarks window with information about the Web page title, location, creation date, and date last visited.
- **Components bar:** You can click items on the components bar to launch other Communicator components.

To expand a folder and view the folder contents, click the + sign to the left of a folder icon. To contract the folder, click the – sign to the left of the folder icon (it appears when the list is expanded).

Adding Bookmarks to Your List

Bookmarks make it easy for you to mark your place while browsing Netscape pages. Getting back to the good stuff—without having to remember and reenter those pesky, long URLs—is as simple as selecting items from a pull-down list. You can add bookmarks to the list or into a folder straight from a favorite Web page, or you can add a bookmark from scratch from the Bookmarks Window.

FROM A WEB PAGE

The easiest way to add bookmarks to your list is by collecting them as you travel. When you come across a place worth visiting again, you can create a bookmark in a snap.

To add a bookmark to your list, do the following:

1. Click the **Bookmarks** icon on the **Location** toolbar.
2. When the **Bookmarks** menu displays, select **Add Bookmark**.

And voila! You're done. New bookmarks are added to the bottom of your list and function as hypertext links. To jump to a bookmarked page, just select any bookmark.

TO FOLDERS

Are you one of those people who likes to keep things neat? You can put new bookmarks right in the proper place by adding them straight to a folder that you've created in the Bookmarks window.

To add a bookmark to a folder, do the following:

1. Click the **Bookmarks** icon on the **Location** toolbar.
2. When the **Bookmarks** menu displays, select **File Bookmark**.
3. When the list of folders appears, as shown in Figure 8-3, select the one you want to place your new bookmark in.

There. That was easy, wasn't it? Bookmarks that have been sorted into folders appear in a cascading list when you select the folder from the **Bookmarks** menu.

TO YOUR PERSONAL TOOLBAR

You can also add bookmarks to your personal toolbar, like the ones shown in Figure 8-4. Adding bookmarks to your personal toolbar helps you jump to

FIGURE **8.3** *Filing a bookmark to a folder.*

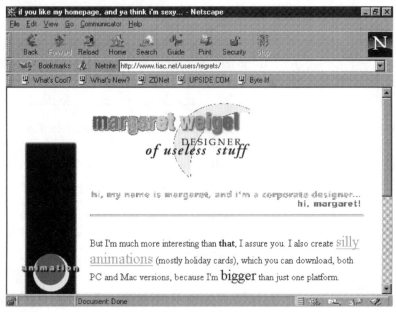

FIGURE **8.4** *Navigator window with bookmarks added to the personal toolbar.*

frequently visited sites more quickly—or reminds you to check certain sites every day, like your company news page.

To add a bookmark to your personal toolbar, do the following:

1. Click the **Bookmarks** icon on the **Location** toolbar.
2. When the **Bookmarks** menu displays, select **File Bookmark**.
3. When the list of folders appears (as shown in Figure 8-3) select **Toolbar Folder**.

When you add bookmarks to the **Toolbar** folder, they appear as icons on the personal toolbar. Personal toolbar icons function as hypertext links.

FROM THE BOOKMARKS WINDOW

If you already know the URL for a particular Web site, you can also enter bookmarks from scratch and add them to your list through the **Bookmarks** window. This can be useful in cases where somebody refers you to a Web site and you don't want to forget the URL.

To add a bookmark from the **Bookmarks** window, do the following:

1. Select **Edit** from the **Bookmarks** menu
2. When the **Bookmarks** window appears, select the item under which you want your new bookmark to appear. If you select a folder, the item appears inside of the folder. If you select a bookmark, the new entry appears below it.
3. Select **New Folder** from the **File** menu.
4. When the **Bookmark Properties** dialog box appears, as shown in Figure 8-5, enter the name of the site, the URL, and a description (the description's optional) in the appropriate text fields.
5. Click **OK** (or click **Cancel** if you change your mind).

The new bookmark will appear on your list.

TIP

You can also add a bookmark to your list by selecting a link from a Web page and dragging it into your Bookmarks window.

Organizing and Editing Bookmarks

Rearranging and organizing bookmarks in the **Bookmarks** window, shown in Figure 8-6, is as easy as clicking and dragging items from one place to another. You can add separators, sort bookmark items in different order, and place them into different folders. Double-click on folders or click on

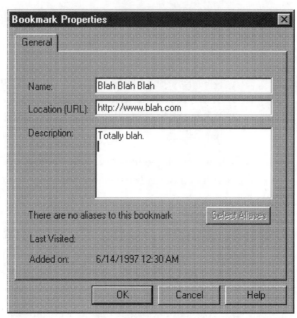

FIGURE *You can add Bookmarks from scratch in the Bookmarks Properties dialog box.*
8.5

FIGURE *Bookmarks window.*
8.6

the + signs to show their contents or click on the – signs to hide folders' contents. You can also create new folders, view bookmark properties, and more.

MOVING BOOKMARKS AROUND

When you add bookmarks to the list or to a folder, the new entry automatically gets added to the bottom of the list. But that doesn't mean it has to stay there. You can go to the Bookmarks window and move your bookmarks around anywhere you want. To move a bookmark to a different folder or a different position on the list, select the bookmark you want to move, drag it to its location, and let go of the mouse.

ADDING SEPARATORS TO THE BOOKMARKS LIST

Separators are horizontal lines that appear in Web pages or on the **Bookmarks** menu. You can add them to group entries by categories or to break down your bookmarks list visually so you can read it more easily.

To add a separator, do the following:

1. **Select the bookmark or folder under which you want the separator to appear.**
2. Select **New Separator** from the **Bookmarks** window's **File** menu.

Although you add separators in the **Bookmarks** window, they only appear in the Bookmarks menu or in the Bookmarks HTML document (I'll explain how Bookmarks work as HTML documents later in this chapter).

SORTING YOUR BOOKMARKS

You can tell the **Bookmarks** window to sort your bookmarks automatically by clicking on one of the four column items. Click once on a column to sort items in descending order, or click twice to sort items in ascending order.

Columns are as follows:

- **Name:** Bookmark or folder title (bookmark titles are usually derived from the Web page title).
- **Location:** The linked bookmark URL.
- **Created On:** The date the bookmark was added to the list.
- **Last Visited:** The last time you visited the page represented by the bookmark.

EDITING YOUR BOOKMARKS LIST

You can also edit your bookmark list from the **Bookmarks** window by selecting folders and bookmarks and choosing options from the **Edit** menu.

The **Edit** menu in the **Bookmarks** window offers the following options:

- **Undo:** Cancels your previous action. You can also use the CTRL+Z (Windows) or CMD+Z (Macintosh) key combination.
- **Redo:** Cancels your undo. You can also use the CTRL+E (Windows) or CMD+E (Macintosh) key combination.
- **Cut:** Deletes selected items and places them on the clipboard so you can paste them in another location if you want. You can also use the CTRL+X (Windows) or CMD+X (Macintosh) key combination.
- **Copy:** Copies selected items onto the clipboard so you can paste them in another location if you want. You can also use the CTRL+C (Windows) or CMD+C (Macintosh) key combination.
- **Paste:** Places items that have been either cut or copied onto the clipboard into the currently selected area. You can also use the CTRL+V (Windows) or CMD+V (Macintosh) key combination.
- **Delete:** Deletes currently selected items without placing them onto the clipboard. You can also use the **Delete** key on your keyboard.
- **Select All:** Selects the entire bookmark list. You can also use the CTRL+A (Windows) or CMD+A (Macintosh) key combination.
- **Find:** Displays the **Find Bookmark** dialog book so you can search for bookmark items by name or location.

WORKING WITH FOLDERS

At some point, you may find that you've added so many bookmarks that your list has become unmanageable. Never fear—let folders come to the rescue. You can break your list down into categories and create folders for them. For example, you can create folders for Web sites and articles with information related to different projects. You can then sort your bookmarks into the folders. When you pull down the **Bookmarks** menu and select a folder, a cascading list appears with the bookmarks that have been added to the folder, as shown in Figure 8-7.

Creating New Folders

You can create and name new folders in the **Bookmarks** window by doing the following:

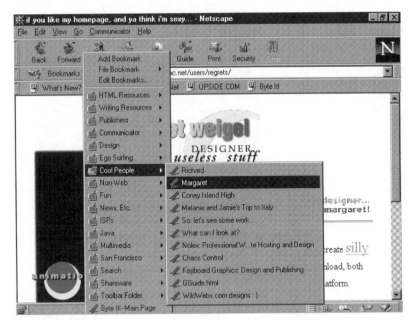

1. Select **Edit** from the **Bookmarks** menu to display the **Bookmarks** window.
2. When the **Bookmarks** window appears, select **New Folder** from the **Bookmarks** menu.
3. When the **Bookmarks Properties** dialog box appears, as shown in Figure 8-8, enter the name of the folder (notice that the URL field is disabled because folders do not function as links) and enter a description or some notes, if you wish, in the appropriate text fields.
4. Click **OK** (or click **Cancel** if you change your mind).

When the new folder appears in the **Bookmarks** window, you can select and drag bookmarks into it from the **Bookmarks** window, or file bookmarks into it from Navigator via the **Bookmarks** menu.

TIP

*Bookmark and folder descriptions do not appear in the **Bookmarks** menu or Bookmarks window. To display descriptions, you have to display the **Properties** window for a selected bookmark or folder by choosing **Bookmarks Properties** from the **Edit** menu. Or you can view your Bookmarks list as a Web page as explained later in this chapter.*

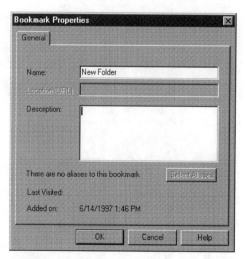

FIGURE *Bookmark properties dialog box.*
8.8

Editing Bookmark and Folder Properties

You can edit bookmark and folder properties—such as titles and descriptions—in the **Bookmark Properties** dialog box any time you want by doing the following:

1. Select a bookmark in the **Bookmarks** window.
2. Select **Bookmark Properties** from the **Edit** menu (Windows users can also use the Alt+Enter key combination).
3. Make your changes and click **OK**.

This can be useful when titles are confusing or when you want to enter some notes to jog your memory about the folder or the bookmarked Web site.

When you add bookmarks to your list from Navigator, the bookmark title is automatically entered based on what the Web designer titled the page. If this title doesn't clearly tell you what topics the site discusses, you can change the title by editing it in the Properties window.

Placing Bookmarks in Multiple Folders

If certain bookmarks fit into multiple categories and you always want to have them at your fingertips, you can make copies of them and paste them into multiple folders.

To copy a bookmark and paste it into a folder, do the following:

1. Select a bookmark from the **Bookmarks** window and choose **Copy** from the **Edit** menu. Or use the CTRL+C (Windows) or CMD+C (Macintosh) key combination.
2. Select a folder from the list by clicking on it.
3. Choose **Paste** from the **Edit** menu. Or use the CTRL+V (Windows) or CMD+V (Macintosh) key combination.

The new bookmark will appear when you open the folder, and the original bookmark will remain in its original place.

Setting a New Default Bookmark Folder

When you add new bookmarks from Navigator, they get added directly to the **Bookmarks** list. However, you can choose a folder for new additions to your **Bookmarks** list so the **Bookmarks** menu doesn't get too cluttered. You can either create a new folder especially for this purpose, or use an existing folder.

To set a new **Default Bookmarks** folder, do the following:

1. Select a folder from the **Bookmarks** window.
2. Select the **Set as New Bookmarks Folder** command from the **View** menu.

When you add new bookmarks by selecting the **Add Bookmark** command from the **Bookmarks** menu while browsing in Navigator, the new bookmark gets added to the new default folder. To reset the default **Bookmarks** folder, return to the **Bookmarks** window, select the top level **Bookmarks for (Your Name)** folder and repeat the steps explained above.

SETTING A NEW DEFAULT BOOKMARKS MENU

When you display the **Bookmarks** menu by clicking the **Location** toolbar's **Bookmarks** icon in Navigator, the menu displays all of the folders and bookmarks on your list. However, you can set any folder you want as the default **Bookmarks** menu.

To set a new default **Bookmarks** menu, do the following:

1. Select a folder from the **Bookmarks** window.
2. Select the **Set as New Bookmarks Menu** command from the **View** menu.

When you return to Navigator and display the **Bookmarks** menu, only the items from the new default **Bookmarks** menu will display. To reset the default **Bookmarks** menu, return to the **Bookmarks** window, select the top level **Bookmarks for (Your Name)** folder and repeat the steps explained above.

SETTING A NEW DEFAULT TOOLBAR FOLDER

As I explained earlier in this chapter, Navigator displays bookmarks in the **Toolbar** folder as icons on the personal toolbar for easy access.

You can choose a new folder as your **Toolbar** folder by doing the following:

1. Select a folder from the Bookmarks window.
2. Select the **Set as New Toolbar Folder** command from the **View** menu.

When you return to Navigator, icons representing the bookmarks inside of the new default **Toolbar** folder will display on the personal toolbar. To reset the default toolbar, return to the **Bookmarks** window, select the **Toolbar** folder, and repeat the steps explained above.

Bookmarks as HTML Documents

You may wonder how Netscape's bookmarks point you automatically to the URLs you select. Surprise! Your bookmarks list is really a hypertext document just like any other Web page. And each bookmark is a link. In fact, you can view your entire bookmark list as a Web page. This works quite well, because knowing that your bookmark list is really just a regular HTML document means that you can easily maintain and use multiple bookmark lists or share your bookmarks with coworkers, friends, and family.

TIP

You can add links from your Bookmarks page—or any HTML document—to email messages and news and discussion groups postings by clicking on the link and dragging it to an open email message window. For more about email and news, see Chapters 10 through 13.

To view your bookmarks as a Web page, do the following:

1. From the **Navigator File** menu, choose the **Open Page** command.
2. When the **Open Page** dialog box appears, as shown in Figure 8-9, make sure the **Open location or file ... in Navigator** radio button is selected and click the **Choose File** button.

3. When the **Open** dialog box appears, browse for your file and click the **Open** button (Figure 8-10).

4. When you return to the **Open Page** dialog box, the directory path to your bookmark file appears (Figure 8-11). Click the **Open** button.

The bookmark list displays in Navigator just like a regular Web page. If you selected the default directories or folders during the Communicator setup routine instead of choosing a different location for Communicator, then users of the Communicator Standard version can find their bookmarks in:

```
C:\Program Files\Netscape\Navigator\Program\
bookmark.htm
```

Communicator Pro users can find their bookmarks in:

```
C:\Program Files\Netscape\Users\your-user-
name\bookmark.htm
```

FIGURE   *Open Page dialog box.*
8.9

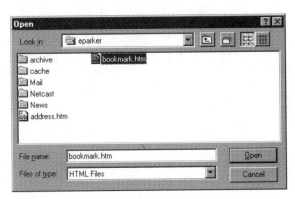

FIGURE   *Open dialog box.*
8.10

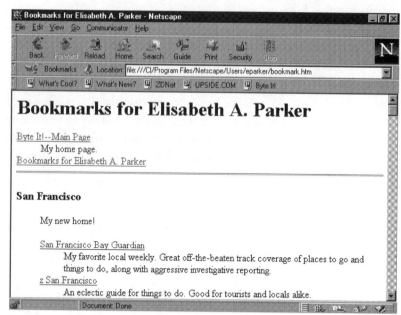

FIGURE *Bookmark list displayed in Navigator as a Web page*
8.11

Bookmarks appear as linked list items. Folders appear as headings. Separators appear as horizontal lines. If you enter a **Description for a bookmark or a folder** in the **Properties** dialog box, the description appears as indented text below the bookmark or folder. You can edit bookmark titles and descriptive text on the **Bookmarks** page either in Composer or by displaying the **Bookmarks** window, selecting individual items and editing their properties in the **Properties** dialog box. When you're finished with your edits, click the **Reload** button in Navigator to display your changes.

You can edit entries on your bookmark list in Composer, but you cannot change the structure or layout of the Bookmarks page or else the Bookmarks menu will no longer work properly.

CAUTION

*Curious about how Web pages and bookmarks work? Take a peek at the source code for the Bookmarks page by selecting Page Source from Navigator's **View** menu. You can also use the CTRL+U (Windows) or CMD+U (Macintosh) key combination.*

TIP

Importing Bookmark Files

You can quickly and easily add other people's bookmark files to your list. Now that you understand that your bookmarks are really an HTML documents with hypertext links, you'll have a better idea of how to work with them. Like text in word processing documents (and HTML files are nothing more than plain text documents), bookmarks and folders can be copied, pasted, imported, exported, and edited.

To import someone else's bookmarks list from your network (with their permission, I hope!) or a bookmark file that someone has given you on disk or sent as an email attachment, into your list do the following:

1. Display the **Bookmarks** window by selecting **Edit** from the **Bookmarks** menu.
2. When the **Bookmarks** window displays, select **Import** from the **File** menu.
3. When the **Import Bookmarks File** dialog box appears, browse for the bookmark list you want to import.
4. Select the **Bookmarks** file and click **Open**.

The new bookmark list appears on your bookmark list as a new folder with the list owner's name ("Bookmarks for Elisabeth A. Parker," for example). To display the new bookmarks list, click the + sign on the left side of the folder.

CAUTION

Importing HTML files that are not *bookmarks files can* really *mess things up!*

Exporting Bookmark Files

"Exporting" sounds like an activity that requires a thorough knowledge of global economics. But never fear. All I'm talking about here is saving a copy of your bookmarks file as an HTML document with a different name. You export your bookmarks as HTML documents so that friends and coworkers can share them. They can then append your list to their own bookmarks files by importing it as described in the previous section, "Importing Bookmarks." You can also maintain multiple bookmark lists by exporting your bookmarks (I'll explain that in the next section).

To export your bookmark list, do the following:

1. Go to the **Bookmarks** window by selecting **Edit** from the **Bookmarks** menu.
2. From the **File** menu, select the **Save As** command.

3. When the **Save Bookmarks File** dialog box appears, enter a name for your bookmark file with the .HTM or .HTML file name extension. You can also choose a different folder for your bookmark file.

4. Click the **Save** button.

You now have an HTML document that you can use as an alternative bookmark list. You can also attach a bookmark file to email messages or save it to a different directory so your coworkers can use it.

Maintaining Multiple Bookmark Lists

You can maintain multiple bookmark lists by exporting and saving bookmarks files under different names as explained in the previous section. When you have multiple bookmark lists, you can choose which list you want to use during a particular session with Navigator. This can be useful in situations where you and your coworkers need to use different bookmark lists for different projects. For example, one project may require you to frequently check up on competitors' Web sites and see what they're doing, while another project may require extensive online research using certain Web sites. Multiple bookmarks lists can also be helpful at home, where Mom, Dad, the two kids, and the dog can all have their own bookmark lists.

To replace your currently active bookmark file with a different one, do the following:

1. Go to the Bookmarks window by selecting **Edit** from the **Bookmarks** menu.

2. When the Bookmarks window displays, select **Open Bookmarks File** from the **File** menu.

3. When the **Open Bookmarks File** dialog box appears, browse for a bookmark file and select it.

4. Click the **Open** button.

The new bookmark list appears in the **Bookmarks** window and on your **Bookmarks** menu.

CHAPTER

9

Finding
Resources

Surfing the Internet can seem overwhelming at times—so much to check out and so little time! You can do research for projects, download software for just about every task, experience cutting-edge multimedia, view a dazzling array of images, play games, subscribe to email newsletters, explore Usenet newsgroups, and even learn how to create your own Web site—without having to leave your computer. Those of you who don't like the idea of never leaving your computer can still use the Internet to plan vacations and business trips, learn how to find out about places to go and things to do across the world or right in your own neighborhood. As you get more familiar with what the Internet has to offer, you can build a bookmark list of your favorite resources.

Now let's get started. This chapter points you towards the following types of resources:

- Search engines
- Shareware
- Usenet newsgroups
- Email subscriptions
- News
- General resources
- Learning HTML
- Fun

Don't worry if your first ventures into cyberspace lead to frequent detours. The Internet has lots of appealing diversions, and getting there is half the fun.

Look for the companies you do business with on the Web—corporate Web sites usually have lots of useful information and resources for their customers. The people who developed your computer's hardware and software, your travel agent, your favorite clothing store, your bank, and others are probably there. For those hectic days at the office, your favorite lunch place may even serve up its daily menu and let you order deliveries by email.

Search Engines

Finding things on the Internet often feels like exploring an exotic city with no road map . . . and possibly no roads. So let's pause here to heave a hearty sigh of gratitude for search engines. Search engines are giant databases that link you to gazillions of Internet sites covering everything under the sun. Whether you're looking for information about buying a car or having one repaired (the Web Garage at `http://www.webgarage.com/`) or a book on a hard-to-find topic (Amazon Books at `http://www.amazon.com/`), search engines can help you find it. If something exists, someone has probably launched a Web site or newsgroup about it. For a long time, search engines mostly existed to help people find Web sites. But now, search engines exist for finding newsgroups and newsgroup archives, businesses and contact information, email addresses, and even information about more specialized topics. In addition, many Web sites with huge amounts of resources—such as the Netscape (`http://home.netscape.com/`) and Microsoft (`http://www.microsoft.com/`)—have their own search engines just for finding material on their sites.

THE NETSCAPE NET SEARCH PAGE

Netscape helps get you started on your Internet travels with a special search page featuring links to many popular search engines, including Excite, Yahoo, Infoseek, and Lycos. You can get to Netscape's **Net Search** page, shown in Figure 9-1, by clicking the **Search** button on your Navigation toolbar. To perform a search, all you have to do is enter key words in the text field and click the **Search** button. If you don't find what you're looking for, click a different tab to use a different search engine.

CAUTION

Netscape's Internet Searches page is a great place to explore search engines. However, searches take longer from here because after you enter your keywords, Netscape's server has to contact the actual search engine's server. For easy access, go directly to the search engine sites and add them to your bookmark list.

The Netscape **Net Search** page displays prominently featured links to four different search engines, and leaves one blank. This is a customizable button that lets you insert a link to any search engine you want, in order to make it conveniently accessible. In addition, you can specify which of the five search engines you wish to display first when you jump to the search page. To customize your page, click the **Customize** link and select your choices from the pop-up JavaScript form window shown in Figure 9-2.

In addition to Netscape's search engine, there are lots of great search engines and directories out there. After experimenting with various search en-

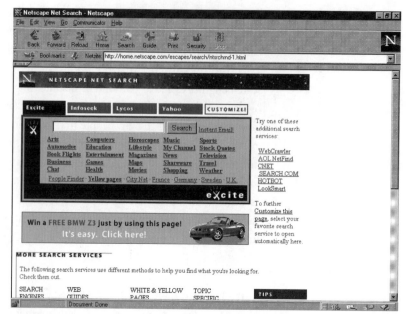

FIGURE *Let Netscape's Search page launch you onto the Web.*
9.1

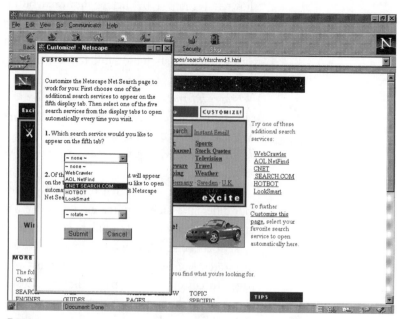

FIGURE *You can customize your Netscape start page.*
9.2

gines, you'll find the ones that work best for you. I describe a few of them for you in the following sections. But keep your eyes open—you can always use another search engine, and new ones keep cropping up all the time.

You can do searches using all of the search engines available on the Web. Resources: Search Engines: All-In-One-Search Page; Go to the All-In-One Search Page at http://www.albany.net/-wcross/all1www.html#WWW.

SOME POPULAR SEARCH ENGINES

Cnet

Cnet (`http://www.cnet.com/`) is the big daddy of Internet resources, and you can find just about anything on its site. Cnet has a search site (`http://www.search.com/`) with categories for everything from finding pages on the Web to finding long-lost pals' email addresses (or maybe that person you have a meeting with next week . . . but you lost her business card), two shareware sites (`http://www.shareware.com/` and `http://www.download.com/`), news, reviews, and more.

Excite

Excite (`http://www.excite.com/`) is one of my favorite search engines. In addition to helping you find Web sites and newsgroups, Excite provides reviews of sites, current events articles, travel information, stock quotes, sports news, horoscopes, and even helps you find Internet channels that you can subscribe to with Netcaster (see Chapter 6).

Web Crawler

The Web Crawler (`http://www.webcrawler.com/`) was developed in 1994 by the University of Washington Computer Science and Engineering Department's Brian Pinkerton. It functions as a program—or Web "spider"—that cruises the Internet in search of information to pull in from Web page text. Web Crawler automatically indexes text entries and feeds them into a database. To use it, enter words related to your topic and click on the **Search** key. You can also choose whether you want your search to turn up a list of 10, 25, or 100 sites from a pulldown menu. The Web Crawler is now owned by America Online and Global Network Navigator.

Lycos

Lycos (short for *Lycosidae*, Latin for "Wolf Spider") was developed at Carnegie Mellon University by Dr. Michael Mauldin. Lycos sends out groups of applications (called "spiders") to look for new Web, Gopher, and FTP sites. The spiders build outlines from the text contained in Web pages and how many times other sites mention the URL, and then add them to the Lycos catalog. To use Lycos, enter your keyword(s) in the text field and click on the **Search** button. Results will appear in order of relevance (how many times your keyword occurs in the text). In addition, it guides you to Web reviews, popular sites, new places to go, and indexes organized by category. Lycos has indexed over 10 million URLs. You can find Lycos at `http://www.lycos.com/`.

Yahoo!

Yahoo! (`http://www.yahoo.com/`) lets you enter searches by keyword or browse through extensive indexes organized by topic. The project began in 1994, when Stanford graduate students Jerry Yang and David Filo realized they were in grave danger of finishing their Ph.D's and entering the real world. Their laborious hours of cruising the Web, cataloging sites, and entering them into a database soon paid off. Yahoo!'s attractive graphics, well-organized index, and collections of links to cutting-edge sites quickly made it one of the Internet's most popular search engines.

Alta Vista

Alta Vista was introduced in late 1995 by computer behemoth Digital Equipment Corporation. Its catalog includes over 9 million Web pages and more than 13,000 newsgroups. Use the pulldown menus to choose whether you wish to search for newsgroups or Web pages and whether to include detailed summaries or brief listings. You can find Alta Vista at `http://altavista.digital.com/`.

Filez

Looking for shareware, a new printer driver, software updates, clip art, new fonts, or technical documentation? You can find all this and more at Filez (`http://www.filez.com/`), as shown in Figure 9-3. What makes Filez unique? Unlike most search engines, it indexes FTP sites rather than Web sites and newsgroups. FTP sites aren't as glamorous as Web sites, but they

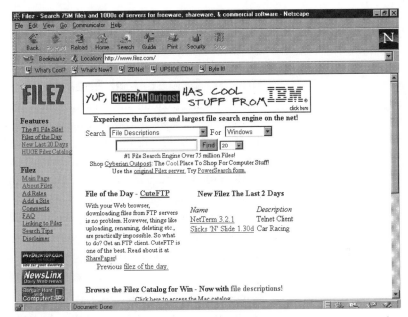

FIGURE
9.3   *Filez at http://www.filez.com/ is a fast search engine that searches FTP sites for lots of shareware and other downloadable goodies.*

serve up lots of goodies. Just about all major universities, software companies, and hardware manufacturers maintain FTP sites that serve up just about everything from software to collections of recipes. Finding things on FTP sites used to be difficult unless you knew the exact URL and file name already (FTP sites don't have text, graphics, and search engines like Web sites do—they only display lists of files). Now, Filez puts FTP offerings at your fingertips. And by the way, Filez performs searches faster than any search engine I've seen yet.

Four11

Looking for a telephone number, business address, or email address? Visit Four11 (http://www.four11.com/). Four11 even has a Net Phone section so you can use it as a Dynamic Lookup Service (DLS) server and use Netscape Conference through them—and see who else is using Netscape Conference (for more on Conference, see Chapters 15 and 16).

You can also look up long-lost friends, old classmates, business contacts, and others at Big Foot (http://www.bigfoot.com/), Who? Where?

(`http://www.whowhere.com/`), or Search.Com's People section (`http://www.search.com/`).

HOW TO USE SEARCH ENGINES

To find the information you're looking for, enter keywords related to your topic in the text fields provided by the search engines. After a few seconds, a list of search results will appear. You can then follow the links. If the links don't point you in the right direction, try searching again with different keywords or use a different search engine. And if you get lost, remember that the main screen's **Back** toolbar button is your friend. While search engines may sound complicated, wait till you try them. Nothing could be easier. Think of it as searching through your local library's card catalog . . . only say goodbye to jotting down those annoying Dewey decimal numbers.

Refining Your Searches

Search engines have an annoying habit of frequently turning up vast quantities of useless and irrelevant information. You can refine your searches by using *Boolean logic*. Named after George Boole, the nineteenth century mathematician who invented mathematical logic, Boolean logic lets you use the operators AND, OR, NOT, and ( ) to narrow down your searches. The word "operators" refers to words that act like commands for refining or expanding your search.

Does this remind you of that pre-algebra class you almost failed back in junior high school (well, OK, maybe you didn't almost fail, but I did)? Fear not—you'll find search engines to be much more useful and fun. Let's say you want to get a job in San Francisco, for example. When I entered San Francisco in the Netscape Net Search query window for the Excite search engine, it turned up 895359 results, as shown in Figure 9-4. Nobody could possibly have time to look at 895359 Web pages.

Excite gave me all of these results because it doesn't know what kind of information I want about San Francisco. Some search engines—like Excite—try to help you narrow down your search. Excite prompts you with additional keywords that you can select by clicking the appropriate checkboxes, and also guides you to some travel resources (since many people look up cities when they want to travel to them). This is very thoughtful of the people at Excite, but they still can't possibly know exactly what you want—which is where Boolean logic comes in.

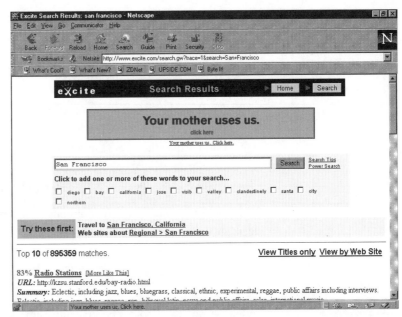

FIGURE *Excite suggests options for refining your search. "Excite, Excite Search, and the*
9.4 *Excite Logo are trademarks of Excite, Inc. and may be registered in various jurisdictions. Excite screen display copyright 1995–1997 Excite, Inc.*

You can narrow down keyword searches with the following Boolean operators:

- **AND:** Using AND narrows down your search. Search results include only documents containing all words combined by the AND operator. By entering San Francisco AND Jobs in the Excite search engine's query window, I narrowed the search down to 3260 results. That's still a lot of sites, but at least most of them are job-related.
- **OR:** Using OR expands your search. Search results include documents containing one or both of the words connected by the OR operator. For example, for information about jobs in general and information about San Francisco, you could enter San Francisco OR Jobs. The OR operator can be helpful when there isn't much information about the topic you're looking for.

Sometimes search engines are unpredictable. When I searched for San Francisco OR Jobs, that should have generated more *results than my search on San Francisco alone. Yet San Francisco alone generated 855359 pages and San Francisco OR Jobs generated 566410 pages.*

NOTE

- **NOT:** Using NOT narrows down your search, but it a different way than by using AND. Search results include only documents that include the first specified word without the second specified word. When I entered San Francisco AND NOT Jobs to find San Francisco information unrelated to jobs, the search turned up 276660 pages.
- **( ):** Parentheses let you group words together to form more complex Boolean queries. For example, many of the search results related to jobs in education. Let's say you want to narrow down job information to noneducational opportunities. Entering (San Francisco AND Jobs) AND NOT Education narrows the search down to 2400 results.

It should be mentioned that although the search engines and Boolean logic are useful, they still don't work perfectly.

Shareware

While writing this book, it became difficult to keep track of all the illustrations. I thought, "Gee, wouldn't it be nice to have an application that displays thumbnails of the images in my folders so I can take a quick peek at them?" I took a quick trip to TUCOWS (`http://www.tucows.com/`) and found, downloaded, and installed Cerious Software, Inc.'s ThumbsPlus for Windows 95 in less than 10 minutes.

If you wish your computer would perform a particular task, chances are that someone out there has created the program you need. The Internet abounds with extensive collections of useful and interesting software for just about any purpose you can think of.

Shareware—which you can download and try before purchasing—usually costs less than $100. In addition, some applications are offered as freeware, which costs nothing at all. Before you turn up your nose and repeat the old adage, "You get what you pay for," remember: Many of today's most popular commercial software packages started off as freeware or shareware. Shareware and freeware are often as useful and well-documented as their commercial software counterparts.

TIP

Even commercial software and hardware providers often serve up free goodies—like printer driver upgrades, utilities, plug-ins, samples, and more—on their Web sites.

When you need shareware, check out the following places:

- **TUCOWS:** This is where I always go to find that perfect utility, HTML editor, and other goodies. Aptly named, "The Ultimate Collection of Winsock Software." TUCOWS has extensive, frequently updated, and well-organized collections of freeware and shareware for Windows users. Unlike other shareware sites, which often only provide a download link, TUCOWS's entries also have links to the software developers' Web sites so you can get more information before downloading. As for Macintosh users, don't let the "Winsock" part of the TUCOWS acronym fool you—there's plenty of software for you too. You can find TUCOWS at `http://www.tucows.com/`.

- **Shareware.Com and Download.Com:** CNET, the lively online computer industry magazine, has a huge collection of links to shareware. You can check out what's new, what's popular, or you can search its database for a specific program. Shareware.Com is located at `http://www.shareware.com/`. It offers a huge database, but not much in terms of description. Download.Com, on the other hand, also offers reviews and information so you can read about the software you're about to download. Download.Com is located at `http://www.download.com/`.

- **ZDNet:** In addition to interesting articles about computers, Ziff Davis' Web site has tons of software, along with editors' picks, files of the day, and exclusives, plus you can either use the index or browse for shareware by topic. To find the latest hot stuff, Windows users can `http://www.hotfiles.com/` and Mac users can go to `http://www5.zdnet.com/mac/download.html`.

- **Jumbo!:** Jumbo boasts a mammoth collection of shareware and freeware for everything from surfing the Internet, helping the kids with homework, managing your finances, doing astrological readings and more. It's friendly, fun, and conveniently organized by software category and operating system. In addition, software listings come with brief descriptions and system requirement information. You can find Jumbo at `http://www.jumbo.com/Home_Page.html`.

TIP

For quick access to your favorite search engines, shareware, multimedia, and other sites, create bookmarks for them. For more on bookmarks, see Chapter 8.

Usenet Newsgroups

Finding newsgroups that suit your interests can seem like looking for a needle in a hay-stack. Fortunately, Usenet's popularity has led to the generation of Web pages devoted exclusively to exploring the wide world of Usenet. Now, you can search for newsgroups by topic, explore their archives, jump to the newsgroup by clicking on hypertext links, or copy the newsgroup's URL onto your clipboard, then search for it in Communicator's Message Center. For more about participating in newsgroups, see Chapters 10 and 12.

The following Usenet resources can help you unravel the anarchic tangle of newsgroups:

- **Zippo's Daily News:** Newcomers to the Internet and Usenet news junkies alike should take a look Zippo's Daily News at: `http://www.zippo.com/`, as shown in Figure 9-5. For those of you who chose not to install a newsreader due to limited system resources, Zippo's DirectRead News feature lets you explore newsgroups and post messages straight from the Web. Zippo can also help you if your ISPs (or network administrators!) don't serve up all the newsgroups you want. Zippo's DirectRead News service is free to the public. To access

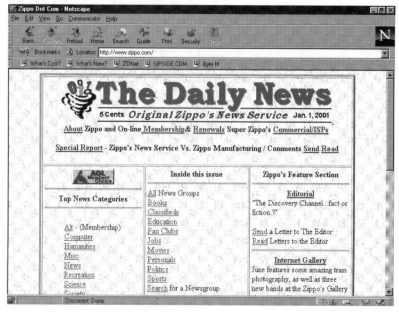

FIGURE *Zippo's Daily News makes participating in newsgroups easy.*
9.5

over 18,000 newsgroups through Zippo's news server, you need to sign up for an account. At the time of this writing, an account costs less than $15 per year.

- **Deja News Research Service:** You can get acquainted with newsgroups by browsing through its archives. With Deja News, you can search for recent Usenet archives by topic, and create a query filter to restrict your search to specific newsgroups, posting dates, or authors. It should be noted here that archive files are documents from libraries of news postings, not the newsgroups themselves. You can find Deja news at `http://www.dejanews.com`.

- `Usenet Info Center Launch Pad`: If you don't feel entirely comfortable with Usenet, stop by Sunsite's Usenet page. Maintained by the University of North Carolina at Chapel Hill and Sun Microsystems, this site hooks you up with helpful information, answers to frequently asked questions (FAQs), a Usenet history, and more. To help you find newsgroups, they have a search engine and links to other resources. You can find the Usenet Info Center Launch Pad at `http://sunsite.unc.edu/usenet-i/`.

Here are some other places to check out.

- **Anchorman:** `http://www.ph.tn.tudelft.nl/People/pierre/anchorman/Amn.html`
- **Where is the Archive for Newsgroup X:** `http://starbase.neosoft.com/~claird/news.lists/newsgroup_archives.html`
- **Usenet News Finder:** `http://www.nova.edu/Inter-Links/`

For more information about participating in newsgroups, see Chapters 10 and 12.

TIP

Remember—the World Wide Web Excite and Alta Vista search engines also help you find Usenet newsgroups.

Email Subscriptions

Want some more email to look forward to? Subscribe to an electronic mailing list. Some lists function as online discussion groups focused on specific topics. Mailing list members exchange questions, answers and information. Discussions are generally moderated by an individual or organization. Other electronic mailing lists operate more like newsletters, with the list's owner sending out periodic updates. Most lists are managed with either ListServ or Majordomo mailing list manager software.

The following resources can help you locate email mailing lists that address topics of interest:

- **Publicly Accessible Mailing Lists (PAML):** This comprehensive source for email subscriptions is one of the most popular on the Internet. Mailing lists are indexed alphabetically by name and by subject, and entries include a brief description and contact information. You can find the PAML site at: `http://www.neosoft.com/internet/paml/`.

- **The List of Lists:** This spiffy mailing list database has been around since the prehistoric Arpanet days and provides you with a search engine and helpful information. Enter your topic of interest. The results include the name of the list and its owner, and a brief description of what the mailing list covers. You can find the List of Lists at `http://catalog.com/vivian/interest-group-search.html`.

- **Tile.Net/ListServ:** You can search through indexes here for email discussion groups by description, name, country, organization, or subject. This site is maintained by the Walter Shelby Group, creators of the Tile Web page authoring program. You can also search for newsgroups and FTP sites from here. You can find Tile.Net/ListServ at `http://tile.net/listserv/`.

You can also try:

- **ListServ Guide for General Users:** `http://www.earn.net/lug/notice.html`
- **Links and Sources for Internet Mailing Lists:** `http://www.cahe.wsu.edu/~pace/lists.htm`
- **Liszt:** `http://www.liszt.com/`.

CAUTION

Subscribing to mailing lists can often result in vast numbers of email messages per week. Before subscribing, make sure you know how to unsubscribe!

Subscribing, unsubscribing, and posting messages to email mailing lists generally requires sending email to the person in charge of the list with specified commands entered in the body of the text. Since procedures vary from list to list, it is important to carefully follow the instructions outlined on the Web site that points you towards your subscription.

News

Thanks to the Web, you can stay up to date on current events all the time—some Web sites update their pages every few hours and sometimes even *more* frequently. Whew! That's a lot to keep up with! If you were *always* 'net surfing for the latest news, you'd never get any work done. However, it's still nice to know these sites are there.

You can stay current on what's happening in the world by visiting the following sites:

- **Touch Today:** Links you to hundreds of online newspapers and magazines, and publishes a daily business paper. `http://www.clickit.com/touch/news/news.htm`.

- **RealPlayer:** Progressive Networks' RealPlayer plug-in lets you play video and audio newscasts. After going to its Web site and downloading the plug-in, you can go back to the site, shown in Figure 9-6, which features links to C-SPAN, ABC News, National Public Radio,

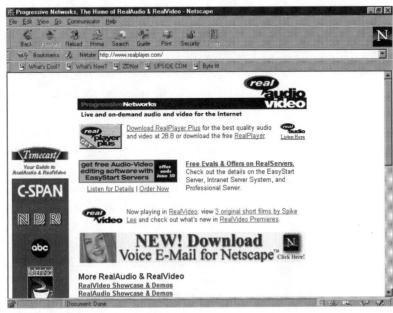

FIGURE *Progressive Networks' RealPlayer site at http://www.realplayer.com/ guides you to*
9.6 *audio and video newscasts that you can play once you have the RealPlayer plug-in.*

and other great news sites that you can download audio and video broadcasts from. `http://www.realplayer.com`.

- **MSNBC:** News junkies can visit MSNBC's Web page to see the results of Microsoft and NBC's partnership. Here, you'll find sections on world, commerce, opinion, science and technology, and more. `http://www.msnbc.com/`.

You can also use search engines to find news that is more specific to your community or your line of work. Many newspapers now publish online as well as in print.

General Resources

The Web abounds with resources for finding interesting places to go, learning more about the Internet and how to use it productively, and designing your own Web site.

Netscape's Product Information page: To get the latest information about Communicator, check the **Frequently Asked Questions** page about things you may be confused about, join Netscape discussion groups, and more, go to Netscape's Product Information page at: `http://home.netscape.com/menu/prodsupp/client/`. You can also find it by selecting **Product Information** and **Support** from the **Help** menu.

- **Indiana University UCS Knowledge Base:** Do you need answers to questions about the Web, Usenet, shareware, FTP, the Internet, or computers in general? You have a good chance of finding detailed information by searching the Indiana University' UCS Support Center Knowledge Base. You won't find souped-up graphics on this no-nonsense site—just straightforward text that tells you what you need to know. You can find the UCS Knowledge Base at `http://sckb.ucssc.indiana.edu/kb/`.
- **NetGuide Magazine:** The online version of NetGuide Magazine keeps you up to date on new developments on the Internet, reviews Web sites and software, and dishes up tips and tricks for using the Internet. You can also search NetGuide's database by keyword for articles on particular topics. You can find NetGuide Magazine at `http://www.netscape.com/`.
- **Safe Kids Online:** Concerned parents and educators can go here for resources on how to guide children as they travel the Internet without taking all the fun out of it. `http://www.safekids.com/`.

- **EFF's (Extended) Guide to the Internet:** The Electronic Frontier Foundation—an Internet activist organization—serves up an extensive guide to just about everything on the Internet. `http://leviathan. tamu.edu:70/0/internet/EFF_Net_Guide/eeg_toc.html`.
- **The Computer Dictionary:** Go here whenever you're stumped by a computer or Internet-related technical term. `http://wombat.doc. ic.ac.uk/foldoc/contents.html`.
- **The Internet Public Library:** They're busily working on posting the text from books and academic text on the Web. `http://ipl.sils. umich.edu/`.
- **Nerd World Media:** Nerd World hosts a large catalog of links to various places to go on the Internet, along with reviews, news articles, and more. `http://www.nerdworld.com/`.

Learning HTML

Has cruising the Web given you a hankering for creating your own Web page? If so, the Web offers a rich array of HTML guides and resources. Whether you're new to the Internet or an experienced Web page author, you can find information geared towards varying levels of technical expertise. The following sites tell you how HTML works, give instructions for adding different features to your page, tell you where to find Web page development tools, and more. Plus we've included an HTML design on the companion CD, the HTML Template MASTER.

You can also learn more about Web pages from the following sites:

- **Netscape Navigator Gold Toolchest:** For help in designing Web pages, along with lots of graphics for backgrounds and buttons, sample pages, design tips, and more, visit `http://home.netscape. com/assist/net_sites/starter/samples/index.html`.
- **Web 66 Cookbook:** Web 66 tells educators everything they need to know for setting up servers and Web sites at their schools—but the rest of us can learn a lot from them too. `http://web66.coled.umn. edu/Cookbook/`
- **The Web Spinners Workshop:** Learn how to do the fun stuff—this site has step-by-step instructions and examples for just about anything you might want to do. `http://dcn.davis.ca.us/~lacarrol/ webspin.html/`
- **A Beginners Guide to HTML:** NCSA, the creators of the first graphical Web browser, help fledgling Web page developers get their

feet wet. `http://www.ncsa.uiuc.edu/demoweb/html~primer.html`

- **Learning Web:** The University of Texas provides its students with easy instructions for creating and posting Web pages. `http://www.utexas.edu/learn/`
- **Writing HTML:** A well-organized beginners' guide for creating Web pages. `http://www.mcli.dist.maricopa.edu/tut/lessons.html`
- **Web Page Design for Designers:** Once you learn how to put pages together, check out this guide to making them look fabulous. `http://ds.dial.pipex.com/pixelp/wpdesign/wpdintro.htm`

While browsing the Web can't substitute for reading an in-depth book or using a training tool like the Template MASTER, HTML-related sites can get you started and keep you updated on the latest developments. For more about creating your own Web pages, see Chapter 17.

Fun

The following sites have no use whatsoever. But their cleverness and originality makes them popular places to visit. Some Web page creators lure visitors with high-tech gimmicks, while others use only text, pictures, and a charmingly skewed world perspective.

Next time you feel a bad mood coming on, lighten up and take a gander at one (or all) of these home pages:

- **The Electronic Postcard Rack:** Choose from a variety of attractive postcards, pick the card you like, write a message, and send it to a friend. After the server notifies your recipient, he or she can go to the pickup window and get the postcard. Yes, it really works. `http://postcards.www.media.mit.edu/postcards/`
- **The Amazing FishCam:** If you've always wanted a fish tank and don't have the money or time, this Web site's the next best thing. `http://www2.netscape.com/fishcam/fishcam.html`
- **Crayon:** Create and post an online newspaper, and see other people's newspapers. `http://sun.bucknell.edu/~boulter/crayon`
- **Tarot:** Feeling uncertain about the future? Go to the Tarot Card site and get a reading. Even if you don't believe in this stuff, the history of Tarot is interesting, and the cards are pretty to look at. `http://www.facade.com/attraction/tarot/`

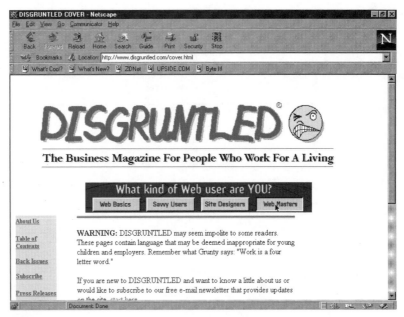

FIGURE *Disgruntled at http://www.disgruntled.com/ says "Work is a four-letter word.*
9.7

- **Center for the Easily Amused:** Tons of useless and fun links to places like "Hillary's Hair," the "Mr. Bad Advice Page," and "My Boss is a #!$#@!." http://www.amused.com/

- **Joe's Apartment:** Visit Joe's apartment, see the cockroaches scurry around, tour the contents of Joe's refrigerator, see a QuickTime movie of Joe's unfortunate date, and more. http://www.joesapt.com/

- **Disgruntled:** Those who hate their jobs should go here. Disgruntled's motto says "Work is a four-letter word." At Disgruntled (shown in Figure 9-7), you'll find real-life work stories, workplace-related news, resources, career tips, humor, and more. Those of you who worry about getting caught cruising the Web can even click on the **Boss** icon to display an innocuous-looking spreadsheet if your supervisor walks by. Or you can subscribe via email. http://www.disgruntled. com/.

Now that you've had a little fun, let's get back to work!

10

Managing Communications with the Message Center

Message Center;Communicator's Message Center provides you with a handy way to manage your email and discussion group messages. Here, you can download messages, access and subscribe to news and discussion groups, organize your email messages into folders, and more. As you'll see in Chapters 11 and 12, you can download, read, compose, and send messages via email or post messages to newsgroups via Netscape Messenger. However, the Message Center is a useful tool for people who exchange lots of email and news/discussion group messages and need to keep track of it all.

This chapter covers the following:

- Viewing the Message Center
- Downloading email, newsgroup, and discussion group messages
- Managing news and discussion groups

This chapter tells you how you can use the Message Center to keep track of your email, newsgroup, and discussion group messages. If you don't have much experience with email and newsgroups, you may want to read Chapters 11 and 12 first.

Viewing the Message Center

The **Message Center** displays a list of all of your email message folders and discussion and newsgroups servers. To view the **Message Center**, as shown in Figure 10-1, click the **Message Center** icon on the Communicator component bar, or select **Collabra Discussion Groups** from the **Communicator** menu in Navigator. By the way, if you already participate in newsgroups, you might wonder what I mean when I talk about "discussion groups." Don't worry—newsgroups and discussion groups are basically the same thing, but the people at Netscape have decided to call Intranet "newsgroups" that are managed with Netscape's Collabra news server "discussion groups" instead.

The Message Center consists of the following elements:

- **Title bar:** Indicates that you're in the message center or displays the title of the currently open message folder, discussion or newsgroup, or message.
- **Menu bar:** Displays menu items from which you can select options.
- **Navigation toolbar:** Displays icons for selecting common tasks to perform in the Message Center.

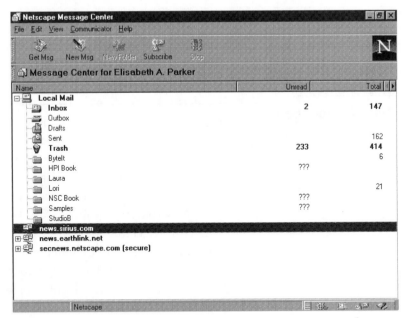

FIGURE *Netscape Message Center.*
10.1

- **Location toolbar:** Displays the name of the current user's Message Center.
- **Columns:** Categories by which information about folders and messages is organized.
- **Display pane:** Displays a list of message folders and discussion and new group servers and other information.
- **Email message folders:** Displays a list of folders that you can sort email messages into.
- **Group servers:** Displays a list of news and discussion group servers.
- **Status bar:** Tells you the status of messages that you're downloading or sending.
- **Components bar:** Displays icons for launching other Communicator components.

The following sections discuss some of these elements in greater detail.

Downloading Email, Newsgroup, and Discussion Group Messages

NAVIGATION TOOLBAR

The Navigation toolbar helps you do the things you'll need to do most frequently from within the Netscape **Message Center**. The Navigation toolbar gives you the following options:

- **Get Messages:** Checks your server for new email and news/discussion group messages, and downloads them. You can also get your email messages from within Messenger, but here you can kill two birds with one stone.
- **New Message:** Displays a new message composition window so you can compose and send messages to individuals or news/discussion groups.
- **Create New Folder:** Displays the **New Folder** dialog box so you can create a new folder for sorting email into.
- **Subscribe:** Displays the **Communicator: Subscribe to Discussion Groups** dialog box so you can search for newsgroups and discussion groups on your server and subscribe to groups that you want to participate in.

In order to participate in news and discussion groups, you must subscribe to them. But never fear—it's easy to subscribe, and with the occasional exception, it's free too.

- **Stop:** Cancels the current download.

MESSAGE FOLDERS

Folders help you keep track of your email. You can create new folders and sort email into the folders manually (as explained in Chapter 11) or create automatic mail filters (as explained later in this chapter). To display the messages in a folder, double-click on a folder icon on the **Message Center** list in the display pane. When the Messenger window for the currently selected folder appears, like the one shown in Figure 10-2, you can view, compose, and reply to email messages (for more about email, see Chapters 10 and 11).

The **Message Center** also comes with the following folders set up for you.

- **Inbox:** The default folder for all incoming email messages. To display new messages after you've downloaded your messages, double-click the **Inbox**.
- **Outbox:** Outgoing messages that haven't been sent yet are stored here. To display outgoing messages, double-click the **Outbox**.

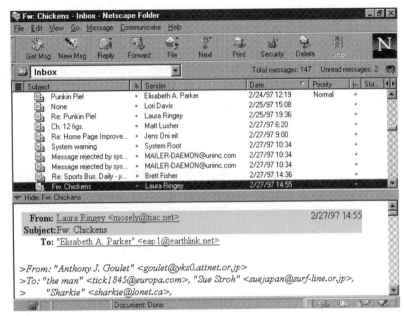

FIGURE *Netscape Inbox Folder contents displayed.*
10.2

- **Drafts:** You can store email messages that you've begun composing but you want to edit later before sending in this folder. To display a list of your unfinished and unsent email messages, double-click the **Drafts** folder.
- **Sent:** When you send messages, Communicator saves a copy in the **Sent** folder (make sure you delete files frequently from the **Sent** folder so it doesn't take up too much space).
- **Samples:** Contains samples of email messages with rich content. The people at Netscape included these samples so you can get an idea of the neat stuff you can do with Communicator.
- **Trash:** Contains deleted emails. To empty your trash, select **Empty Trash Folder** from the **File** menu.

GROUP SERVERS

The **Message Center** also displays the news and discussion group servers currently available to you. News and discussion group servers store and maintain newsgroups so you can subscribe to them. Netscape makes a special server application called Collabra, which is especially designed to work with Communicator via an organizational Intranet. When newsgroups are created and managed with a Collabra server on an Intranet, the people at Netscape call them Collabra discussion groups. However, Communicator can handle any kind of news or discussion group.

This list can consist of:

- **Your primary group server:** At least one list item with an icon representing a news server should appear in the **Message Center** display pane. This is the default news server specified in your Preferences (for more about Preferences, see Chapter 5). This could be an in-house discussion groups server available through your company or your Internet Service provider's news server.

- **Discussion group servers associated with your organization:** The network administrator at your company or organization may have designated one or more news and discussion group servers that you can access.

- **Other news servers:** You can also access newsgroups that are not offered through your ISP or organization's server. For example, Netscape maintains its own news server with newsgroups that address all sorts of topics related to Netscape products. When you click on a newsgroup link, the Collabra news reader component launches and displays the newsgroup postings. The new server is automatically added to the **Message Center** display pane's list of servers.

You can find Netscape user groups (NUGgies) at Netscape's NUGgies page at `http://help.netscape.com/nuggies/server.html`.

VIEWING COLUMN INFORMATION

The **Message Center** columns gives you information about your folders so you can keep track of your messages, and whether you've been keeping up with your email:

- **Name:** Lists folder and discussion/newsgroup names.
- **Unread:** Displays the number of unread messages within email message folders and news/discussion groups.
- **Total:** Displays the total number of messages within email message folders and news/discussion groups

To view information about individual news or discussion groups that you subscribe to (I'll explain how to subscribe to news and discussion groups later in this chapter), you can display the groups by clicking the + sign next to the news server icon.

MANAGING EMAIL MESSAGES

The **Message Center** also makes it easy for you to keep track of your email messages. You can create, rename, move, and delete folders for keeping messages organized; compress folders to save some disk space without having to delete messages; search for messages and email addresses, and more.

Creating, Renaming, Moving, and Deleting Folders

Sometimes you need to add or rename folders, while other folders become obsolete when an event or project is completed. Fortunately, you can work with folders in the **Message Center** the same way as you would use folders and directories on your computer.

To create a new folder, do the following:

1. Click the **New Folder** button.
2. When the **New Folder** dialog box appears, enter the name of the new folder in the **Name:** text field.
3. Select a location for the folder by selecting the name of a folder from the **Create as a sub folder of:** pulldown list (the new folder is created inside of the selected folder—to add the folder to the main list, select the default **Local Mail** option).
4. Click **OK.**

To rename a folder, do the following:

1. Select a folder.
2. Choose **Folder Properties** from the **Edit** menu, or use the ALT+Enter key combination.
3. When the **Folder Properties** dialog box appears, enter a new name in the **Name:** text field.
4. Click **OK.**

*You can also compress the messages in the folder by clicking the **Clean Up Wasted Space** button.*

TIP

To move a folder, do the following:

1. Select a folder.
2. Select **Move Folder** from the **View** menu.
3. When the pulldown list appears, select the folder you want to move the current folder to.

You can also select a folder icon and drag it into another folder icon. When you move a folder into an existing folder, a + sign appears next to the higher-level folder. To expand the list of folders to display sub folders, click the + sign. To collapse the list, click the – sign that appears at the top of the expanded list.

To delete a folder, do the following:

1. Select a folder.
2. Choose **Delete Discussion Group** from the **Edit** menu (this command also deletes folders).
3. When the **Change rule to reflect new folder location?** dialog box appears, click **OK** (the new folder location is the **Trash**).

You can also simply select the folder and press the **Delete** key.

Compressing Folders

Email messages are usually tiny, but they can add up quickly! Fortunately, you can save yourself some disk space without having to delete your folders by compressing them.

To compress an individual folder, do the following:

1. Select a folder.
2. Choose **Folder Properties** from the **Edit** menu, or use the ALT+Enter key combination.
3. When the **Folder Properties** dialog box appears, click the **Clean up wasted disk space** button.
4. Click **OK**.

To compress all of your folders, choose **Compress Folders** from the **File** menu.

Search Messages

Oh no! You have a meeting to go to but you can't remember exactly where the meeting is. Fortunately, you still have that email message or groups posting with the meeting announcement *somewhere*. Now, if only you could find that email . . . Let the **Message Center**'s search function come to the rescue!

To search for an email message, do the following:

1. Select **Search Messages** from the **Edit** menu.
2. When the **Search Messages** dialog box appears, as shown in Figure 10-3, select a folder or group to search from the **Search for items in:** pulldown list (leave the default **Local Mail** selected to search all of your folders and groups)
3. Select a message element (sender or subject) from the **where the** pulldown list. This determines what part of email messages are searched.
4. Select an option from the second **where the:** pulldown list (contains, is, begins with, ends with).
5. Enter the name or keyword you want to search for in the text field.
6. Click the **Search** button.

By selecting elements, you create a phrase that tells the search application what to look for. For example, the search criterion shown in figure 10-3 says:

```
Search for items in Local Mail where the sender
contains "Lori."
```

In other words, I'm looking for all email on my local mail directory that was sent to me by someone who has "Lori" as part of her first or last name.

Search results are generated in a text window that appears within an expanded **Search Messages** dialog box. For additional search options, you can click the **More** button. To clear the current search criteria and start over, click the **Clear Search** button. For helpful hints, click the **Help** button.

FIGURE *Search Messages dialog box.*
10.3

Searching for Email Addresses

Email addresses can be hard to find and keep track of. Fortunately, the **Message Center**'s search capabilities makes finding people's email addresses easy. You can search a Lightweight Directory Access Protocol (LDAP) directory on your network or a public LDAP directory. The LDAP directory on your network at work lets you look up email addresses for coworkers and other people whom your company works with. Public LDAP directories on the Internet let you search for other individuals. Anyone can help others find them by visiting public Internet directories' Web sites and registering their information.

To search for an email address, do the following:

1. Select **Search** directory from the **Edit** menu.
2. When the **Search** dialog box appears, as shown in Figure 10-4, select an LDAP directory from the pulldown list. The pull-down list includes popular publicly accessible directories like Four11 and InfoSpace. In addition, if your organization provides an LDAP directory on its server, that directory also appears on the list.
3. Select a search criterion from the **where the:** pulldown list—such as a name, organization, or email address.
4. Select a second search criterion from the second pulldown list, such as contains, doesn't contain, or begins with.
5. Enter a name or keyword in the text field.
6. Click the **Search** button.

By selecting elements, you create a phrase that tells the search application what to look for. For example, the search criterion shown in Figure 10-4 would say, "Search for items in the Four11 Directory where the name contains Lori" In other words, I'm searching for an email address for someone who has "Lori" as part of her first or last name. Search results are generated in a text window that appears within an expanded **Search Messages** dialog

FIGURE   *Search dialog box.*
10.4

box (however, this may turn up people named "Lori," but also people named "Lorianne" or "Lorinda"). For additional search options, you can click the **More** button. To clear the current search criteria and start over, click the **Clear Search** button. For helpful hints, click the **Help** button.

CREATING MAIL FILTERS

If you receive a lot of emails from a particular person or with a consistent subject line that refers to a particular project, you can tell the **Message Center** to automatically sort these incoming messages into a designated folder so you don't have to move the messages manually (Chapter 11 tells you more about sending and receiving email and moving mail to different folders).

To create a mail filter, select **Mail Filters** from the **Edit** menu. When the **Mail Filters** dialog box appears, click the **New** button.

When the **Filter Rules** dialog box appears, as shown in Figure 10-5, enter the following information:

1. Enter the name of your filter in the **Filter name:** text field.
2. Choose one of the following options from the **If the** pulldown list:
   - **Sender:** If you frequently receive email from the same person, try filtering mail by sender.
   - **Subject:** If you frequently send and receive email with the same heading in the subject line (for example, "The Huge Conference" or "Weekly Meeting"), try filtering mail by subject line.

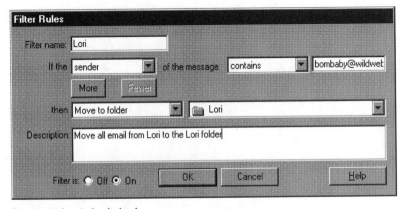

FIGURE   *Filter Rules dialog box.*
10.5

- **Body:** You can also sort mail by keywords that appear in the body of messages.
- **Date:** Filters email by date received.
- **Priority:** You can also sort email by levels of priority, so you don't skip over those urgent messages by mistake (Chapter 11 talks more about assigning priority levels to outgoing messages).
- **To:** Of course, all your email comes addressed to *you*. So at first glance, this option doesn't make sense. But if you subscribe to electronic mailing lists that send messages to people as a group (such as list@blahblah.com), this option can help you keep messages from your electronic mailing list separate from the rest of your mail.
- **CC:** You can also filter incoming mail by who the message is cc'd (carbon copied) to.

3. Choose an option for the **of the message:** pulldown list. In most cases, you would choose the **contains** option.

4. Enter an email address, name, filter, subject line, phrase, or keyword in the text field.

5. Select an action from the **then** pulldown list, then select an option from the adjacent pulldown list. In most cases, you would choose the **Move to folder** option, and would then select a folder from the pulldown list.

6. Enter a description of the mail filter in the **Description** text area (this is optional) and click the **Filter is: On** radio button to activate the filter.

Click **OK** to keep your filter, or click **Cancel** to cancel the filter. If you get stuck, just click the **Help** button. As when searching for an email address or an email message (as explained earlier in this chapter) when you specify filter rules, you basically create a sentence that tells the mail filter what to do. In the example shown in Figure 10-5, I applied the following filter rules:

```
If the sender field of the message contains the
words "bombaby@wildwebs.com", then move the
message to the Lori folder.
```

When you return to the **Mail Filters** dialog box, as shown in Figure 10-6, you can create more filters, edit the currently selected filter, or delete the currently selected filter. You can also set priority levels for which filters should be applied if email messages conform to more than one filter criterion.

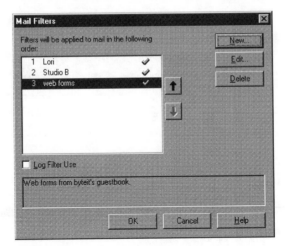

FIGURE *Mail filters dialog box.*
10.6

You can do the following from within the **Mail Filters** dialog box:

- **Rearrange filter priorities:** You can move filters up or down on the **Filters will be applied to mail in the following order list** by selecting a filter name and clicking the up or down arrow buttons.
- **Create additional mail filters:** To specify more mail filters, click the New button and follow the procedure outlined previously.
- **Edit filters:** To change mail filter criteria, select a filter from the list and click the **Edit** button to display the **Filter Rules** dialog box.
- **Delete filters:** To delete a mail filter, select a filter from the list and click the **Delete** button.

The **Mail Filters** dialog box also displays a filter description for the selected filter (if you provided a description for the filter in the **Filter Rules** dialog box) and enables you to create an automatically generated document that keeps track of how often you use your filters by clicking the **Log Filter Use** checkbox. When you're finished making changes, click **OK**.

Managing News and Discussion Groups

In addition to folders for email messages, the **Message Center** also displays news and discussion group servers and subscribed news and discussion groups, as shown in Figure 10-7. When you click on the + sign next to the discussion or newsgroup server items, the subscribed newsgroups available

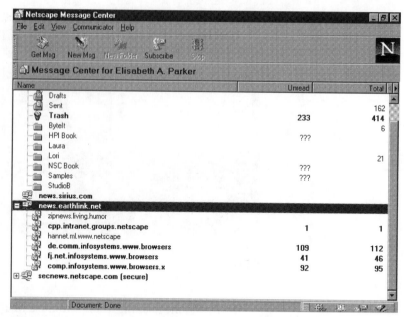

FIGURE *Message Center with news server selected and subscribed groups displayed.*

10.7

on that server display. From the **Message Center**, you can download new messages, search for and subscribe to new newsgroups, display news/discussion group postings in the **Messenger** window, and more.

GETTING NEWS/DISCUSSION GROUP MESSAGES

To download messages from all of the news/discussion groups and from the email server, click the **Get Messages** toolbar button. To download new messages from a particular news or discussion group server, double-click on the server item in the display pane.

SUBSCRIBING TO GROUPS

If you like a particular news or discussion group and plan on participating in it frequently, then you can subscribe to it. When you subscribe to a news or discussion group, it appears as an item on your list of newsgroups (which you can display by clicking the + sign next to the appropriate server list item—if you haven't subscribed to any newsgroups from a particular server yet, the + sign does not appear).

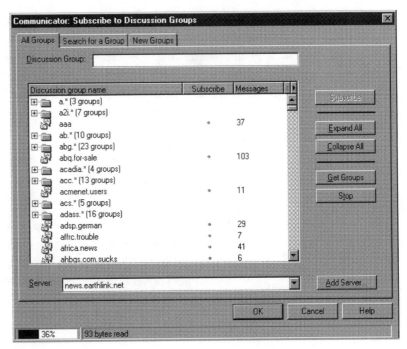

FIGURE   *Communicator: Subscribe to Discussion Groups window.*
10.8

To subscribe to a news or discussion group, do the following:

1. Select **Subscribe to Discussion Groups** from the **File** menu.
2. When the **Communicator: Subscribe to Discussion Groups** window appears (with the **All Groups** tab selected), as shown in Figure 10-8, select a server from the pulldown **Server: list** (you may only have one news server to choose from).
3. Enter the name of the news or discussion group you want to subscribe to in the **Discussion Group** text field.
4. If the group is available on the selected server, you'll jump straight the group on the **Discussion group** scrolling list, where it appears as a selected item. To subscribe to it, click the **Subscribe** button. A check mark appears next to the subscribed newsgroup in the **Subscribe** column.
5. When you're finished subscribing to newsgroups, click **OK** to return to the **Message Center**.

The newly subscribed news or discussion group appears as an item beneath the selected news or discussion group server. You can also subscribe to newsgroups straight from the Web. When you click on a link to a newsgroup, Messenger launches and downloads messages. The new group and the group's server appear as items on the **Message Center** list in the display pane.

Getting Groups

If this is the first time you've accessed your news server, you need to download a list of newsgroups available on your server before you can subscribe to anything. To download the list of newsgroups, do the following:

1. Select **Subscribe to Discussion Groups** from the **File** menu.
2. When the **Communicator: Subscribe to Discussion Groups** window appears (with the **All Groups** tab selected), as shown in Figure 10-8, select a news server from the **Server:** pulldown list.
3. Click the **Get Groups** button.

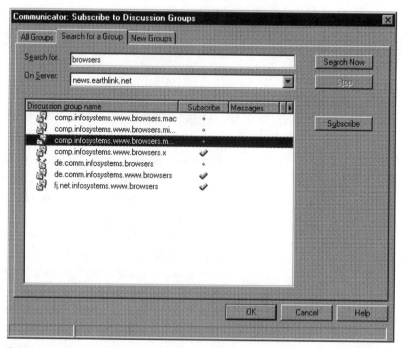

FIGURE
10.9
Communicator: Subscribe to Discussion Groups window with the Search for a Group tab selected.

4. When the list of available groups finishes downloading, you can sub-scribe to some of them, or click **OK** to return to the **Message Center**.

It may take a few minutes to download all of the groups.

Some servers have thousands of newsgroups to choose from! Fortunately, when you get groups so you can view the list, Communicator doesn't actually download messages from all the newsgroups! It only downloads the list, along with messages from the groups you've subscribed to.

Finding Groups

Sure, subscribing to groups sounds easy. But how do you find any groups to subscribe to? If you're lucky, you know the name of the group *and* the group happens to be available on the server. But most of the time, we aren't so sure of what we're looking for.

There are three ways to find newsgroups:

- **Search for them on the Web:** The popular Excite (`http://www.ex-cite.com/`) and Alta Vista (`http://www.altavista.digital.com/`) search engines both provide options for searching for news-groups. Once you find a link to a group that interests you, you can subscribe by simply clicking on the link. This downloads postings and launches Netscape Messenger.
- **Scrolling through discussion groups list:** When viewing the Com-municator: Subscribe to Discussion Groups window with the **All Groups** tab selected, a list of groups available on the selected server dis-plays. You can locate groups by scrolling down the list until you find a group with a name that sounds relevant to the topic you want to find a group for. The only problem is that most servers host hundreds and thousands of groups. Scrolling could get awfully tiresome.
- **Use the Subscribe to Discussion Groups search feature:** You can also search for discussion groups by launching the Communicator: Sub-scribe to Discussion Groups window and clicking the Search for a Group tab, as shown in Figure 10-9.

To search for discussion groups from the **Communicator: Subscribe to Discussion Groups** window, do the following:

1. Select **Subscribe to Discussion Groups** from the **File** menu.

2. When the **Communicator: Subscribe to Discussion Groups** window appears, click the **Search for a Group** tab.

3. When the **Search for a Group** window appears, as shown in Figure 10-9, enter a word that describes the topic you're interested in (for example, if you want to find a group that discusses Web browsers, enter the word "browsers" or "browser") in the **Search for:** text field.

4. Select a server from the **On Server:** pulldown list.

5. Click the **Search Now** button.

If your keyword appears in any group titles, the groups appear as list items. To subscribe to groups on the list so you can download messages and see what the groups are like, select a group, and click the **Subscribe** button. Subscribed groups appear with a checkmark next to them. When you're finished searching and subscribing, click the **OK** button.

Downloading New Groups

People are always launching new discussion and newsgroups. But how do you find out about them? Wouldn't that be like looking for a needle in a haystack? Nope. Finding groups that have recently been added to your server is as easy as displaying the **Communicator: Subscribe to Discussion Groups** window and clicking the **New Groups** tab, as shown in Figure 10-10.

To display a list of new groups that have been added to the server since the last time you checked, select a server from the pulldown **Server:** list and click the **Get New** button. To subscribe to a group so that you can download and view messages, select a group from the list and click the **Subscribe** button.

Unsubscribing from Groups

If you decide a group isn't something you wish to participate in, you can unsubscribe from it. Simply select it from the list of items in the **Message Center** display pane and press the **Delete** key. When the dialog box appears to confirm that you want to unsubscribe to the group, click **OK.**

ADDING A SERVER

Servers can only carry so many groups. Your server may not offer all of the groups you want. That's OK, because you can access groups from different servers. All you have to do is add a new server to your list. As long as the

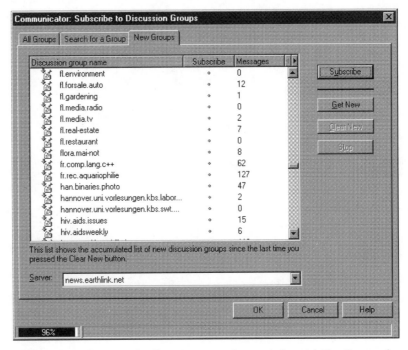

FIGURE *Communicator: Subscribe to Discussion Groups window with New Groups tab*
10.10 *selected.*

newsgroup you wish to subscribe to is freely accessible, this is no problem
(some servers charge you a monthly fee for membership and you can only access their newsgroups if you're a member). When you subscribe to a newsgroup from a different server by clicking on a link from a Web page, the new
server appears on the **Message Center** list automatically.

If you need to access a specific news or discussion group server, you can
also add the server manually by doing the following:

1. Select **Subscribe to Discussion Groups** from the **File** menu.
2. When the **Communicator: Subscribe to Discussion Groups** window
   appears with the **All Groups** tab selected, click the **Add a Server** button.
3. When the **New Discussion Groups Server** dialog box appears, as
   shown in Figure 10-11, enter the name of the server in the **Server:** text
   field.
4. Enter the port number in the **Port:** text field. With most news and discussion group servers, the port number is 119. If it's a secure server, the
   number is generally 563.

FIGURE **10.11** *New Discussion Groups server dialog box.*

5. Click the **Secure** checkbox if you're adding a secure server (a server that uses security protocols), and click the **Always use name and password** if the server requires a name and password.

Click the **OK** button when you're finished entering information to return to the **Communicator: Subscribe to Discussion Groups** window.

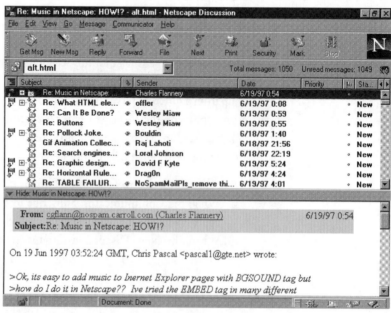

FIGURE **10.12** *Netscape Messenger window displayed with messages from the alt.html newsgroup—an excellent place to get help if you're thinking of designing Web*

DISPLAYING NEWS/DISCUSSION GROUP MESSAGES

In order to participate in news and discussion groups, you need to launch the Netscape Messenger window so you can view, reply to, compose, and send messages. You can do this the same way you displayed the contents of your email message folders earlier in this chapter—double-click on a group listed in the **Message Center** pane to open the Messenger window, as shown in Figure 10-12. The list of messages appears, with the message text displayed for the selected message list item. There is also a toolbar so you can easily read and post messages. And fortunately for us, Messenger handles both newsgroups and email so we don't have to learn two different applications. We'll talk about participating in newsgroups in greater detail in Chapter 12.

11 Emailing with Messenger

Even people who don't like computers much and rarely explore the Web or participate in news and discussion groups *love* email. With Communicator's Messenger component, you can compose, send, and receive email; keep messages organized; and easily access email addresses through the address book and Intranet or Internet directory services. It has a simple, intuitive interface that's easy for novices to master, while experienced users will find all of the features they like about other email programs they've used. You can even send and receive attached documents, live active content files, images, and URLs with working hypertext links.

This chapter covers the following:

- Viewing the Messenger window
- Getting messages
- Composing messages
- Sending email
- Replying to and forwarding messages
- Organizing your messages
- Sorting messages
- Marking messages
- Creating new folders
- Moving, copying, and deleting messages

And best of all, Communicator serves all of your Internet needs in one integrated package. And as you'll see in Chapter 12, you can also use Messenger to participate in news and discussion groups.

Email and news/discussion groups work very similarly, only groups store messages on the server instead of sending them to everyone individually so people can view them all. Once you know how to send, receive, and compose email, participating in groups will come easily to you.

Viewing the Messenger Window

Let's take a look at the Netscape Messenger window, as shown in Figure 11-1. Opening it is easy—just click the **Mailbox** icon on the Communicator component bar. You can also open the Messenger window for a particular email message folder by double-clicking on a folder in the Message Center, as explained in the last chapter.

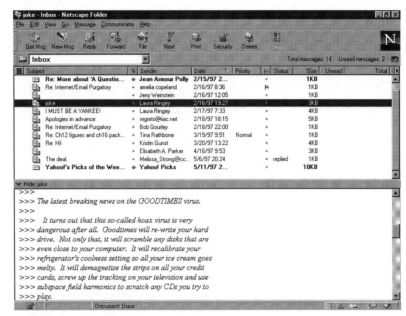

FIGURE *Netscape Messenger window.*
11.1

The Messenger window consists of the following components:

- **Title bar:** Displays the subject line and folder or group name for the currently selected message.
- **Menu bar:** Displays menu items.
- **Navigation toolbar:** Provides clickable icons for common tasks, including:
  - **Get Msg:** Downloads messages from server.
  - **New Msg:** Displays **Message Composition** window so you can compose a new message.
  - **Reply:** Displays a pulldown list with options for replying to messages.
  - **Forward:** Displays a **Message Composition** window with the message text included so you can forward messages.
  - **File:** Displays a list of folders so you can pick one to file the currently selected message into.
  - **Next:** Selects the next message on the list and displays it in the message display pane.

- **Print:** Prints the current message.
- **Security:** Displays security information for the current message (for more about security, see Chapter 18).
- **Delete:** Deletes the currently selected message.
- **Stop:** Cancels the current download.
- **Location toolbar:** Displays options for moving to different message folders and discussion groups, including:
  - **Folders and groups window:** Click the little arrow next to the folders and groups window to display a list of other email message folders, and news and discussion groups so you can select and view them in the Messenger window (for more about folders, see Chapter 10).
  - **Folder/group statistics:** Displays the total number of messages and the total of unread messages for the current folder.
  - **View Message Center:** Click to display the **Message Center** (for more about the **Message Center**, see Chapter 10).
- **Columns:** Display a list of categories by which message information is organized, including the email subject, sender, and date. I'll explain columns in greater detail later in this chapter.
  - **Show/hide columns:** Click the right and left arrows to show or hide columns.
- **Message list:** Displays a list of messages along with information about each message. To view a message in the message display pane, select an item from the list by clicking on it. To view the message in a separate window, double-click the list item.
- **Show/hide message:** You can hide the currently displayed message in the message display pane by clicking the **show/hide message** icon. To display the message again, click the icon again.
- **Message display pane:** Displays the currently selected message on the message list.
- **Status bar:** Provides information about the current download or the currently selected message, such as whether messages are downloading or not.
- **Component bar:** You can access other Communicator components by clicking on the component bar icons.
- **Scroll bars:** When your message list or the currently selected message is longer than what displays in the message list and message display panes, scroll bars appear.
- **Close box:** Click to exit the Messenger window.

The Messenger window makes it easy for you to receive, view, compose, and send messages from your email correspondents and from news and discussion groups.

You can keep track of people you frequently exchange messages with by entering their email address and other information in your Address Book. For more about using the Address Book, see Chapter 14.

TIP

Getting Messages

Unless you've specified otherwise in your Email and News Preferences (as explained in Chapter 5), Communicator automatically downloads your email and news/discussion group messages when you launch Messenger. You can also get messages any time you want by clicking the **Get Messages** button. The first time you download messages, a dialog box may appear and request your password.

When Communicator downloads messages, the **Getting New Messages** dialog box appears, as shown in Figure 11-2. The status bar also displays a message to inform you that messages are downloading. If, for some reason, you decide not to download your messages, you can click the **Cancel** button.

VIEWING INCOMING MESSAGES

Incoming email messages usually download to your **Inbox** folder (except for ones that meet criteria that you set when creating mail filters, as explained in Chapter 10) and appear on the message list. New incoming messages that you haven't read yet are indicated by bold text, a neon green diamond icon, and a closed envelope icon. Messages that you have read appear with normal, unbolded text, a grey diamond icon, and an icon that looks like an open envelope with a letter. To read a message, you can select it from the message list and read it in the message display pane, or you can view the message in a separate window by double-clicking on the message list.

VIEWING MESSAGES IN OTHER FOLDERS AND GROUPS

To view a message in another folder or group, click the arrow next to the folders and groups window on the **Location** toolbar, and select an item from the list when it displays.

OPENING ATTACHED FILES

One of the great things about email is the ability to send attached files, such as images and word processing documents. Attached files appear as links in the body of the message. If someone sends you a message with an attached file, don't panic.

To open an attached file, do the following:

1. Open the message in a separate window by double-clicking on it.
2. When the message appears in a separate window, as shown in Figure 11-3, an attached file icon appears, along with a link and information about the attached file, including the application that created it.
3. Double-click on the link to the attached file.
4. When Navigator launches and the **Warning: There is a Potential Security Hazard Here** dialog box appears, you can choose to open the file right now by selecting the **Open the File** radio button, or you can choose to save it to a folder on your computer so you can find it later by clicking the **Save it to Disk** radio button.

*Don't worry about this dialog box. Communicator's just trying to protect you. If you're worried about your computer's security, then don't open attached files from strangers. If you find this dialog box annoying, deselect the **Always ask** before downloading file checkbox.*

5. If you choose the **Save it to Disk** option, a **Save** dialog box appears so you can save the file and open it later.
6. If you choose the **Open the File** radio button, Navigator either launches the file (if it knows how to handle that particular type of file),

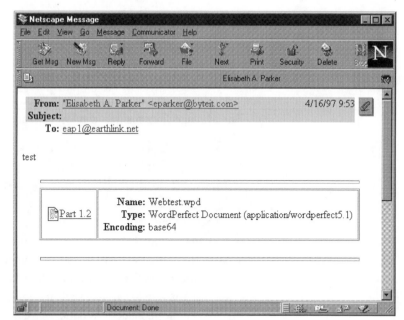

FIGURE *Message with attached file opened in a separate window.*
11.3

or it displays a dialog box so you can browse for an application that can open the file, then launches the file. For more about Navigator and file types, see Chapters 5 and 7.

If you'd prefer to simply save the file and open it later without opening Navigator first, do the following:

1. Click the attached file link with your right mouse button (Windows) or click the link and hold the mouse key down (Macintosh) until the pop-up menu appears.
2. Choose the **Save Link As...** option from the list.
3. When the **Save As...** dialog box appears, browse for a folder to save the file into.

If you receive attached files frequently, you may want to create a folder especially for them.

Composing Messages

To compose a new email message, click the **New Message** icon on the Navigator toolbar or use the CTRL+M (Windows) or CMD+M (Macintosh) key combination to display the **Message Composition** window, as shown in Figure 11-4. The **Message Composition** window provides options for sending and addressing messages, formatting text, adding objects, and attaching files.

The **Message Composition** window contains the following elements:

- **Title bar:** Displays the subject line of the current message.
- **Menu bar:** Displays menu items.
- **Message toolbar:** Displays options for sending, composing, and editing messages.
  - **Send:** Sends current message.
  - **Quote:** Quotes text from the previously read message and places it in the current message so you can respond to it.
  - **Address:** Displays the Address Book so you can select addresses that you've entered, or search for addresses on a directory service (for more about address books, see Chapter 14).

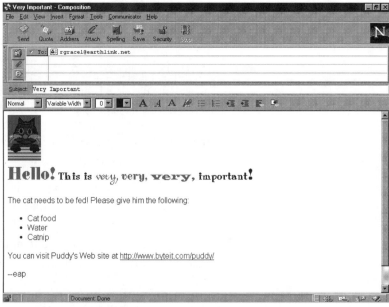

FIGURE *Message Composition window.*
11.4

- **Attach:** Displays a list of options for attaching files (I'll tell you more about attaching files later in this chapter).
- **Spelling:** Checks the spelling in your message.
- **Save:** Saves the current message to your **Drafts** folder instead of sending it, so you can work on it later.
- **Security:** Displays security options (for more about security, see Chapter 18).
- **Stop:** Cancels the sending of a message (if you click it fast enough!).
- **Address messages tab:** Displays lines for entering email addresses of the individuals or groups you wish to send the message to.
- **Attached files tab:** Displays information about any files that you've attached.
- **Message sending options Tab:** Provides additional options for sending messages.
- **Subject:** Enter a subject line here—this should be a two- or three-word description of what the message is about.
- **Formatting toolbar:** Provides options for adding styles and other formatting attributes to text, and inserting objects directly into the message (as opposed to attaching them), including the following:
  - **Paragraph Style:** Displays a pulldown list from which you can apply headings, body text, and other paragraph formatting attributes to selected text.
  - **Font:** Displays a pulldown list from which you can apply a font to selected text. Be careful when choosing fonts. Some Web browsers can't display fonts. Nor can people view your fancy fonts unless they have the same font installed on their systems.
  - **Font size:** Displays a pulldown list from which you can apply font sizes to the selected text to make it larger or smaller.
  - **Font color:** Displays a dialog box with a color palette so you can apply colors to the selected text.
  - **Bold:** Bolds the selected text.
  - **Italics:** Italicizes the selected text.
  - **Underline:** Underlines the selected text.
  - **Remove all styles:** Removes all formatting and style attributes from the current document.
  - **Bullet list:** Formats selected text as a bulleted (unordered) list.
  - **Numbered list:** Formats selected text as a numbered (ordered) list.

- **Decrease indent:** Moves the indentation for the selected list closer to the left side of the page.
- **Increase indent:** Moves the indentation for the selected list further from the left side of the page.
- **Alignment:** Displays a pulldown list of alignment options so you can align the selected text left, right, or center.
- **Insert object:** Displays a list of objects that you can insert, such as links and images.
- **Page display:** Displays the current Web page.
- **Status bar:** Displays a description of toolbar icon functions when you pass your mouse over toolbar icons.
- **Close button:** Closes the Composer window for the current document.
- **Composition pane:** Displays the message you are currently working on.

Composing Messages

To compose and send a basic message with no fancy stuff—just text—do the following:

1. Make sure the **Address Messages** tab is selected (it displays by default)
2. Enter the recipient's email address or a news or discussion group address in the **Address Messages** tab **To:** text field, or click the **Address** icon to display the Address Book window and search for an address (for more about the Address Book, see Chapter 14).
3. Jot down a brief description of your message topic in the **Subject** text field.
4. Type your message in the message body window.
5. Click the **Send** button.

Well, that wasn't too difficult, was it?

*If you're offline, you can choose to send your message to your **Outbox** folder instead of logging on to your server and sending it right away. To send your message later, select **Send Later** from the **File** menu. The next time you go online and download messages, Messenger sends messages waiting in the **Outbox**. This is called deferred delivery. For more about working with email and news messages offline, see Chapter 13.*

COMPOSING MESSAGES FOR MULTIPLE RECIPIENTS

Sometimes you'll need to send the same message to more than one person. For example, if you're planning a meeting you wouldn't want to write separate messages to everyone.

To send messages to multiple recipients, do the following:

1. Enter a recipient in the **To:** field as you would with a basic message, then press the **Enter** key.
2. When the **additional To:** button appears below the first one, click it with your mouse key and hold it down to display a pop-up list with the following options:
   - **To:** Addresses message to the primary recipient of the message.
   - **Cc:** Sends "carbon copies" to additional recipients (the term is a holdover from less technically inclined times when people made carbon copies of correspondence for additional recipients).
   - **Bcc:** Sends "blind carbon copies" to additional recipients whose addresses cannot be seen by the other recipients.
   - **Group:** For sending messages to a news or discussion group.
3. When you select an option from the pulldown list, the button name changes and you can enter the additional recipient's email address in the text field.
4. Follow the previous steps to add more names or discussion groups.

With carbon copy (Cc) and blind carbon copy (Bcc) recipients, you don't need to create a new text field for each of them. You can enter the email addresses and separate them with commas.

ATTACHING FILES

You can attach files to email messages, including word processing and HTML documents, images, URLs, multimedia files, and more. Unlike other email programs, Messenger handles file attachments as linked objects in the body of the message so your recipient can find and open them more easily (if they have an email program that can also handle attachments this way).

To attach a file, do the following:

1. Click the **Attach** icon on the **Message** toolbar.
2. When the pull-down menu appears, choose one of the following options:

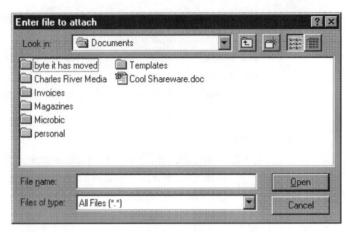

FIGURE *Enter file to attach dialog box.*
11.5

- **File:** Displays the **Enter File to Attach** dialog box shown in Figure 11-5 so you can browse for the file you want to attach. When you find the file you want, select it, click the **Open** button, then click **OK**.
- **Web page:** Displays the **Specify a Location to Attach** dialog box so you can enter a URL or local HTML file. When you finish entering the location, click **OK**.
- **Address Book card:** Attaches your address book card (for more about address book cards and how to create them, see Chapter 5).

To view information about files that you've attached to the current message, click the attached files tab.

Don't attach files unless you're absolutely *positive that your recipient has the application needed to open it. Attachments can also take forever to download for people with slow Internet connections.*

CAUTION

SELECTING MESSAGE SENDING OPTIONS

You can display additional options that you can select before sending your messages by clicking the **Message Sending Options** tab, as shown in Figure 11-6. These options enable you to encrypt and digitally sign messages, choose the HTML or plain text format, set priorities for messages, and more.

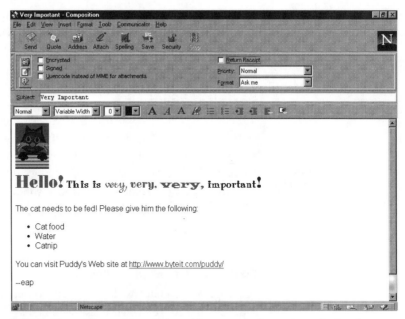

FIGURE *Message Composition window with message sending options tab selected.*

11.6

Message sending options are as follows:

- **Encrypted:** Click to encrypt your message (your recipient must have access to your public key—for more on security and encryption, see Chapter 18).

- **Signed:** Click to digitally sign your message with a certificate (for more on security, see Chapter 18).

- **Uuencode instead of mime for attachments:** When you're sending email to someone who prefers Uuencoded messages, select this check-box to Uuencode your message and any attachments. Messenger defaults to Multipurpose Internet Mail Extensions (MIME) format, which makes it possible to open files in Navigator or Messenger, and to send email messages back and forth. Uuencode is an older system for exchanging email and attached files.

- **Return Receipt:** Requests a return receipt to prove that the message was sent and received when you click the **Return receipt** checkbox.

- **Priority:** You can select a level of priority (from highest to lowest) from the pulldown list. Priority levels display beneath the **Priority** column in the Messenger window's Message list.

- **Format:** You can choose plain text (recommended when sending messages people who don't use Communicator) or HTML from the pull-down list.

SAVING MESSAGES

If you get interrupted while typing a message, you don't have to send it right away. You can save the message and work on it later. To save a message that you're composing, click the **Save** button. This places your message in the **Drafts** folder. You can return to your message by selecting the **Drafts** folder from the Messenger **Folders and Groups** window on the **Location** toolbar. When the **Drafts** folder Message list appears, you can open your message in the composition window by double-clicking on it.

FORMATTING MESSAGES

Messenger is integrated with Composer, so not only can you send, receive, and reply to messages, you can also send messages that look just about as attractive as Web pages—like the message we looked at earlier in this chapter in Figure 11-4. How does this work? Communicator lets you format email messages as HTML documents. This may seem like a lot of fluff, but if you exchange dozens of messages every day, a little formatting can make them easier to read.

Don't send HTML-formatted email messages to people unless you're sure they can receive HTML-formatted messages.

CAUTION

You can indicate whether contacts listed in your Address Book prefer to receive HTML-formatted messages. For more about the Address Book, see Chapter 14.

TIP

    I won't go into a lot of detail in this section because all of the **Message Composition** window's tools are also available in Composer, which is discussed in Chapter 17. However, this section can give you a quick introduction.

    You can select the **Message Composition** window's HTML options from the **Formatting** toolbar and perform the following types of tasks.

- **Format text:** All of the items on **Formatting** toolbar except for the last one are for making text look nicer. You can choose HTML tag styles, fonts, font sizes, colors, text styles, and more. To apply formatting to text, select the text you want to format, then select an option from the **Formatting** toolbar.

- **Embed objects and make links:** You can also make links, create targets (so you can make links to areas within your email message), insert images, add horizontal rules, and design tables. Select the area where you wish to create the link or place the object, click the **Insert Object** icon on the **Formatting** toolbar, and select an option from the pulldown list to display the appropriate dialog box.

For more about working with text, links and objects, see Chapter 17.

Replying to and Forwarding Messages

When you receive messages, you can respond by composing a message from scratch, typing all the text, and entering the person's email address, or you can do things the easy way. With Messenger, you can reply to messages and incorporate quoted text, or you can forward messages to share information with friends, family, and colleagues (this comes in especially handy when someone sends you a good joke). You can respond to messages straight from the Messenger window by selecting the message from the message list and clicking the **Reply** or **Forward** button on the Navigation toolbar, or you can open the message in a separate window by double clicking on it, as shown in Figure 11-7, and choose an option from there.

To reply to a message, do the following:

1. Select a message and click the **Reply** button on the **Navigation** toolbar.
2. When the menu appears, choose **Reply to Sender** (sends the reply to the author only) or **Reply to Sender and All Recipients** (sends the reply to the author and anyone else the author sent the original message to).
3. When the Composition window appears, as shown in Figure 11-8, voila! Everything is set up for you. The author's email address appears in the **To:** text field, the author's subject line is entered (preceded with RE: for "reply"), and other recipients' (if you chose **Reply to Sender and All Recipients**) names should appear in the **Cc:** text field. Quoted text from the message also appears in the **Message Composition** pane unless you chose not to automatically quote text in your Message Preferences (for more on preferences, see Chapter 5).
4. If the quoted message from the sender does not appear, click the **Quote** toolbar icon. Quoting text places text from the previously read message in your message. To make it easier for you to distinguish

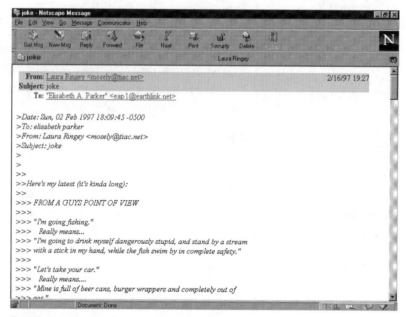

FIGURE *Message opened in a separate window.*
11.7

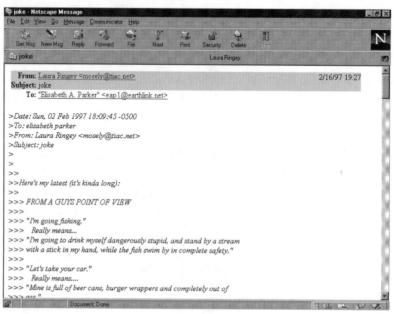

FIGURE *Message reply set up in the Composition window.*
11.8

quoted text from new text, the quoted text appears with > signs at the beginning of each line.

5. Type a reply. With quoted text, you can reply to messages line by line, so the author remembers what you are referring to.

6. When you're finished typing your message, click the **Send** button.

TIP

Sometimes you don't need to quote entire paragraphs to jog someone's memory. After all, long email messages take longer to download and upload, plus they take up disk space. To make messages easier to read, you can delete parts of the quoted text. Long-time emailers and newsgroupies indicate deletions by replacing text that they've cut out with: <SNIP!>

To forward a message, do the following:

1. Select a message from the Messenger window's message list.
2. Click the **Forward** toolbar icon.
3. When the **Message Composition** window appears, the subject line is entered (preceded with a FW: for "Forward") but the **Message Composition** pane is blank. Address the message in the **To:** text field and click the **Quote** icon to place the quoted text in your **Message Composition** pane.
4. When the quoted text appears, you can also type a little note preceding it to explain why the recipient may appreciate the message.

Click the **Send** button to send the message.

Organizing Your Messages

The last chapter on the **Message Center** talked about organizing your messages, but you can also do these things straight from Messenger, and more. You can red flag messages to remind yourself that they contain important information, mark a message as unread if you've just skimmed over it, create folders and move messages into them, and sort mail by various categories.

Sorting Messages

If you look closely at your Inbox, you may notice there's a lot more to the message list, as shown in Figure 11-9, than a mere list of messages. By looking at the message list, you can tell which messages you haven't read yet, which messages are urgent, which messages you've replied to, and more.

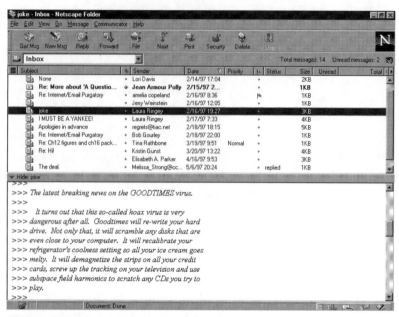

FIGURE   *The Messenger window's Message list organizes message information into*
11.9   *columns.*

Message information is displayed in the following columns:

- **Subject:** Displays the message's subject line.
- **Green diamond icon:** Indicates whether you have read a message or not. Green diamonds appear next to unread messages and gray diamonds appear next to messages that you've already read. Unread messages also appear in bold text.
- **Sender:** Displays the sender's name and email address.
- **Date:** Displays the date the message was sent.
- **Priority:** If the sender has indicated a priority level for the message (on a scale of Lowest to Highest), it is indicated here.
- **Red flag icon:** You can mark messages with a red flag to indicate them as extra-important to you.
- **Status:** Indicates whether you have replied to the messages.
- **Size:** Displays the size of the email message as measured in Kilobytes (KB).

You can adjust the size of columns by selecting a column divider and dragging your mouse to the left or the right.

TIP

Messenger defaults to displaying messages on the list in order of date, but you can sort messages by any of these categories by clicking on a column. Sometimes being able to display messages by sender, subject, or priority level can come in handy.

Marking Messages

Think of marking messages as the modern-day equivalent of tying a string around your finger to remind you of something.

To mark a message with a little red flag, do the following:

1. Select a message from the message list.
2. Select **Flag** from the **Message** menu.

You can also mark messages as unread by doing the following:

1. Select a message from the message list.
2. Select **Mark** from the **Message** menu.
3. When the menu displays, select the **Mark as Unread** option.

This often comes in handy because after you leave a message on the message list selected for a few seconds, Messenger marks it as read—whether you've read it or not!

Creating New Folders

What happens when your **Inbox** folder starts getting full but you don't want to delete many messages? Or when you want to save a newsgroup message for future reference? Add a new folder and put your messages in it. You can create new folders, name them, and move messages into them to manage your correspondence better. For example, you might want to keep emails with agendas for the weekly department meeting in one folder.

To create a new folder from the Messenger window, do the following.

1. Select **New Folder** from the **File** menu.
2. When the **New Folder** dialog box appears, enter the name of the folder in the **Name:** text field.
3. If you want to place the new folder within an existing folder, select a folder from the **Create as subfolder:** pulldown list.
4. Click **OK**.

When you return to Messenger and click the **Folder and Groups** window arrow to display your list of folder and groups, the new folder appears on the list. To delete a folder, select it and press the **Delete** key.

Moving, Copying, and Deleting Messages

Email and group messages can get out of hand pretty quickly, especially if you're an electronic pack rat like me and feel like every single message contains vital information or brilliant examples of correspondence that should be saved for posterity. Messenger provides you with a variety of ways to handle and organize your correspondence. You can delete messages, move messages, or copy them to folders.

To move a message to a different folder, do the following:

1. Select a message from the message list.
2. Select **File Message** from the **Message** menu.
3. When the list of folders appears, select a folder.

To copy a message to a different folder so the message still exists in the current folder, do the following:

1. Select a message from the message list.
2. Select **Copy Message** from the **Message** menu.
3. When the list of folders appears, select a folder.

To delete email messages, do the following:

1. Select an email message.
2. Press the **Delete** key.

CHAPTER

12

Participating in News and Discussion Groups

If you haven't had a chance to participate in news and discussion groups, you should try it. Think of them as dynamic online gathering places where people get together and talk about everything from aliens to Zen. Some newsgroups are served up on the Internet and allow anyone to read and post messages, while other news servers require paid membership for access to more specialized topics and quality control. In addition, many organizations—including schools, nonprofits, and businesses—run internal newsgroups on their Intranets to enable people who hardly ever (or never) get to see each other communicate. The people at Netscape call these discussion groups. Organizations can also purchase and install Netscape's Collabra server, which provides enhanced features for managing discussion groups.

This chapter covers the following:

- What are news and discussion groups?
- Newsgroup categories
- Displaying group messages
- Downloading and reading messages
- Posting messages
- News and discussion group etiquette
- Acronyms and Emoticons

If you already participate in news and discussion groups, rest assured that Communicator offers all of the features you like about other news reader applications. If you've upgraded from Netscape Navigator, you will also find that Communicator has made lots of improvements. And if you've never participated in a news or discussion group in your life, dive in—the water's just fine! Thanks to Messenger, which handles email and group messages similarly, participating in groups is as easy as sending and receiving email. In fact, group discussions and email work very similarly. Only with news and discussion groups, all messages get sent to the server, rather than to an individual. When you download groups, all messages display in Messenger so everyone can follow the discussion.

If you haven't read Chapter 11, "Emailing with Messenger" yet, go back and take a look at it. Chapter 11 takes you through the basics of downloading, composing, replying to, forwarding, and sending messages. You also need to know these things in order to participate in groups.

What Are News and Discussion Groups?

When compared with the World Wide Web's flash and dazzle, news and discussion groups look like that computer nerd from tenth grade who seemed weird—and who now probably makes a lot more money than either of us. Sure, the Web gets all the press and has all the bells and whistles, but there's more to news and discussion groups than meets the eye. They're anything and everything. You can find groups that ask and answer questions about the software you just bought, groups that exchange information and tips about your profession, and groups that talk about business, politics, hobbies, music, television shows, and more.

A BRIEF HISTORY

News and discussion groups go a long way back. Before Intranets gathered steam, most newsgroups were publicly accessible and available via the Internet (and thousands, maybe millions, still are). People called this global network of newsgroups "Usenet." Usenet started out back in 1979 when two graduate students—Tom Truscott of Duke University and Jim Ellis of the University of North Carolina (UNC)—wanted to distribute and exchange information among members of the UNIX development community. UNIX is the powerful, but not very user-friendly, operating system used to run servers and handle large amounts of data.

Truscott and Ellis teamed up with Steve Bellouin and Steve Daniel and created a protocol called UNIX-to-UNIX CoPy (UUCP), along with conferencing software to link users at Duke and UNC so they could talk. This first newsgroup could only handle a few postings per day, but the idea slowly caught on. In 1981, Berkeley College graduate student Mark Horton and a friend, Matt Glickman, wrote a new version of the software to handle large volumes of messages. Since then, Usenet has exploded into thousands of newsgroups. Most servers now use the newer Network News Transfer Protocol (NNTP) but UUCP is still in use today.

HOW NEWS AND DISCUSSION GROUPS WORK

Newsgroup messages are stored on a server and made available to subscribers to the group (to learn how to subscribe to groups, see Chapter 10). News and discussion group participants can download and read postings and respond to them by sending their own messages, which in turn get posted to the server.

Although the Web looks fancier, groups offer an excellent medium for participating in discussions and asking and answering questions in real time. The difference between moderated and unmoderated groups should also be noted here. Some groups—particularly those dealing with sensitive topics—have moderators. Moderators read all of the messages before making them available on the server. With unmoderated groups, your messages appear on the server almost immediately after you send them (though you need to download messages again in order to read new postings).

TIP

Read the FAQs, Jack! "FAQ" stands for "frequently asked question." Most news and discussion groups (and many other Internet resources) make FAQs available to users. FAQs provide answers to commonly asked questions and basic information about the resource itself. Read the FAQ before asking these types of questions so other users don't get annoyed with you.

Newsgroup Categories

BASIC CATEGORIES

Usenet newsgroups are divided into basic hierarchies (categories) that give you an idea of the types of topics discussed. Newsgroup URLs include the newsgroup name and hierarchy, so you can get a basic idea of what topics the group discusses. For example, the name `comp.home.misc` indicates that this newsgroup discusses miscellaneous home computer topics.

TIP

News and discussion group names are the same as their URLs. That makes things easier, doesn't it?

Listed below are the major newsgroup hierarchies:

- **Misc:** A variety of topics that don't quite fit in with the other categories.
- **Rec:** Recreation-related topics including travel, sports, and hobbies.
- **Soc:** Discusses sociology issues and has an academic bent.
- **Talk:** Eclectic, chatty discussions on a variety of topics.
- **Comp:** Discussions, questions, and answers for computer-related topics.
- **Sci:** Innovations, research, and issues in the scientific community.
- **Alt:** Newsgroup topics that don't fit in with the more established communities described above.

Starting a Misc, Rec, Soc, Talk, Comp, or Sci newsgroup requires a vote of approval from members of other newsgroups. But anyone can launch an

Alt newsgroup. And many people do. Maybe this explains titles like `alt.coffee`, `alt.cyberpunk`, and `alt.books.beatgeneration`. Some of the people running newsgroups wind up in the Alt hierarchy because they can't get approval from the other groups, while others don't even bother applying.

OTHER TYPES OF NEWSGROUPS

In addition, a host of other networks, company, and local newsgroups exist. These groups are hosted on servers owned by independent organizations. In many cases, you can access these groups from the host's Web page. Some groups charge for access, but many don't. Here are a few places worth checking out:

- **Netscape User Groups (Netscape NUGgies):** Whether you're a newbie (a newcomer to the Internet), a network administrator, or a programmer, you can participate in lively discussions and get help on just about any topic related to Netscape products. For more information and links to the newsgroups, visit `http://help.netscape.com/nuggies/` (these newsgroups are very popular, so the first download takes a while).
- **Clari.Net:** Although Clari.Net charges a low fee for access, it carries many specialized topics and daily updates from periodicals around the world. For more information, visit Clari.Net Corporation's Web site at `http://www.clari.net/`.
- **Zippo's Daily News:** Visit its Web site `http://www.zippo.com/` and get your feet wet in the world of newsgroups. You can access some groups for free—and for a low yearly fee, Zippo's Daily News gives you access to tens of thousands of newsgroups. In addition, it features a special protocol that lets you read news and post messages straight from the Web.

Finally, many organizations host their own groups, which you can jump to via their Web pages (if the groups are publicly accessible).

FINDING PUBLIC NEWSGROUPS

If a newsgroup that you want to participate in isn't available from your server, or you can't find a group that discusses a topic you're interested in, don't give up hope. You can search for publicly available groups on the Web and access them by clicking on links. Both Excite (`http://www.excite.com/`) and Alta Vista (`http://www.altavista.com/`) provide options for you to search for newsgroups.

Displaying Group Messages

You can display the news and discussion groups available on your server, search for groups, and subscribe to them through the **Message Center**, as explained in Chapter 10. Once you subscribe to some groups, you can access them through the **Message Center** (as discussed in Chapter 10) or through the Messenger window (as discussed in Chapter 11).

To access a news or discussion group from the **Message Center**, as shown in Figure 12-1, do the following:

1. Click the **Discussion Groups** icon on the component bar, select **Message Center** from the **Communicator** menu, or use the CTRL+Shift+1 (Windows) or CMD+Shift+1 (Macintosh) key combination.

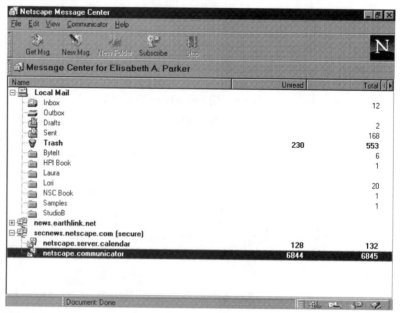

FIGURE *Message Center with group selected.*
12.1

2. When the **Message Center** window appears with the server list at the bottom, click the + sign next to a server to display your subscribed groups.

3. Double-click a group name to open the group in the Messenger window.

To open a group straight from the Messenger window, do the following:

1. Click the **Mailbox** icon to display the Messenger window, select **Messenger Mailbox** from the Communicator menu, or use the CTRL+2 (Windows) or CMD+2 (Macintosh) key combination.

2. When the Messenger window appears, click the **Folders and Groups** window's arrow button to display a list of folders and groups, as shown in Figure 12-2.

3. Select a group from the list.

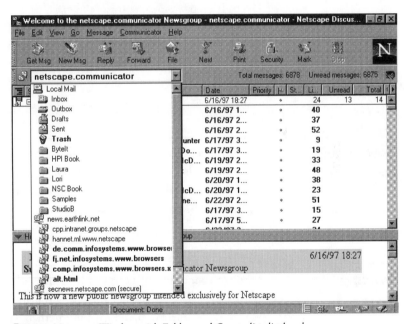

FIGURE *Messenger Window with Folders and Groups list displayed.*
12.2

When messages from the selected group appear in the Messenger window, as shown in Figure 12-3, you can begin reading, composing, and responding to messages.

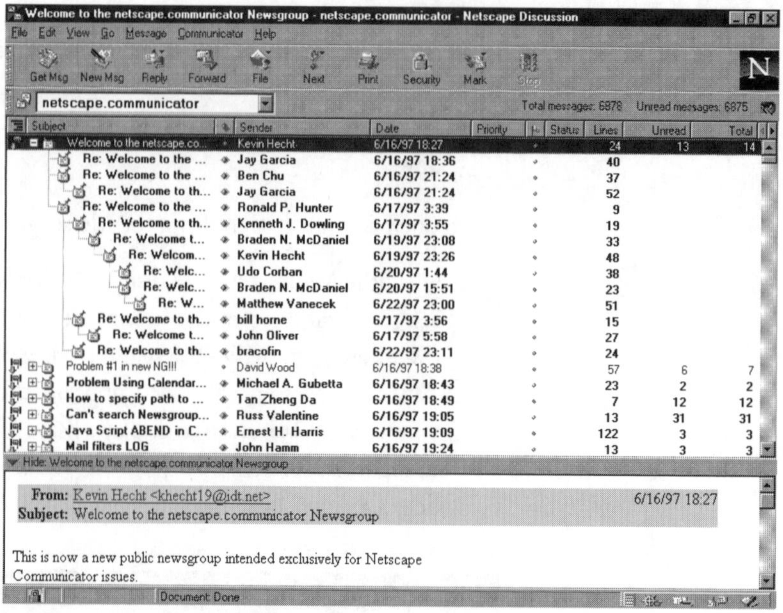

FIGURE **12.3**   *Netscape's netscape.communicator newsgroup displayed in Messenger window.*

Downloading Messages

To download new messages from all your group servers (and your news server too), click the **Get Messages** toolbar icon, select **Get Messages** from the **File** menu and choose the **New** option, or use the CTRL+T (Windows) or CMD+T (Macintosh) key combination.

Reading Messages

If you're connected to the Internet, then you can access all public newsgroups as well as any discussion groups available on your organization's Intranet . . . in theory. Because your Internet service provider or network administrator has to download all of the messages from groups to its server every day, and because there may be concerns about content, you may have to access a group from a different server via the Web, or request that your ISP or network administrator carry the group.

When you open a group in Messenger, as shown in Figure 12-3, it looks similar to what appears when you display the contents of an email message folder, with a few differences. The toolbar and columns offer a couple of additional options, and messages are often organized into threads (which I'll explain shortly). Threaded messages are organized as indented lists below the original message item.

To read messages, select a message from the message list to display it in the message display pane. You can also double-click the message to display it in a separate window. For details on toolbar options, see Chapter 11.

UNDERSTANDING MESSAGE INFORMATION

When you view messages in the **Message** window, messages display in the message list. As with email messages, information about each message is organized into columns. You can view more columns by clicking the left arrow button at the far right of the columns bar or view fewer columns by clicking the right arrow button at the far right of the columns bar.

Message information is displayed in the following columns:

- **Subject:** Displays the message's subject line. Messages followed by threads appear with a + sign next to them. Unread messages are accompanied by an icon that looks like a comic balloon with a thumbtack. Read messages appear with a plain comic balloon.
- **Green diamond icon:** Indicates whether you have read a message. Green diamonds appear next to unread messages and gray diamonds appear next to messages that you've already read. Unread messages also appear in bold text.
- **Sender:** Displays the sender's name and email address.
- **Date:** Displays the date the message was sent.
- **Priority:** If the sender has indicated a priority level for the message (on a scale of lowest to highest), it is indicated here.
- **Red flag icon:** You can mark messages with a red flag to indicate them as extra-important to you.
- **Status:** Indicates whether you have replied to the messages.
- **Lines:** Displays the number of lines in each message.
- **Unread:** Displays the number of unread messages in a message thread.
- **Total:** Displays the total number of messages in a message thread.

You can adjust the size of columns by selecting a column divider and dragging your mouse to the left or the right.

TIP

Messenger defaults to displaying messages on the list in order of date, but you can sort messages by any of these categories by clicking on a column. Sometimes, being able to display messages by sender, subject or priority level can come in handy.

FOLLOWING MESSAGE THREADS

What do the + signs next to messages on the message list mean? A + sign indicates a news thread. Threads are discussions on particular topics, organized under the same subject heading. When you respond to a message and don't change the subject line of the original message, your message is added to the thread. If you click on a + sign next to a message, message list items threaded the original posting appear as indented list items, and the + sign chances to a – sign.

NAVIGATING MESSAGES

Personally, I like cruising groups randomly and reading messages when the subject line catches my eye. But if you're a stickler for chronological order (or just plain old order!), you'll like Messenger's navigation options. To read through messages, click the **Next** button with the downward arrow.

You can also participate in groups offline by downloading messages and logging off, reading and replying to messages, then logging on again to send outgoing messages and download new messages. (For more, see Chapter 13.)

You can also determine how the **Next** arrow picks up messages by clicking it with the right mouse button and choosing from the following options when the menu appears:

- **Next Message:** Moves to the next message on the message list and displays it in the message display pane.
- **Next Unread Message:** Moves to the next unread message on the message list and displays it in the message display pane.
- **Next Flagged Message:** Moves to the next red-flagged message on the message list and displays it in the message display pane.
- **Next Unread Thread:** Moves to the beginning of the next unread thread on the message list and displays it in the message display pane.
- **Next Group:** Moves to the next group in the message list and displays the first message in that group in the message display pane.

• **Next Unread Group:** Moves to the next unread group in the message list and displays the first message in that group on the message display pane.

MARKING MESSAGES

To mark messages, select a message from the message list, click the **Mark** toolbar icon, and select from the following options:

• **As unread:** Marks selected message as unread.
• **As read:** Marks selected message as read.
• **Thread read:** Marks selected message's entire thread as read.
• **All read:** Marks all messages in group as read.
• **By date:** Displays a dialog box so you can enter a date. Marks all messages as read up to the date you enter.
• **For later:** Temporarily marks selected message as read so you can skip it for now. The next time you view the newsgroup, the message appears as unread.

Posting Messages

After you've spent some time reading messages, you might start wanting to participate. You can post messages similarly to the way you send email, with slight differences. If you compose a message from scratch, select **New Message** from the toolbar. Then click the **To:** button (with the **Address Message** tab selected) with your mouse, and select **Group** from the menu. When the **Group** button appears, enter the group's URL (which is also its name).

Replying to messages is also easy. When you see an interesting message, click the **Reply** button to display the following options:

• **Reply to Sender:** Sends reply only to the person who sent the message (this option is good in situations when you want to share information with a fellow group participant, but don't feel the information would be of value to everyone in the group).
• **Reply to Sender and All Recipients:** Sends reply to the sender, the newsgroup, and any other recipients specified in the sender's posting.
• **Reply to Group:** Sends reply only to the group.

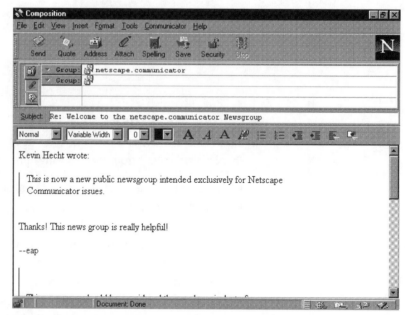

FIGURE *Replying to a message in the Message Composition window*
12.4

- **Reply to Sender and Group:** Sends reply to both the sender and to the group.

When you reply to messages or compose new messages, the Message Composition window appears, as shown in Figure 12-4.

When getting your feet wet with groups and posting messages, try alt.test.yer.posts (most news servers carry it). This newsgroup is exclusively devoted to users who want to see if they're doing everything properly. You can also use this group to experiment with attached files and multimedia so you can make sure they work before making group members irate.

TIP

News and Discussion Group Etiquette

Participating in groups is like entering any other social environment. You want to get along with everyone, find out some useful information, network, and make friends. Since you don't want to accidentally offend anyone, it is best to keep a low profile at first. Read through messages and get a feel for what this group likes to discuss and how they interact with each other. After a while, you'll be ready to jump in.

When exploring the wonderful world of groups, consider the following:

- **Moderated or unmoderated:** Unmoderated groups tend to be more fast-paced and freewheeling, while moderated groups tend to stay more on topic—but postings often don't get updated for a few days. Figure out what style meshes with you so you don't get impatient.
- **Treat people as you want to be treated:** Don't sling epithets at someone when that person's opinion differs from yours. It makes the world a less friendly place and also makes you look bad. Remember that there are humans behind those funny-sounding email addresses.
- **Make sure you want to participate:** Before posting to groups, hang around for a while and read messages to make sure you want to get involved. The best groups rely on a good mix of solid contributors and a sense of community. When too many people post a couple of messages here and there, then disappear, it creates a transient feel that is bad for the group.
- **Before you ask, check the FAQs:** Most Usenet groups post lists of Frequently Asked Questions (FAQs) on their sites. Before posting a general question, see if you can't find the answer you want in the FAQs first.
- **Multiple postings look like Spam:** Spam means electronic junk mail (nobody remembers where exactly the term came from). When you send messages to multiple groups, other participants often think it's unimportant and skip the message. You're better off taking the time to send individual messages to groups.
- **To email or to post?:** When answering people's questions or getting into discussions with them, think about emailing your answer directly to the person instead of posting it. If you think your message would be useful to everyone in the group, send the message to the group. Otherwise, send a message to the individual only.
- **Approach humor with caution:** Some kinds of humor don't always come across the right way in writing. Sarcasm often backfires (though you can use emoticons to get around this)
- **Improve your writing style:** When posting to groups, approach it as though you were writing a press release or a business letter. You don't have to write like William Shakespeare. Just keep your subject lines and messages lively and concise.

These rules aren't too hard to follow, and have helped make many groups into pleasant, informative, online communities.

Acronyms and Emoticons

When browsing through groups (and reading email) you'll often come across strange acronyms and characters composed of keyboard symbols. The acronyms stand for terms commonly used on the Internet. The symbols are "emoticons" (or, occasionally, typos!), which represent facial expressions and emotions that otherwise would not come across in the digital world.

Here are a few of the most commonly used Internet emoticons and acronyms:

- :-)   Smile
- ;-)   Smile with a wink
- <G>   Grin
- :-(Frown
- >:-(Angry frown
- :-O   Yelling
- **BTW:** By the Way
- **FYI:** For Your Information
- **WRT:** With Respect To
- **IMHO:** In My Humble Opinion
- **TTFN:** Ta Ta for Now
- **LOL:** Laughing Out Loud
- **FOFL:** Falling on Floor Laughing
- **ROFL:** Rolling on Floor Laughing
- **Flame:** Angry email or posted messages. This term isn't an abbreviation, but people use it frequently.

Depending on which groups you participate in, more of these abbreviations and emoticons will come your way. If a few of them stump you, check the group's FAQs.

CHAPTER
13
Email, News, and More for People on the Go

The person who coined the phrase "Time is money" probably had an Internet account. If you pay an hourly fee for online time, share Internet access, need to use your telephone for other things besides connecting to the Internet, or you're taking your laptop off the road, then you'll enjoy being able to work offline. Offline? Well, sure you have to connect to the server to download and upload data. But you don't need to be online to read messages, view channels, or work with your calendar. You can connect to the server, upload and download everything you need while connected, and then disconnect. You can then read and reply to email and group messages (Chapters 10–12), view channel information (Chapter 6), and review your Calendar agenda (Chapter 6) offline. When you are ready to send your messages, download new channels, and reconcile your Calendar, you can connect again.

This brief chapter tells you how to download and work with the following types of Internet and Intranet content offline:

- Email and news
- Netcaster
- Calendar

Email and News

Some times reading and responding to all of your email and groups messages can take a while. And before you know it, your whole family's yelling at you to quit hogging the phone or your coworkers start nagging you because they can't connect. You can save yourself the hassle by downloading all of your email and groups messages and then perusing them offline at your leisure.

To download your email and groups messages so you can read them offline, do the following:

1. Select **Go Offline** from the **File** menu.
2. When the **Download** dialog box appears, as shown in Figure 13-1, you can tell Communicator to download mail, discussion groups (this takes care of newsgroups, too), and to send your outgoing messages by selecting the appropriate checkboxes.
3. If you don't want to download messages from *all* your news and discussion groups (some of them have an *awful* lot of messages), click the **Select Items For Download...** button.

FIGURE *Download dialog box.*
13.1

4. When the **Discussion Groups** dialog box appears, as shown in Figure 13-2, you can select the groups you wish to download and click **OK** to return to the **Download** dialog box.

5. From the **Download** dialog box, click the **Go Offline** button to return to Communicator.

FIGURE *Discussion Groups dialog box.*
13.2

Now, you can go take a quick coffee break while Communicator downloads your messages and logs off from the server. Unless you have tons of messages, going offline shouldn't take more than five or ten minutes. For more about email and news, see Chapters 10 through 12.

Netcaster

Netcaster is ideally suited for offline browsing because Web pages served up by channels get stored in your computer. So when you click on links, the new pages appear more quickly than if you were navigating ordinary Web pages. To browse channels offline, you must first subscribe to them. For more about channels, see Chapter 6.

To browse channels offline, do the following:

1. Launch Netcaster by selecting **Netcaster** from the **File** menu.
2. When Netcaster appears, click the **Options** button below the **Channel Finder**.
3. When the **Options** window appears with the **Channels** tab selected, select a channel from the list and click the **Update Now** button, as in Figure 13-3.
4. When that channel finishes updating, you can download additional channels.
5. Click **OK** to return to Netcaster.

When you disconnect, you can browse channels at your leisure. This works best when you don't exit Netcaster before browsing.

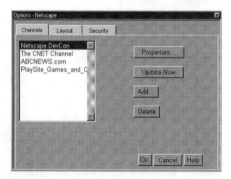

FIGURE *Options window with Channels tab selected.*
13.3

Calendar

If your office uses Calendar (for more about Calendar, see Chapter 21) then you'll get accustomed to checking your agenda frequently. However, you may not be connected to the server all the time. That's OK. You can work with your agenda offline, and then connect to the server periodically to reconcile your agenda with everyone else's on the network.

To work offline with Calendar, you first need to choose your offline preferences. First, launch Calendar by selecting **Calendar** from the **Communicator** menu.

When the Calendar window appears, do the following:

1. Select **Preferences** from the **Edit** menu, then choose **Offline** from the list.
2. When the **Off-line Preferences** window with the **Location** tab selected appears, as shown in Figure 13-4, click the **Browse** button to find your offline file location, and click the **Create directory if none exists** checkbox.
3. Click the **Download** tab, as shown in Figure 13-5, and choose a download period that you want to download entries from by entering numbers and selecting a period of time from the pulldown list. Then choose a download option for when you exit Calendar and disconnect by selecting the appropriate radio button.

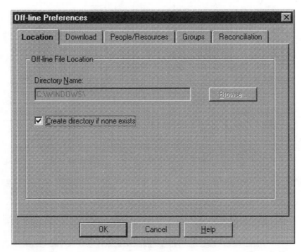

FIGURE   *Offline Preferences window with Location tab selected.*
13.4

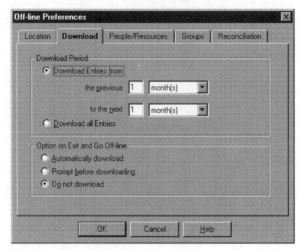

FIGURE
13.5
Offline Preferences window with Download tab selected.

4. Click the **People/Resources** tab, as shown in Figure 13-6, and select any agendas you need from the list.
5. Click the **Groups** tab, as shown in Figure 13-7, and choose whether to download no groups, all groups, or selected groups by clicking the appropriate radio button. If you choose the **Select Groups** radio button, click the **Load** button to load groups. When the groups appear on the

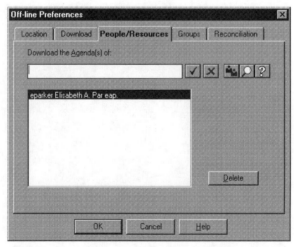

FIGURE
13.6
Offline Preferences window with People/Resources tab selected.

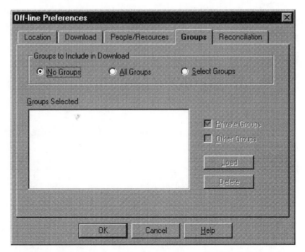

FIGURE *Offline Preferences window with Groups tab selected.*
13.7

list, you can select groups you don't want to download and click the
Delete button.

6. When you get back online, both your agenda and other agendas on
   the server will change and you have to reconcile them. Click the **Reconciliation** tab, as shown in Figure 13-8, and select options for how
   reconciliation and possible scheduling conflicts should be handled.

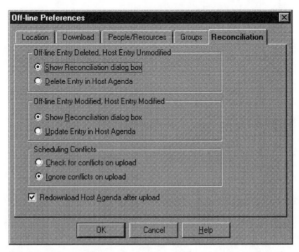

FIGURE *Offline Preferences window with Reconciliation tab selected*
13.8

Calendar "groups" aren't news and discussion groups—they're work groups with agendas.

7. Click **OK** to return to Calendar. If you get stuck or confused, click the **Help** button.

These options apply whenever you launch Calendar while disconnected from the server.

14 Keeping Track of Contacts with Your Address Book

C an't remember everyone's email addresses? Thanks to Communicator's address book, you don't need to. After all, how could we remember email addresses for all the people we exchange messages with over the course of a day? You can set up an address book for people that you correspond with frequently. Once you add their contact information to your list, sending email becomes as easy as displaying your little online rolodex and clicking the name you want. The Address Book is integrated with both Messenger (Chapter 11) and Netscape Conference (Chapters 15 and 16), so you never have to fumble through little scraps of paper and business cards in your briefcase, purse, wallet, or backpack to find people's email addresses again.

This chapter covers the following:

- Address book basics
- Adding entries to your Address Book
- Editing contacts
- Deleting contacts
- Importing Address Books
- Exporting your Address Book
- Creating mailing lists
- Addressing messages

Address Book Basics

Your address book makes it easy for you to keep track of your contacts. You can add new people to the list, create a mailing list so you can send messages to multiple recipients, search for people on a directory, and more. To display the Address Book window, as shown in Figure 14-1, select **Address Book** from the **Communicator** menu, or use the CTRL+Shift+2 (Windows) or CMD+Shift+2 (Macintosh) key combination.

The **Address Book** window has the following elements:

- **Address Book toolbar:** Contains options for adding and editing your correspondents' contact information, searching for addresses, sending messages, and making telephone calls by clicking the following toolbar icons:
  - **New Card:** Displays the **New Card** window so you can add a new contact to your Address Book.

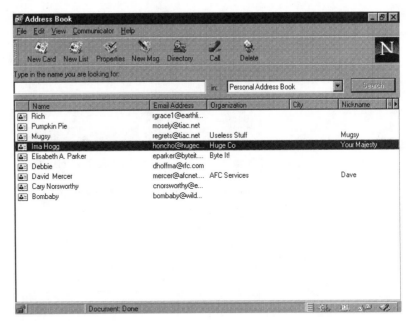

FIGURE *Address Book window.*
14.1

- **New List:** Displays the **Mailing List** dialog box so you can create a group of multiple recipients that you can address and send the same message to.
- **Properties:** Displays the card for (recipients' name) window for the selected item on your recipients list so you can edit contact information.
- **New Message:** Sets up a new message and displays the **Message Composition** window with the selected recipient's address entered in the **To:** window so you can compose and send email, as shown in Figure 14-2.
- **Directory:** Click to display the **Search** dialog box with additional options for searching for users who you want to send messages to and add to your Address Book, as shown in Figure 14-3.
- **Call:** Displays the **Netscape Conference** dialog box, as shown in Figure 14-4 so you can set up a conference call with the selected re-

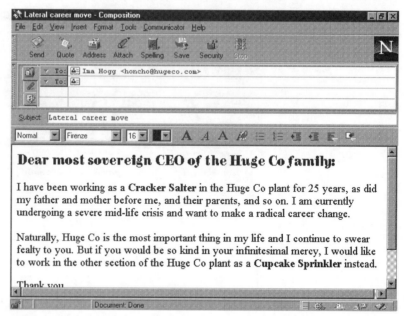

FIGURE **14.2** *Click New Message to set up an outgoing message for the selected recipient in your Address Book.*

FIGURE **14.3** *Click Directory to display the Search dialog box.*

cipient in your Address book (for more about Netscape Conference, see Chapters 15 and 16).

- **Delete:** Deletes selected recipient from the Address Book.
- **Location toolbar:** You can search for an address in your Address Book or in a local network or Internet directory service by entering a name in the text field and selecting an address book or directory service from the pulldown list.

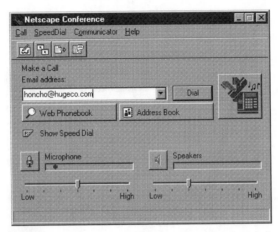

FIGURE *Click Call to display the Netscape Conference dialog box.*
14.4

TIP

If you work for an organization that runs an Intranet with Netscape server products, you and your coworkers can make your address books available to other users. Available address books also appear as items on the Location toolbar's pull-down list.

- **Columns:** Displays information about recipients list items by category.
- **Recipients list:** Displays your contacts along with contact information.

Adding Entries to Your Address Book

To add names and addresses to your address book, do the following:

1. Click the **New Card** icon on the **Address Book** toolbar.
2. When the **New Card** window appears with the **Name** tab selected, as shown in Figure 14-5, enter the recipient's name, email address, and other information in the appropriate text fields.
3. You can also click the **Prefers to receive rich text (HTML) mail** checkbox to remind yourself that this person can handle messages with fancy formatting (as explained in Chapter 11).

FIGURE *New Card window with Name tab selected.*

14.5

NOTE

If you plan on making your address book available to other users on your network, then you should fill in information as completely as possible so that other users can search for the recipient more easily.

4. Click the **Contact** tab, as shown in Figure 14-6 to display text fields for additional contact information you can enter (the window name also changes to **Card for**).

5. Click the **Netscape Conference** tab to choose Dynamic Lookup Service (DLS) server options so you can teleconference with the recipient, as shown in Figure 14-7. You can select the following options from the **Address:** pulldown list:

- **If you don't know whether the contact has a preferred DLS server,** choose Netscape DLS Server from the **Address:** pulldown list. You can then make conference calls to other Netscape Communicator users through Netscape's DLS server.
- **Specific DLS Server:** If you know the person's DLS server address, select **Specific DLS Server** from the list and enter the DLS server's URL in the text field below.

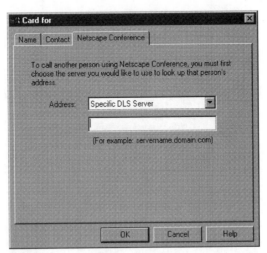

FIGURE *Card for window with Contact information.*
14.6

- **Host Name or IP Address:** You can also enter a host name or IP address by selecting **Host Name or IP Address** from the pulldown list and entering the information in the text field below.

Click **OK** to add the name to your recipients list and to return to the Address Book window.

FIGURE *Card for window with Netscape Conference tab selected.*
14.7

ADDING ENTRIES FROM MESSENGER

When you receive email and group messages, you can also add contact information to your Address Book straight from the message.

To add contact information directly from an email message, do the following:

1. From the Messenger window, select a message from your message list.
2. Select **Add to Address book** from the **Message** menu.
3. Choose **Sender** to add only the sender's address or **All** to add carbon copy (Cc:) recipients of the message as well.

If the sender also uses Communicator and has attached a business card, additional information (such as organization, title, and snail mail address) is added to your address book as well. Otherwise, only that person's name and email address are added.

Editing Contacts

When you need to change a contact's information, do the following:

1. Display the Address Book window and select the contact from the recipient list.
2. Click the **Properties** button.
3. When the **Card for (name of contact)** window appears, as shown in Figure 14-8, you can make your changes.

FIGURE   *Card for (name of contact) window.*
14.8

Click **OK** to save your changes and return to the Address Book window.

Deleting Contacts

To delete contacts from your Address Book, select a contact from the recipients list and click the **Delete** toolbar icon.

Importing Address Books

Like bookmarks (as discussed in Chapter 8), address books are HTML documents. This means that you can either view them as Web pages or easily import other people's address books into your own address book. This can come in handy when your boss needs you to send messages to a bunch of contacts whose information you don't have. People can send you their address books via email as attached files, or you can search for coworkers' address books on the network (with their permission, of course!).

To import an address book, do the following:

1. Select **Import** from the **File** menu.
2. When the **Import address book file** dialog box appears, as shown in Figure 14-9, browse for the address book (by default, address books are named `address.htm`).

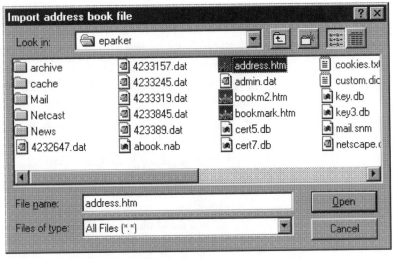

FIGURE *Import address book file dialog box.*
14.9

Click **OK** to import the address book's contacts and return to the Address Book window.

Exporting Your Address Book

If your organization has an LDAP-enabled server so users can search for people's addresses and other data, then you can make your address book contacts available to other users. How is this different than letting colleagues import your address book? When you export your address book, it is added to the LDAP searchable database so other users can search for your contact's email addresses and other information.

To export your address book, do the following:

1. Select **Save As...** from the Address Book window's **File** menu.
2. When the **Save As** dialog box appears, name your file with the .LDIF file name extension and browse for a directory on the network to save it to.
3. Click **OK**.

Before you export your address book, ask your network administrator for instructions on what to name the file and where to save it.

Creating Mailing Lists

If you frequently send messages to multiple recipients—such as people you're working on a project with or a group of friends and family members—you should consider creating a mailing list. For example, you could put all of the people with whom you're planning a big event in a group called "The Big Event" and the people you correspond with about Project X in a group called "Project X." When you need to send these groups of people mail, you can select the entire group from the Address Book recipients' list instead of selecting each name individually.

To create a mailing list, do the following:

1. From the Address Book window's toolbar, click the **New List** toolbar icon.
2. When the **Mailing List** dialog box appears, as shown in Figure 14-10, name the mailing list, give it a nickname, and enter a brief description in the appropriate text fields.

FIGURE *Mailing List dialog box.*
14.10

3. Type a name from your Address Book on each line of the list in the list area (each name needs to be entered exactly as it appears on the list).

Click **OK** to save your changes and return to the Address Book window. You can add or delete names from the list when you need to by selecting the **Mailing List** item by selecting it from the recipients list and clicking the **Properties** toolbar icon to display the **Mailing List** dialog box again.

Addressing Messages

Once you create your address book by making a list of names, addressing your outgoing email messages is easy. To enter addresses in the **Message Composition** window, do the following:

1. Click the **Address** button.
2. When the **Select Addresses** dialog box appears, as shown in Figure 14-11, select a name from the scrolling list, then click the **To:**, **Cc:**, or **Bcc:** button.
3. When all of the recipients' names appear in the **This message will be sent to:** list, click **OK** to return to the **Message Composition** window.

FIGURE *Select address dialog box.*
14.11

4. To remove a recipient from the list, select his or her name and click the **Remove** button.

There. That was pretty easy, wasn't it?

CHAPTER

15

Setting up for Conference Calls

Someday, life will be like "The Jetsons" (the futuristic cartoon that was popular back in the 70's). No one will commute, we'll all video-conference and telecommute. We won't even have to go halfway across the country (or the world) to visit dear old Grandma and Grandpa, we'll just make a Gigabit connection and display full-motion real-time video on our wall-size monitor. Then we can schmooze to our heart's content.

But, for now, we'll have to be satisfied with the plain old small screen, blocky video and delayed audio coming out of our machines, realizing it's still light years ahead of what was available two years ago. Of course, if we're lucky enough to all have Pentiums on our desktops and a high-speed network installed, maybe we can actually do some serious conferencing.

Communicator's Conference application is both a client component of Netscape Communicator and the name of one of Netscape's SuiteSpot Servers. You don't necessarily have to buy the Conference server to use the Conference client, but you must have a server available. Fortunately, Four11 at `http://www.four11.com` offers a publicly accessible Conference directory so those of us who don't just happen to have our own Conference server can still make online telephone calls.

CAUTION

If you already chat with friends, family, and colleagues with Netscape CoolTalk—the latest version of Netscape's online conferencing software—you should keep CoolTalk installed. Unfortunately, Conference is not backward-compatible with CoolTalk.

This chapter covers the following:

- What's Conference?
- What you need to run Conference
- Setting up Conference
- Conference features
- Making a telephone call
- Learning Voice Mail messages

What's Conference?

Conference is a component of Netscape's Communicator, and you get it at the same time that you download Communicator from the Netscape Web-Site. When you install Communicator, Conference gets installed right along with it (unless you do a custom install and leave it out). With Conference, you can make telephone calls via the Internet by entering email addresses, provided the other people have Conference set up as well. Before you can make a connection, you and the person you're calling must be connected to the Internet or the same in-house network and have the Conference software running.

If you've ever used Internet Relay Chat (IRC) software or participated in online forums with America Online, Compuserve, or Prodigy, then you already have an idea of what you can do with Conference. IRC and online forums let users log-on to a channel or conference room or forum at a particular time. Visitors could then have ongoing conversations with multiple participants where messages flew back and forth as fast as participants could type. However, IRC technology allowed only text communications. Conference uses similar technologies and even has a text Chat feature, but it goes much further than that. You can actually talk in real-time to the person on the other end, you can share a whiteboard, you can transfer files, and you can browse the Web together. The only thing you can't do (at least for the time being) with Conference is talk to more than one person at a time.

What You Need to Run Conference

You need a microphone and speakers in order to run Conference. You also may need to purchase a sound card if your system doesn't have built-in audio support. You can get by with 8 MB of RAM and a 14.4 Kilobits per second (Kbps) modem. We recommend running a powerful, multitasking operating system (like Windows 95), a 28.8 Kbps or faster modem, and plenty of RAM (16MB or more). Conference works best when you have a dedicated connection to the Internet or to a Network so you can keep the application running and people can call you without having to make prior arrangements with you. However, you can use Conference with a regular dial-up account if you're resourceful!

Setting up Conference

Before you can use Conference, it needs some information from you. If you or your network administrator has not set up Conference yet, the Setup Wizard automatically launches when you try to launch it. To launch Conference from within Navigator, select **Conference** from the Communicator menu (Figure 15-1). The Setup Wizard guides you through the process of entering settings and testing your microphone and speakers.

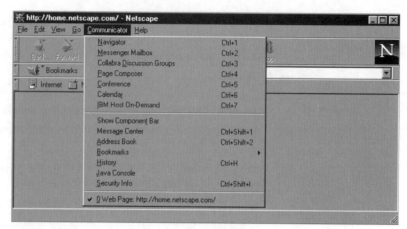

To launch Conference, choose Conference from the Communicator menu.

Now, let's see the Setup Wizard in action as it takes us through the following steps.

- **Read the introduction:** The Setup Wizard provides several dialog boxes to give you introductory information and to confirm that you want to continue with the setup. Click the **Next** button to move forward.
- **Create an online business card:** When the **Setting up Your Business Card** dialog box appears, as shown in Figure 15-2, you can create a special conference call business card for yourself. When you call someone, the information that you enter here appears on the other person's computer so that person can identify you. You can create your business card by doing the following, and clicking the **Next** button when you're through:
  - Enter your name, email address, and other contact information in the appropriate text fields.
  - You can also jazz up your online business card by adding a picture—such as a photograph or company logo in the picture frame. The image displays in the **Answering mode** indicator box in the Netscape Conference main window. You can do this by either clicking the folder button to browse your computer's folders for the image file. Or you can click the **Paste** button to paste an image from your clipboard. The image must be formatted as a .GIF, .JPG, or .BMP file and should be approximately the same size and pro-

FIGURE   *Netscape Conference—Business Card setup screen.*
15.2

     portions as the picture frame. The name of the image appears in the
     Photo: text field.

- You can also choose not to create a business card, leave all the information blank, and click the **Next** button to move on. But that's no fun.

- **Choose a DLS server to handle your conference calls:** When the Setting Your Directory Preferences dialog box appears, as shown in Figure 15-3, you need to specify a default where Dynamic Lookup Service (DLS) server is located. DLS servers maintain a phone book database with names and email or IP addresses so you can search for people's "phone numbers" from within Conference. To choose your directory preferences, do the following, then click the **Next** button:

  - **Select a DLS server from the pulldown list following the DLS Server prompt:** You need to be registered with a DLS server in order for Conference to work—but never fear: If your ISP or company network doesn't have a DLS server, Netscape provides you with a few. The default directory preferences settings specify the

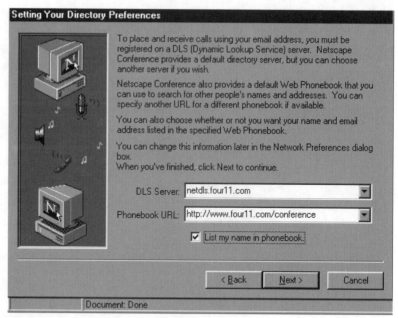

To place and receive calls using your email address, you must be registered on a DLS (Dynamic Lookup Service) server. Netscape Conference provides a default directory server, but you can choose another server if you wish.

Netscape Conference also provides a default Web Phonebook that you can use to search for other people's names and addresses. You can specify another URL for a different phonebook if available.

You can also choose whether or not you want your name and email address listed in the specified Web Phonebook.

You can change this information later in the Network Preferences dialog box.
When you've finished, click Next to continue.

DLS Server: netdls.four11.com

Phonebook URL: http://www.four11.com/conference

☑ List my name in phonebook

< Back   Next >   Cancel

Document: Done

FIGURE **15.3** *Specify a DLS Server and Phonebook URL in the Setting Your Directory Preferences dialog box.*

Four11 DLS server, but there are also others you can choose from. Your ISP or network administrator also may have added a DLS server name to your list.

• **Select the DLS server's corresponding URL from the pulldown list:** DLS server databases run from Web pages, so in addition to selecting a DLS server, you need to select the DLS server's corresponding URL. You can do this by selecting the URL from the pulldown list following the **Phonebook URL:** prompt. The default directory preferences settings specify the Four11 DLS server's URL, `http://www.four11.com/conference/`.

• **Choose to list your name in the DLS server's phone book:** To add your name and email address to your DLS server's directory, leave the **List my name in phonebook** checkbox selected.

• **Tell Conference what type of connection you have:** When the **Specify Your Network Type** dialog box appears (Figure 15-4), the Setup Wizard asks for information about your type of Internet connection and modem speed (for more about modem speeds, see Chapter 3).

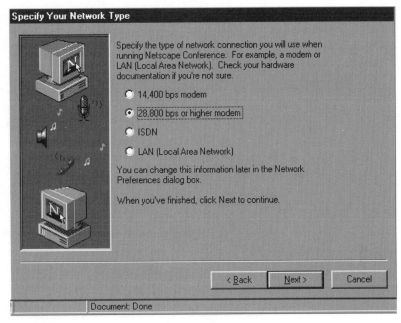

FIGURE *Specify Your Network Type dialog box.*
15.4

You can choose one of the following options, then click the **Next** button to move on:

- **14,400 bps modem:** Choose this option if your modem has a 14.4 Kbps (Kilobits per second) data transfer speed. If you plan on using Conference frequently, you should also consider getting a faster modem.

- **28,800 bps or higher modem:** Choose this option if you have a 28.8 Kbps, 33.6 Kbps, or 56 Kbps modem speed.

- **ISDN (Integrated Digital Services Network):** ISDN setups transfer data at a *minimum* speed of 64 Kbps—that's twice as fast as what most of us get. High-speed ISDN lines are more expensive, but are slowly becoming more affordable and more accessible.

- **LAN (Local Area Network):** If you connect to the Internet through your organization's network, then choose this option.

- **Wait for Conference to find your sound card:** As explained earlier in this chapter, you need a sound card in order to use Netscape Conference. When the **Detecting Your Sound Card** dialog box appears, as

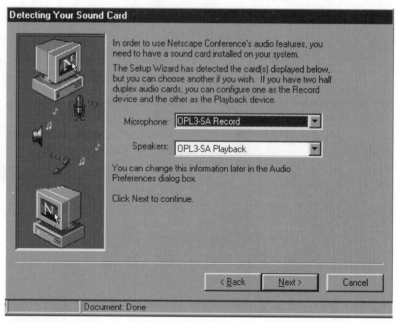

FIGURE   *Detecting Your Sound Card dialog box.*
15.5

shown in Figure 15-5, wait for the Setup Wizard to find your audio devices. This happens automatically for Windows 95 users and Macintosh users (Macintoshes come with sound built in). Windows 3.1x users can select their type of microphone and speakers from the **Microphone:** and **Speakers:** pulldown lists. When you're finished, click the **Next** button.

If you have a full-duplex sound card, you can send and receive audio simultaneously, but if you have a half duplex card you can only send or receive at any given time. Conference employs a feature that automatically switches between send and receive (for half duplex cards) to make it sound like full duplex, or you can perform this operation manually if you like. To turn this feature on (it's the default, by the way) use the Playback/Recording Autoswitch preference.

- **Choose to test your audio devices:** Once the Setup Wizard finds your sound card, microphone, and speakers, it tests them for you. When the **Testing the Audio Levels (Screen 1 of 2)** dialog box appears, you can either choose to allow the Setup Wizard to adjust your audio lev-

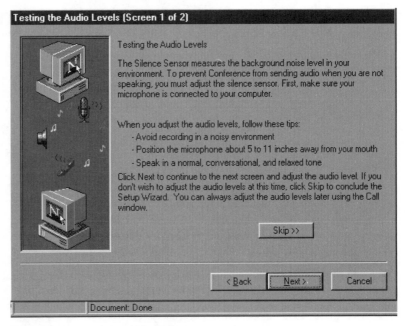

FIGURE *Setting Noise Levels dialog box.*
15.6

els (Figure 15-6) by clicking the **Next** button, or skip the test by clicking the **Skip** button.

Conference won't work until you let it test and adjust your audio levels, so you might as well do it now.

CAUTION

- **Test Your Audio Devices:** When the **Testing the Audio Levels (Screen 2 of 2)** dialog box appears, as shown in Figure 15-7, do the following, then click the **Next** button:
  - Click the **microphone** button to activate your microphone.
  - Begin talking into your microphone. The green bar that appears when you speak is called the Volume Meter. The red control is the Silence Sensor.
  - If the Volume Meter extends past the right of the Silence Sensor, then you're all set, and you can click the **Next** button to move on.
  - If the Volume Meter does *not* extend past the right of the Silence Sensor, then some quick adjustments are in order. You can adjust the Silence Sensor by moving the red control on the outgoing audio

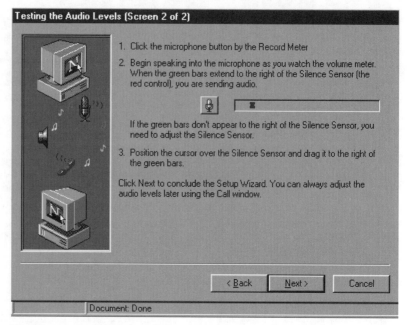

FIGURE *Noise Level Adjustment dialog box.*
15.7

meter so that the Volume Meter (which represents audio levels) only displays when you are actually talking, not during ordinary background noise.

The last Setup Wizard dialog congratulates you for successfully setting up Conference. Click the **Finish** button and you're all done!

You can change your settings at any time by selecting Preferences from the Call menu in the Netscape Conference main window.

TIP

By the way, if you have trouble sending and receiving during a Conference session, there's a good chance that you have your Silence Sensor set incorrectly. This often happens with half duplex sound cards. Remember that half-duplex sound cards can't send and receive audio simultaneously. The purpose of the Sensor is to detect when you are not speaking, so the Playback/Recording Autoswitch can switch you to Receive. The Silence Sensor does this by monitoring the sound entering your microphone. If you've set the Sensor too low, it will interpret background noise as you are talking, and keep the Playback/Recording Autoswitch on Send.

TIP

Conference Features

Now that you've set up Conference, let's have some fun! When you launch Conference, the Netscape Conference window appears, as shown in Figure 15-8. You will probably notice that Conference is jam-packed with features. Fortunately, it's easy to use once you get the hang of it. This section gives a brief overview of the things you can do with Conference. The next two sections tell you how to dial up a number and leave a voice mail message.

You can do the following from the **Conference** window:

- **Share whiteboarding:** Conference's whiteboard feature gives you a way to exchange data in a highly visual and interactive way. You can take screen captures of the contents of any application window—for example, an image or a spreadsheet that you're working on—and display it on the whiteboard so your colleague can view it. Or vice versa. The two of you can then use shape, drawing, and text tools to make comments and suggestions. To use the shared whiteboard, click the **Whiteboard** toolbar button. In order to share the whiteboard, you and your colleague must both have the whiteboard feature activated.

- **Browsing together:** Let's say you and a colleague are collaborating on revamping your company's Web site and viewing other pages for inspiration. Or the two of you are discussing late-breaking news that affects your industry. Or, OK, not all of us use the Web for work—you could even be talking about a favorite hobby and exchanging information

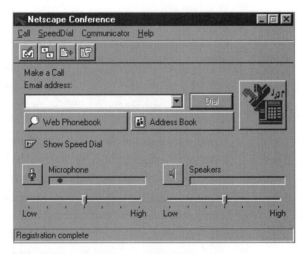

FIGURE *Netscape Conference main screen.*
15.8

about related Web sites. Collaborative browsing lets you view Web pages simultaneously so you can talk about them. When both of you have Navigator running, one of you can jump to a Web page and the other person goes there, too. Pretty neat, huh? To use the collaborative browsing feature, click the **Collaborative Browsing** toolbar button. In order to browse collaboratively, you and your colleague must both have the Navigator and the collaborative browsing feature activated.

- **Exchange files quickly:** Conference also gives you an easy way to exchange files back and forth. It's much more intuitive than using an FTP folder and much faster than sending emails with attachments. With Conference's file exchange feature, you can easily send, receive, and collaborate on files. To use file exchange, click the **File Exchange** toolbar button. In order to use file exchange, you and your colleague must both have it activated.

- **Exchange real-time text messages:** Those of you who chat regularly in online forums know the benefits of sending text messages back and forth in real time. This can be especially useful if you or some of your colleagues have a slow Internet connection or a half duplex sound card. To use the chat feature, click the **Chat** toolbar button. In order to have text chats, you and your colleague must both have the chat feature activated.

- **Make telephone calls:** To make a telephone call, enter an email or IP address in the **Make a Call Email address:** text field, then click the **Dial** button.

- **Search the DLS server for addresses:** To look up an address while connected to the Internet or a network with a DLS server, click the **Web Phonebook** button and enter a first and last name.

- **Display your address book:** You can also display your address book by clicking the **Address Book** button. For more about using your address book, read Chapter 14.

- **Show speed dial numbers:** You can create a custom list of speed dial numbers and display them by clicking the **Show Speed Dial** icon.

- **Check the status of current tasks and connections:** As with Navigator and other Communicator applications, a quick glance at the status indicator tells you what's going on with a current task or your connection.

- **Adjust audio levels:** You can use the **Adjust Microphone Sensitivity** and **Adjust Speaker Sensitivity** sliders to adjust audio levels while engaged in a conference call.

- View the other party's picture, and determine whether you can receive calls: The **Answer mode** indicator tells you what answering mode you have Conference set to. You can select answer mode settings from the Conference Window's **Call** menu to determine how Conference should handle incoming calls. In addition, if the party that you're speaking to has selected an image to display through the Setup (as explained earlier in this chapter) or Netscape Conference Preferences window, the image displays in this box. For more about the **Answer mode** indicator, see the next chapter.

The next chapter tells you how to use Conference in greater detail. In addition to all of the goodies already included with Conference, Netscape plans to introduce H.323 video in the release version of this product. H.323 is a widely used standard for video conferencing. Digital video offers the advantages of visual communications. Alas, most of us will need speedier modems in order to use digital video to its fullest.

Making a Telephone Call

Making telephone calls with Conference is a piece of cake. First, both you and the person you're calling need to have Netscape Conference installed. In order for the person to be able to receive your telephone call, that person must also be connected to the Internet and have Conference running. Obviously, this works best in work situations where users are connected to the network all the time. However, with a bit of advance planning, Conference works great for ordinary Internet users as well. I have an ordinary 28.8 Kbps modem and access the Internet through a dial-up ISP. Yet, I've managed to have ordinary telephone conversations and successfully use Conference's other features. All you need to do is set up a time for making and receiving telephone calls with the parties involved.

To make a telephone call, do the following:

1. Enter an email or IP address following the **Make a Call Email address** text field.
2. Click the **Dial** button.
3. If the person you're trying to reach is online and has Conference running, his or her phone will ring. Otherwise, a dialog box appears asking if you'd like to leave a voice mail message.

If you don't recall someone's email or IP address, you can look it up in your DLS server's directory by clicking the **Web Phonebook** button. Or you can click the **Address Book** button to display your address book.

Leaving Voice Mail Messages

If you know the person you're calling isn't available, you can choose to send a voice mail message. Conference voice mail messages only work when you send them to other Conference users. The **Voice Mail** option appears when you make a phone call and the recipient isn't available, as described in the previous section, or you can choose to send a voice mail message straight from the **Communicator** menu.

To leave a voice mail message, do the following:

1. Select the **Voice Mail** option from the **Communicator** menu in Conference's main window.
2. When the **Recipient email address needed** dialog box appears, as shown in Figure 15-9, enter an email address and click **OK**.
3. When the **Netscape Voice Mail:** dialog box appears, as shown in Figure 15-10, begin recording your message.
4. Click the **Record** button with the red circle icon to begin recording your message and speak into your microphone. The audio indicator shows whether your message is being recorded.
5. Click the **Stop** button with the white square icon to stop recording your message. You can play your message back by clicking the **Play** button with the white triangle icon.
6. To send your message, click the **Send** button. Or click the **Cancel** button to cancel your message.
7. When the email message composition window appears with the voice mail message embedded, as shown in Figure 15-11, you can enter text in the message and click the **Send** button.

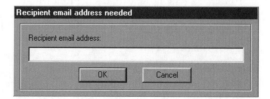

FIGURE *Enter an email address in the Recipient email address needed dialog box.*
15.9

FIGURE
15.10   *Record and send your message when the Netscape Voice Mail dialog box appears.*

When the **Send** dialog box appears, you can choose whether to send the message as an HTML or a plain text document. If you're sure that your fellow Conference users use Communicator's Messenger component to receive

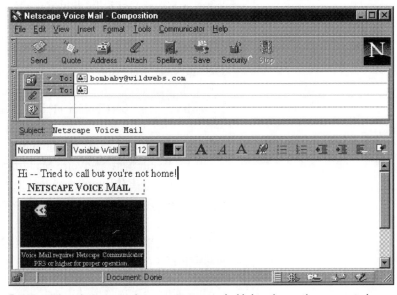

FIGURE   *When the voice mail message appears embedded in the email message window,*
15.11   *you can add some text if you want and send it to your recipient.*

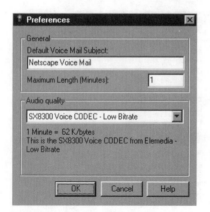

FIGURE *Editing Voice Mail Preferences.*
15.12

their email, choose the HTML option. The voice mail message will be embedded in their document so they can play back the message by double-clicking on it. If your message recipient uses a different client, play it safe and select the **Plain Text** option so they can open it as an email attachment file.

You can also set preferences through the **Voice Mail Preferences** dialog box, shown in Figure 15-12. To display the **Voice Mail Preferences** dialog box, select **Preferences** from the Netscape Voice Mail dialog box's **Edit** menu, and choose from the following options:

- **Default Voice Mail Subject:** When you send email, you can enter a subject line so recipients can see what topic the message discusses (for more about email, see Chapter 11). You can enter a default subject for email messages with embedded or attached voice mail messages by entering it in the **Default Voice mail Subject:** text field. For example, I entered "Default Netscape Voice Mail from Elisabeth Parker" here.

- **Maximum Length (Minutes):** Audio files take up lots of space, so you should make your messages short and sweet. You can specify a maximum message length in minutes in the **Maximum Length (Minutes)** text field. If your message runs over, Netscape Voice Mail cuts it off and displays a warning dialog box.

- **Audio Quality:** You can specify levels of audio quality from the **Audio quality** pulldown list. Low bit rates mean low quality and higher bit rates mean higher sound quality. Bit rate refers to the number of times per second that sound recordings are sampled and digitized.

Don't use higher audio quality settings unless you and the people you use Conference with have high-quality sound systems and high-speed connections.

Click **OK** to save your changes. If you find these options confusing, never fear. The default settings work well for most users.

CHAPTER

16 Using Netscape Conference

L ike a kid with a brand new toy, you're all psyched to have Netscape's Conference all set up. You know you can connect, chat, talk, whiteboard, transfer files, and browse together. But how do these tools work in actual practice? Are they just neat and cool, or do they offer real money and time-saving features that can give you and/or your company an edge? *That* is the $64,000 question. It's tempting to play with Conference, particularly the first time you use it. But to get the most out of it (you don't want your network administrator, parents, roommate, or spouse to take it away!), you should figure out when, why, and how to use it. Fortunately, this chapter can reassure personal and business users. Although Conference has some limitations, it can save you money on your long distance telephone bills and help you communicate more productively with more of a personal touch. I use a Windows 95 computer with 32 MB of RAM, 100 MHz processor speed, a 28.8 modem, SoundBlaster sound card, and a dial-up Internet connection. And everything runs smoothly. And although my system may be slightly more beefed up than some users', it certainly isn't hugely impressive, expensive, or more advanced than what many people are using these days.

This chapter discusses the following:

- Getting in touch with Conference
- Speed dialing
- Finding email addresses
- Using the Whiteboard
- Browsing together
- Transferring files
- Chatting with text messages

Getting in Touch with Conference

You've probably been to some sort of conference in your field before. Ideally, people from around the country, or even the world, travel to some sunny locale, check into upscale hotels, dress up, and share industry information with each other in between brunches, lunches, parties, and other happenings. Netscape Conference may not offer quite as much excitement, but does make it possible to communicate in new and exciting ways. If you have a dedicated connection to the Internet or your network, then you should have Conference running all the time. To launch Conference, select **Conference** from the **Communicator** menu from any Communicator compo-

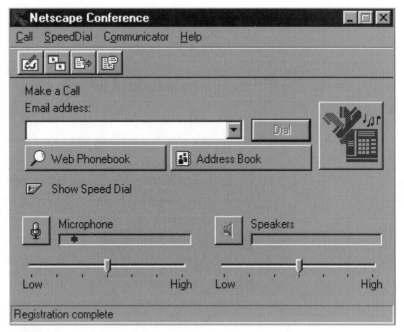

FIGURE *Netscape Conference main window.*
16.1

nent window. To jog your memory about the basic overview of Conference provided in Chapter 15, the Conference main window appears as shown in Figure 16-1. For more details on what each of the items in the Conference main window does, see the previous chapter.

Naturally, the most important thing about any type of communication is how people can contact and exchange information with each other. With email, newsgroups, and Web pages, you can upload pages or send messages at any time, and the person receiving the information can view it at any time. In fact, one of the most appealing things about email is the fact that you never get put on hold or have to leave voice mail messages because people don't have to actually *be* there in order to communicate with each other.

Conference is different. Even though you're on the Internet, the other person still has to be around to answer the phone in order for the two of you to talk. When you make a phone call, the other person has to be connected to the Internet and have Conference up and running in order for you to connect to them. When you "dial" up someone by entering his or her email or IP address in the Netscape Conference main window, the "phone" "rings" on that end. The receiving party's system "answers" the phone, and that person's picture appears where the Answer Mode indicator is currently located. If the person has not chosen an image to display (as discussed in Chapter 15), a question mark displays instead. If the person you're trying to reach is not connected and does not have Conference running, a dialog box displays and asks if you want to leave a voice mail message.

RECEIVING TELEPHONE CALLS

'Tis blessed to give as well as to receive. However, you should still specify how you want Conference to handle incoming calls. Think of it as your on-line secretary that will either announce calls and ask if you want to take them, automatically let callers through, or hold all of your calls. Telling Conference how to handle calls is easy. All you have to do is select an item from the **Call** menu in the Netscape Conference main window.

The **Call** menu provides the following options for handling incoming calls:

- **Always Prompt:** Tells Conference to display a dialog box that tells you who is calling and asks if you want to take the call. If you choose not to answer, the caller can leave a voice mail message. Select this option if you want to screen your calls or if you're frequently away from your desk. When you select the **Always Prompt** option, the Answer mode indicator appears as shown in Figure 16-2.
- **Auto Answer:** Automatically puts the call through. Select this option if you generally take most calls and are going to be at your desk for a length of time. When you select the **Auto Answer** option, the Answer mode indicator appears as shown in Figure 16-3.
- **Do Not Disturb:** Tells the caller that you're unavailable. Select this option if you don't want to take any calls. When you select the **Do Not Disturb** option, the Answer mode indicator appears as shown in Figure 16-4.

You can easily change answer modes depending on your schedule and your mood. You can get your voice mail messages along with the rest of your email.

MAKING TELEPHONE CALLS

Chapter 15 briefly introduced you to making a telephone call, but this section explains things in greater detail. Making telephone calls is easy. But re-

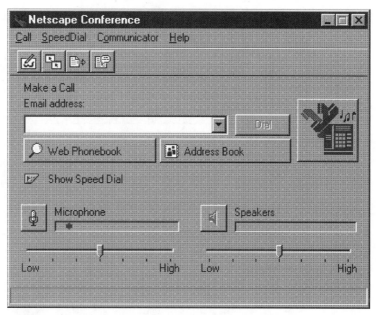

FIGURE   *Answer mode indicator displaying Conference in Always Prompt mode.*
16.2

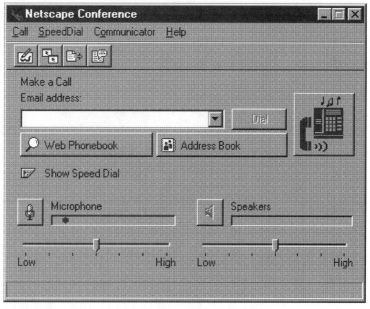

FIGURE   *Answer mode indicator displaying Conference in Auto Answer mode.*
16.3

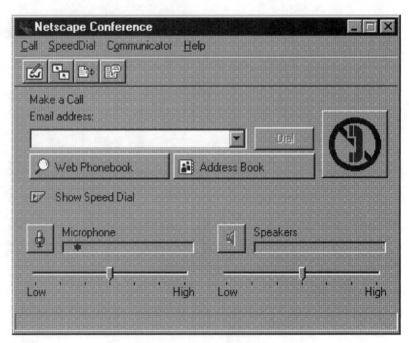

FIGURE
16.4
Conference in Do Not Disturb Answer mode.

member that both you and the other user must be connected to the Internet and running Conference.

To make a telephone call, do the following:

1. Enter the person's email address in the Netscape Conference Window's **Make a Call Email address:** text field, and click the **Dial** button.
2. When the **Pending Invitation** dialog box appears, wait for the call to go through. When it does, either an image or a question mark appears in the Answer mode box.
3. You can then begin talking and using Netscape Conference—just make sure you're speaking directly into the microphone!

If the call does not go through, the **Voice Mail** dialog box appears, as shown in Figure 16-5, and asks if you want to leave a voice mail message. You can then click **Yes**, and record your voice mail message as described in the last chapter.

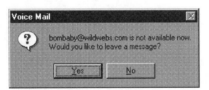

FIGURE *If the person you're calling is unavailable, a Voice Mail dialog box appears and*
16.5 *asks if you want to leave a message.*

Speed Dialing   Like all modern phones, Conference comes with a speed-dial function. With
speed dialing, you can access the six people you call the most often by clicking on a button. To display your speed-dial buttons, as shown in Figure
16-6, click the **Show Speed Dial** button in the Netscape Conference window. To hide the speed-dial buttons, click the **Hide Speed Dial** button (it
appears where the **Show Speed Dial** button was).

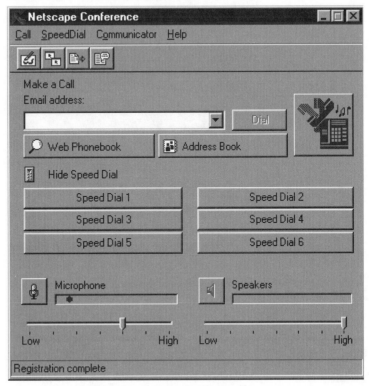

FIGURE *Netscape Conference main window with speed-dial buttons displayed.*
16.6

To create your own speed-dial buttons, do the following:

1. Select a speed-dial item from the Netscape Conference main window's **Speed Dial** menu. List items are named Speed Dial 1 through Speed Dial 6, and the button names change when you customize them.
2. When the cascading menu appears, select **Edit.**
3. When the **Speed Dial Edit** dialog box appears, as shown in Figure 16-7, enter the person's name in the **Name:** text field and the email address in the **Email:** text fields Your default DLS server should automatically appear following the **DLS server:** prompt. If you have the person's IP address, enter it following the **Direct address:** prompt instead of entering an email address.
4. Click **OK.**

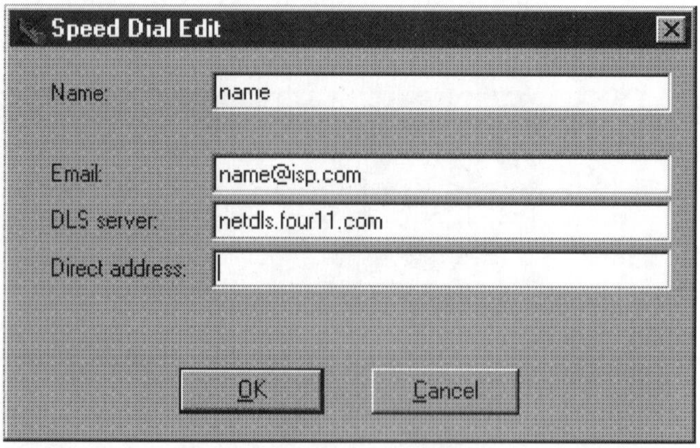

FIGURE *Speed Dial Edit dialog box.*
16.7

The next time you display your speed-dial buttons, a button with the person's name will appear. When you want to dial that number, click the appropriate speed-dial button.

Finding Email Addresses

How do you find someone's email address unless you know it? Fortunately, Conference makes this easy. And now you'll find out how Dynamic Lookup Service (DLS) servers come in handy. DLS servers are set up to be integrated with your teleconferencing software so you can find email addresses on the fly. You can either look up email addresses via search engines on the Web or search straight from your Address Book.

You can search for email addresses in the following ways:

- **Straight from your personal Address Book:** You can contact people who you already have listed in your Address Book (to learn how to create an Address Book, see Chapter 14). To dial up people from your personal address book, do the following:

  1. Click the **Address Book** button in the Netscape Conference main window to display your address book, as shown in Figure 16-8.
  2. Make sure the **Personal Address Book** option is selected from the pulldown list on the right.
  3. Select an entry from your Address Book list.
  4. Click the **Call** button to dial the currently selected email address.

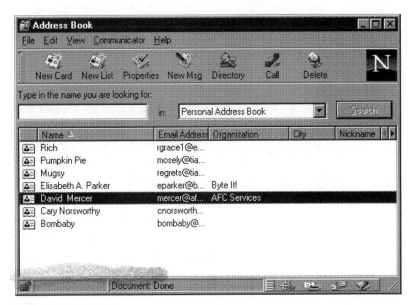

FIGURE *Address Book list.*
16.8

- **Search for people on a DLS server:** DLS servers make it possible to search for email addresses in your Address Book, view search results, and dial up email addresses straight from the list of search results. To search for someone on a DLS server, do the following:

  1. Enter a name in the **Type in the name you are looking for:** text field.

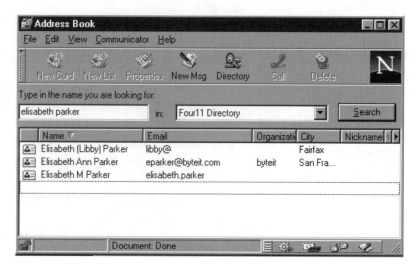

FIGURE *Searching for people on a DLS server through your Address book.*
16.9

2. Select a DLS server directory from the pulldown list on the right.
3. Click the **Search** button.
4. When the list of matches displays, as shown in Figure 16-9, select one and click the **Call** button.
5. If you don't find a match, you can select a different directory server and start over again. You can use WhoWhere, Big Foot, InfoSpace, and a host of other good directories with lots of listings.

- **Perform an advanced search:** You can also do more sophisticated searches by clicking the Address Book's **Directory** toolbar button to display the **Search** dialog box shown in Figure 16-10.
- **From the Web:** You can also search for addresses straight from the Web. Four11 (http://www.four11.com) and other directory com-

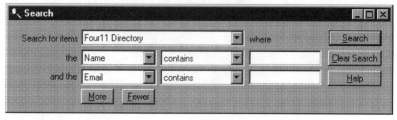

FIGURE *You can use the Search dialog box for more detailed searches.*
16.10

panies all let you search and register your own address (so people can find you) free of charge. A good place to start looking for search directories is the PeopleFinder section of CNET's Search.Com, located at `http://www.search.com/`.

Using the Whiteboard

The whiteboard, as shown in Figure 16-11, is one of my favorite Conference tools. You can use it to display images and take pictures of whatever is happening on your computer screen so you and the person you're conversing with can look at things and discuss them together. Whether you want to show pictures of the kids to Grandma and Grandpa, or get feedback on graphs, handouts, and presentations for tomorrow's big meeting, the whiteboard can help. It even comes with all the tools you need for highlighting items and making edits and comments. Just think—you have this whole screen waiting blankly for you to fill it with anything you want (wow!). To launch the whiteboard, click the **Whiteboard** toolbar button in Conference's main window. When you launch the whiteboard, the other person's whiteboard launches automatically—or vice versa.

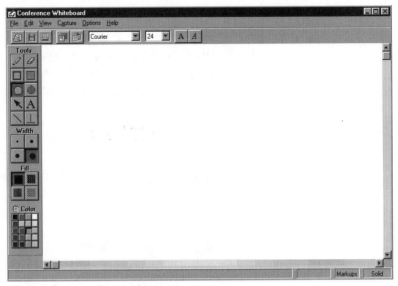

FIGURE *Netscape Conference whiteboard.*
16.11

The **Conference Whiteboard** window consists of the following components:

- **Work Area:** The main part of the whiteboard where you display files and work with them.
- **Menu bar:** Provides items that you can select to display pulldown menus with lists of commands.
- **Toolbar:** You can select basic options from the **Conference Whiteboard**'s toolbar, including:
  - **Open:** Displays the **Open File** dialog box, so you can select a .GIF, .JPEG, .BMP, or .TIF image to display on the whiteboard.
  - **Save:** Displays the **Save** dialog box so you can save the current whiteboard as an image.
  - **Print:** Prints the current whiteboard.
  - **Copy:** Displays a selection box so you can draw a rectangle around the part of the whiteboard you want to copy.
  - **Paste:** Pastes the part of the whiteboard you most recently copied.
  - **Font Name:** To select a font for entering text, select a font name from the pulldown list.
  - **Font Size:** To select a font for entering text, select a font size from the pulldown list.
  - **Bold and Italic buttons:** Click to bold and/or italicize text.

The tools palette gives you the flexibility to create just about any kind of markings and comments on your whiteboard. The person to whom you are connected will immediately see your mark-ups (and vice versa). You can highlight, erase, point to items, type comments, draw freehand lines, filled or unfilled shapes, and straight lines. You can also choose what colors you use. The tools palette offers the following options:

- **Freehand line:** Draws a line in any shape using the currently selected line width and color.
- **Eraser:** Erases lines, shapes, and text, but not pictures that have been imported or captured to the work area.
- **Rectangle:** Draws the outline of a rectangle using the currently selected line width and color.
- **Filled rectangle:** Draws a filled rectangle using the currently selected patterned fill and color.
- **Circle:** Draws the outline of a circle using the currently selected line width and color.

- **Filled circle:** Draws a filled circle using the currently selected patterned fill and color.
- **Pointer:** Click to display an arrow to highlight items in the work area by clicking on them. When you deselect the **Pointer** tool, the arrow disappears.
- **Text:** Click to enter text in the work area. Text appears in the currently selected font name, font size, style (if bold or italic is selected), and color.
- **Diagonal line:** Draws a diagonal line using the currently selected line width and color.
- **Straight line:** Draws a straight vertical or horizontal line in the currently selected line width and color.
- **Line width:** Sets the size of the line for unfilled shapes and lines.
- **Fill:** Applies the current selection to filled shapes.
- **Colors:** Applies the current selection to text, lines, and fills.

The next two sections tell you how to do some neat stuff with the whiteboard.

IMPORTING AND CAPTURING IMAGES TO THE WHITEBOARD

The real power of the whiteboard becomes apparent when you start importing images or taking *screen captures* and displaying them in the work area. "Taking screen captures" means telling an application to take pictures of other programs running on your computer. It's amazing that you can no longer need to be in the same room, or spend time sending email attachments back and forth to discuss projects! Let's say you have a chart or graph in Excel, a block of text in Word, or the cover photograph for your annual report. If it's a draft, you want to share it with others and get immediate feedback about the changes they might like to see. If everyone has digital signature files or stylus devices, you can even get people to sign off on approvals on the spot!

To import an .JPEG, .GIF, .BMP, or .TIF image to display it in the whiteboard work area, do the following:

1. Click the **Open** button or select **Open** from the **File** menu.
2. When the **Open** dialog box appears, as shown in Figure 16-12, browse through your folders for the image file.
3. Select an image and click the **Open** button.

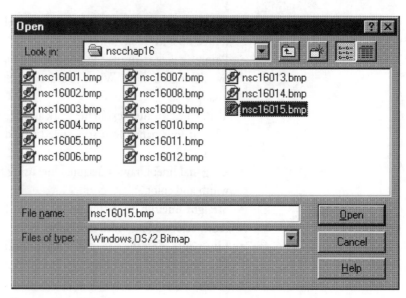

FIGURE *Open dialog box.*
16.12

When the image appears in the work area, you and the person you're talking with can view and comment on it.

To capture an image of a file in an application window to display it in the whiteboard work area, do the following:

1. Open the file from within the application you created it in.
2. Select **Capture** from the menu bar and choose one of the following options:
   - **Screen:** Captures a picture of your entire desktop.
   - **Window:** Captures the active application window.
   - **Region:** Displays a cross-hair selection tool so you can draw a rectangle around a particular region on your computer screen.
3. When you select a capture option, the whiteboard minimizes so you can capture the image.
4. When the whiteboard reappears, a cross-hair and selection box appear so you can place the capture wherever you like and click on an area of the screen to display it.

Figure 16-13 shows how my colleague David Mercer of AFC Services and I collaboratively viewed and marked up a capture of a Web page with graphed data in the whiteboard work area.

OTHER WHITEBOARD BASICS

There are also a few other things you should know about using the whiteboard to make things easier for you. You can clear the work area when it gets too cluttered, paste text and images selected from other applications, zoom in and out, save a copy of the current work area, and adjust the work area size.

- **Clearing the whiteboard work area:** After a while, the work area gets messy. You can clear your markups by selecting **Clear Markups** from the **Edit** menu. Or you can clear the entire Whiteboard by selecting **Clear Whiteboard** from the **Edit** menu.
- **Pasting text and images selected from other applications:** You can paste text and images that you have selected and copied onto the clipboard from other applications by selecting **Paste Text** or **Paste Picture** from the **Edit** menu.

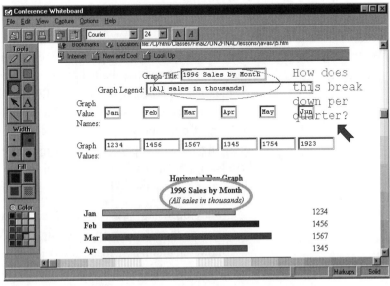

FIGURE *Whiteboard work area with screen capture and markups.*
16.13

- **Zooming in and out:** To zoom in for a close-up view, and zoom out again, you can select options from the **View** menu.
- **Save a copy of the current whiteboard work area:** If you just got everyone to sign off their approval for a project—or a friend or family member showed you some fun photographs—you sure don't want to lose what you have in your work area! To save everything on the current work area as an image, click the **Save** toolbar button or select **Save** from the **File** menu to bring up the **Save** dialog box.
- **Adjust the work area size:** To adjust the work area size, select **Canvas Size** from the **Options** menu. When the **Canvas Size** dialog box appears, enter values in the height and width fields. Values should be entered in pixels. Pixels are a unit of measurement used in the computer world, and their size varies depending on a person's type of computer and monitor. However, 70 to 100 pixels roughly equals an inch.

To end your whiteboarding session, click the **Close** box in the upper right-hand of the Whiteboard window, or select **Close** from the **File** menu.

CAUTION

Go slowly when making any changes to the whiteboard or work space—especially when deleting items or placing images on top of items your colleague may still need to look at. Remember that everything you do happens on the other person's computer, too!

Browsing Together

There's nothing like browsing the Web to find great information in a hurry. But telling someone else about a particular Web site sometimes just doesn't do the trick, and spelling out a long URL or trying to tell them which link to click can get real boring, real fast. But never fear, Conference is here. Just click the **Collaborative Browsing** toolbar icon, and the **Collaborative Browsing** window appears, as shown in Figure 16-14 (though you must have Navigator launched in order for this to work).

To start cruising the Web in tandem, choose from the following options:

- **Start Browsing:** Just click the **Start Browsing** button and you'll be leading the other person on a tour of the Web. Before they go along, however, they'll have to agree (a dialog box will pop up on their screen and ask if they agree to browse with you or not). Meanwhile, if you suddenly land on a URL you've never heard of, that's because the other person can guide you to Web pages, too.

FIGURE   *Conference Collaborative Browsing window.*
16.14

- **Control the Browsers:** If you're a real control freak, or need to take someone to several sites in a row, select the **Control the Browsers** checkbox to make them follow your lead (and make sure you click it first!).
- **Sync Browsers:** Even when you've designated yourself the Head Browsing Honcho, if the other party decides to go off to another URL, he or she can still do so. If you want to get back to reading from the same page, just click the **Sync Browser** button, and the other person will go to your location.

To stop browsing together, click the **Close** button.

Transferring Files

If you'd like to exchange files while you're working together, there's no need to open an FTP program and try to figure out where you can send the files so the other person can download them. Nor do you have to send them back and forth as email attachments. Just click the **File Exchange** toolbar button in the Conference main window, and the **Conference File Exchange** window appears, as shown in Figure 16-15.

To send a file or several files to the other party, do the following:

1. Click the **Open File** button, or select **Add to Send List** from the **File** menu.
2. When the **Add to Send List** dialog box appears, browse for your file, and click the **Open** button.

FIGURE   *Conference File Exchange window.*
16.15

3. When all the files you want to send appear on the **File(s) to send** list, click the **Send** button.

You can also choose options for sending and receiving files. You can choose the following items by selecting them from Conference File Exchange's **Options** menu:

- **Compress:** Leave this item selected to compress your files so they transfer more quickly.
- **Pop Up When Receive:** Leave this item selected so that File Exchange launches automatically when someone sends you a file. Otherwise you might forget to check.
- **ASCII:** If you're sending plain text files with no formatting whatsoever, then choose ASCII.
- **Binary:** If you're sending any other type of file, choose **Binary**.

Receiving files from the other party happens automatically (unless you have **Pop Up When Receive** selected from the **Options** menu, though you won't know you've received a file!). When someone sends you a file, it appears on the **File(s) received** list the next time you launch Conference File Exchange.

To save a file that someone has sent you, do the following:

1. Select an item from the **File(s) received** list.
2. Click the **Save** button.
3. When the **Save** dialog box appears, choose a folder to save the file into and rename it if you want.

Try this yourself—you'll find that File Exchange offers a fast and easy way to transfer files back and forth.

Chatting with Text Messages

Conference Text Chat, as shown in Figure 16-16, harks back to Conference's roots in Internet Relay Chat (IRC), as mentioned in the previous chapter. Ordinarily you would want to conduct your conversations using the microphone and speakers, but there are some circumstances when you may find the text chatting feature quite useful. For instance, suppose you

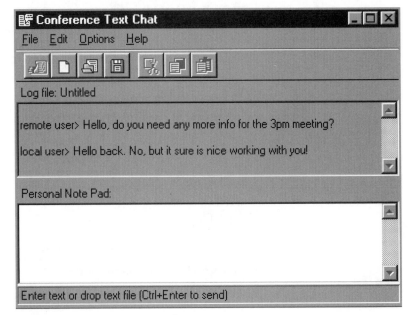

FIGURE *Conference Text Chat window.*
16.16

need to exchange detailed information involving numbers, or passwords, technical material, or complex instructions that can get garbled (even if the voice connection is good)? Typing text and sending it back and forth ensures that you're communicating actively and productively.

To launch Conference Text Chat, click the **Conference Text Chat** button. When you launch it, the other person's Conference Text Chat launches along with yours.

To send a text message, do the following:

1. Type some text in the **Personal Note Pad** area at the bottom of the **Conference Text Chat** window.
2. Click the **Send** button.

You'll see your words posted in the **Log file** area (the gray text area above the Personal Note Pad area). When your partner responds, that person's words also appear in the **Log file** area. You can review the entire conversation by scrolling up and down the **Log file** area, along with captions showing who said what (you're the local user, they're the remote user)

To add a text file to the log file so the other person can view it, do the following:

1. Click the **Include** button.
2. When the **Open** dialog box appears, browse for the text file you want to add.

I don't recommend pasting long text files here, and documents with formatting will not work. Use File Exchange if you need to send more complicated files.

CAUTION

To save a record of your text conversations, do the following:

1. Click the Save button.
2. When the **Save** dialog box appears, browse for a folder and name the log file.

You can also cut, copy, and paste plain text to and from the clipboard with the **Cut, Copy,** and **Paste** buttons.

CHAPTER

17

Building Web Sites with Netscape Composer

"Billions and billions." The late Carl Sagan coined that phrase to express the vastness of the universe and the stars and galaxies in it. Looking around on the Web, you could easily apply the same phrase to the number of Web sites and their individual pages. Some of these many Web pages are works of art, others are plain and simple, and some look downright tasteless. The subjects, design, motivation, and objectives are as varied as the people inhabiting this planet. In fact, I believe there will come a time when personal Web pages are as common as names, and most of the information produced in organizations will be published on the Web or on an organizational Intranets.

But wait! Doesn't designing and maintaining a Web site take at least a little programming knowledge? Well, yes and no. Sure, designing, organizing, and maintaining a complex, high-end Web site takes considerable expertise. But with tools like Composer, pretty much anyone can assemble basic Web pages or update and edit information. Composer provides you and your coworkers with a handy tool for quickly creating new Web pages and making changes to existing ones. It's extremely easy to use—even for complete novices.

Composer doesn't do everything (no single tool does), but it is quite capable of producing a satisfactory Web site. Moreover, anyone familiar with a word processor can easily master the basics of using Composer—such as creating new HTML documents, opening existing pages, entering and formatting text, and adding images. And since Composer makes it easy for an administrative assistant or department head who doesn't know a lot about servers and Web pages to create pages for daily announcements, reports, and such, the application is ideal for use on office Intranets.

Composer belongs to a class of software known as HTML editors. Some HTML editors require that you work directly with HTML documents, while others (such as Composer) use a WYSIWYG environment. WSYIWYG (What You See Is What You Get) means that you can work directly with Web pages and view them as you work, instead of having to write the HTML code and view finished pages separately in Navigator.

Among Composer's features are:

- **WYSIWYG development environment:** You can create pages that look exactly as they will appear in Navigator. This means that you don't have to know HTML in order to create Web pages (I'll explain what HTML is later in this chapter).

- **Built-in upload and download capability:** You can work with Web pages straight from the server, and download and upload Web pages, graphics, and other elements straight from Composer without having to use a separate FTP application.
- **Image import capability:** Composer automatically converts Windows Bitmap (.BMP) images to the JPEG format. Web browsers are only capable of displaying JPEGs and GIFs.
- **Drag and drop capability:** You can add links (URLs), images, and other files by simply clicking on them and dragging them into your pages.

With Composer, as shown in Figure 17-1, anyone from the novice to the professional can create polished Web pages quickly, with a high degree of control over the finished product. If you know HTML, you can also use a separate HTML or text editor to work with the code directly. If you don't know HTML, never fear—with Composer, you don't have to worry about it.

FIGURE *Composer window with a simple Web page that took about a minute to create.*
17.1

This chapter covers the following:

- What is Composer?
- Web site development
- HTML—A Short Course
- Using Composer
- Uploading pages

Composer is a component of Netscape Communicator (both the standard and professional versions). It installs automatically when you install Communicator (although you can use the custom install feature of Setup to leave it out if you like). The application may look slightly different depending on what operating system you use, but Composer's features are basically the same for Windows 95, Windows 3.1x, and Macintosh users. To begin working with Composer, click the **Composer** icon on the component bar, or select **Composer** from the **Communicator** menu. But first, I'd like to give you a little background information.

What Is Composer?

The Composer window, as shown in Figure 17-1, looks like a cross between the Navigator Web browser and a word processing application. It provides you with all the options you need to create, design, save, publish, and print a basic Web page. Because Composer is so well-integrated with Navigator, it also displays pages exactly as they would appear in Navigator. However, if you incorporate live content, such as Java applets and multimedia, you need to preview them in Navigator. Composer displays where the live page elements are placed, but does not load and run them (it would be hard to work with a bunch of Java applets and multimedia singing and dancing across your page!).

The **Composer** window contains the following elements:

- **Title bar:** Displays the name of the current Web page.
- **Menu bar:** Displays menu items.
- **Composition toolbar:** Displays the following toolbar icons for commonly performed tasks for working with Web pages, including:
    - **New:** Creates a new HTML document.
    - **Open:** Displays the **Open** dialog box so you can browse for and open and HTML document.
    - **Save current HTML document:** Displays the **Save** dialog box so you can save and name the current HTML document.

- **Publish:** Displays the **Publish** dialog box so you can enter a Web site or FTP address, your password and user name, and other information Composer needs in order to upload your page to the server.
- **Preview:** Displays your page in Navigator (this is useful if your page contains live content and you want to make sure it works properly before uploading it to the server).
- **Cut:** Deletes selected page element and pastes it to the clipboard.
- **Copy:** Copies selected page element to the clipboard.
- **Paste:** Pastes page element from clipboard into the selected part of the page.
- **Print:** Prints current page.
- **Find:** Displays the **Find** dialog box so you can search for an item of text on your page.
- **Link:** Creates a link for the selected page element.
- **Target:** Creates a target for the selected page element so you can create links within the current HTML document (this is useful for longer documents, so users don't have to keep scrolling around—for example, you could create a table of contents and link each item to the appropriate section of the page).
- **Image:** Displays the **Image Properties** dialog box so you can insert images and designate image properties, such as how text aligns around the image, and places an image at the insertion point (where you place your cursor on the page).
- **Horizontal line:** Inserts a horizontal line at the insertion point. Horizontal lines are useful for dividing pages into sections.
- **Table:** Displays the **Tables** dialog box so you can create a table. Tables are ideal for page design and layout, or for creating column lists.
- **Spelling:** Runs a spell check for the current page so you can avoid errors.
- **Formatting toolbar:** Provides options for adding styles and other formatting attributes to text, including the following:
  - **Paragraph style:** Displays a pulldown list from which you can apply headings, body text, and other paragraph formatting attributes to selected text.
  - **Font:** Displays a pulldown list from which you can apply a font to selected text. Be careful when choosing fonts. Some Web browsers

can't display fonts. Nor can people view your fancy fonts unless they have the same font installed on their systems.

- **Font size:** Displays a pulldown list from which you can apply font sizes to the selected text to make it larger or smaller.
- **Font color:** Displays a dialog box with a color palette so you can apply colors to the selected text.
- **Bold:** Bolds the selected text.
- **Italics:** Italicizes the selected text.
- **Underline:** Underlines the selected text.
- **Remove all styles:** Removes all formatting and style attributes from the current document.
- **Bullet list:** Formats selected text as a bulleted (unordered) list.
- **Numbered list:** Formats selected text as a numbered (ordered) list.
- **Decrease indent:** Moves the indentation for the selected list closer to the left side of the page.
- **Increase indent:** Moves the indentation for the selected list further from the left side of the page.
- **Alignment:** Displays a pulldown list of alignment options so you can align the selected text left, right, or center.
- **Page display:** Displays the current Web page.
- **Status bar:** Displays a description of toolbar icon functions when you pass your mouse over toolbar icons.
- **Close button:** Closes the **Composer** window for the current document.

If this seems a bit confusing at the moment, never fear. Things will become clearer as you continue reading this chapter.

SETTING COMPOSER PREFERENCES

Remember how I talked about setting preferences back in Chapter 5? Here's a little refresher course. This section gives you some more ideas about setting Composer's preferences to make it easier for you to work with pages. Composer Preferences are divided into two categories: Composer and Publishing. The Composer preferences allow you to specify default settings for working with pages on your computer, and the Publishing preferences let you specify how you want Composer to handle pages when you upload them to the server.

You can set your preferences by selecting **Preferences** from the **Edit** menu within any Communicator component. If you're new to Web publishing, you might not be sure yet about what options would work best for you. That's OK. You can always edit your preferences in the future, when you get more acquainted with Web publishing and Composer.

The **Composer Preferences** window, as shown in Figure 17-2, lets you customize the following settings:

- **Set the Author Name associated with your Web documents:** Enter your name here. This information does not display in the Web page itself. But if someone needs to know who authored the page, they can look at the source code (by selecting **Page Source** from the **View** menu) and find your name inside the header tag. If your network administrator has set up a search engine on the server, entering your name here enables your coworkers to locate all pages created by you.

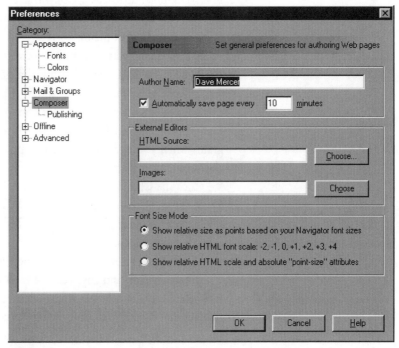

FIGURE *Composer Preferences window, accessible from either Communicator Preferences*
17.2 *or from Composer's menu (Edit, Preferences).*

- **Set the frequency of automatic saves, or disable this feature:** Select the checkbox and enter a number of minutes to enable this feature. The default is to automatically save the current page every ten minutes. With automatic saves, you won't lose your work if your system crashes or you have a power outage.
- **Specify an external HTML source code editor:** Composer's a nifty application, but it doesn't let you work directly with your HTML source code. If you know HTML and enjoy working with a particular Web page design tool, you can tell Composer to launch that editor when you need it. To choose an external HTML source code editor, do the following:
  1. Click the **Choose** button (next to the **HTML Source:** text field)
  2. When the **Choose an External HTML Editor** dialog box appears, browse for the application's executable file.
  3. Select the file and click **Open**.
  4. Click **OK** to return to the **Preferences** window.

  The directory path and application file name is entered in the HTML Source: text field. Once you select an HTML editor, you can use it to edit a page currently open in Composer by selecting **HTML Source** from the **Edit** menu.

- **Specify an Image editor:** If you work with an imaging program that can handle .BMP, .GIF, and .JPEG images—like Adobe Photoshop (http://www.adobe.com/), Corel PhotoPaint (http://www.corel.com/), or Jasc System's Paint Shop Pro (http://www.jasc.com/)—you can tell Composer to automatically launch these programs when you need to edit images that appear on your pages. To choose an external image editor, do the following:
  1. Click the **Choose** button (next to the **Images:** text field).
  2. When the **Choose an External HTML Editor** dialog box appears, browse for the application's executable file.
  3. Select the file and click **Open**.
  4. Click **OK** to return to the Preferences window.

  The directory path and application file name is entered in the Image: text field. Once you select an Image editor, you can use it to edit images that appear on your Web page by double-clicking on an image. When the Image Properties window displays, click the **Edit Image** button.

- **Specify the method used to display font sizes:** There are two ways of specifying font sizes in HTML. The **Font Size Mode** options determine which type of font sizes will appear on the pulldown list of font sizes so you can select from them. You can specify regular font sizes such as 12, 18, or 24 points as you would with a word processing document, or you can specify standard HTML font sizes that display relative to other fonts in the HTML document, such as –2 or +2. When choosing font sizes from the toolbar in Composer, the numbers available to select from can be set here.

To choose your **Font Size Mode** option to determine what font sizes appear in Composer's pulldown font size list, select one of the following radio buttons:

- **Show relative size as points based on your Navigator font sizes:** Enables you to format your text with regular font sizes such as 12, 18, and 24 points. When you use regular font sizes, it gives you greater control over your HTML document's appearance, but only cutting-edge browsers like Netscape Navigator and Microsoft Internet Explorer can display them.

- **Show relative HTML font scale: –2,–1,0,+1,+2,+3,+4:** Enables you to format your text with standard HTML font sizes that are interpreted and displayed correctly by most Web browsers. The actual sizes depend on the type of browser, computer, screen resolution settings, and monitor used by visitors to your page.

- **Show relative HTML scale and absolute "point size" attributes:** Enables you to select either type of font size options. If you publish publicly accessible pages to a server that is connected to the Internet, you should use the relative HTML font scale. If everyone in your organization uses Netscape Communicator, and you only publish your pages to a closed organizational Intranet, you can get fancier with your formatting and use regular font sizes as measured in points.

The **Publishing Preferences** window, as shown in Figure 17-3, lets you enter settings for the following:

Publishing Preferences is a subcategory of Composer Preferences. To display the Publishing option on your Preferences Category: list, click the + sign next to the Composer list item.

- **Set Composer to adjust links automatically:** Select this checkbox to ensure that links on Web pages saved from remote sites will continue to work from your local site. Composer automatically formats all links

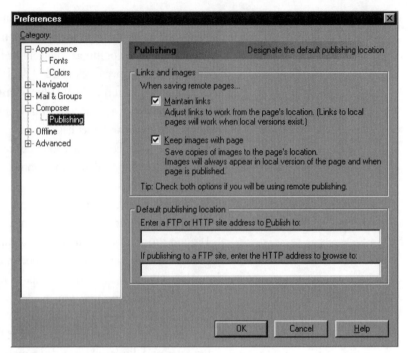

FIGURE *Composer's Publishing Preferences.*
17.3

as *absolute* URLs (such as http://www.yoursite.com/) instead of
making paths relative to directories within a site (such as changing
news/daily/announce.html to http://www.yoursite.com/
news/daily/announce.html). If you're a beginner, you should select this option. If you have more experience working with Web pages,
you can leave this option deselected so that Composer won't change
your links. However, if you leave this option deselected, some links
may not work until you upload the page to the remote directory.

- **Keep images with the pages:** When working with pages on a remote
  server, select this checkbox to tell Composer to save a copy of the images associated with the remote page in your local directory, along
  with the HTML files. Once again, people who have more experience
  with Web pages may want to leave this option deselected. Especially
  if—like many Web site developers—you store your images in a separate directory (if Composer keeps making copies of images every time
  you work with a page, you'll end up wasting a lot of disk and server

space). If you leave this checkbox deselected, then the images will *not* appear on the page when you work with it on your computer, but they should work perfectly fine when you upload it to the server again.

If you've ever run across a Web page full of graphics that you wanted to save for later use, you know what a hassle this is if all you've got is the right mouse button for saving images. Composer can save the entire document at once, and that can save you valuable time even if you're not going to publish the page later.

- **Enter a FTP or HTTP site address to publish to:** Unless your computer also happens to be a Web server (which isn't the case with most of us!), you will generally have to upload your page to a remote server. This means entering either the Web site URL for your page or an FTP site and directory in the Enter a FTP or HTTP site address to publish to.
- **If publishing to a FTP site, enter the HTTP address to browse to:** If you entered an FTP address in the previous text field, you'll need to also enter the HTTP address (your Web site URL).

If you aren't sure of your FTP and HTTP site addresses, get in touch with your network administrator or with your Internet service provider's technical support department.

Web Site Development

Before we start actually using composer to build a Web page, let's take a few minutes to talk about how Web pages work. Ever find a really gorgeous, graphical Web page, loaded with buttons, animation, scrolling text, and all the rest of the gee-whiz stuff, only to discover that you can't find what you're looking for? All the bells and whistles in the world won't help your organization if the site doesn't help users find the information they need or help you and your coworkers work more productively.

Whether you're designing a site for your entire department, generating just a few reports or weekly announcements, or creating pages just for the fun of it, you should think about the following:

- **Objectives:** Exactly what do you hope to accomplish with your site? Is it for entertainment, is it a catalog, or is it meant to inform? Perhaps it's a combination of these. Try to define the purpose (or purposes) in writing, and if possible estimate the number of hits or the feedback you are trying to achieve.

- **Audience:** Who will be using your site, and what characteristics define them? Is your intended audience younger or older, well-to-do, highly educated, mostly male, or mostly female? Are your pages for use outside of your organization—or for a specific department within your organization? Marketing types call these factors demographics, and attempt to equate them to "hot buttons"—images, ideals, and language that particular groups identify with. You don't need to hire a market research firm necessarily, but "speaking the language" (both in writing and visually) of your intended audience is an important part of effective communication.

- **Design:** Think about how you want to lay out your page and how to organize it so users can find information easily. I can remember the days when many Web sites only included a few pages with basic information. Now, many sites consist of thousands of pages and even have special server applications that generate custom pages on the fly depending on information entered by the user via an electronic form. Even if hiring a professional Web designer isn't in your budget for now, you can still take the time to ensure that users can easily locate and read information, and that they don't become lost or confused while navigating your site.

- **Content:** What information do you want to include and how do you expect people to use it? Who will provide the information you want to include, how frequently should you update pages, and who will maintain your pages and make sure that your site functions properly? Broken links, out-of-date information, poor spelling, bad grammar, and poorly written content that neither instructs nor informs are surprisingly common on Web sites. The people who generate information need a clear idea of what is expected from them and need to know how to use Composer in order to get the job done.

- **Feedback:** How will users communicate with you or conduct transactions? Users can send email, fill out forms, make queries to a database, or simply accept cookies (for more about cookies, see Chapter 18). Each of these actions provides information about the user to you, and, in some fashion or another, requires a corresponding action on your part. User feedback is also important in terms of maintaining your site's appeal and usefulness. Make arrangements for someone to respond to email messages, keep your database up-to-date and functioning properly, and don't sell anything online or encourage people to send away for information unless you have some sort of fulfillment system in place.

An excellent Web site doesn't have to be outlandishly expensive to be effective, but careful consideration of the factors involved can save you (and your users) a great deal of time and frustration. Keep in mind that Web pages are interactive—people can click on links and go where they want. Web pages are not a static display of information. If that's all you want, a billboard is probably more effective. Interactive communication is the forte of the medium, and that's a whole different ballgame.

HTML—A Short Course

HTML stands for HyperText Markup Language. The reason it's called a markup language relates to the old word processor style of marking up a text file with special codes (called tags) that provide instructions for displaying or printing text. For example, you can use HTML tags to make text <B>**BOLD**</B>, or <I>*ITALICIZED*</I>, or <FONT SIZE=+4>LARGER</FONT>, or <FONT SIZE=-1> smaller</FONT>. The markup tags also make HTML documents searchable because they also contain information about the document and document elements.

HTML documents can be created with any basic text editor (such as Notepad for Windows or Simple Text for Macintosh) that can save plain text documents with the .HTML or .HTM file name extension. You can either enter HTML tags as you enter the text, or you can compose the text of your document first and add tags later. When you finish, you can save the file and then view it with a Web browser. The browser interprets the tags and displays the text with the special formatting you've called for.

HTML does more than help you format text. It also includes tags for telling images where to display; linking specified text and images to different pages so users can click on them to go to a different location; and embedding live content—such as multimedia and Java applets; and more. And innovative technical folks are constantly figuring out new things that people can do on the Web. You're only limited by the capabilities of your browser. Fortunately, Navigator's always on the cutting edge. Web browsers display and load page elements according to the instructions included in the tags. HTML documents and page elements are stored in directories on a server that is connected either to the Internet or to an Intranet.

A PEEK AT HTML SOURCE CODE

If you take a look at the HTML source code of a Web page by selecting **Page Source** from the **View** menu, you'll see something similar to Figure 17-4. Remember the simple Web page you saw in Figure 17-1 earlier in this chapter? This is what HTML documents are made of. But how can anyone remember all those tags? Well, some people do, but thanks to Composer, you don't have to. Composer does all this HTML coding for you—but understanding how these codes work can make it easier to work with Composer.

HTML tags consist of commands enclosed by angle brackets (or more commonly known as the greater-than and less-than signs). The opening tag contains no slash, while the closing tag contains a slash to indicate the end of the formatting specified by the opening tab. Think of opening and closing tags as bookends that specify commands that apply to all of the text and other elements between. For instance, the <B> tag begins a bold section of text, and the </B> tag ends the section. If you don't use the closing </B> tag, the BOLD section continues until it encounters an ending </B> tag or the file

```
Netscape                                                                    _ □ ✕
<HTML>
<HEAD>
   <META HTTP-EQUIV="Content-Type" CONTENT="text/html; charset=iso-8859-1">
   <META NAME="Author" CONTENT="Dave Mercer">
   <META NAME="GENERATOR" CONTENT="Mozilla/4.0b4 [en] (Win95; I) [Netscape]">
   <TITLE>Fisrt Composer Page</TITLE>
</HEAD>
<BODY>

<CENTER><I><FONT SIZE=+2>Building Web Pages</FONT></I></CENTER>

<CENTER><I>with</I></CENTER>

<CENTER><I><FONT SIZE=+4>Composer</FONT></I></CENTER>

</BODY>
</HTML>
```

FIGURE *The source code for the simple HTML document shown in Figure 17-1.*

17.4

ends. As you can imagine, leaving off the ending tag can quickly mess up your pages. One of the reasons HTML editors are popular is they automatically apply the tags correctly and prevent this type of error. It should also be noted that not all HTML tags require a beginning and ending tag, though most do. For example, image source tags (<IMG SRC="image.gif">) stand alone.

Common HTML tags fall into the categories listed here:

- **Document tags:** The <HTML>...</HTML>, <HEAD>...</HEAD>, and <BODY>...</BODY> tags are what make your Web page a Web page. The <HTML> tag tells the browser to display the document as a Web page and the </HTML> closing tag tells the browser where the document ends. The <HEAD>...</HEAD> tag encloses document information that does not display in the browser but that can be helpful to users searching for information. The <BODY> tag specifies default text and can also contain attributes for displaying a page background, and colored text and links. The </BODY> closing tag specifies the end of an HTML document. When you create a new Web page, Composer enters these tags for you.

- **Title and Meta tags:** The <TITLE>...</TITLE> and <META> tags are also automatically generated with Composer. The text in between the <TITLE> ...</TITLE> tags displays in the title bar for each page. <META> tags (they stand alone and have no closing tags) specify document information, such as the author of the page.

- **Text formatting tags:** You can select text, then choose formatting tags from Composer's **Formatting** toolbar to arrange your text in a pleasing manner. Formatting tags include the commands for centering, bolding, and resizing text. You'll use them extensively in any Web site you create.

- **Form tags:** You can build online, interactive forms and buttons with forms tags. Unfortunately, Composer does not have any options for creating forms so you would have to get a separate HTML editor or enter the codes by hand.

- **Table tags:** These were designed for the display of spreadsheet type data (columns and rows) but quickly became the most extensively used formatting tags available. Tables, particularly without borders, offer unmatched precision and flexibility for the placement of other elements on your page. You can create a table by clicking the **Table** icon on the **Composition** toolbar.

- **List tags:** Formats text as bulleted (unordered) and numbered (ordered) lists. You can format text as indented lists by selecting the text and clicking the **Bullet List** or **Numbered List** on the **Formatting** toolbar.
- **Link tags:** Specifies hypertext links for the selected text or page element so users can click it to go somewhere else. To specify a link, select text or an image and click the **Link** icon on the **Composition** toolbar to display a dialog box where you can enter a URL.
- **Image Tags:** Determines where the browser should display images. To insert an image, click the **Image** icon on the **Composition** toolbar to display a dialog box that lets you browse for the image you want to place and specify properties for the image.
- **Frameset:** A frameset document tells the browser to display documents in separate frames. Frames are very popular on the Web, but unfortunately Composer does not support frames (though naturally, Navigator can display them). But never fear. You can still edit documents on Web sites with frames because each frame contains a stand-alone document. You just won't be able to view them unless you preview the set of documents with Navigator.

Of course, there are hundreds of HTML codes out there. However, these are the ones you'll use the most often—even though you won't *know* you're using them because Composer makes Web pages so easy.

Using Composer

To launch Composer, first start Communicator, and then click the **Composer** icon on the component bar or select **Composer** from the **Communicator** menu. You can open an existing Web page in Composer if you need to make edits, or you can start from scratch. Composer opens to a new blank page by default when you launch it.

To open a new page after closing a page, or while another page is open, do the following:

1. Click the **New Page** icon.
2. When the **Create New Page** dialog box appears, you can choose from the following options:
   - **Blank Page:** Opens a blank page.

- **From Template:** Displays the **New Page From Template** dialog box so you can browse for a template you or a coworker has already created. Or you can click the **Netscape Templates** button to jump to some nifty samples that Netscape lets you download from its Web site. When you're finished, click **OK.**
- **From Page Wizard:** Launches a series of dialog boxes that take you through the steps of creating a basic page, and prompts you to select options. This works similarly to the Setup Wizard explained in Chapter 3.
- **Open Local File:** Displays the **Open** dialog box so you can look for an existing Web page on your computer or on the network. A copy of the selected Web page opens as a new document. When you're finished, click **OK.**

3. When the new page appears, you can begin working.

To open an existing Web page on your computer (that's also called a "local file") and make changes to it, do the following:

1. Click the **Open** button.
2. When the **Open** dialog box appears, select a page and click the **Open** button.
3. When the page appears, you can begin working.

To open an existing Web page on a server, do the following:

1. Select **Open Page** from the **File** menu.
2. When the **Open Page** dialog box appears, select the **Composer** radio button.
3. Enter a URL in the text field and click the **Open** button.

When you open a Web page from a remote site, the page downloads to your computer so you can work with it. You can also open a local file by clicking the **Choose** button and browsing for the Web page when the **Open** dialog box appears.

To save a Web page that you've been working on, do the following::

1. Click the **Save** button on the **Composition** toolbar.
2. When the **Save** dialog box appears, enter a name for your Web page document along with the file name extension (such as "mypage.html") and click **OK.**

Page Title

Enter a title for the current page

Sample Web Page

The page title identifies the page in the window title and in bookmarks.
Page titles can have spaces and special characters in them.

You can change the title in the Page Properties dialog box.

[OK]   [Cancel]

FIGURE *Page Title dialog box.*
17.5

3. When the **Page Title** dialog box appears, as shown in Figure 17-5, enter a title in the text field and click **OK**. The information entered in the text field displays in the title bar when people view it in their browsers.

When saving documents, you can name them anything you want. But you must include the .HTML or .HTM file name extension or else your Web site will not work. In addition, you should be aware of the fact that UNIX servers are case sensitive (it can tell the difference between capital letters and small letters in file names) but Windows NT servers aren't. This means that if your Internet service provider or network administrator runs a UNIX server, `new.html` and `NEW.HTML` are completely different files. On the other hand, on Windows NT, if you had a document called `new.html` on the server and you uploaded a different document called `NEW.HTML`, the first document would be replaced. Being aware of this issue can help you avoid a lot of problems when saving and naming your documents.

Are you creating a Web site from scratch? Remember that you need to name your welcoming page (the page that everyone gets to first when they enter your URL) `index.html`. *The index document tells the browser where the site is located.*

TIP

ENTERING PAGE PROPERTIES

You can set or edit page properties in the **Page Properties** window. Page properties include general document information, such as the page title and the author, and page color schemes. To display the **Page Properties** window, select **Page Colors and Properties** from the **Format** menu.

General Options for Page Title and Meta Tags

To display the **General Page Properties** window, as shown in Figure 17-6, select the **General** tab. You can enter text in the following text fields:

- **Title:** Enter the text that you want to appear in the browser's title bar while the user is viewing it.
- **Author:** Enter your name here (in some cases you might enter the name of the person in charge of your department or project).
- **Description:** You can enter a brief description of the Web page here.
- **Keywords:** Enter a few keywords that people may use to search for the information you have available on your page, and separate each word with a comma.

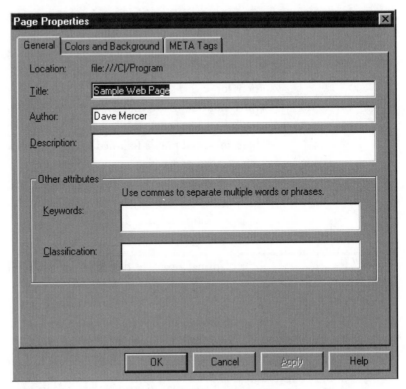

FIGURE *Page properties, general tab, for setting title and Meta tag attributes.*
17.6

- **Classification:** Enter a classification for your page (for example, if your page conforms to a rating system, you should enter that information here).

Composer formats the information entered in the **Author**, **Description**, **Keywords**, and **Classification** text fields into META tags that are included within the <HEAD> opening and closing tags. But what use is a bunch of text that doesn't even get displayed in people's browsers? META tags make it easier for Internet and Intranet search engines to properly classify and rank your Web page, which means that people who want or need what you have to offer will be more likely to find your page. How do Internet search engines find your Web site? Some search the Web randomly in search of new pages and automatically catalog the new information, while others let you submit your URL so they can explore your site. To register with search engines, visit their sites, and fill in the forms they provide (for more about search engines, see Chapter 9).

Colors and Background Options for Page Color Schemes

You've seen Web pages with snazzy-looking backgrounds, text, and link colors, haven't you? Now you can create some fancy pages, too. You display options for setting the background color, text color, and link colors by clicking the **Colors and Backgrounds** tab in the **Page Properties** window, as shown in Figure 17-7. The default is to use either a gray background with black text, blue links, and purple followed links. If you don't have the greatest design sense, don't worry. Netscape was even kind enough to supply a variety of color schemes for easy use. Just click the **Color Schemes** selection box and make your choice from the twelve available (Figure 17-8).

The **Colors and Background** window provides options for customizing the following:

- **Normal Text:** The default color for body text.
- **Link Text:** The color for links.
- **Active Link Text:** The color links turn when the user clicks on them.
- **Followed Link Text:** The color links turn after the user clicks on them and visits the locations they lead to.
- **Background:** The color of the page background

And if you want to use a background image as a texture, use the **Choose File** button in the **Background Image** area of the window to select the file.

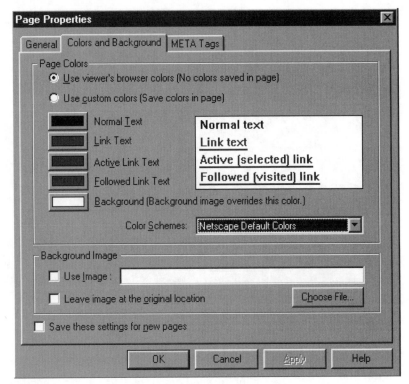

FIGURE   *Page properties, colors, and backgrounds.*
17.7

If you want to make sure it stays at its original location instead of moving to the folder the current page resides in, select the **Leave image at the original location** checkbox. To use the current settings for future pages, select the **Save these settings for new pages** checkbox.

When you click the color box associated with the text item, the color palette displays as shown in Figure 17-8 (left). To pick a custom color, click the color palette's **Other** button to display the **Color** dialog box shown in Figure 17-8 (right). When you finish selecting colors, you can view your new color scheme in the preview area.

TEXT LAYOUT

Let's assume we're going to enter the text content into the body of our page, and then insert the images later. You can type the text in, copy and paste it

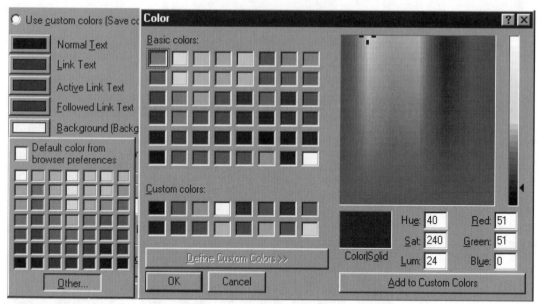

FIGURE   *The color chooser and the custom color builder, accessible from any Color box.*
17.8

in, or drag and drop it in. Chances are, a good portion of the text you need
to enter already exists in some text or word-processing document, so it's better to spend a few minutes locating it, rather than trying to compose and
type it all in from scratch. You can then copy the text from the original document onto the clipboard, paste it into the current HTML document, and
format it. Now, let's take a close up look at the **Formatting** toolbar, as shown
in Figure 17-9 and discuss the available options in greater detail

From left to right, your choices are:

- **Style:** This selection box lets you choose which style to apply to your
  text. For instance, if you'd like a heading of a certain size, choose headings from size 1 to size 6 (one being the largest and 6 being the small-
  est). While headings and text can both be sized using font size,
  headings qualify as a separate style because they are automatically
  boldfaced and, unlike regular text, they include a blank line before and
  after themselves.

- **Font:** You probably have plenty of fonts available on your machine to
  choose from, and they should be included in the list inside this selection box. You'll notice that there are also two settings that begin the

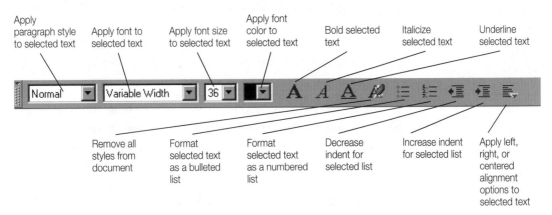

FIGURE *The Composer formatting toolbar, for setting text attributes.*
17.9

list, labeled **Variable Width** and **Fixed Width**. If you choose either of these, your text will be displayed in whatever font *the reader's* browser is set to for these fonts.

- **Font Size:** In Windows, you can set the font size display to be relative to the point size of the default Navigator font, relative to the HTML font scale, or both. The choice you made in **Preferences** will be displayed here. Simply choose another font size here to change font sizes for text you are typing (or have already entered and then selected).

- **Color:** Text color can be set here. When you click this down arrow, you'll see the colors available, and also be given the option to choose more colors or create new ones. You can either set the color for text you have yet to type, or select some text and change its color, in a manner similar to choosing the style and size of the text.

- **Bold, Italics, and Underlined:** Either set these attributes for text you are going to begin typing, or select the text and change these attributes. All it takes is a click of these buttons.

- **Remove Style Settings:** Sets the style back to its defaults for any selected block of text. For instance, if you've set a block of text styled as Heading 1 (font size = 24) to a font size of 36, clicking this button will set it back to a font size of 24.

- **Bulleted and Numbered Lists:** You can create a bulleted or numbered list using these buttons.

- **Decrease/Increase Indent:** You can increase or decrease the indent of a paragraph using these buttons.
- **Alignment:** This button reveals three alignment settings; left, center, and right in that order. Click to set for selected text or text yet to be typed.

Another way to implement these selections is by using the menu to display the **Character Properties** dialog box by selecting **Character Properties** from the **Format** menu, or directly using the other **Format** menu choices (**Font, Size, Style, Color,** etc.). You can also select text and right-click it to display these screens.

If you display **Character Properties** dialog box, as shown in Figure 17-10, you'll see three tabs (**Character, Link,** and **Paragraph**). We'll discuss **Link** in the next section, but for now, notice that you have some additional choices in the dialog box that weren't available from the **Formatting** toolbar. For example, you can select other bullet styles (open circle, open square) using the **List Style** choices on the **Paragraph** tab. And, as shown in Figure 17-11, you

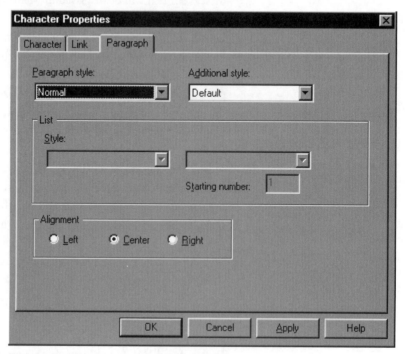

FIGURE *Character Properties, Paragraph tab.*
17.10

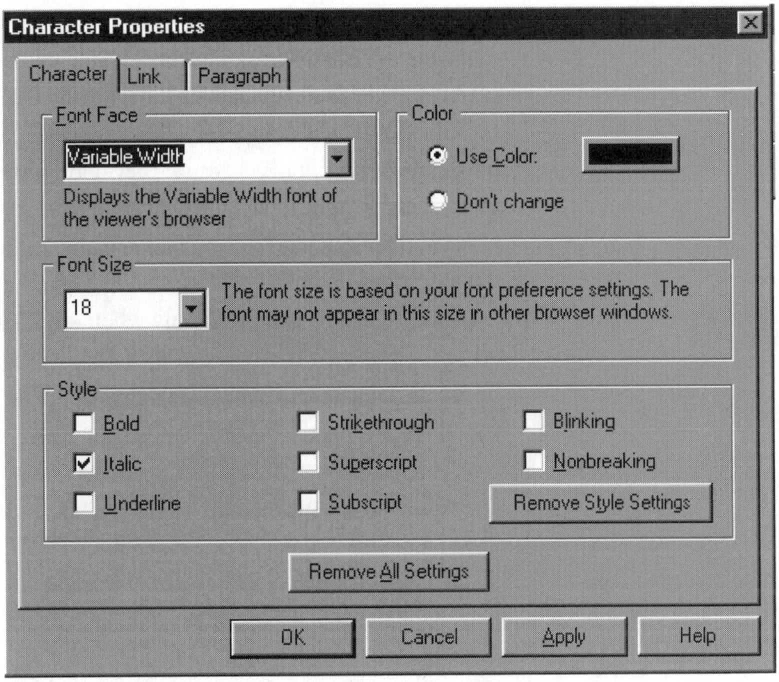

FIGURE *Character Properties, Character tab.*
17.11

can use the **Character** tab to set text to display as strikethrough, superscript, subscript, blinking, or nonbreaking.

CHECKING YOUR SPELLING

Once you have entered your text, Composer will check your spelling. Click **Tools, Check Spelling** and the spell checker will run. Possibly misspelled words will appear in the top text box, and suggestions will appear below that. Click **Replace** to replace them (or all of them) and enter them in your dictionary if you like. If Composer's spell checker finds no misspellings, just click the **Done** button to exit the spell checker.

MAKING LINKS

Also called Hyperlinks, links are hypertext links that take your browser to other locations within the same page (file), to other pages (files) on your hard drive or your Webspace, and to other URL locations anywhere on the Internet/Web. When browsing a Web site, links can be identified by the icon displayed at the cursor (usually a little hand with a pointing finger appears). Linked text generally appears as highlighted in a different color and underlined. Links are popular because they allow the writer to give the reader or user access to additional information easily. Instead of reading in a linear fashion, users can "surf" or browse, usually finding the information they are looking for more quickly (but certainly not always).

Within a link you must specify where the user will "go" (what file or target will be opened in the browser upon clicking the link) and what text or image on the current page will *be* the link. The path to the file or target is contained within the HTML tag for the link and is surrounded by quotes, as in <A HREF="myfile.htm">, and the text or image to be linked is between the beginning tag and the ending tag, as in <A HREF="myfile.htm"> `This is the Link</A>`.

Links can be *relative* or *absolute*, meaning you can specify:

- Just the filename if the target or file is in the same directory (relative).
- Just the filename and directory path relative to the current location (relative).
- The entire URL, such as `http://www.mycomp.com/files/my-file.htm` (absolute).

A *target* is a special kind of tag that can be placed within the same file or another file. It allows you to set a link to go to the same file or another file *and scroll to an exact location within the file*.

To make a link, do the following:

1. Select some text or an image as the link.
2. Click the **Link** icon from the **Composition** toolbar.
3. When the **Character Properties** window appears with the **Link** tab selected, as shown in Figure 17-12 (if you select an image, then the **Image Properties** window appears with the **Link** tab selected), you can do the following:
   - Enter the text you wish to include within the link in the **Enter text to display for a new link:** text field (if you have already selected text, the text displays here).
   - Select a file to make a link by entering a URL in the **Link to a page location or local file:** text field, or click the **Choose File...** button to display the **Choose File** text box.

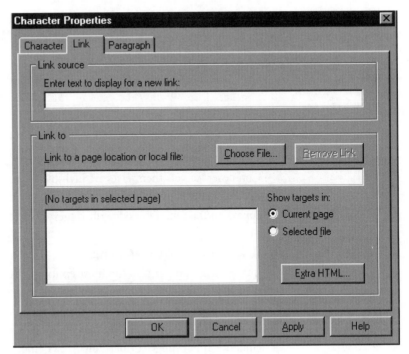

FIGURE *Character Properties, Link tab.*
17.12

- If you're linking to a target in the current page or in the selected file, you can display available targets and select from them by selecting the appropriate radio button. Targets are places that you can link to within an HTML document.

Targets are useful for linking to specific parts of a Web page—either in the current page or in a different page. You can also enter additional HTML code by clicking the Extra HTML button. This isn't usually necessary, but comes in handy when you make links to Java applets.

To create a target, do the following:

1. Open the file you intend to link to.
2. Place the cursor where you want the target to appear, and click the **Target** icon on the **Composition** toolbar, as shown in Figure 17-13.
3. When the **Target Properties** dialog box appears, enter a name for the target in the text field.
4. Click **OK**.

FIGURE   *The Composition toolbar.*
17.13

Composer uses icons to indicate targets, but these icons only display in Composer (targets themselves are invisible to the browser). Then when you make a link to that page, the name of the targets available on that page will appear on the **Link** tab as described previously for you to set your links to.

A LITTLE ABOUT IMAGES

Images make up perhaps the most exciting part of many Web pages, and they serve a variety of functions. Pictures, charts and graphs, icons, backgrounds/textures, symbols, paintings, 3D logos, and various other elements of a Web page can all be inserted as image files. GIF (the CompuServe Graphics Interchange format) and JPEG (the Joint Photographic Experts Group format) are the two formats browsers can display. Composer can also convert .BMP files to .JPEGs.

But where do you find images? Common ways to obtain images are:

- **Using a digital camera or a scanner:** Scanning (using a scanner) and taking pictures with a digital camera are really very similar in terms of image capture, although the technology and techniques required are different. In both cases, your image is captured and digitized, from paper (or something flat) if you use a scanner, and from the real-world if you use a digital camera. When scanning, keep in mind the precautions we mentioned about copyrights.
- **Drawing or painting on your computer:** Creating your own images may be worthwhile, depending upon your level of skill and your needs, but keep in mind that the more sophisticated programs have a fairly steep learning curve, and even then you might need the services of a professional graphic artist.
- **Buying images on CD-ROM:** If you buy images on CD-ROM, make sure they are royalty-free, otherwise you will owe money for every usage.

- **Browsing the Web:** If you get your images from the Web, make sure they are offered free (and the person offering them owns the rights). Otherwise, you may end up on the wrong end of a copyright lawsuit.

However you obtain your images, you need to convert them to GIF or JPG for use on your Web page. These formats are used because they are compressed image formats; uncompressed image formats such as TIFF result in file sizes so large they take forever to download on the Web at 28.8 (the most common modem speed used).

Compression in the case of GIF and JPG means a loss in image quality, but I've never had serious problems using either format. If you're unsure, try them both and fiddle around with the compression settings in your image editing programs to get the best results.

If you use the GIF format, there are several special attributes you can add to your images:

- **Transparency:** Makes the background color of your image files transparent (allows the background color of the page to show through). Since all graphics files are rectangular, this is a nice effect when you have a primary object in the image file that is some other shape.
- **Interlacing:** Your graphics file begins to display before all the image data has arrived, resulting in the appearance of faster downloads.
- **Animation:** Several files are combined into one and played back (displayed in succession) quickly. If the files are similar but some elements have "moved" slightly, the eye is deceived into the appearance of motion.

However, to do this, you need an image editor like Adobe PhotoShop, Corel PhotoPaint, or PaintShop Pro, and a GIF animation program like GIF Construction Set to create the animations.

Inserting Images

To insert an image put the cursor at the location on your page where you want the image to appear and click the Composer toolbar's **Image** icon. When the **Image Properties** window (with the **Image** tab selected) appears, as shown in Figure 17-14, you can add your image and set properties for it. Adding an image is simple. All you have to do is choose a file by either entering a URL and file name or by clicking the **Choose File** button to display the **Choose File** dialog box so you can browse for the image you want.

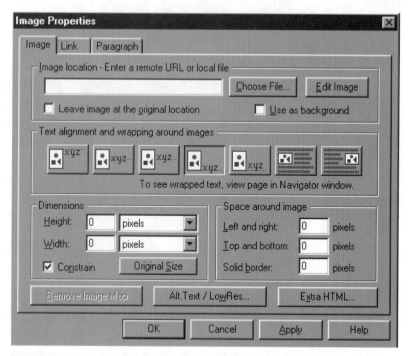

Image properties, Image tab, for setting image attributes prior to insertion.
17.14

But the **Image Properties** window also offers you lots of useful options for working with images, including:

- **Image location:** You can enter a directory path or URL that points to your image, or click the **Choose File** button to display the **Choose File** dialog box so you can find your image and add it to the page.
- **Edit Image:** To edit your image with your favorite graphics application, click the **Edit Image** button (you can tell Composer what you favorite graphics application is by entering it in the Preferences window, as explained earlier in this chapter and in Chapter 5.
- **Leave image at the original location:** You can either copy the file from its present location or leave it where it is. Composer will check or uncheck this box according to your settings in Preferences, but you also have the opportunity to override that choice for the current Web page through this window.

- **Use as background:** You can also elect to use the image as a background image by checking the **Use as Background Image** box in this dialog box.

- **Text alignment and wrapping around images:** You can tell Composer how to align text with the current image by selecting a button. Each button displays a preview of how the text would align with the image if you selected it.

- **Dimensions:** You can also add the height and width values for your graphics in pixels by entering the height in the **Height:** field and the Width in the **Width:** field. This is a good idea because graphics download faster when you specify the height and width. The only problem is that Composer doesn't do it for you, so you would have to view your image in an imaging application by clicking the **Edit Image** button get the pixel measurements, return to the Image Properties window and enter the dimensions manually.

- **Space around image:** You can also specify the amount of space around your image by entering pixel values in the **Left and right:** and **Top and bottom:** text fields. If you wish to display a border around your image, you can enter a number of pixels for the border width in the **Solid Border:** field.

- **Remove Image Map:** Removes image map formatting from the image tag HTML coding, but you may have to edit the HTML source to completely rid your document of any traces of the image map code.

- **Alt. Text/Low Res:** Displays the **Alternate Image Properties** dialog box in which you can enter the following in the appropriate text fields:

  - **Alternative Text:** You can enter text that displays before an image finishes loading, or when a browser cannot display images. This way, although the user can't see the image, he or she can still figure out what the image is supposed to be and how to navigate your site. Considering the number of people who access the Internet with those little personal information managers, specifying alternative text is a very good idea.

  - **Low resolution image file name and path:** When choosing detailed images with large file sizes (which take a lot of time to download), you can also specify a less detailed image with a smaller file size. This low resolution image displays while the larger image is still downloading so the viewer doesn't have to wait for the large image to download before getting an idea of what your layout looks like. When the larger image finishes downloading, it replaces the low resolution image.

- **Extra HTML:** Opens a dialog box for entering additional HTML associated with the image—such as an image map or JavaScript.

CREATING TABLES

Composer has extensive table creation and manipulation capabilities. Tables give the Web page builder extensive control over the layout of elements on the page and are typically used without borders to achieve stunning visual results, both within HTML editors and by manual HTML programmers. To begin building a table, place the cursor where you want the table to appear and click to set the insertion point, then click the **Table** icon from the **Composition** toolbar.

When the **New Table Properties** dialog box appears, as shown in Figure 17-15, you can do the following:

- **Set the number of rows and columns for your new table:** Enter a number of rows in the **Number of rows:** text field, and enter a number of columns in the **Number of Columns:** text field. You can go back and change these settings at any time to add or delete rows or columns.
- **Set the Table Alignment:** You can choose whether to align your table to the left, center, or right of the current page by selecting the appropriate radio button.
- **Caption your table:** Enter text here to create a caption for your table. When you click **OK** to insert the table and return to the current page, the caption appears as an empty text box outlined with a broken line above the table. You can enter the text for your caption directly onto the page in this box.
- **Set border line width:** If you'd like the table border to be visible, select the **Border line width:** checkbox and enter a pixel value in the text field.
- **Set cell spacing:** Cell spacing is the distance from one cell to another. If the border is visible, it appears to grow between the cells as you increase the cell spacing by entering a pixel value in the text field.
- **Set cell padding:** Cell padding is the distance between the contents of a cell and the border around it. An increase here will make the con-

FIGURE *The New Table Properties dialog box, for setting table attributes.*
17.15

tents appear farther and farther from the cell walls as you increase the cellpadding by entering a pixel value in the text field.

- **Set table width and height:** You can constrain the table's width and height by entering a percentage or pixel value.
- **Equalize column widths:** Use this feature if you want equal column widths. Otherwise, columns adjust their width to fit cell contents.
- **Set table background attributes:** You can set colors and background image files for your tables similarly to how you create page colors and background image files (as explained earlier in this chapter).

You can set properties for rows or for individual cells using the same dialog box and the row or cell tabs. Each row or cell can have individualized alignment and color settings, and cells can span several rows or columns. These settings make your table very versatile for placing elements on your page in a visually pleasing way.

Uploading Pages

Whew! Wipe the sweat from your brow, all the hard work's over and you can get some rest now, right? Wrong! Unless you've been working directly on a Web server, you still need to upload your page to the server and check it again to make sure everything works. Fortunately, Composer makes it easy to upload your files.

To upload your files, Click the **Publish** icon on the **Composer** toolbar. When the **Publishing** dialog box appears, as shown in Figure 17-16, enter the following information:

- **The page title and file name:** You shouldn't need to enter any text here—this information displays automatically in the **Publishing** dialog box's **Page Title:** and **HTML Filename:** text fields.

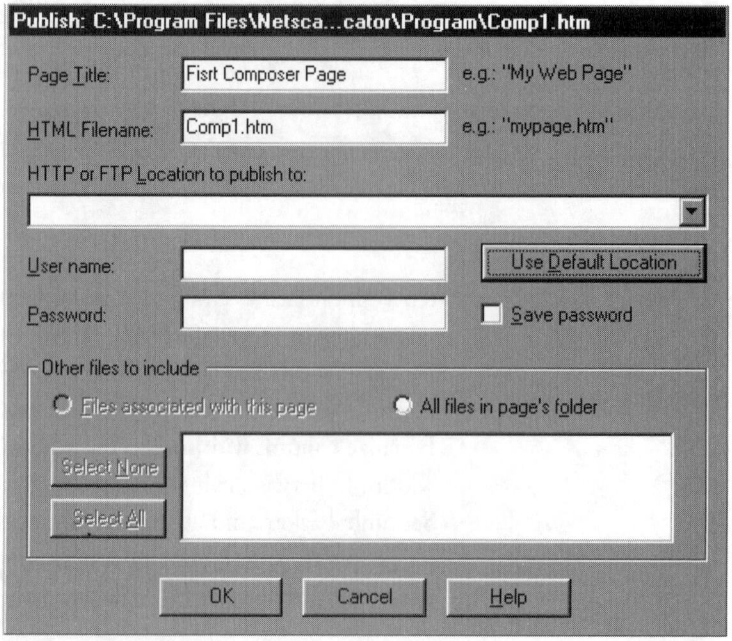

FIGURE *The Publish dialog box, for setting the publishing location and other attributes*
17.16

- **Page location:** Enter a Web page or FTP site URL in the HTTP or FTP **Location to publish to** text field. If you've recently published pages to the same location that you intend to publish to, you can select the location from a list of recent URLs. To display the list of URLs, click the arrow button to the right of the text field. If you created a default location in your preferences (as explained earlier in this chapter) click the **Default Location** button.
- **User name and password:** Enter your user name and password in the appropriate text fields so you can access your server. If you use the same password all the time, as most of us do, you can click the **Save password** checkbox so you don't have to keep entering it.
- **Other files you want to upload:** You can also download other files besides the current Web page. Click the **Files associated with this page:** radio button to include all images and page elements that go with the current page. To include all files residing in the same folder, click the **All files** radio button. The selected files appear in the list area.

When you're finished selecting options, connect to the server by going online (if you haven't already), and click the **OK** button.

For those of you familiar with using FTP to transfer files, you know that you can transfer files in either ASCII or binary format. HTML files, being text files, can be transferred in either format, but image files must use the binary format, so Composer's default FTP format is binary.

TIP

Why FTP?

There's more than one way to upload and download files from a server. FTP programs have been around long before the Web and are still popular. But since the Web is so fabulous and you can download with Navigator and upload with Composer, why would anyone use File Transfer Protocol (FTP) any more?

Well, FTP applications and material stored on FTP servers aren't as pretty or easy to navigate as the Web. FTP servers can't even display text, let alone images. When you view the contents of an FTP server—even with Navigator—only a list of downloadable files appears. But FTP programs let people do things that you can't do with Communicator. FTP servers and client applications let you upload files as well as download them. Sure, Composer does let you upload your Web pages. But what if you need to upload material that is unrelated to your Web page?

Let's say you need to send someone a large file—like an application, presentation, image, or brochure layout. Well, you could find an envelope and stamps and send it via snail mail (oh no, not *that*!). Or you could try sending it as an email attachment—but email doesn't always handle large attached files very well. So how do you send the file? If one of you has a Web or FTP folder, you can upload files to the folder, and the other person can download them. In addition, Composer likes to store Web pages and images in the same folder or directory. What if you prefer to keep your images in a separate directory?

FTP to the rescue! With FTP programs, you can organize your Web site the way *you* want, not the way Communicator wants. FTP applications like Cute FTP (Windows) and Fetch (Macintosh) also provide an easy way for people to exchange and distribute files that are too large for Web pages. As long as both parties have access to an FTP directory, they can exchange large files quickly and easily.

Organizations that frequently exchange files this way generally set up special servers and directories for this purpose. Some FTP servers require passwords and restrict access to authorized individuals, while others let you log on *anonymously* to download and (depending on the server) upload files. Anonymous FTP servers let you log on with "anonymous" as your user name and your email address as your password.

You can find and download CuteFTP (Windows) or Fetch (Macintosh) via Shareware.com's search engine at `http://www.shareware.com/`.

18

Security Features and Doing Business Online

The prospect of conducting business on the Internet has always generated excitement. Yet somehow, merchants and consumers keep dragging their feet. However appealing a worldwide, searchable mall with hypertext links and online forms sounds (to some of us, at least), people feel nervous about submitting their credit card numbers online or sending confidential data via email. Fortunately, Netscape and other businesses have put a high priority on making the Internet a more secure place.

Security technology also has uses beyond turning us into pasty-faced, cybermall rats who never leave the house. Organizations and individuals can now feel more confident about exchanging data and providing a range of complex online services. There is not as much danger of hackers tampering with servers, and there is a measure of protection against downloadable computer viruses and assorted online charlatans.

Finally, there's more to security technology than credit card numbers and confidential data. Many Web sites use Java, JavaScript, multimedia, and other types of live content to make their pages more interactive, useful, responsive, and fun for users. The only problem with live content is that while it loads in Navigator, all kinds of stuff downloads to your computer. In most cases, live content is harmless, yet some people feel distrustful about allowing this kind of access. Netscape's security features also help you protect your computer from potential hazards by warning you when your computer is about to receive data.

This chapter covers the following:

- Security features
- Software security
- Object signing
- Secure data transfers
- Digital certificates
- Cookies
- Doing business online
- Setting security preferences

Security Features

Exchanging data via the Internet can help make life easier, more productive, and more fun. But it also poses risks. To alleviate concerns about transacting business, exchanging confidential data, and downloading software and active Web page content via the Internet, Netscape has built the following security features into Navigator:

- **Secure Sockets Layer (SSL) Protocol:** You can shop online and submit confidential data to a secure server and Navigator will warn you if the server doesn't implement secure protocols. When you send information from a secure server, the information automatically *encrypts* itself until it reaches an authorized destination. Encryption scrambles the data so unauthorized people can't read it during transmission.

- **Secure Multipurpose Internet Mail Extensions (S/MIME) support:** When you submit data via an electronic form on a secure server, messages are automatically encrypted. If you register with a *certificate authority* like VeriSign, you can also send encrypted email messages that can only be decoded by users that you authorize.

- **Certificate Server:** Netscape also has a certificate server available to network administrators who want to issue certificates to users to ensure secure communications. I explain certificates and certificate authorities in more detail later in this chapter.

- **Secure Server Support:** Communicator supports most commonly used network and Internet security technologies.

- **Security status indicators:** Navigator also displays security information in the status bar, warns you when you're about to submit data to a site that doesn't use security technologies, allows you to display security information about a particular Web page, and alerts you to possible security hazards.

- **Software security:** Navigator also alerts you to possible security hazards to your computer when you download data so you can determine whether you want to proceed.

- **Object signing:** Netscape is also working with developers on an *object signing* system that would enable developers to certify their software as safe for downloading. This would help Navigator to determine which software and other downloadable content is safe for downloading.

I'll explain how to set your Security preferences, and we'll talk about how these features work in detail later in this chapter.

Certificate authorities are organizations that can issue certificates for assuring that software and other downloadable Web page content is safe, and for enabling individuals and organizations to communicate privately.

Software Security

Web pages keep getting fancier these days. Some people worry about accidentally transmitting computer viruses to their computers or downloading corrupted active content files that foul up their computer system. Although this rarely happens, it's better to be safe than sorry. You can choose to disable different types of active content like Java and JavaScript through the Advanced Preferences window, as explained in Chapter 5 (to display the Preferences window, select **Preferences** from the **Edit** menu). As I explain later in this chapter, you can also set security preferences by clicking the **Security Status** icon (the little lock) in the left corner of Navigator's status bar. In addition, when you click a link to download a file, or when Navigator encounters unfamiliar active content types, Navigator displays a **Security Information** dialog box, as shown in Figure 18-1.

The **Security Information** dialog box provides the following options:

- **Show this alert next time:** Leave this checkbox selected if you want the **Security Information** dialog box to display every time you click a link to download a file. If you find the dialog box to be more annoying than useful, deselect the checkbox by clicking on it.
- **Continue:** Click to go ahead with your download.
- **Cancel:** Click to cancel your download.

As time goes on, you'll be able to gather certificates from trusted vendors and Web sites to ensure the safety of files before downloading them.

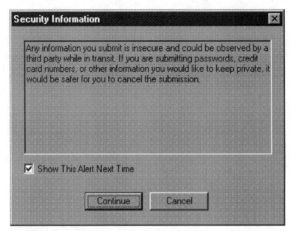

FIGURE *Security Information dialog box.*
18.1

Back up your system frequently! This is the best possible way to ensure your computers security from potential hazards. Even before everyone started using the Internet, bad things happened to people's computers.

Object Signing

Netscape is also working with software companies, Internet site content developers, and certificate authorities to implement an *object signing* system. With object signing, creators of downloadable Internet site content can apply to certification authorities who verify their files as safe for downloading. When you land on a page with active content files or click a link to download a file, a dialog box with a certificate appears. A certificate tells you who published the software, who issued the certificate, and when the software expires. Certificates also offer options for continuing or canceling the download, and telling Navigator not to display this dialog box the next time you download software that has been developed by the same publisher or certified by the same organization.

There's only one problem with object signing and certification: Object signing cannot work unless programmers agree to get their files certified. And unless getting certification is affordable and quick, and there's a compelling reason to do it, why would anyone go through the hassle? At the time of this writing, I couldn't even find any certified downloadable files to show you what a certificate looks like. So until digital certification catches on, we'll have to rely on our own judgment.

Secure Data Transfers

Communicator supports common secure server protocols, including Netscape Communications Corporations Secure Sockets Layer (SSL), which means that if you shop at a Web site with security features implemented on the server, you can safely fill out the online order form and give out your credit card number, or any information you want, without worrying. Secure servers protect your data from unauthorized tampering.

How to Tell if a Site Is Secure

If a Web page asks you to sign a little guest book form and have a nice day, then it probably doesn't matter whether a Web site is secure. But if you plan on making a credit card purchase or sending confidential data, then you should double check. Fortunately, Navigator makes it easy for you.

TIP

In general, entire Web sites aren't secure, only the specific pages that request confidential data. If you jump to an online store's welcoming page and see an open lock in the status bar, don't worry. If the page on the online order form that requests your credit card number isn't secure, then you can start worrying. It should also be noted that some online merchants take your order information on an insecure page, and then send you to a secure site that takes your credit card information and processes it.

There are three ways to tell whether you can safely transfer your data:

- **Look at Navigator's security indicator:** A quick glance on the left-corner **Navigator** status bar (at the bottom of the Navigator window) tells you whether the site is secure. A closed lock icon indicates a secure site. An open lock icon indicates an insecure site.
- **Display Netscape Security Information:** Click the lock in the lower left-hand corner of the status bar to display the Security Information window, as shown in Figure 18-2. Or you can select **Security Info**

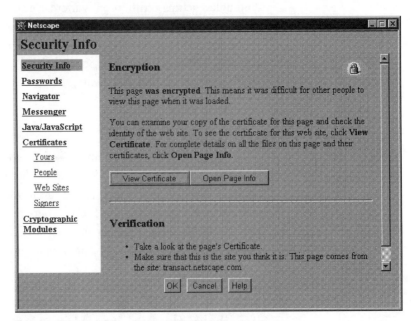

FIGURE *Security information about Netscape's General Store page.*

18.2

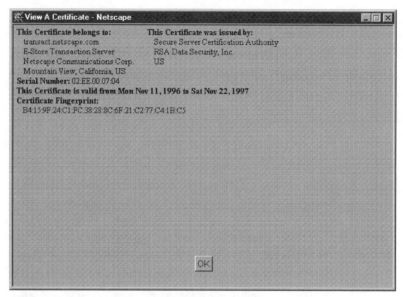

FIGURE *Netscape's General Store page security certificate.*
18.3

from the **Communicator** menu or use the CTRL+Shift+I (Windows) or CMD+Shift+I (Macintosh) key combination. For more details, click the **Open Page Info** button. To display the certificate, as shown in Figure 18-3, click **View Certificate**. To proceed, click **OK**. To cancel, click **Cancel**.

- **Security Information dialog box:** If you forget to check, never fear. If you submit data to an insecure site, navigator displays the **Security Information** dialog box and warns you, so you can choose whether to proceed.

You can also view detailed information about any Web page by selecting **Page Info** from the **View** menu or using the CTRL+I (Windows) or CMD+I (Macintosh) key combination.

Digital Certificates

Tomorrow's cybermalls might not accept credit cards. Instead, we will pay for purchases with personal *digital certificates*. With digital certificates, you get a unique identification number from a certification authority like VeriSign (http://www.verisign.com/). This number is linked to your credit card number, but only you and the certification authority have access to both the digital certificate *and* your credit card information. The certificate gets stored in your computer to verify that you are who you say you are. In the future, personal certificates may also be linked directly to your bank account, so those of you who don't have credit cards can pay with digital money.

Meanwhile, online businesses also need certification in order to assure that visitors know that their site is secure and that they're authorized to take online orders. This way, when you transact business on a Web site, both parties can trust each other.

You can get a personal certificate from VeriSign's Web site at `http://www.verisign.com/`. There are several levels of security, but the $6.00 per year Level One option should be adequate for most of us. In addition, network administrators who use the Netscape Certificate Server can also issue certificates to assure levels of access and private communications to authorized users. Certificates also enable you to send encrypted messages to people who have the same certificate as you. By ensuring that both the merchant and the customer are trustworthy and qualified to follow through on their transactions, certification authorities like VeriSign facilitate commerce on the Web. VeriSign is an offshoot of RSA Data Security, an innovator in security technology.

HOW DO CERTIFICATES WORK?

The client authorization process takes secure server technology one step further. It uses encryption as a sort of secret code. With encryption, your digital ID gets scrambled when you send it, and can only be *un*scrambled by authorized parties who have the key code. This helps deter potential hackers and cyberthieves from intercepting your private information. Your digital certificates, which verify your identity, are stored in your computer (you can view them in the Security Information window), along with certificates for people, organizations, and Web sites that you communicate with or visit regularly.

Encryption technology has been around for a long time, and most security schemes are based on it. With *public key* encryption, users have a *public* key and a *private* key. Individuals and organizations would post their public key on the Web server so visitors can send information confidentially. If you visit an online merchant with a secure Web site, you would use its public key to place an encrypted order with your digital ID number.

The merchant would use its private key to decrypt your order and process it . . . but *wait*! The merchant still doesn't have your money *or* your credit card number. He or she only has your personal certificate, which ensures them that you *can* pay. Now, the merchant must get clearance from the authority that issued your digital ID. When the certifying authority verifies the legitimacy of both parties, the sale goes through.

About Encryption

Phil Zimmerman wrote a freeware encryption program called Pretty Good Privacy (PGP), so people can send private messages and store confidential data. PGP doesn't involve certification authorities. You or anyone can use it (if you can figure out how) by giving your public key to people you wish to exchange files with.

PGP-encrypted code is virtually impossible to break. In fact it works too well. The U.S. government viewed PGP's ability to encrypt coded messages as a threat to national security, classified PGP as dangerous munitions, and pressed charges against Zimmerman. Instead, the government prefers Clipper Chip encryption, because, if necessary, its agents could decode messages.

Fortunately, the government dropped its charges against Zimmerman. But the debate over individuals right to privacy vs. the problems PGP poses for law enforcement rages on. Why would anyone need to encrypt messages unless he or she is a drug dealer, international spy, or some other kind of criminal? Plenty of legitimate reasons exist for privacy, including the storage of confidential tax, legal, medical, and psychiatric records. Or perhaps the correspondence of high-profile politicians conducting their illicit (but perfectly legal) affairs.

If you want more information about PGP, Zimmerman, or electronic privacy issues, go to Yahoo's Pretty Good Privacy page at `http://www.yahoo.com/Computers_and_Internet/Security_and_Encryption/`, then click on the Pretty Good Privacy link.

Cookies

Cookies is an innocuous-sounding name for something that many people find quite sinister. When you visit pages on a Web site or fill out forms, you leave a trail of data crumbs behind you. Web servers that are able to generate cookies use these crumbs to figure out your surfing habits and preferences while you're visiting their pages. The server then generates a little data file called a cookie and stores it on your computer to help it remember you. The next time you land on that site, a custom-tailored Web page with links to your favorite parts of the site appears. Before you get alarmed, I should mention that these servers can only gather information generated *while you're visiting that particular Web site*. They can't follow you around the Internet.

ACCEPTING OR DECLINING COOKIES

On the one hand, cookies are interesting because they enable Web sites that you frequently visit or transact business with to respond to your needs. For example, if the server notices that you always go to a particular document, it may jump you to that particular document first, so you don't have to click on a lot of links to get there. Some Internet service providers and other companies like Earthlink (http://www.earthlink.net/) and others even invite you to fill out forms so you can generate custom home pages with links to your favorite topics.

On the other hand, some people see cookies as an invasion of their privacy. When we give our information to servers intentionally or unintentionally, the information can be used to target advertising toward us. Personally, I find that the benefits of customized pages outweigh the annoyance of scrolling past a Webvertisement targeted towards whatever sort of consumer the server thinks I am. Occasionally, the ad even interests me enough to make me click on the link. It would be great if everyone created and surfed Web pages just for fun and nobody cared about money or advertising. Unfortunately, that planet has not been discovered yet.

If you don't like the idea of cookies, you can tell Navigator to warn you before accepting them, or not to accept them at all, in the **Advanced Preferences** window, as shown in Figure 18-4. To display the **Advanced Preferences** window, select **Preferences** from the **Edit** menu, then select **Advanced** from the list when the **Preferences** window appears. For more about Communicators preferences, see Chapter 5.

NOTE

You may find that many of the Netcaster and Marimba channels (as discussed in Chapter 6) use cookies to determine what kind of information you want delivered to your desktop.

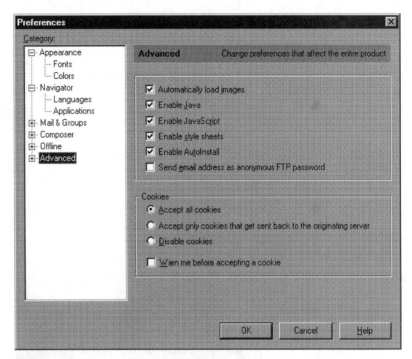

FIGURE *You can tell Navigator how to handle cookies in the Advanced Preferences*
18.4 *window.*

Doing Business Online

The Web may seem like lots of fun, but it can also help you get things done. You can do some shopping, plan business trips and vacations, track the status of orders and shipments, get tech support for software products, do research, and more straight from the Web. Powerful server capabilities, flexible programming tools like Java and JavaScript, and security technologies help companies, schools, and other organizations provide complex and highly sophisticated services over the Internet and via networks. For example, extensive inventory and customer databases can now be securely maintained, accessed, and automatically updated online.

PURCHASE PRODUCTS AND SERVICES ONLINE

Is it really safe to shop on the Web? Few technologies work perfectly, but secure servers and Navigator still offer a reasonable guarantee that your confidential information will *stay* confidential. To a certain degree, it's a matter of trust and what you feel comfortable with. If you make credit card purchases over the telephone, as many people do, then you can feel pretty good about ordering products over the Internet.

If you're too busy for shopping (or prefer to spend your time doing something else), you can quickly find what you want and order it online. Office-Max Online (http://www.officemax.com) and Staples Virtual Office Superstore (http://www.staples.com) boast huge selections of office and computer supplies. If you're looking for just the right thing Excite's Shopping Reviews page (http://www.excite.com/Reviews/Shopping/) discusses everything from gardening to kids. The Big Book (http://www.bigbook.com/) provides an online database for locating online shopping malls, companies, and products. Before you buy online, it wouldn't hurt to know your rights as a consumer. The Consumer Information Center site, as shown in Figure 18-5, gives you the lowdown and points you towards resources.

FIGURE
18.0
You can get lots of free information for consumers and small businesses, learn about your rights as a consumer, and get advice from the Consumer Information Center site at http://www.pueblo.gsa.gov.

MAKE PLANS AND FIND OUT WHAT'S GOING ON

The Web also helps you see what's going on and make plans. Whether you're taking a vacation or traveling for business, chances are that the airline you wish to book a flight on, the hotel you want to stay in, and the city you're visiting all have Web pages. The International Travel Network (`http://www.itn.net`) lets you register for a free membership; view available flights, accommodations, and car rentals; search for the best prices; and make reservations on the spot.

The Web can also help you keep track of what's going on in your community. You can find out what's going on at your children's schools, search for continuing education opportunities, find out how you or your company can contribute to the community, stay up to date on issues that affect you and your business, and more. For example, San Francisco County's official Web site, CitySpan (`http://www.ci.sf.ca.us/`), as shown in Figure 18-6, links you to a wide variety of community and government resources.

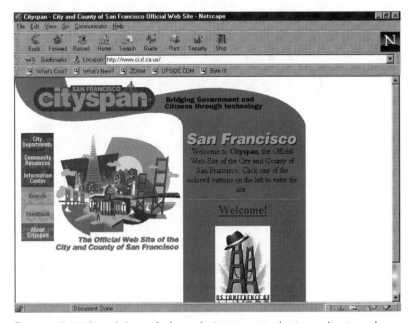

FIGURE **18.6** *The Web can help you find out what's going on in the city you live in or plan to visit.*

TRACK SHIPMENTS

If you frequently send and receive packages, you can use the Web to check up on your shipments. Federal Express (`http://www.fedex.com/`), United Parcel Service (`http://www.ups.com/`), and Airborne Express (`http://www.airborne-express.com/`) all provide special software so you can check up on the status of packages that you've either sent or that you expect to arrive.

GET TECH SUPPORT AND CUSTOMER SERVICE

Are you having trouble with your software or hardware? Before you reach for the phone and prepare to stay on hold forever, check the company's Web site (if you don't know the URL, you can use a search engine to look it up). Most companies publish frequently asked questions and answers (FAQs), instructions, and troubleshooting guides. In addition, they often post downloadable software upgrades, utilities, and other goodies. And guess what? Online customer service isn't just for high tech companies any more. Even the conservative company, L.L. Bean has a Web site now (`http://www.llbean.com/`)!

Setting Security Preferences

If you wind up using certificates a lot, frequently access the Internet and communicate through a secure server, want to send encrypted messages, or are concerned with security in general, you can set security preferences through the **Security Information** window. To display the **Security Information** window, click the **Security Indicator** icon that looks like an open or closed lock in the left corner of Navigator's status bar, or select **Security Info** from the **Communicator** menu. When the **Security Information** window displays (as shown in Figure 18-2 earlier in this chapter) you can view and edit settings by selecting items from the list.

The **Security Information** window provides the following options:

- **Security Info:** Displays security information about the current Web page, as explained earlier in this chapter.
- **Passwords:** If you share your computer with other people or others can access data on your computer via your office network, you can create a password so people can't access your private messages and certificates. To display the **Passwords Security Information** window, as shown in Figure 18-7, select **Passwords** from the list. To create a password for

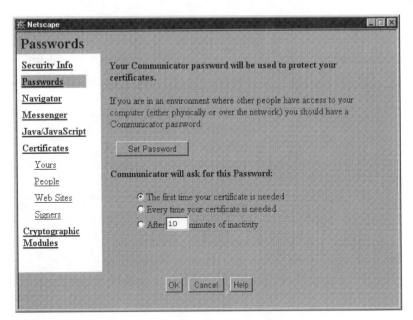

FIGURE   *Passwords Security Information window.*
18.7

yourself, click the **Set Password** button. To specify when Communicator should prompt you for your password, select the radio button you want following the **Communicator will ask for this Password:** prompt.

- **Navigator:** You can specify security settings for Navigator in the **Navigator Security Information** window, as shown in Figure 18-8. To display the Navigator Security Information window, select **Navigator** from the list. Here you can tell Navigator to display warnings when dealing with encrypted pages by selecting or deselecting the appropriate checkboxes from the **Show a warning before:** list, and specify when Navigator should identify you to Web sites requesting certificates. In addition, you can choose advanced Security (SSL) configurations by selecting the Enable SSL (Secure Sockets Layer) v2 or Enable SSL (Secure Sockets Layer) v3 and clicking the corresponding **Configure** button (in general you wouldn't have to do this—your network administrator would enter these settings for you).

- **Messenger:** You can control security settings for your email messages in the **Messenger Security Information** window, as shown in Figure 18-9. To display the **Messenger Security Information** window,

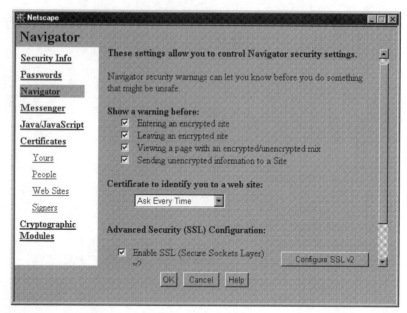

FIGURE *Navigator Security Information window.*
18.8

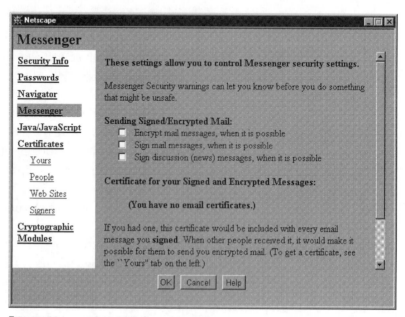

FIGURE *Messenger Security Information window.*
18.9

select **Messenger** from the list. From here, you can tell Messenger when to encrypt and sign outgoing email messages and discussion group messages by selecting the appropriate check box. *Signing* messages means including your email certificate so your recipients can reply to you with encrypted messages in turn. If you don't have an email certificate, the **Yours Security Information** window tells you how to get one.

• **Java/JavaScript:** When more software and Web page content developers start using object signing certificates, you can grant or refuse access to Java applets and JavaScript scripts through the options in the Java/JavaScript Security Information window, as shown in Figure 18-10. To display the Java/JavaScript Security Information window, select Java/JavaScript from the list. When you decide to trust Java applets and JavaScript scripts from a particular vendor, you can add that certificate to the scrolling list. To view a certificate, click the **View Certificate** button. To delete a certificate, click the **Remove** button. To edit the access privileges granted to a certificate, click the **Edit Privileges** button.

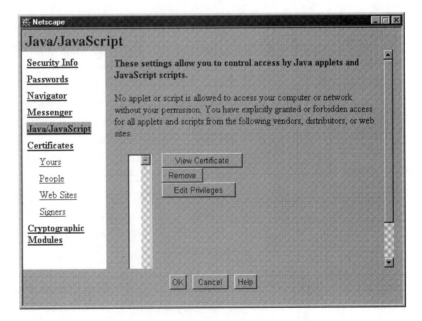

FIGURE *Java/JavaScript Security Information window.*
18.10

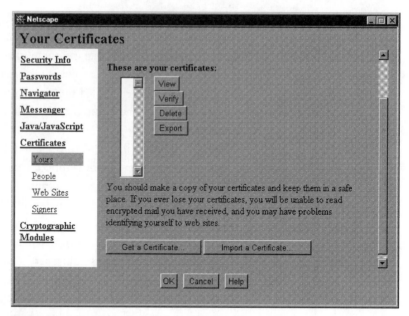

FIGURE *Your Certificates Security Information window.*
18.11

- **Certificates:** The **Certificates Security Information** window explains how you can obtain and use digital certificates. To display the **Certificates Security Information** window, select **Certificates** from the list.
- **Yours:** **Yours** is a subcategory of the **Certificates** section. You can obtain view, verify, delete, export, and import certificates through the options in the **Yours Security Information** window, as shown in Figure 18-11. To display the **Yours Security Information** window, select **Yours** from the list. To obtain a certificate, click the **Get a Certificate** button and follow the instructions that appear. As you gather certificates, they appear as items in the scrolling list. The buttons that appear alongside the scrolling list offer options for viewing, verifying, and deleting selected items. You can also export certificates by clicking the **Export** button.

Exporting your certificates as a backup copy is a good idea. You should always have an extra copy of them in case you lose them for some reason. You can then use the Import a Certificate button to reinstall them.

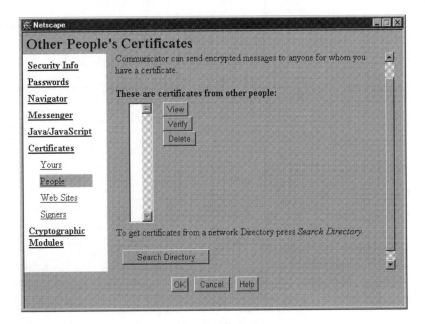

FIGURE   *Other People's Certificates Security Information window.*
18.12

- **People:** You can also store other people's certificates in the **People** (Certificates) **Security Information** window, as shown in Figure 18-12, so you can send encrypted messages to them. To display the **People Security Information** window, select **People** from the list. Other people's certificates appear as items on the pulldown list. You can also view, verify and delete certificates by selecting the appropriate buttons. If your office uses Netscape's Certificate server, you can also get certificates from other people on a network who authorize you to have access to them by clicking the **Search Directory** button.
- **Signers:** The scrolling list in the **Certificate Signers Certificates Security Information** window, as shown in Figure 18-13, displays a list of certification authorities. To display the **Certificate Signers Security Information** window, select **Signers** from the list. You can choose whether to accept signers and what degree of access to give them by selecting an item from the list and selecting the **Edit**, **Verify**, or **Delete** button.

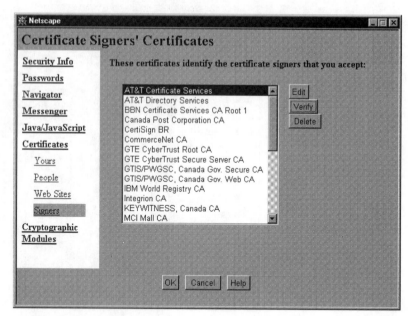

FIGURE *Certification authorities.*
18.13

- **Cryptographic Modules:** Communicator comes with its own encryption technology. To edit or add other cryptographic modules (methods for encrypting), choose options from this window. To display the **Cryptographic Modules Security Information** window, select **Cryptographic Modules** from the list.

When you're done with these changes, click the **OK** button.

19 Administering Your Network

If, you work in a corporate environment, chances are there's talk about setting up an *Intranet*. As Chapter 1 explains, Intranets work just like the Internet, only they're closed networks for in-house use. Often, people who
are connected to an Intranet are also connected to the Internet. And why not?
Web pages, email, newsgroups, and the Internet's other features make communicating, exchanging data, looking up information, and other things you
have to do at work easy, efficient, and (dare we say it?) even *fun*. Plus, it saves
lots of paper. Since Internet technologies are already designed so that people
with different operating systems can share, distribute, publish, and access
data across networks, they can easily be used for groupware purposes as well.

And chances are that you and your coworkers will use Netscape server
products to set up your company Intranet. Netscape servers work hand in
glove with Communicator's various clients. After all, Netscape didn't develop Communicator in a vacuum. The strategy all along was to build both
sides of the equation. With Netscape's server products, you can do all kinds
of things, like set up and distribute customized versions of Communicator
that point users toward company-related resources and jump users to the
company home page, instead of Netscape's, as shown in Figure 19-1; automate Web page updates based on data inputted by your coworkers; create
special newsgroups for coworkers or customers (when you create an in-house
newsgroup, it's called a *discussion group*); and more.

This chapter covers Netscape's various server products and talks about
how you can use the tools that come with Windows NT and Netscape's
SuiteSpot and Communicator to administer and manage your Intranet. If
your company currently uses a UNIX system, these tools are also available
for various versions of UNIX.

This Chapter covers the following:

- Netscape SuiteSpot server products
- Windows NT tools for managing servers
- The Netscape Administration Kit (NAK)
- Setting global Communicator preferences with the Configuration
  Editor
- Using the Install Builder

Every network is different and telling you everything you need to know
would require writing another book. However, this chapter can get you
started in creating an integrated Netscape server that has all of the capabilities you need.

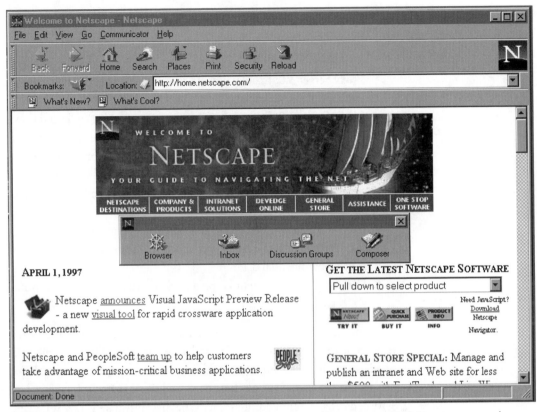

FIGURE   *When users launch Navigator, it automatically jumps users to Netscape's page. With Netscape server tools, you*
19.1   *can distribute customized versions of Communicator that guide users to work-related resources instead.*

Netscape SuiteSpot Server Products

Netscape's solution for server-side components is called SuiteSpot. It's actually a collection of server products that Netscape has either bought or constructed. These server products make the most of open, Internet-based technologies so that even coworkers and customers who use non-Communicator Internet clients (for example, many people use Microsoft's Internet Explorer for Web browsing and Qualcomm's Eudora to send and receive email) can access resources. In addition, Netscape's SuiteSpot tools help you develop well-integrated services both in-house and on the Internet at large and help you make the most of Communicator's capabilities. You don't necessarily have to buy all of the servers to use the components of Netscape Communicator, but you must have servers available for any components you wish to use.

In a nutshell, the SuiteSpot servers are:

- **Enterprise Server 3.0:** For setting up and managing a Web server.
- **Messaging Server 3.0:** For setting up a secure email messaging system.
- **Proxy Server 3.0:** Enables users to access the Internet through your organization's firewall.
- **Media Server 1.0:** For broadcasting real-time streaming audio and video.
- **Calendar Server 1.0:** For group scheduling and project management.
- **Collabra Server 3.0:** For setting up in-house discussion group forums.
- **Catalog Server 1.0:** For automatically indexing and cataloging Web pages, discussion group postings, and other data uploaded to the server so users can find information quickly.
- **Certificate Server 1.0:** For issuing certificates and passwords to users for different levels of access to confidential information, or for submitting confidential data.
- **Directory Server 1.0:** For keeping track of shared resources, like printers, servers, and applications.

In addition to the SuiteSpot servers, Netscape has also released some development tools, named LiveWire and LiveWire Pro. These visually oriented products allow Intranet developers to create and maintain large, complex Web sites and to link those pages and sites to Oracle, Informix, and Sybase databases. In addition, Netscape has integrated LiveWire and LiveWire Pro with JavaScript, a lightweight scripting language that enables non-programmers to add powerful capabilities to their Web sites. With JavaScript, you can create sophisticated forms that let users generate pages on the fly that display the content they're looking for, add exciting new page design elements, and more.

TIP

If you're interested in working with JavaScript but don't know any programming, try out Netscape's Visual JavaScript. At the time of this writing, Visual JavaScript was still in the early stages of development. But it promises to make creating JavaScript pages that integrate with Netscape server tools or existing CGI scripts and Java Applets almost as easy as Web browsing. For more information and a trial download, visit Netscape's home page at http://home.netscape.com/. *Also try the JavaScript CD Cookbook included on the companion CD*

Once you install the servers you choose, you'll be managing your Intranet and servers using the tools that come with the servers and also Windows NT. Essentially, you'll want to monitor your network performance, control access, maintain security, and perform routine maintenance. Netscape SuiteSpot includes an Administration Kit as well, and it can greatly ease the burden of administration.

WHERE TO GET SUITESPOT

SuiteSpot server tools don't come with Communicator—you need to purchase them separately. You can find out more about SuiteSpot server products (along with trial and beta versions) on the Netscape Web Site at `http://home.netscape.com/`. You can get information and even trial copies of some of them, as well as order them online. The server products run on Windows NT and UNIX. For the purpose of this book we'll look at Windows NT products, and use Communicator to demonstrate how the Communicator products look and feel when interacting with the servers. Since Communicator runs on just about every operating system you can think of, it doesn't matter what kind of computer your users have. They'll all have equal access to your network services.

SUITESPOT SERVERS
Enterprise Server 3.0

The primary function of Enterprise Server 3.0 is to provide Web services to your users, meaning it runs as a Web server for your Intranet or Internet applications. It includes support for HyperText Transfer Protocol (HTTP) for publishing and serving Web documents; the ability to use CGI scripts, server extensions, Java, and JavaScript to create dynamic Web pages; LDAP (Lightweight Directory Access Protocol) so users can look up their coworkers' email addresses and other important information through Messenger's Address window; and other integrated text search functions. Installation consists of simply loading the setup files and clicking. Obviously, there's more to it than that, but we can talk about installation in depth a little further on, during our discussion of Calendar and Collabra in the next two chapters.

Unsurprisingly, there are several features found in the Enterprise Server you can use to create, modify, publish, and maintain Web sites. For instance:

- **Workgroup Publishing:** People throughout the company can publish information and collaborate on Web sites.
- **WebSite Access Control:** Administrators can set access levels for users.

- **One-Button Publishing:** Authorized users can edit and update pages straight from the server with Composer.
- **LiveWire:** Powerful server-based features and integration with JavaScript and databases are enabled for online ordering, search engines, dynamic Web pages, and more.

Messaging Server 3.0

Essentially, Messaging Server 3.0 is Netscape's mail server, meaning it supports the Standard Mail Transport Protocol (SMTP) email capabilities any organization requires. Typical functions include sending and receiving of email, remote processing of email, and delivery status notifications. If you already have a Local Area Network (LAN)-based, proprietary email system in place, you'll need to migrate to Netscape's Messaging Server. But the advantages can make the trip worthwhile. For starters, you won't be tied to a proprietary (read expensive) email system. You can integrate the Messaging server with any SMTP, MIME, and IMAP4 client, because these are open, Internet standards that are not owned by Netscape. The Messaging Server also supports Lightweight Directory Access Protocol (LDAP) and Secure Sockets Layers (SSL) 3.0. LDAP means you can set up the network so users can find network resources easily (for example, directories like `http://www.four11.com/`, that let you search for people's email addresses so you can email or call them for a teleconference). SSL enables secure, private communications for exchanging and accessing confidential data, online ordering, and more.

Proxy Server 3.0

Originally, the term firewall meant a physical wall separating a dangerous area from a relatively safe area, as in the engine compartment of a car from the occupant area. Today, if you hear someone talking about a firewall, chances are they are discussing the software used to protect a company's internal network from the wild and untamed Internet. This way, only authorized users can access critical data on your company's network. A proxy server allows users inside your firewall to make a request for information that resides out on the Internet. It then fulfills the request, either from the WebSite on the Internet or from the documents it has *replicated* internally, by proxy.

Media Server 1.0

Media Server allows you to publish and broadcast high-quality stereo audio (and soon video, too!) over the Internet at speeds as low as 28.8 Kbps. How can this be possible? Well, it's already happening. Take Progressive Networks RealAudio (`http://www.realaudio.com/`), for example. Progressive Networks puts out a server product designed to "stream" audio (and video) over the Internet and offers a free plug-in so we can listen to it (for more on plug-ins, see Chapter 7).

"What's streaming?" you ask. Well, back in the old days of the Web, downloading and playing audio or video files required two separate operations. The Webmaster would create a link to an audio file in HTML documents. If you clicked on that link, your browser (depending upon how it was configured) would either download the file and launch your audio player, or ask if you'd like to save the file to your computer. This meant that the entire file had to be downloaded prior to playback. Back in the days of mostly 14.4 bps modems, that could really put a damper on your enjoyment of the sounds.

Of course, bright software designers immediately began working on a solution: streaming audio. Companies like VDONet (`http://www.vdonet.com`) have also made breakthroughs with streaming video. Streaming multimedia means that the files (which are *enormous*) get compressed, served up from the Web site with a server specifically designed for that purpose, and then played back *while downloading* with a plug-in player. No waiting for the file to completely download and the player to launch; it all happens in real time. Live audio and video streaming makes live broadcasts possible on the Web.

Of course, with Media Server content and Navigator, users don't even have to download and install a plug-in, since Communicator has Media Server capabilities built in.

The entire set of tools includes:

- Media Server: For serving up the content.
- Media Player: For receiving and playing the content.
- Media Converter: For encoding (compressing) multimedia files for the Web.

Calendar Server 1.0

Another important component of Netscape Communicator is the Calendar client, which, of course, would be pretty useless without a corresponding

Calendar server. The Calendar client alone allows you to do some impressive scheduling functions for yourself, such as keeping track of meetings, holidays, and to do lists. But no one lives in a vacuum, and as painfully boring as they can be, meetings are frequently vital to efficient communications in larger organizations.

But getting people together across the company (especially when the company is spread across the country), even just for a conference call, is extremely difficult at times. What with downsizing, rightsizing, and plain old slash-and-burn-until-the-cash-flows, no one has much "spare time" to waste.

Enter Netscape's Calendar Server 2.0. You can set it up to help users manage their time across an organization. The Calendar Server keeps track of everyone's entries in the Calendar client so users can more easily schedule meetings and use of office resources within the company. You can even set the server up so that project managers and department heads can make entries on their coworkers' calendars. This is much easier than passing around a printed memo that might get thrown in the trash. The Calendar Server also allows for custom configuration so you can keep some events or tasks private.

Collabra Server 3.0

As Chapter 20 explains in greater detail, Usenet is made up of many thousands (20,000 and counting) of discussion groups, each focusing (so they hope) on a particular topic. Usenet is the bulletin board, discussion group, and gossip gabfest of the Internet. You can read the posted messages, post messages of your own, and follow discussions via threads (messages related to one another by reply and re-reply). It's current, it's topical, and it can be informative and fun. Then again, you often have to wade through *spams* (useless postings that are unrelated to the topics being discussed) and *flames* (angry messages in response to a previous posting) to find the information you want. Many newsgroups start off strongly with lively, informative discussions, then deteriorate in quality when less responsible people start posting.

With Netscape Collabra Server 3.0, you can set up and administer discussion groups, enable users to post HTML material, complete with images, audio, and other multimedia. It also includes search capabilities that make the process of archiving postings and searching for topics by keywords easy and intuitive. Now imagine being able to set up your own private newsgroup on your Intranet, strictly for use by company employees and perhaps some outsiders you designate. Or even for your customers. For example, if some departments and outside consultants in scattered locations are collaborating on a big project, you could set up a newsgroup so colleagues could ask questions, exchange information, and post updates. Or you could create a newsgroup for board members and strategic partners. You can also set up discussion groups to support your customers. Many of the most useful newsgroups on the Internet are set up and run by companies who want to support users of their products. Microsoft (`http://www.microsoft.com/`) and Macromedia (`http://www.macromedia.com/`) both have their own news servers. While discussions in public forums can often get out of hand, you can restrict access and maintain quality control.

Catalog Server 1.0

People have likened the Internet to a library with its books stripped of their covers and Dewey Decimal numbers and strewn all over the floor. I suppose that's what it feels like some days, but I rarely have a problem finding what I want because I use Yahoo!, Webcrawler, or some other convenient (and free) search service (for more about using search engines, see Chapter 9).

Shortly after installing your Intranet, you'll notice that just about anything that can be posted will be posted. Many network managers have found that their Intranet quickly expands exponentially in size towards the *terabyte* range (a terabyte is a billion gigabytes—imagine a thousand billion floppy disks piled up in a room). Even if you have a relatively simple Intranet, managing the constant flow of information can prove time-consuming and frustrating.

Wouldn't it be nice if all the data were arranged catalog fashion, so you could categorize information from broad topics to finely focused ones, and enable users to quickly find exactly the information they need? Netscape's Catalog Server 1.0 was designed with that in mind. It provides your users with a friendly search interface, so they can easily access data. You can also set up the Catalog Server so it automatically maintains and updates the catalog, and searches the network for new material—such as Web pages, news postings, calendar entries, and more—on the network. You'll also like it, because no programming is necessary.

Certificate Server 1.0

If your users frequently work with confidential information, you should consider getting the Certificate Server. If you've used a bank machine recently, then you're already somewhat familiar with how the certificates security scheme works. You go to the ATM, feed your bank card to it, enter your PIN number (password), and the bank machine (hopefully!) gives you cash. Almost all of us conduct financial transactions via ATMs and feel perfectly safe in doing it because there are two levels of security at work: You have to have the correct bank card *and* you have to have the correct password. Someone can't just steal your bank card and use it, or figure out your password and enter it because one won't work without the other.

With certificates, a person accessing your system needs the proper certificate as well as the password, providing extra strong security. You can also issue different types of certificates to users depending on what level of access they need. In addition, with Netscape Certificate Server 1.0, your users only have to remember one password to access their mail, news, and other server services, rather than having a separate password for each service. You'll do less maintenance and enable users to get their work done more efficiently.

Directory Server 1.0

Last, but certainly not least, is the Netscape Directory Server 1.0. Its primary function is to find and maintain a list of resources available on your network, and publish that list to anyone with access. Notice we're talking resources here—such as servers, printers, and applications—not data. As strange as it may sound, these types of resources can get lost on a network without some kind of specialized directory server to locate them and call them up when users need to use them. Directory Server 1.0 uses Lightweight Directory Access Protocol (LDAP), just like the other SuiteSpot servers, for lookups. LDAP's primary advantage is that it is an open standard for requesting and managing directory information, meaning it should be easier to use with products from multiple vendors.

Windows NT Tools for Managing Servers

If you're working with a Windows NT server, then you're in luck. The Windows NT server package comes with some useful tools, including the Performance Monitor and the User Manager. You can use these in addition to Netscape's server products. Monitoring the performance of your network could be very difficult, if you had to read printouts of all the statistics to figure out usage patterns and anticipate problems. Unless you take a speed reading course, just one day's worth of data can be too much to handle. Fortunately, the Performance Monitor and the User Manager make it easy to keep track of things.

The Windows NT Performance Monitor, not only records all vital statistics, but also displays them graphically in real time. In most cases, a quick glance is all you need to get a grasp of the situation. Each colored line represents a type of activity. While it takes a little getting used to, once you're accustomed to the meaning and acceptable range of each activity you can spot significant variations quickly.

The Windows NT User Manager, helps you set up accounts for different levels of access and assign levels of access by group. The User Manager's graphic display makes it easy for you to view and edit different users and groups.

The Netscape Administration Kit (NAK)

Netscape Communicator is designed from the ground up to function with your network. And naturally, Communicator works best when used with Netscape server products. One of the most important products is the Netscape Administration Kit (NAK), which makes it easy for network administrators and Internet service providers to create and distribute customized copies of Communicator over networks with all of the necessary access levels and passwords, custom toolbar buttons, and bookmarks for accessing company-related resources and other specialized features built in. The administration kit also allows central management from the server, so you can automatically update everyone's settings at once, instead of having to enter them manually on each user's computer. Busy managers with little knowledge of networks will jump for joy when they see how easily they can get their departments up and running on their Intranet, while experienced network administrators will appreciate the NAK's ease of use.

The NAK helps you do many things, including the following:

- Create and distribute self-installing Communicator files across networks.
- Customize the Start and Search Page.
- Create a custom Bookmarks list that jumps users to company-related resources.

- "Brand" Netscape with your company's logo in the upper-left hand corner of the Navigator window.
- Include or exclude features and add-ons.
- Include other programs in the installation package.

This section takes you on a quick tour of the NAK's features and gives you a basic introduction to how it works. Once again, this book shows Netscape's server tools in relation to a Windows NT server. However, Netscape has strong roots in the UNIX community and all of its products are available for various versions of UNIX.

The NAK consists of the following components:

- **The Configuration Editor:** A set of HTML documents and forms that prompt you for information and that automatically generate a configuration file based on your input. The configuration file contains the Communicator preferences settings that are deployed across your network.
- **AutoAdmin:** A Communicator Pro component that works in tandem with the Administration kit. It looks for the configuration file stored on the server and automatically updates the settings for your users based on your input.
- **The Java Archive (JAR) Packager:** Enables you to deploy Java applets across your network to enhance network services.
- **The Install Builder:** Helps you build a customized Communicator installation package.
- **Online Documentation:** The NAK comes with a set of HTML documents that take you through the steps of using the NAK and can help answer any questions you might have.

Of course, you'll need to develop a knack for using the NAK, but once you do, you'll wonder how you ever managed without it.

Setting Global Communicator Preferences with the Configuration Editor

I work in a perfect organization. No one ever changes software preferences without permission, no one ever uses illegal software, downloads untested shareware without the administrator's permission, connects to a personal email server, or forgets proxy settings. Of course, the company I work for consists only of myself and three computers. If you work with other human beings, you know that administration can be a real nightmare, even without anyone deliberately messing around. It's not that you want to be a control freak, it's just that without some control there's simply no way one person (or even one person with a small staff, if you're lucky) can keep a network secure and running smoothly.

The NAK helps you get around these problems by enabling you to pre-set Communicator preferences before distribution, as well as update settings via the server. The first step in creating and updating customized versions of Communicator is to enter settings in the Configuration Editor. And guess what? Using the Configuration Editor is as easy as selecting items from a scrolling list and filling Web page form items. The Configuration Editor launches in Navigator as a Web page, as shown in Figure 19-2.

LAUNCHING THE CONFIGURATION EDITOR

Launching the Configuration Editor means opening a Web page called `top.htm` (located in the `Adminkit\conf_ed\` folder), rather than launching an executable file. To open the Configuration Editor, do the following:

1. Launch Navigator.
2. Select **Open Page** from the **File** menu.
3. When the **Open Page** dialog box appears, click the **Choose File** button.
4. When the **Open** dialog box appears, browse for your Adminkit folder and open it, then locate the `conf_ed` folder and open it, then select the `top.htm` document and open it.

When `top.htm` displays in Navigator, as shown in Figure 19-2, you can begin configuring settings for your installed base of Communicator clients.

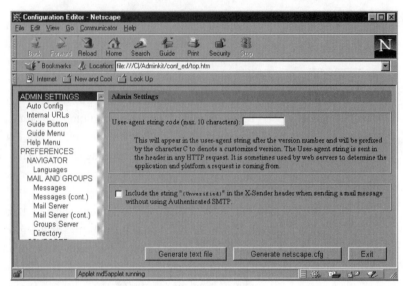

FIGURE *You can enter new server settings with the Configuration Editor, a set of HTML*
19.2 *documents that you can launch in Navigator.*

GENERATING CONFIGURATION FILES

You may notice that the Configuration Editor document in the Navigator
main window works similarly to setting Communicator preferences from
within Communicator (see Chapter 5). When you select the item you want
to change from the left frame's scrolling list, a new form appears in the right
frame. When you enter and change settings, your entries are written to the
configuration file—a text document named `netscape.cfg` that contains a
list of all the preferences you have selected. The configuration file is included with each Communicator setup file to automatically generate your
preferences settings during installation. Depending on the option you
choose, the Configuration Editor automatically generates JavaScript code
based on your input. JavaScript puts even more powerful server management
tools into your hands so you have greater control over Communicator clients
on the network.

*Wonder what the configuration file looks like and how it works? Launch Note
Pad or another text editor, open up the* `netscape.cfg` *document, and take a
look.*

TIP

The Configuration Editor offers as many options as there are organizations. After all, everyone has unique networking needs. Rather than discuss all of the items on the Configuration Editor page's scrolling list, this chapter highlights the ones that relate to common server administration issues.

The Configuration Editor helps you do the following:

- **Control server access:** The Admin Settings main page (shown in Figure 19-2) provides options for setting up "user-agent" strings so the server can identify individual users when they log on. In addition, you can keep users from accessing an unauthorized mail server (for example, to get their personal email) by setting up the Email X-Header to include "Unverified" when not sending with Authenticated SMTP.

- **Automate distribution of preferences settings:** The AutoConfig page settings help you set up a URL that links to a master configuration file from which Communicator automatically downloads its preferences settings at specified intervals. Doing this requires creating a master AutoConfig file document with the .jsc file name extension. The big advantage is that you can change the settings of every client (aimed at this URL) by changing the settings on this file just once.

NOTE

Keep in mind that to use the AutoConfig options, you'll still have to include an individual config file with each new install of Communicator you issue in order to get it to point to the master config file.

- **Customize toolbar link buttons:** When users click on the Navigator toolbar's Netscape logo in Navigator, they jump to Netscape's home page at `http://home.netscape.com/`. Wouldn't you rather have users jump to your organization's home page instead? Go to the Internal URLs page, shown in Figure 19-3, and enter a new URL in the **Animation logo URL** text field. You can also enter new default URLs for the **Search button** and the **Plug-in Finder** (the default page that Navigator goes to when the user doesn't have the right plug-in for loading Web page content).

- **Create custom guide and help menu links:** One of the primary advantages of having an Intranet in the first place is that it can ease company newcomers into the scheme of things with online training and access to company resources. If your company is like many, it's growing and changing rapidly, and staying connected is critical. As the sys-

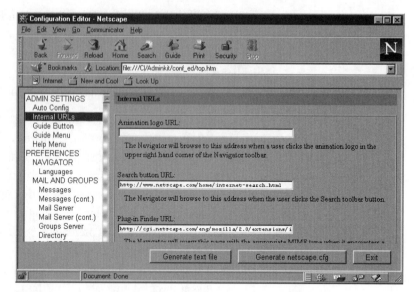

FIGURE *You can customize toolbar link buttons from the Internal URLs page.*
19.3

tem administrator, you can help people get accustomed to the unique way you do business by setting some of the places to go. You do this by redefining the description and underlying URLs for the nonrequired **Directory** and **Help** menu entries. The About Netscape entry is the only required entry on the **Help** menu. You can create custom links for the **Guide Button**, the **Guide Button** menu, and **Help** menu pages to guide users to company resources and training materials.

- **Deploy Preferences settings across networks:** Remember the Communicator Preferences settings from Chapter 5? Now it starts to really get interesting. The **Preferences** page, shown in Figure 19-4, and the pages organized beneath it on the scrolling list give you options for setting Communicator Preferences, determining which applications launch on startup, and locking users out of certain Communicator components. You can also determine whether they can select particular tools and menu choices.

- **Browser and Languages:** This group of pages provides options for setting and locking the default start page and history list options. In addition, network administrators for organizations with interests around the globe can configure the Language preferences (for more about Language settings, see Chapter 5).

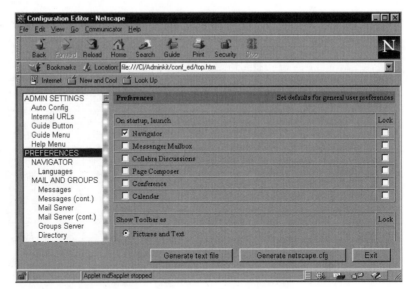

FIGURE *The Preferences pages help you control who uses what.*
19.4

- **Mail and Groups:** As Chapter 5 discusses, users cannot access email or discussion groups until they set their mail and news preferences. For beginners, this can prove terribly confusing and time consuming. You can get users up and running faster by setting their Mail and Groups preferences for them. The Mail and Groups preferences tell Communicator how to handle email and newsgroups. At the very least, you should set up the **Mail Server** and **Groups Server** entries, as shown in Figures 19-5 and 19-6. Users can generally figure out how to enter basic information but probably won't know the name of the mail and news servers.

- **Link users to a default Directory page:** If you have an LDAP directory set up so users can search for each other's email addresses and contact information, then you can specify a link to it on the Directory page. This way, users throughout the company can find each other's email addresses by simply clicking the **Directory** button in their address book. You can also create links to other LDAP directories like http://www.four11.com. For more about Communicator's address book, see Chapter 14.

- **Streamline Web publishing:** Allowing users to compose and upload Web pages to the server facilitates collaboration, teamwork, and effec-

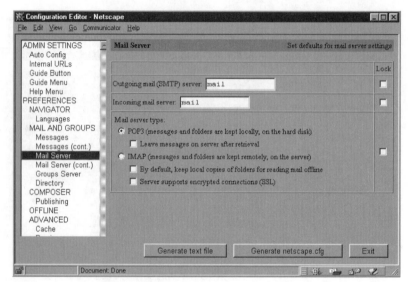

FIGURE *Mail Server preferences page.*
19.5

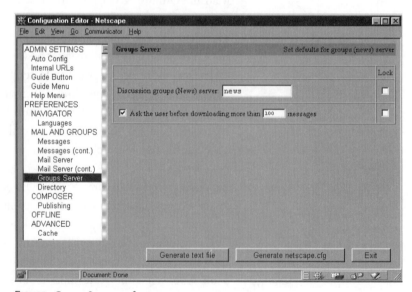

FIGURE *Groups Server preferences page.*
19.6

tive communication among company employees—the main reason for having an Intranet. But as an Administrator, you need some degree of control over where and how users are publishing. The **Composer** page, as shown in Figure 19-7, goes a long way toward accomplishing that end by letting you set the author's name, the template URL (for creating new documents using previously built templates), and the frequency of saves. In addition, you can create a default directory for page uploads and also enter a setting for automatic link adjustment so links stay updated.

- **Preset Communicator connection modes:** The **Offline** page lets you designate a work mode for how Communicator connects to the network. There are three choices on this window, **Online Work Mode**, **Offline Work Mode**, and **Ask the User**. Basically, you can set Communicator to be connected all the time, to allow the user to connect at will, and to give the user a choice at startup. You can set up these options depending on your company's needs.

- **Address potential bandwidth problems:** The **Advanced** page, as shown in Figure 19-8, along with the **Cache**, **Proxies**, and **Disk Space** pages, all help you determine what types of content can be down-

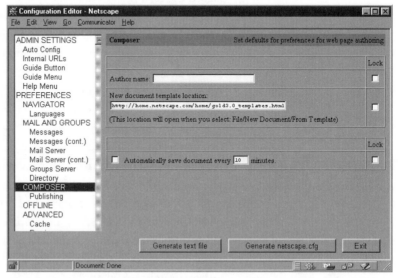

FIGURE

19.7   *The Composer page has options for setting up the user's name and guiding him or her to a default template document so that person can generate Web pages easily.*

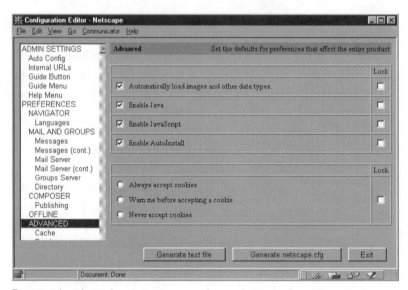

FIGURE 19.8 *The Advanced page gives you control over what types of content users can download.*

loaded and how much demand Communicator clients are allowed to place on the server. For a more detailed discussion of these options and what they mean, see Chapter 5. In addition, you can click the **AutoInstall** option so you can deploy automatic software installations across the network.

• **Adjust cache and disk space reserved for Communicator:** The Cache folder holds visited pages so you can return to them frequently during a session without having to download them again. In order to keep Communicator running smoothly, the cache is set to a fixed size on the hard disk (and in the RAM of your machine as well). You can adjust the size of the RAM cache, the hard disk cache, and also the frequency with which pages are compared (for updates) to pages on the network on this window. The **Disk Space** page, as shown in Figure 19-9, is for setting message parameters, such as size and number of email and newsgroup messages that can be received, and how long messages can be stored on the server.

• **Set up access to proxy servers:** Proxy servers enable users to access the big bad world of the Internet through firewalls—security software that

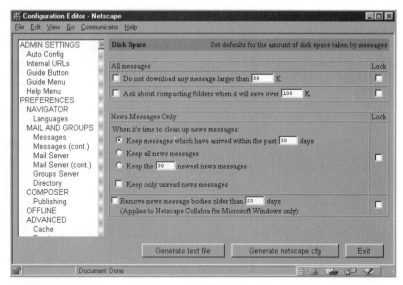

FIGURE *The Disk Space page helps you control the size of messages that users can receive*
19.9 *and automate the cleaning out of old messages.*

protects the server from unauthorized tampering and potentially damaging downloads. For more about proxy servers, see the "How Proxy Servers Work" section.

• **Enter password settings:** You can enter default settings for entering passwords in the **Passwords** page, as shown in Figure 19-10.

SETTING UP CONFIGURATION FILES

Now that you've entered your customized settings with the Configuration Editor, you can use them in a couple of ways. Options include setting up a Master AutoConfig file that enables you to update settings automatically over the entire network or create a Local Config file that you can distribute to users with the Communicator installation program.

You need to include local configuration files with Communicator installation files. When Communicator is installed (either automatically or by the user), the customized settings are applied during the setup process. You can create different configuration files to accommodate the needs of different user groups. And remember that if you want to link users to a Master Auto-

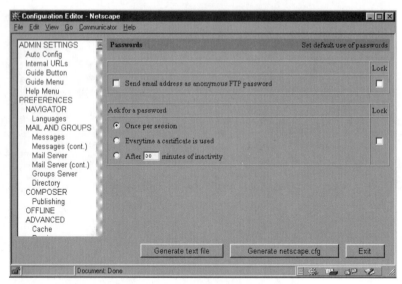

FIGURE *You can enter password settings on the Passwords page.*
19.10

Config file, then you need to provide a URL in the AutoConfig page in the Admin Settings section.

To create a local configuration file, do the following:

1. Click the **Generate text file** button.
2. Save the file with a name and the `.cfg` file name extension.
3. Or, if you want the file to be "locked" so users can't change any settings, click the **Generate netscape.cfg** button to save a file with the `.lck` extension.

Using a Master AutoConfig file makes life easier and you can create multiple versions to accommodate access needs for different users. To create a master AutoConfig file that automatically updates Communicator client preferences settings from a single file, do the following:

1. Click the **Generate text file** button.
2. Save the file with a name and the `.jsc` filename extension.
3. Make sure you save it with the directory path and file name (URL) you specified in the AutoConfig page.

The NAK also lets you load and change settings for previously built configuration files in the Configuration Editor.

How Proxy Servers Work

In addition to the options discussed in the previous section, the Configuration Editor's **Proxies** page helps you manage user access through your proxy server. Proxies are common in Intranet installations, because they function with your firewall to allow safe and secure access to the Internet. Nothing is perfect, of course, but at least proxies give you an extra measure of security while offering your users the ability to get out and cruise around a little. You can set which proxies to use across the board here (or use no proxy at all), and allow the user to manually set the proxy if you desire.

Your customized proxy configuration is actually a script stored at a particular URL on a server. When a user makes a request, instead of directly contacting the Internet, the request travels to that URL, runs the script to determine the correct proxy to use, and then makes the contact. By storing the proxy configuration on a server in a central location, you can easily update proxy information for many users (if you've ever tried to get your users to simultaneously update their proxy data, you know what a blessing this is). By creating different versions of the proxy config URL, you can allow different users different levels of Internet access.

The Internet, being the Internet, is the largest, most diverse, and probably the most comprehensive source of online information available, and for the most part it's free. No organization can afford to be isolated from this resource. At the same time, the Internet is also available to everyone out there, including those who would damage your company, steal secrets, or overload you with garbage. Eventually, it seems to me that there will be a variety of levels of Internet access, each with its own speed, cost, and restrictions. Until that time, however, many of us will use firewalls to protect our internal systems from predators, hackers, and junksters.

Having a firewall is no guarantee of safety, but at least it provides some measure of control over what goes in and out of your network. A typical firewall setup uses proxies to send and receive data from the Internet, and you can configure proxies for Navigator components, both manually and automatically. The default configuration is no proxies. You can also tell Communicator to go through various proxies depending on who is being contacted, designate several proxies as backups to the primary proxy, and use URL wildcard matching to determine the correct proxy for a given protocol.

Using the Install Builder

Once you create and save your configuration files, you can build your customized installation files with the Install Builder. The Install Builder is an application included with the Netscape Administration Kit that takes your custom configuration files, the components of Communicator you select, and Install shield files and builds your disk, CD-ROM, or network-based installation. You can build 16- and 32-bit Windows installers simultaneously, and you can build installers for Macintosh and UNIX users as well. The process is fairly straightforward, with a few things to watch out for.

The basic steps go something like this:

- Copy your config file to the appropriate directory.
- Customize Installer itself.
- Launch the Install Builder and choose options.
- Enter the path to the Custom Directory.
- Enter the path to the Media Target Directory.
- Select the modules (such as Communicator components and plug-ins) to be included.

Now, let's roll up our sleeves and get down to business.

- After you generate your custom configuration file, you copy it to a directory that has been set aside for your installer package. In order to incorporate your settings, the Install Builder needs to access the configuration file during the creation of your installer. This directory is:

```
Install Builder\Custom\32bit\Nav40\Program
```

If you're creating a version for Windows 3.1x, substitute 16bit for 32bit in the directory path. Macintosh and UNIX installers will also have different entries here.

- Next, use a text editor to make the changes you desire in the Install Builder itself, such as the names in the Product Setup window, etc.

These changes are made in the `Setup.ini` file, located in:

```
Install Builder\Custom\32bit\Installer directory
```

- Launch the Install Builder application.
- When the **Install Builder** dialog box appears, as shown in Figure 19-11, select the 32-bit and/or 16-bit checkboxes (for Windows 95 and NT and/or Windows 3.1x) and distribution media (disk, CD-ROM, or network)
- Click the **Browse** buttons and find a directory so the Install Builder knows where to find the customized files and where to output the final product.
- Click the **Configure** button to display the **Setup Configuration** dialog box shown in Figure 19-12 and select the Communicator components and plug-ins you wish to install, then click **OK**.
- When you return to the **Netscape Install Builder** dialog box, click the **Create** button.

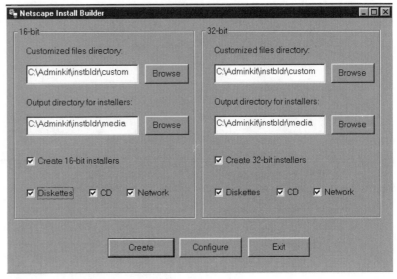

FIGURE *Netscape Install Builder dialog box.*
19.11

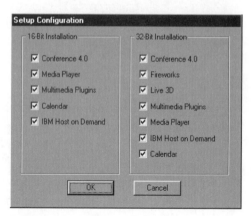

FIGURE *Setup Configuration dialog box.*
19.12

- When the next dialog box appears, click **Make Media** and choose to store the output either as a self-extracting executable file for network distribution, a CD-ROM disk, or a series of 3.5″ disks.

And voilà! The Install Builder assembles your customized setup file!

20 Setting up Newsgroups with Collabra

S o, you don't know much about servers and all of the sudden you have to set up an in-house news server. Or maybe you're experienced in server matters, but it's still a big job nonetheless. Whatever you do, you will have to stay on top of things and do some studying and experimenting. But thanks to Collabra, you can get the job done with minimal pain. Collabra server, as we've already discussed, is part of Netscape's SuiteSpot family of Internet and Intranet server software. It performs newsgroup services for your network. An admin server is also installed with Collabra server to help you manage administrative functions. Network News Transfer Protocol (NNTP) is the open standard of the Internet for forming discussion groups, and Netscape's Collabra server uses it to provide all the discussion group services needed to make an effective solution.

TIP

Newsgroups and discussion groups work the same way. Only newsgroups are served up to the public via the Internet and discussion groups are set up on Intranets for authorized users.

Among Collabra server's features are:

- **Setup and administration tools:** Help you set up and manage news and discussion groups.
- **Support for rich content:** Post and receive HTML-formatted messages with working links, images, attached and embedded multimedia, Java and JavaScript files, and more.
- **Searching and monitoring tools:** Make it easier for you to locate postings, track server performance, and locate potential trouble spots.
- **Security features:** Keep discussions private and limit access to allow participation only from authorized individuals.
- **Replication capability:** Make some or all of your discussion groups available on other servers and accept news and discussion groups from other servers.
- **Support for NNTP compliant clients:** Using Network News Transfer Protocol (NNTP), a standard protocol, means that even users who do not have Communicator and who use other news clients can read postings and send messages.

With Collabra, you can create and manage your own discussion groups within your Intranet, meaning you can select a topic (perhaps employee benefits, pricing for your latest products, etc.) and create a discussion group that focuses on that topic. Then, you can moderate and manage that group so that it remains an vital part of the overall communications in your organization.

If you get confused or lost, just click the Help button for the current page for more information.

In addition, Collabra comes with an administration server called Admin that helps you set up and keep track of your users and groups, and perform other normal administrative functions. In addition, both the Collabra server and the admin server support Lightweight Directory Access Protocol (LDAP) so users can interact with a directory service, if you have one set up. Or you can use the local directory database that ships with the Administration server. Like the Netscape Administration Kit (NAK) and most of Netscape's other server products, Collabra and Admin run as a set of Web pages with buttons and electronic forms.

Collabra is available for UNIX and Windows NT. And since you administer Collabra with a set of Web pages, UNIX and Windows NT versions run similarly. However, this chapter shows Collabra running on Windows NT.

This chapter covers the following:

- Getting the Collabra and Administrative servers
- The Administrative Server
- Managing users and groups
- Managing keys and certificates
- Cluster management
- Setting up and configuring Collabra server
- Discussion group
- Replication management
- Collabra News server maintenance

If you get stuck, visit Netscape's Nuggies page at `http://help.netscape.com/nuggies/server.html`. *Nuggies stands for Netscape Users Groups—this page has links to newsgroups about Netscape's server products, including Collabra.*

Getting the Collabra and Admin Servers

You can download a trial or for-purchase version of Netscape's Collabra Server 3.0 from the Netscape home page (`http://home.netscape.com/`). Collabra is available for Windows NT and UNIX. The screens and features you load may differ somewhat from what this chapter describes, depending upon the version you receive and the machine you run it on.

Collabra Server 3.0 actually consists of the news server itself and an administration server. The Admin server is used to perform routine administrative functions, such as setting up users and groups, while the news server performs the work of creating and managing the discussion groups. You can also install additional news servers and delete news servers with the Admin server.

The Admin Server

INSTALLING WITH THE SETUP WIZARD

Before you can set up your Collabra server, you have to go through the installation routine, and then configure the Admin server. Fortunately, installation is easy. The Setup Wizard guides you through the process and prompts you for instructions. You can then fill in the requested information in the text fields and click the **Next** button to move on to the next step. Launching the Setup Wizard is easy too. Just double-click on the Collabra setup executable file and it starts running.

As you follow the Setup Wizard's instructions, you'll be asked for the following data:

- **User Name and Password:** Enter your desired Admin server user name and password.
- **Server Port:** Enter the appropriate port number. In most cases, the number is TCP/IP Port 119 for a standard server and 563 for a secure server.

Server ports aren't like physical parallel ports—the ones people use for printers and modems. Think of them more as channels for handling different types of data transfers and communications.

- **Collabra Server Unique ID:** Assign an identification code for the Collabra server. This can consist of numerical or text characters, or a combination of the two.

- **Administration Server Port:** The Setup Wizard automatically selects a server port. Make a note of this number.
- **SMTP Server:** Enter the name of your email server.
- **Email Address:** Enter the email address where you want the server to direct messages to the administrator.

When you're finished entering your settings, the Setup Wizard builds the Admin Server, load the files for the Collabra server, and places menu choices on the **Start** menu for a Collabra Readme file and the Admin Server, and displays a program group. To get started, click on the **Admin Server** menu choice. Navigator launches automatically, and the Netscape **Server Administration** main page displays in the browser, as shown in Figure 20-1.

You must have Netscape Navigator/Communicator or another Java-compatible browser loaded and ready to run, because administration is performed via the browser.

Like Netscape's other server products, the Admin and Collabra servers consist of sets of Web pages that provide you with electronic forms for se-

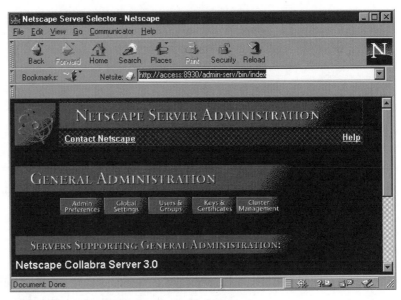

FIGURE *Netscape Server Administration main page.*
20.1

lecting, entering, and editing options. This familiar interface makes your job a little easier—even if you're new to this sort of thing.

LAUNCHING

Right now, you don't need to think about launching the Admin server because you can launch it straight from its program group when you finish setting up with the Setup Wizard. In the future (with Windows NT), you can simply click the **Start** button, select the **Programs** folder, and choose the **Netscape** icon to display the cascading menu of Netscape applications. Click the **Administration** option and the Netscape **Server Administration** page launches in Navigator.

As for the URL, the Setup Wizard sets it up as a port number in the form of standard `http://` syntax, as in `http://localhost:28657/`. The port number entered is the randomly chosen port number that you saw during the Collabra setup process (did you remember to make a note of it?).

CONFIGURING

Before you set up your Collabra news server, you need to configure the Admin server. The Netscape **Administration Server** main page displays a set of buttons for **General Administration** options. When you click one of the **General Administration** server options buttons, a framed page appears, like the one shown in Figure 20-2. The General Administration categories display in the top frame, the list of options for the selected category display in the left frame and the currently selected page appears in the right frame.

The **General Administration** options are as follows:

- **Admin Preferences:** Provides options for access and error log files, security and passwords, and shutting down the server.
- **Global Settings:** Global settings let you configure a directory service, or use the local directory database that comes with Collabra. You can also restrict access to the Server.
- **Users & Groups:** The **Users & Groups** functions let you create, find, edit and delete users, groups and organizational units.
- **Keys and Certificates:** For security purposes, **Keys and Certificates** lets you run a command line program creating **Key Pair** files, set **Key Pair** passwords, request and install certificates, and convert News Server 2.0 (Collabra's predecessor) certificates.

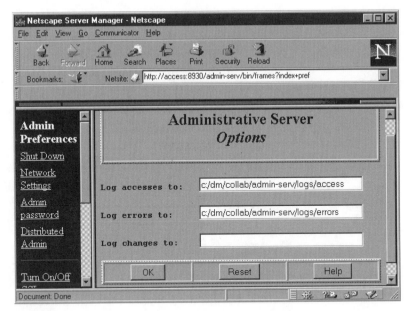

FIGURE   *You can configure and edit server settings by selecting categories and filling in*
20.2   *electronic forms.*

- **Cluster Management:** Cluster management choices let you control several Collabra servers as a cluster.

And remember, if you get confused or stuck, you can always click on the **Help** button for more information.

ADMIN PREFERENCES

The **Admin Preferences** setting helps you create basic settings for administering and accessing the server. To set up your Administration preferences, click the **Admin Preferences** button underneath the **General Administration** heading. When the new page appears, a list of **Admin Preferences** settings appears in the left frame. To choose an option, select an item from the list.

The **Admin Preferences** frame set offers the following options:

- **Shutting Down the Admin Server:** If it's an emergency and you need to shut down the server, choose the **Shut Down** option from the list in the left frame, then click the **Shut down the administrative server!** button when it displays in the right frame.

- **Network Settings:** When you select the **Networks Settings** item from the list in the left frame, the **Administrative Server Daemon Configuration** page appears in the right frame. This allows you to enter a different Admin server port if you need to.

Depending upon how many services you are running on your server, and what ports they use, there may be times when you want to change the Server Port number, but considering how many ports you have at your disposal there's a good chance you'll never use this option. You may want to change it occasionally just to keep security tight.

- **Password and Access Control:** When you select the **Password and Access Control** item from the list in the left frame, the **Administration Server Access Control** page appears in the right frame. Here you can enter options determining which hostnames and IP address are allowed access (in case you need to access the server from a different account or a different computer), and you can create an authentication user name and an authentication password. When anyone attempts to access the server, the server prompts that person for the user name and password that you specify here.

- **Distributed Administration:** When you select the **Distributed Administrators** item from the list, the **Distributed Administration** page appears. *Distributed administration* means enabling one or more of your colleagues to administer the server as well. In most cases, you should allow at least one other person access because you probably need to sleep, eat, and leave the office occasionally. Here, you can choose whether to activate distributed administration. If you activate distributed administration, you need to specify an administrator group name (setting up user groups is explained later in this chapter). You can also specify whether to allow access to end users.

- **Turn SSL On/Off:** Secure Sockets Layer (SSL) is an industry standard secure connection protocol that allows two SSL-capable machines to communicate securely. Data can still be intercepted, but since it's encrypted, it won't be readable. SSL encrypts your data before sending it across the Internet (or Intranet), and it is deciphered at the other end after being received. If you set the server to run in secure connection mode, all incoming connections will be decrypted.

For this to work you must create an alias (discussed in Keys and Certificates).

- **Security Preferences:** Here you can specify whether to activate encryption capabilities and choose whether to be compliant with Secure Socket Layers (SSL) protocol version 2, version 3, or both. You can also choose which cipher types (for encryption) to allow.

- **Logging Options:** Selecting **Logging Options** prompts you for information about where to store log files. As you can see, the access logs and error logs are set to be stored default directories during setup, but the change log has no directory specified. If you'd like to specify a directory for this log, make the entry in the **change log** text field. Log files are automatically generated lists of things that happen on the server—such as accesses (the number of times people access the server, and what IP addresses they accessed the server from, and what data they downloaded from or uploaded to the server), errors (the number of errors that occurred and what the errors were), and changes to the server (such as new installations or directories that are added or removed). For example, Figure 20-3 shows what an error log looks like. Log files are crucial for keeping track of server performance and anticipating problems before they occur.

- **Access Log Review:** Displays the last specified number of successful accesses to the server. The Admin log gives you access to data about what your Admin server has been doing. You can see the time and date of actions taken and a message telling you what the actions were.

- **Error Log Review:** Displays the last specified number of errors that occurred on the server. The error log, like the Admin log, gives you access to data concerning any errors noted, including the time and date of the error, and an error message.

GLOBAL SETTINGS

Global settings help you integrate the Admin server and Collabra with a Lightweight Directory Access Protocol (LDAP)-compliant database or directory so users can find each other's email addresses and search for newsgroup postings and archives by keyword. Depending on your organization's needs, you can either install your own LDAP directory server (such as

Number of errors to view? 25

Only show entries with:

| OK | Reset | Help |

Last 25 errors:

[05/Jun/1997:14:38:18] failure: Failure initializing Listen Sockets
[05/Jun/1997:14:44:49] failure: Failure initializing Listen Sockets
[09/Jun/1997:15:52:13] warning: for host 127.0.0.1 trying to GET /admin-
)
[09/Jun/1997:15:52:13] failure: cgi_send:cgi_start_exec D:/Netscape/Serv
[11/Jun/1997:11:21:50] security: for host 127.0.0.1 trying to GET /, bas

Document: Done

FIGURE *Error log file.*
20.3

Netscape's directory server), or use the local directory database that is installed automatically with Collabra and the Admin server. To access global settings, click the **Global Settings** button on the top frame beneath the **General Administration** heading.

The **Global Settings** options are as follows:

- **Configure Directory Service:** When you select **Configure Directory Service** from the list in the left frame, the **Configure Directory Service** page appears in the right frame, as shown in Figure 20-4. Here you can select the **Local Database** or **LDAP Directory Server** radio button depending on where your directory service is located. You can also enter a base directory name for a local directory in the text field.

- **Restrict Access:** When you select **Security Preferences** from the list in the left frame, the **Administration Access Control** page appears in the right frame. You can select a server from the pulldown list and create an access control list by clicking the **Create ACL** button. When the **Access Control Rules** page loads (it's a JavaScript script), you can specify actions, users and groups, hosts, and programs that are either allowed or not allowed to access the directory service.

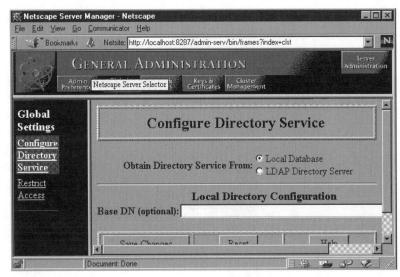

FIGURE *Configure Directory Service page.*
20.4

Managing Users and Groups

Now that you've got your Admin server set up and configured, it's time to get everyone in the office up and running. This means setting up users and groups. In order to do this, you first need to create new users and enter all of their information. You should then assign users to groups. Groups make your life easier, because you can determine user needs by group and set levels of access by group rather than having to set levels of access for each user. *Setting levels of access*, means determining who gets access to what resources and data available through the Collabra server. For example, you may not want to make a top-level management discussion group available to entry-level employees. To access the **Users and Groups** frame set, click the **Users & Groups** button beneath the **General Administration** heading.

For **Users and Groups**, the allowed functions are:

- **New User:** To add a new user, select the **New User** option to display the **New User** page, as shown in Figure 20-5. You can then click the **Create User** button to add a new user, and enter his or her information, such as first name, last name, user ID (user name) password, and email address. To edit information about a current user, click the **Create and Edit User** button.

FIGURE *New User page.*
20.5

- **Manage Users:** The **Manage Users** page makes it easy for you to locate users on your database. To access the **Manage Users** page, click the **Manage users** option. It looks a lot like the **Find** dialog box in your word processing application. To locate one of your users, enter his or her name in the **Find user** text field and click the **Find** button. Search results display in the current frame. The form also includes more advanced search options.
- **New Group:** To add a new group, click the **New Group** option to display the **New Group** page. Here, you can click the **Create Group** button to display a dialog box that prompts you for information about the users you wish to add to the group. When you're finished adding members to the group, you can return to the **New Group** page and enter a group name and a description in the appropriate text fields. To edit existing groups, click the **Create and Edit Group** button.
- **Manage Groups:** This works similarly to the **Manage Users** page. You can search for groups by name when you need to display or edit them. To display the **Manage Groups** page in the right frame, click the **Manage Groups** option on the list in the left frame.
- **Organizational Unit:** Use this menu choice to create organizational units. In a nutshell, organizational units are part of the Distinguished Name structure inside your directory service (or the local directory database). Each entry has a Distinguished Name associated with it,

and adding organizational units can help further define a person or group within your company.

- **Manage Organizational Unit:** You can find, edit and remove organizational units with this menu choice.
- **Import:** Use this option to import directory databases.
- **Export:** Use this option to export directory databases.
- **Convert 2.0 Database:** If you've been running News Server 2.0 (Collabra's predecessor), you can use the Convert 2.0 database options to instantly convert News Server 2.0 directory databases to the format required by Collabra Server 3.0.

Groups are particularly useful for administering multiple users, because once you've created the users you can add them to groups. Then you can assign properties to the group as a whole, rather than making assignments to each individual user as they enter the system. Organizational units are created and managed in much the same way as groups.

Keys and Certificates

Collabra Server uses the Secure Sockets Layer (SSL) protocol to enable security. When the server is running in secure mode, security can be established between the server and any other client that is also SSL enabled (and many common clients are). Running SSL enables login authentication and transmission encryption. In order to run SSL, you must first generate what's called a *key pair*, the public and private key combination that identifies you. You must run your key pair file generator program from the command line. Your key pair file will be generated with a password. Your next step will be to create an alias for the key pair file.

For **Keys and Certificates**, the allowed functions are:

- **Create Alias:** Creates an alias for an existing key pair file and certificate file.
- **Remove Alias:** Removes existing aliases.
- **List Aliases:** Lists existing aliases.
- **Generate Key:** Generates a key pair file. This screen will run the key pair file generator from the command line at the path you enter.

You must have a key pair file program installed to generate a key pair file.

- **Change Key Password:** Changes the password for an existing key pair file.
- **Request Certificate:** To request a certificate, go to the **Request a Server Certificate** page, as shown in Figure 20-6. Choose **New certificate** or **Certificate renewal**, the method you'd like to use to contact the Certificate Authority (CA) of your choice, and enter the alias and key pair file password you intend to use. Fill in the rest of the data (common identification data about you) and click **OK** (for more about security and certificates, see Chapter 18).
- **Install Certificate:** Once you obtain or renew a certificate, you need to install it. The **Install Certificate** page offers options for selecting who the certificate is for and entering the name of the certificate, the file name where the message resides, and the text of the message. After the certificate is installed, you can enable encryption. For more information about encryption, see Chapter 18, or select the **Encryption** topic from the **Help** menu.
- **Manage Certificates:** Helps you search for certificates so you can view them or make changes.
- **Convert 2.0 Cert Dbase:** Use this option to convert your certificate database in News Server 2.0 (Collabra's 3.0) to work with your new Collabra Server 3.0.

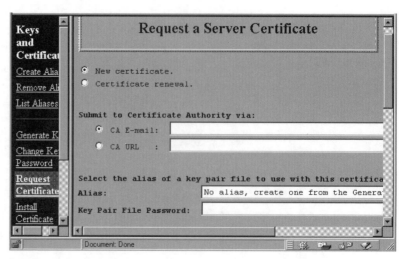

FIGURE **20.6** *Request Certificate.*

Cluster Management

If you have (or intend to have) more than one news server on your Intranet, you may find it advantageous to configure a *cluster* of news servers. This allows you to administer all the servers in the cluster from one administrative server on your machine, called the master Admin server. All the servers must be installed prior to configuring a cluster, and each one requires an Admin server to be installed as well. Your Admin server becomes the master server, and you can log in with the appropriate user name and password to access the Admin servers associated with the other news servers.

The **Cluster Management** options are as follows:

- **Cluster Control:** Use this menu choice to find the server you want to manage and select it. Then you can perform many of the same management functions that you can do for the Collabra Server on your own machine, such as start and stop, use configuration files, and so on.
- **Add Server:** Add a remote server by entering its name and port number. Choose the protocol to be used; either `http` for normal servers or `https` for secure servers.
- **Modify Server:** Find the server you want to modify and change host names, port numbers, and protocols when you change these items in the remote administration servers.
- **Remove Server:** Find the server you want to remove and remove it.

Setting up and Configuring the Collabra Server

Now that the Admin server is fully configured just the way you want it, it's time to configure the Collabra server itself. The Collabra files are loaded when you install the Admin server, but you still need to install the Collabra server through the Admin server. To install the Collabra server, return to the **Admin Server** main page and select the **Create New Netscape Collabra Server** option. When the Netscape **Collabra Server Installation** page displays, as shown in Figure 20-7, your Admin server settings appear in the text fields. All you have to do is click **OK** and Collabra server sets itself up.

WORKING WITH COLLABRA SERVER

Once you've set up the Collabra server, the **Collabra Server** page appears, as shown in Figure 20-8. As with the Admin server, the Collabra server displays as a set of framed Web pages. The main server functions appear as buttons

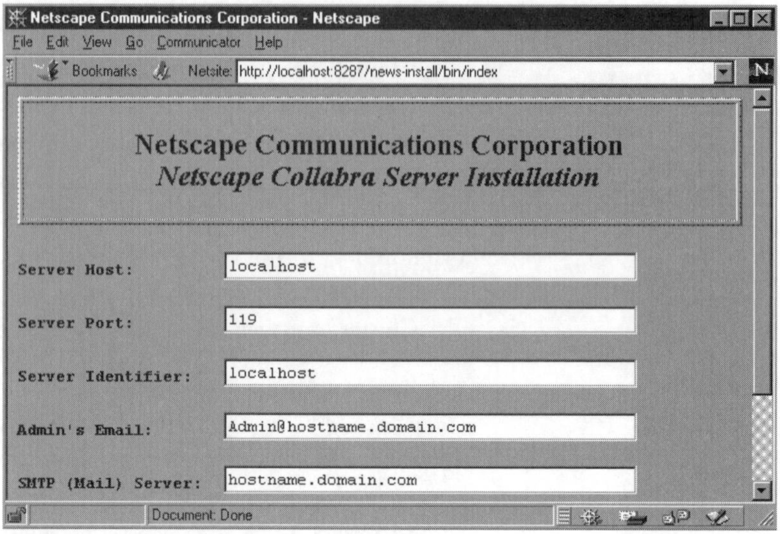

FIGURE **20.7**   *Installing the Collabra server from Admin server.*

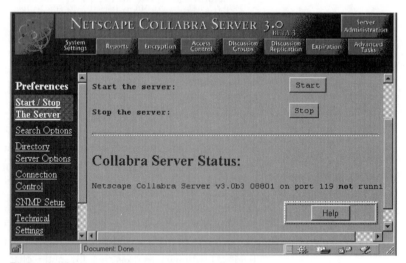

FIGURE **20.8**   *Collabra server.*

in the top frame. When you select a button, a list of options appear in the left frame, and a page for the selected list item appears in the right frame.

Collabra server lets you work with the following:

- **System Settings:** You can enter the message of the day (a daily message that gets posted to discussion groups), or choose to stop or start the server (sometimes you'll need to stop the server when something goes wrong).
- **Reports:** Provides options for viewing various reports, creating directories for logging data to these reports, examining disk usage statistics, and setting the email addresses for notifying you of conditions on your server.
- **Encryption:** Activates connection security.
- **Access Control:** Allows you to set access controls on users and groups for particular discussion groups and lets you define moderator and management roles for users.
- **Discussion Groups:** Create and manage discussion groups and control discussion groups, as well as setting indexing properties.
- **Discussion Replication:** If you send outgoing messages or accept incoming messages, you can control replication functions from this frame set.
- **Expiration:** Create and manage expiration policies for your articles.
- **Advanced Tasks:** Create, view and manage process feeds, perform recovery actions, and cancel individual articles.

SYSTEM SETTINGS

To view, create, or edit your system settings, select the **System Settings** button from the top frame. When the list displays in the left frame, you can select from the following options to display the following pages:

- **Start/Stop The Server:** Here, you can start or stop the server and also view the current server status.
- **Search Options:** When the Collabra server is running, the Searching server is active. The Searching server allows full-text searches across multiple discussion groups, and, if you enable profiling, the results can be stored in a virtual discussion group that looks just like any other discussion group. You can also choose searching and profiling.

- **Directory Server Options:** If you use a directory server, you may want to provide a UserID and password so Collabra server can identify itself to the directory server when users search for addresses through their messaging clients.

- **Connection Control:** Displays the Collabra server status (again), options for rejecting posts, replication connections (for setting up your discussion groups on other servers), and reader connections. You can also enter a text message that displays an explanatory alert message that appears to users who attempt to connect unsuccessfully. For example, if you choose to reject connections while you're toiling away at a problem with the server, you can enter a message that says something like, "Sorry. The discussion groups server is temporarily down. Thank you for your patience."

- **SNMP Setup:** Simple Network Management Protocol (SNMP) is used to monitor IP devices across a network. For your Collabra server to be visible you must indicate an SNMP configuration in the **SNMP Setup** page. Enter a description of your server in the **Description** text field, your organization's name in the **Organization** text field, the physical location of the machine in the **Location** text field, and the server administrator's name in the **Contact** text field. Next, select the **SNMP Monitoring On** option. That's all there is to it.

- **Technical Settings:** Provides options for setting background tasks. Background tasks take place without necessarily notifying you that they are happening. They can, however, affect system performance, so the settings you use should be fine-tuned for your system and your requirements. For instance, if your system sends mail to other systems, you can specify how frequently you'd like this action to be taken. Your choices are between 5 and 60 minutes, with the default being 60 minutes. More frequent sends keep other systems more up-to-date, but also place a heavier load on your system. Updating profiles (search results) operates in a very similar manner.

- The **Technical Settings** page offers the following options:
  - **Background Task options:** You can get display names from **Directory Server** and **Perform Daily Tasks**. Display names are pulled from the directory server at the interval of your choice (from 5 minutes to 60 minutes), and you can choose a time for running the `news.daily` program (try to choose a time of day when demands are low).

- **Limits:** Lets you specify a timeout period. The server automatically closes a newsreader connection after the timeout period has expired with no new requests. The default is 25 minutes (1500 seconds). If system resources are at a premium, set this figure lower, perhaps 10 minutes (600 seconds). This ensures that users who connect to discussion groups, get distracted by a phone call, and forget about their connection disconnect automatically instead of inadvertently tying up the server all day. You can also specify **Maximum Newsreader Connections** (the number of people who can access discussion groups simultaneously) and **Maximum Article Size** (the largest file size for postings—this helps discourage people from adding large, bandwidth-hogging message attachments).

The maximum article size limits the size (in bytes) of the articles that will be accepted by post or from another news server. The default value is 1,000,000 bytes (1 MB), but in actual practice you may find this high. Let your available hard drive space and the requirements of your organization be your guide (for example, if your coworkers need to exchange multimedia files frequently, 1MB is inadequate and you should set the value even higher).

- **Organization Name:** Here you can set the organization name, which will be automatically attached to any posted article by default.
- **Changing the Port Number:** You can change your server port number, but be careful. Many other clients may be affected by such a change. If your server is being fed by other servers, make sure to change the port numbers there as well.
- **Changing the Spool Directory Location:** The spool directory is the location on your system where all articles are kept, in hierarchical order. For each level of newsgroup there is a subdirectory under the spool directory. Here, you can specify a different directory.
- **Message of the Day:** Displays a text box where you can enter a new message each day (or however often you like). Enter your message and click **OK**. That's it.

REPORTS

Like any good server, your Collabra server performs the daily maintenance processes you specify, keeps track of what was done, and can generate reports based upon these actions. To view, create, or edit your report settings, select the **Report Settings** button from the top frame. When the list displays in the left frame, you can select from the following options to display pages:

- **View Daily Report:** The **Daily Report** page shows you whether the server is started or stopped, whether it is accepting replication and newsreader connections, the file system status (including disk space usage), the size of your log and history files, numbers concerning article lines processed, articles retained, expired entries, archival log information, and server statistics.
- **View Server Log:** Enter your search criteria for log entries, as shown in Figure 20-9, to view log files entries matching that criteria. This feature is provided for those times when you are searching for a particular subset of all log entries and you may not be sure what logs they reside in or how many (if any) there are.

Messages each have a priority number (lower is higher priority) in the server log, and messages in red indicate some action is required right away. In the discussion replication log, urgent messages are also colored red.

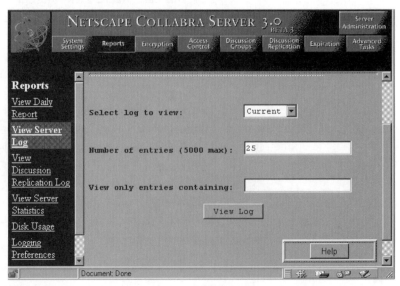

FIGURE *View Server Log.*
20.9

- **View Discussion Replication Log:** Provides options for selecting which log files you want to display and lets you set the maximum number of entries a log may contain. You can select which entries to view based on your search criteria. One event in a log file takes up one line and shows the date and time the message was sent, the process name, and the message itself in quotes.

  Processes that send messages often are:

  - **innd:** The main server process
  - **nnrpd:** Spawns threads for each newsreader
  - **nntpsend:** Creates discussion group batches
  - **innxmit:** Transmits the batches
  - **indexer:** Indexes articles for full-text searches
  - **newstime:** Schedules jobs for the server
  - **ns-admin:** The administration server process
  - **ctlinnd:** Performs basic admin functions outside Collabra server

- **View Server Statistics:** Here, you can search for types of server statistics, specify the date and time frame from which to retrieve them (or you can simply request all available statistics), and display summaries for user groups, hosts, and discussion groups.

- **Disk Usage:** Click the **Run Summary** button to display a summary of disk space usage, as shown in Figure 20-10. Disk usage statistics include the amount of disk space used by the Collabra server and discussion groups as a percentage, disk space usage in KB, the number of articles stored, and the number of subdirectories, along with statistics for incoming articles (the in.coming file), outgoing articles (the out.going file), indexes (the over.view file), and archived articles (the news.archive file—if you archive discussion group postings). This information is your key indicator about how the space on the server's hard drive is being used. It helps you determine how to set your expiration frequency for postings, when to increase your hard drive space, and gives you an indication of which newsgroups are most popular.

- **Logging Preferences:** Provides options for specifying the number of log cycles and the level of log details for your reports.

- **Mail Notices:** Specifies the email address for mail notifications.

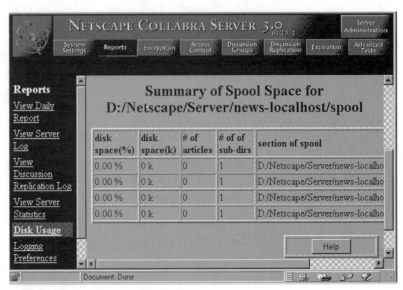

Summary of Spool Space for
D:/Netscape/Server/news-localhost/spool

disk space(%)	disk space(k)	# of articles	# of of sub-dirs	section of spool
0.00 %	0 k	0	1	D:/Netscape/Server/news-localho
0.00 %	0 k	0	1	D:/Netscape/Server/news-localho
0.00 %	0 k	0	1	D:/Netscape/Server/news-localho
0.00 %	0 k	0	1	D:/Netscape/Server/news-localho

FIGURE *Disk usage statistics.*
20.10

ENCRYPTION

Before turning encryption on, you need to have a certificate installed and an alias. The **Encryption** page only provides one option—**Activate Connection Security** (see Figure 20-11). Here, you can turn encryption on and off, and also enter the port number for encryption in the text field. If you're going to run the server with encryption turned on, use port number 563.

SERVER ACCESS CONTROL

The **Server Access Control Options** page, as shown in Figure 20-12, enables you to set up authentication procedures for accessing discussion groups in which users exchange confidential data. Authentication means that someone logging in must enter a valid user name and password. This type of authentication can be difficult or easy to overcome, depending upon how well-kept your user's usernames and passwords are. Obviously, if everyone uses his or her first name as a password (and writes it on a Post-it note and leaves it stuck on his or her monitor), you may need to implement more stringent authentication measures to enable private discussions amongst authorized users. You can accomplish this with certificates. Authentication by certificate requires users to log in from computers that have certificates installed. So not

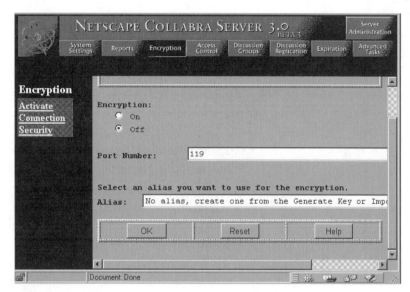

FIGURE *Activate Connection Security page.*
20.11

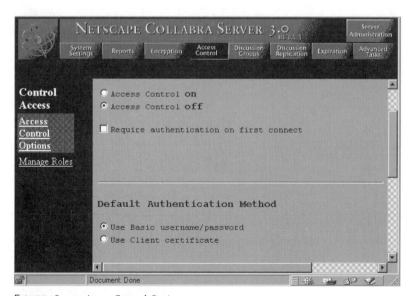

FIGURE *Server Access Control Options.*
20.12

only do they need a valid username and password, they must be on the right machine as well. Authentication by certificate requires a secure server.

To view, create, or edit your access control options, select the **Access Control Options** button from the top frame. When the list displays in the left frame, you can select from the following options to display the following pages:

- **Access Control Options:** Here you can set access control on or off, and set the required authentication time, and the authentication method (user names and passwords or certificates).
  - The first step in enabling access control is to turn it on by clicking **Access control** on. You should also require authentication on the first connect by selecting the checkbox. This means that all users have to authenticate when they first connect to the server.
  - If you don't have a secure SSL-enabled server, your only choice for authentication is the basic user name and password method. Implementing client certificates requires a secure (SSL) server.
  - You can further restrict access by limiting the hostnames that can connect. This restricts the hostnames (other computers) able to connect to your server those you specifically enter. For example, you may want to only specify company server host names and outside Internet account host names for a few coworkers who telecommute or are away from the office frequently. To restrict access, select **Enable host connection control** and enter the hostnames you wish to allow.
  - The **Do not resolve IP addresses into hostnames** keeps your server from translating the IP addresses into hostnames. However, this means that your server reports will only contain IP addresses (not the actual hostnames). This could make it more difficult to determine who is accessing your discussion groups, and if you've specified a limit for hostnames that can connect, you will have to enter IP address rather than hostnames in the textbox provided.
- **Manage Roles:** The **Roles** page, as shown in Figure 20-13, enables you to assign roles to your users. Once you have enabled access control, your users cannot access your discussion groups unless you have assigned roles to them. Roles can be assigned to users after you have created them (and their associated user groups). We have already discussed defining users and user groups, so let's discuss the roles that may be assigned.

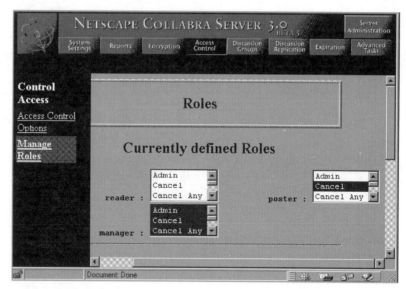

FIGURE *Manage Roles.*
20.13

Some roles are predefined, and you can create more. All roles take on one or more permissions, and permissions define each role. The permissions available are:

- **Admin:** Specifies access control by discussion group (and that group's lower level groups)
- **Cancel:** Allows the user to cancel his or her own discussion group postings
- **Cancel Any:** Allows the user to cancel any postings
- **Moderate:** Allows the user to moderate a discussion group—which means they can view postings before they appear on the discussion group and determine which ones are appropriate.
- **Newgroup:** Allows the user to create or remove any lower level group of discussion group
- **Post:** Allows the user to post to the discussion group
- **Read:** Allows the user to read messages posted to the discussion group but doesn't allow the user to post messages
- **View:** Allows the user to see that the newsgroup exists, but doesn't allow the user to access it
- **The predefined roles are Reader, Poster, and Manager:**

- **Manager:** Has all permissions
- **Poster:** Has Cancel, Post, Read, and View permissions
- **Reader:** Has Read and View permissions

You can see what permissions are available to groups on your list by selecting them from the scrolling list. To create a new role with customized settings, scroll down to the **Add New Role** section of the **Manage Roles** page. Here, you can enter a name for the role, select the permissions you'd like that role to have, then click **OK**. The new role will be defined and visible in the **Currently Defined Roles** scrolling list.

Discussion Group Management

The whole purpose of running a news server for your Intranet is to enable folks to discuss important issues and projects with each other—and to get to know one another. While the near real-time aspect of discussion groups is exciting, the fact that it's not face-to-face contact can actually help people communicate more effectively. With discussion groups, people can review discussions when they have time to do so and can think before they respond to postings. Discussion groups can also create a sense of teamwork among coworkers on different floors, different buildings, or different parts of the world.

To view, create, or edit your **Manage Discussion Groups** settings, select the **Manage Discussion Groups** button from the top frame. When the list displays in the left frame, you can select from the list of options to display the following pages:

- **Manage Discussion Groups:** Managing discussion groups entails setting access control rules for each discussion group and assigning roles to the users. The **Manage Discussion Groups** page, shown in Figure 20-14, helps you locate user groups and display the access control settings for them. If you have created a group or groups, you can select one of them by entering the group name in the text field and clicking the **Access Control Rules** button. When the **Access Controls Rules** page displays, you can make selections and changes to the rules currently in force.
- **Import Discussion Groups:** From time to time you may want to import discussion groups from other locations, such as another server or a remote host. Here, you can choose which way you want to import the

FIGURE   *Manage Discussion Groups.*
20.14

discussion group and what groups you want to import. To import a discussion group from another server or remote host, click the radio button for that option, then specify which groups you'd like to import (you can use DOS wildcards), and click **OK**. The **Discussion Group Creator** text box tells you who created a given group and requires no entry. The names of the discussion groups in the active file—a list of the discussion groups that are on that server—then appears in the frame.

- **Full Text Indexing:** When you create an index, users can search for articles (postings) on the server by key word, topic, and name. To index articles for searching, enter a name, a batch size, and a search pattern identifying the discussion groups to index in the text fields. Collabra then creates an index. You can also enter the names of the groups to index rather than a search pattern, if you like.

Replication Management

This kind of replication refers to outgoing discussion groups. Depending upon the size and scope of your Intranet, you may want to *replicate* articles from one news server to another so coworkers in other offices, partners, and others you wish to communicate with can also participate in your discussion groups. For example, you may want to create a customer support discussion group and replicate it to an Internet news server. Likewise, there may be other servers that carry work-related discussion groups your users would like to participate in. These are called incoming discussion groups.

The Collabra news server supports push feeds, meaning that it can send news feeds to other servers and receive news feeds sent to it. It cannot poll other servers and request news feeds, however, or respond to requests for news feeds from other servers (pull feeds). News servers communicate with each other via *control articles*. Control articles are discussion group articles with special headers (control headers) or subject lines. The network administrator sets up control articles to determine how other servers handle the discussion group.

You can also maintain control over your server by specifying that control articles be emailed to you rather than automatically executed, but it is easier to administer replicated internal discussion groups if you allow automatic execution. With automatic execution, incoming discussion group changes are replicated to your server without your having to intervene.

To view, create, or edit your **Discussion Replication** settings, select the **Discussion Replication** button from the top frame. When the list displays in the left frame, you can select from the list of options to display the following pages:

- **View/Manage Replication Hosts:** You can view a list of the discussion groups you are currently sending, as well as the replication hosts you are sending them to. If you'd like to remove a replication host, select from the list and click the remove button.
- **Configure Replication Host:** Displays a page with options for setting up a new replication host or editing a current one, as shown in Figure 20-15.

  To configure a replication host, do the following:

  1. Enter a hostname, such as `yournews.yourco.com` or enter the IP address in the **Remote server host name** text field.
  2. Choose which discussion groups to send by selecting them from the pulldown list. Selected groups appear in the **Discussion groups** text area below.
  3. Select the **Use port 119** radio button (most news servers use port 119), or select the **Use this port:** radio button and enter the remote server port number in the text field.

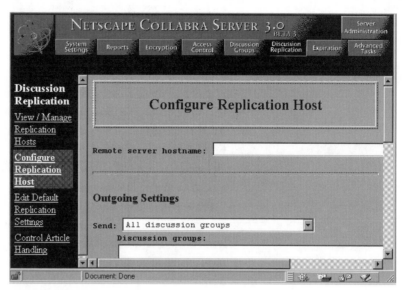

FIGURE   *Configure Replication Host.*
20.15

4. Select an SSL (secure server) setting if applicable. In most cases, you should select the **Use SSL** setting of this server to ensure that your postings conform to its security settings. If you choose the **Remote Server Uses SSL**, your server will send encrypted transmissions (it can send encrypted transmissions whether it's running in secure mode or not). Or select the **Remote server does not use SSL** to keep Collabra from sending an encrypted transmission to a non-secure server.

5. Determine your incoming settings (control articles). You can specify which groups you will accept *control articles* for, and what to do when your server receives them in the **Incoming Settings for Control Articles** section of the page. Control articles are entries that refer to different kinds of data that replicating servers send back and forth. This section provides control articles for *newgroup* (new discussion groups) and *rmgroup* (automatic removal of deleted discussion groups). An asterisk (*) in the top **newgroup** and **rmgroup** text fields means that you want to accept control articles for all discussion groups. You can also specify what to do when control articles arrive by entering a command in the **When newgroup control**

articles arrive: and **When rmgroup control articles arrive:** text fields. I'll explain this in greater detail shortly.

- When you're finished selecting options, click **OK.**

If you choose to use the SSL setting currently active for your server and the remote server has a different setting, you will receive error messages.

- **Edit Default Replication Settings:** Here, you can edit the default replication settings or choose which groups (or none) to send selecting groups from the pulldown menu.
- **Control Article Handling:** Here, you can specify control articles for *checkgroups* (lists valid discussion groups within a hierarchy), *sendsys* (requests a description of your discussion group replication) and *version* (requests the name and version of your server). You can select options for these types of control articles from the pulldown list

CONTROL ARTICLES AND OPTIONS FOR CONTROL ARTICLES

Control articles are discussion group messages that determine how servers handle replication. You can also tell your server how to deal with incoming and outgoing control articles by entering commands or by selecting settings. These settings can be entered manually in a text field or selected from a pulldown list.

Control article types are as follows:

- **newgroup:** Refers to new discussion groups added by the replicating server
- **rmgroup:** Refers to discussion groups that have been deleted from the replicating server
- **checkgroups:** Lists valid discussion groups within a hierarchy
- **sendsys:** Describes your discussion group replication
- **version:** Requests the name and version of your server

The **Discussion Replication** pages include settings for handling the control articles listed above. To specify a method for responding to control articles, you need to enter or select one of the following commands:

- **create group:** Automatically replicates new discussion groups that have been created on the replicating server.

- **send mail to admin:** Sends you an email requesting discussion group creation or deletion before groups that have been created or deleted on the replicating server are added to or deleted from your server
- **make log entry:** Enters requests from replicating servers in the log file
- **ignore:** Automatically ignores requests from replicating servers

Collabra News Server Maintenance

News server maintenance, as opposed to administrative maintenance, is concerned with keeping the discussion groups on your server fresh and vibrant and ensuring good server performance. This means you need to run regular reports with server statistics and configure the server to determine when old articles should expire. After all, you can imagine what your hard drive might look like if you never erased old files (you *do* erase old files periodically, don't you?). Of course, deleting articles on a regular basis and running reports could take all day. Fortunately, the Netscape Collabra server's **Expiration and Advanced Tasks** options display pages help you automate these processes. Once you tell Collabra how to check discussion groups, handle expiration dates, and perform process feeds, it performs these functions automatically each day.

DETERMINING ARTICLE EXPIRATIONS

Determining when and how articles posted to discussion groups should expire revolves around how important certain discussion groups and sets of articles are for the user groups within your organization, and how long the topics discussed will be relevant. For example, articles posted to a Human Resources discussion group that address questions about company policies and benefits probably remain relevant for a longer period of time than articles posted to a discussion group focused on an upcoming event. Information that remains valid for a long time should be purged less frequently than information that quickly goes stale. You also need to determine your server's capacity for handling demands—such as the amount of disk space on the hard drive. Popular discussion groups that receive hundreds of posted messages per day need to have more frequent expirations than discussion groups that contain fewer messages.

To access your expiration options, click the **Expiration** button in the top frame. When the list of expiration options appears in the left frame, you can select list items to display the corresponding page in the left frame. You can set the expiration policy for all discussion groups or for individual groups. You can let articles expire automatically after a specified amount of time on the server, or you can cancel them by deleting them manually.

For **Expiration**, the allowed functions are:

- **View Manage Expiration Policies:** Displays your expiration policies for the various discussion groups on your server. Until you customize your settings, the default expiration policy displays. The default is to obey the expiration headers (automatically delete articles whose expiration dates have been reached) and expire articles without headers after 10 days. The **View/Manage Expiration Policies** page displays when you click the **Expiration** button, or when you select the **View/Manage Expiration Policies** item from the list that displays in the left frame.

- **Create a Custom Expiration Policy:** You can set the server to obey expiration headers, expire articles without headers after a certain number of days, keep all your articles for a set length of time that you can specify, or never expire the articles. To display the **Create a Custom Expiration Policy** page, as shown in Figure 20-16, select the **Create a**

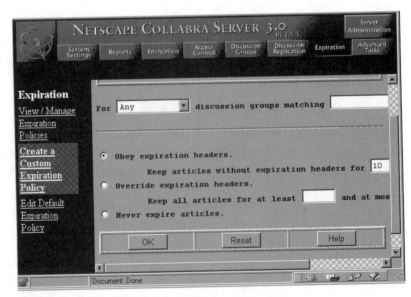

FIGURE *Create a Custom Expiration Policy.*
20.16

Custom Expiration Policy list item. When you're finished making changes, click **OK**. To cancel changes, click **Reset**.

The primary caveat here is that, eventually, with regular use your hard drive will become full. If you choose to never expire articles, you'll have to decide what you want to do with them.

- **Edit Default Expiration Policy:** If you plan on handling expirations for most discussion groups in the same manner, you can make life easier for yourself by changing the news server's default expiration policies instead of making changes to each discussion group. The **Default Expiration Policy** page offers the same options that display in the **Create a Custom Expiration Policy** page. Only the changes you make apply automatically to all discussion groups, unless you change the settings for them manually in the **Create a Custom Expiration Policy** page. To display the **Edit Default Expiration Policy** page, click the **Edit Default Expiration Policy** item from the list in the left frame. When you're finished making changes, click **OK**.

ADVANCED TASKS

The set of pages for Advanced Tasks provide you with options for recovering information and settings when something goes wrong on your server and for handling process feeds. Process feeds are applications that work with your Collabra server to handle mundane discussion groups management tasks automatically. To view your **Advanced Tasks** options, click the **Advanced Tasks** button in the top frame.

Advanced Tasks offers four options:

- **Recovery:** The **Recovery** page, shown in Figure 20-17, provides options for recovering vital Collabra server files when something goes wrong with your system. The **Recovery** page appears automatically when you click the **Advanced Tasks** button. or you can click the **Recovery** option from the top of the list in the left frame.

  You can do the following from the **Recovery** page:

  - **Run the** `news.daily` **program:** `News.daily` runs the daily tasks for maintaining the Collabra server, such as producing a status report, removing old articles, maintaining the active file and history file, and rotating the log files. You can force the server to do all

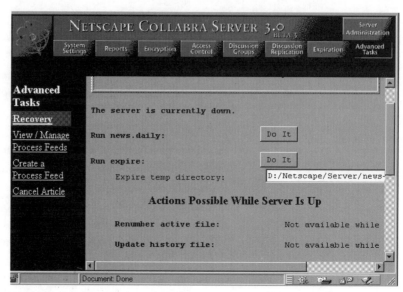

FIGURE *Advanced Tasks Recovery page.*
20.17

maintenance activities immediately, or expire articles immediately by running `news.daily` at any time. `News.daily` can be run whether the server is up or down. To run `news.daily`, click the **Do It** button following the **Run news.daily:** prompt.

• **Run expire: Expire** purges discussion group articles from your system, and also purges references to them from the discussion group's history file (according to the settings of your configuration). If you are running out of disk space or have reset your configuration settings, you should run expire. You can run it any time, whether the server is up or down. To run the expire program, click the **Do It** button following the **Run expire:** prompt. You can also specify a new temporary directory for expired files by entering the directory path in the **Expire temp directory:** text field.

• The Recovery page also provides options for actions you can only take when the server is up and running:

• **Renumber the active file:** The active file lists all the discussion groups on your server, high and low articles numbers, and a flag indicating the type of group. Before remaking the active file, try renumbering it. This may clear up any problems you are experiencing.

- **Update the history file:** The history file lists the articles you have stored and possibly expired, and contains data about article creation times, message ID's, and article locations. Try rebuilding the history file (rather than updating or remaking it) if you are experiencing difficulties with it (such as performance problems or file corruption).

- **Remake the active file:** Remaking the active file or the history file can be very time consuming. And settings, like flags indicating moderated groups, will be lost. Perform these actions only if you have tried renumbering the active file or rebuilding history indexes.

- **Rebuild history indexes:** You can also tell Collabra to rebuild your history index files for your discussion groups.

- **Remake the history file:** Recreates history files for your discussion groups.

- **Remake search indexes:** Recreates search indexes so users can search for discussion groups and articles on the server.

- **View/Manage Process Feeds:** Lists any process feeds that you have defined, or indicates that you don't have any process feeds defined. Process feeds are programs which Collabra Server can send articles to. These programs can perform actions upon specified articles—such as archiving them to a directory, including them with other data, and more.

- **Create a Process Feed:** Provides options for identifying process feeds and specifying how to run them, as shown in Figure 20-18. Setting up a process feed requires you to enter and select options for the following:

  - **Process feed identifier:** Enter the name of the process feed in the text field (no spaces or punctuation marks are allowed).

  - **Run this process:** Enter the path name to the program that executes the process, along with any command-line arguments you include in the text field. When the process activates, it reads the message ID and location of the articles you send.

 The more processes you run, particularly if there are a great many articles incoming, the higher the load on your system.

  - **What information to send to process:** Choose the type of pathname you want to send to the process by selecting either the **Send full pathname to process** or **Send spool relative pathname to**

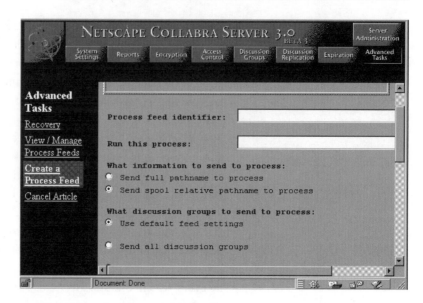

FIGURE *Advanced Tasks Create a Process Feed.*
20.18

process radio button. A relative pathname means the path relative
to the spool, while the absolute pathname begins at the server's
root directory.

- **What discussion groups to send to process:** To stick with current
  process feed settings, select the **Use default feed settings** radio button. To process all of your discussion groups, click the **Send all discussion groups** radio button. To send all discussion groups, but
  exclude a few of them, click the **Send all discussion groups except:**
  radio button, and enter your list of excluded discussion groups in
  the text field. To process a few, select discussion groups, click the
  Send only these discussion groups: radio buttons and create a list
  of discussion groups in the text field. To disable to current process
  feed, click the **Disable this process feed:** radio button.

- **Advanced Specification:** If you need to run a process for a group of
  articles that can best be selected by using pattern matching with
  wild cards, click the **Advanced Specification** radio button.

- To save your settings, click the **OK** button. To cancel your changes,
  click the **Reset** button.

- **Cancel Article:** You can cancel articles by selecting the **Cancel Article** item from the list in the left frame. When the **Cancel Article** page appears, enter the message ID for the message you want to remove in the **Message ID:** text field and click the **OK** button. To cancel your entry, click the **Reset** button.

Server Configuration Files

The Collabra configuration files are stored in the server root directory. These files perform a variety of functions, from configuring the Admin server to specifying the Collabra server version information. Netscape's documentation warns against changing these files unless you're experienced in working with servers. Let your conscience (and your capacity for risky adventures) be your guide.

Following is a list of configuration files:

- **ns-admin.conf:** Server configuration file
- **contrl.ctl:** Specifies handling of control messages
- **dblist.ini:** Defines the path, language, etc.
- **distrib.pats:** Adds distribution header to articles (if none exists)
- **expire.ctl:** Removes old articles
- **extensions:** Defines supported NNTP extensions
- **gateways:** Lists email addresses for news-to-email gateway groups
- **hosts.nntp:** Lists replication hosts sending news to your server
- **inn.conf:** Server configuration file
- **moderators:** Lists email addresses for moderators
- **motd:** Message of the day file
- **news feeds:** Specifies sending of incoming discussion groups to other sites
- **newsgroups:** Contains descriptions of discussion groups
- **newstime.conf:** Controls how and when nntpsend and news.daily run
- **nnrp.access:** Controls access to NNTP sites
- **nntpsend.ctl:** Specifies the default list of sites fed by nntpsend
- **nenews.conf:** Configures variables and path names for commands and utilities
- **overview.fmt:** Used by newsreaders to get to articles
- **passwd.nntp:** Contains hostname and password information
- **prettynames:** Lists discussion groups and their display names
- **searches:** Lists indexed discussion groups
- **snmp.conf:** Stores information about SNMP configurations
- **subscriptions:** Lists default discussion groups
- **system.ini:** Contains search engine configuration information
- **version file:** Collabra server version information

21

Enterprise Scheduling with Calendar

Real-time contact is what calendars are all about. Whether you're planning a face-to-face meeting, a conference call, or even a birthday party, calendars help us plan and track our lives. Although Netscape Calendar is definitely a modern invention, even ancient civilizations created calendars to track and schedule agricultural tasks, religious ceremonies, and other events. We might think of calendars as onerous taskmasters or as an organizational blessing, but regardless how we feel about them, they are indispensable.

In today's organization, meetings can be one of the most unproductive forms of communication. Scheduling them can be just about impossible, given the demands not only on everyone's time but on the resources required as well—such as conference rooms, tables and chairs, audio and visual equipment. And meetings aren't the only issue. What if two or more departments need to use the photocopier all day to meet deadlines? And with more and more offices hiring independent contractors and more workers telecommuting these days, how can anyone coordinate projects and deadlines?

Here's where Netscape Calendar comes into the picture. For an individual user, Calendar is a nifty personal scheduling tool. For users connected by an organizational Intranet with Netscape Calendar server running, Calendar becomes a powerful enterprise scheduling tool that keeps track of individuals, groups, projects, and resources across the network. In order to use the Netscape Calendar client's full range of features, you must have the Calendar server loaded and running somewhere on your network.

TIP

If you get stuck, visit Netscape's Nuggies page at `http://help.netscape. com/nuggies/`. *Nuggies stands for Netscape Users Groups—this page has links to newsgroups about Netscape's products, including Calendar and Calendar server. And of course, there's always the Help system.*

This chapter gets you started with using Calendar and also tells you how to set up and configure the Calendar server. Topics covered include:

- What are Calendar and Calendar server?
- Getting started with Calendar
- Accessing individual and group agendas
- Getting and installing the Calendar server
- Running the Calendar server

Calendar only comes with the Pro version of Communicator, not the Standard version.

What Are Calendar and Calendar Server?

Calendar is a Netscape Communicator Pro component designed to work on an organizational network that has the Netscape Calendar server running. The Calendar server is part of the Netscape SuiteSpot collection of server tools, which is available through Netscape's Web page at `http://home.netscape.com/`. If you aren't on a Calendar server-enabled network, the Calendar client can work nicely as a personal scheduling application, but you won't get the full range of Calendar services. Basically, the Calendar server manages a database consisting of each user's calendars installed on the network. When you enter a lunch meeting in the 12:15 PM slot for a specific date, the Calendar server keeps track of the information you enter. When coworkers check the Calendar server to see when you're available, they can see that you have a meeting scheduled. Similarly, when you schedule meetings, you can also specify which room and which resources you plan on using, so others can check to see if resources are available.

Your individual Calendar client has a "home" server, similar to an email mailbox. Your calendar may exist on the server or on your desktop machine, and you can synchronize them whenever a network connection is made. If everyone's calendar is on the same server, free time searches are performed on the server, but if users are spread across several servers, your "home" server will poll the other servers individually and present the results to you in a unified manner. The Netscape Calendar product uses the vCalendar format (developed by Versit Corporation), along with Transmissions Control Protocol/Internet Protocol (TCP/IP) and Simple Mail Transfer Protocol (SMTP). The people at Netscape hope that this format will become the standard for calendaring. And I hope so, too, because if more people buy Netscape products, more people will buy my books.

Before you can use Calendar on a network, you need to set up a user profile—or have your network administrator set one up for you. For more about setting up a user profile, see Chapter 3.

Getting Started with Calendar

Once you have the Calendar product installed on your system, connected to the Calendar server, and properly set up for use, you can begin working with it. You can enter your own scheduling information, access coworkers' calendars, and get updated information from the server. To launch Calendar, launch Navigator and select **Calendar** from the **Communicator** menu. When the Netscape **Calendar Sign-In** dialog box appears, as shown in Figure 21-1, enter your user name and password. You'll also need to select the name of the server running calendar from the pulldown list (if you're working with Calendar off-line, select the **Off-line** option). If you don't know this information, ask your network administrator.

When Calendar appears, as shown in Figure 21-2, it shows a day view calendar (you can also view your calendar by week or month), an agenda list, and the recurring entry (if you've created one). First, let's take a quick look at Calendar and talk about what all the elements in the Calendar window do.

The **Calendar** window contains the following elements:

- **Title Bar:** Displays the name of the person for whom the user profile is set (for more on user profiles, see Chapter 3).
- **Toolbar:** Displays toolbar buttons for accessing your In tray, printing, and creating, editing, and viewing tasks, events, and daily notes.
- **Date Control Bar:** Provides options for viewing and navigating your daily **Agenda** page.
- **Agenda Page:** Defaults to the **Day** view, which displays a list of entries that you can view, edit, and enter. You can also switch from the **Day** view to the **Month** or **Week** view.
- **Task List:** Provides a list of ongoing tasks that you and your coworkers specify.

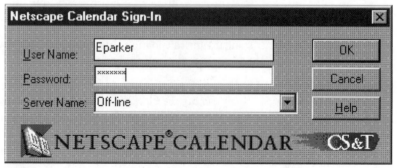

FIGURE *Netscape Calendar Sign-In dialog box.*
21.1

FIGURE *Calendar default view.*
21.2

- **Daily Note:** You (or your supervisor) can create daily, weekly, or monthly notes to remind you of things that need to be done at specified intervals.

The toolbar buttons may look unfamiliar if you've never used a scheduling application before, but they do the following:

- **Open In Tray:** Displays **In Tray** with incoming and outgoing **Calendar** entries.
- **Open Agenda:** Displays a dialog box so you can search for and edit your own agenda or an agenda that you have been allowed access to or are designated to enter settings for.
- **Open Tasks:** Displays a dialog box so you can search for and edit your own task list or a task list that you have been allowed access to or are designated to enter settings for.
- **Open Group Agenda:** You can also search for and view agendas for work groups.

- **Go to Entry:** Displays a dialog box so you can specify a Calendar entry you want to check—such as an important upcoming meeting.
- **View Day:** Displays your daily agenda, as shown in Figure 21-2. This is the default display when you launch Calendar.
- **View Week:** Displays your agenda for the entire week. To return to the default Calendar display with your daily agenda, click the **Close** button.
- **View Month:** You can also display your agenda for the entire month.
- **Decrease Time Slot:** Time slots are set up in 15 minute intervals. But life doesn't happen in 15-minute intervals! You can decrease individual time slots in 5-minute increments by selecting a time slot in your daily agenda and clicking the **Decrease Time Slot** button.
- **Increase Time Slot:** You can increase individual time slots in 5-minute increments by selecting a time slot in your daily agenda and clicking the **Increase Time Slot** button.
- **Icons On/Off:** Entries in your agenda appear alongside icons that represent the type of entry. You can make the icons disappear or reappear by clicking the **Icons On/Off** button.
- **Agenda Entry Colors:** Agenda entries are also color coded by status. As explained later in this chapter, when coworkers make calendar entries, you can accept items, refuse items, or accept items tentatively. The color codes also remind you of whether you've confirmed entries by accepting or refusing them. But who can remember all these color codes? You don't need to. Just click the **Agenda Entry Colors** to jog your memory.
- **New Agenda:** Click to display a dialog box that enables you to add a new agenda entry to your calendar.
- **New Task:** Click to display a dialog box that enables you to add a new task entry to your calendar.
- **New Day Event:** Click to display a dialog box that enables you to add a new day event entry to your calendar.
- **New Daily Note:** Click to display a dialog box that enables you to add a new daily note to your calendar.
- **Print:** Click to print the currently displayed agenda page.

Don't worry if you don't understand what all these items mean. I explain everything in greater detail later in this chapter.

Calendar also provides a Date Control bar so you can find things in your calendar more easily. The Date Control Bar provides the following options:

FIGURE   *You can search for a specific day by clicking the Open Calendar button on*
21.3   *the Date Control bar.*

- **Move back one week:** Jumps you back to the previous week's agenda page.
- **Move forward one week:** Jumps you forward to the following week's agenda page.
- **Move forward one day:** Jumps you to the next day's agenda page.
- **Move back one day:** Jumps you to the previous day's agenda page
- **Open Calendar:** Displays a miniature calendar, as shown in Figure 21-3, so you can look for a specific day by selecting a month and year from the pulldown lists and then clicking a date.
- **Make rows shorter:** Click to shorten the rows in your daily agenda so you can view more rows.
- **Make rows taller:** Click to make the rows in your daily agenda taller so you can view entries in greater detail.

TIME MANAGEMENT

Before we get into working with Calendar, let's talk a little about time management first. For starters, it's a good idea to arrange your activities according to description, priority, date, duration, and status—especially since this is similar to how Calendar organizes activities. For example, you could make a list like the one shown in Table 21-1.

In a lot of ways, Netscape Calendar isn't much different than the daily planner you keep on your desk or in your briefcase, purse, or backpack. When planning activities, you should consider the following:

TABLE 21.1   A Piece of Your Daily Routine

Description	Priority	Date*Time	Duration	Status
Meeting	1	1/1/97*3PM	2 Hours	weekly
Party	2	1/1/97*5PM	2 Hours	pending

- **Description:** Describe activities in a way that helps you remember what they are.
- **Priority:** Calendar also encourages you to prioritize activities (for example, of course a business meeting is more important than a party, even though we wish things were the other way around!).
- **Date and time:** When entering events, you should specify the date and time. When entering projects, you should specify the due date.
- **Status:** Calendar also offers options for specifying the status of events and projects—for example, whether an event occurs on a monthly or weekly basis, or the percentage of a project that has been completed.

Table 21-1 shows why it's important to plan a little before entering data. You need to attend both activities, but you've left yourself no time to travel from one to the other. Calendar helps you check for time conflicts and also makes your schedule easier to visualize so you can spot potential problems. It's a good idea to incorporate bits and pieces of time into your schedule (you don't have to tell everyone the real activity, just make it sound official) so you can give yourself breathing room between functions, and travel time between locations, and perhaps still have a life as well (keep dreaming, right?).

TIP

You can also export and import your agenda so you can view it off-line on a different computer that has Communicator Pro but isn't connected to the server, or even with a Personal Information Manager. For more about working with Calendar offline, see Chapter 13.

CAUTION

Everything you enter in Netscape Calendar gets advertised to others on the network—so this is not *a good place for jotting down a reminder about that upcoming job interview with your company's competitor.*

HANDLING CALENDAR ENTRIES IN YOUR IN TRAY

If you're using Calendar on a network, then you won't be the only person trying to make entries in your calendar. Therefore, you should check your **In**

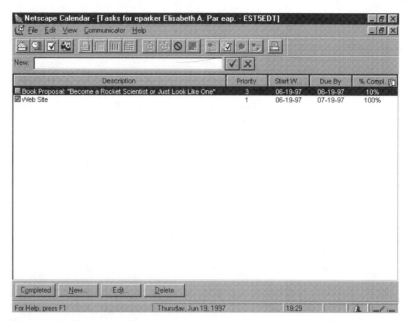

FIGURE *The Calendar In Tray.*
21.4

Tray throughout the day. To display your **In Tray**, as shown in Figure 21-4, click the **In Tray** button. Your online **In Tray** works a lot like plain old analog. It contains a folder with your name—and folders with other people's names on it, if the server administrator has designated you as someone who is authorized to make entries for coworkers.

Your user **In Tray** contains the following folders:

- **New Entries:** New agenda items for your calendar. You can view each item by double-clicking on the agenda item to display a dialog box with further information.

- **Entries you've accepted:** Entries from your **New Entries** folder that you choose to accept.

- **Entries you've sent out:** Entries that you've made on other people's calendars and have sent out.

- **Entries you've refused:** Entries that you've turned down.

To open a folder, select and double-click it. To view items in your folders, double-click on them. Items are represented by icons that indicate daily notes (reminders of things that have to be done every day), holidays, agenda entries, day events (events that take all day), and recurring entries (tasks or events that need to be performed or attended at specified intervals).

Accepting and Refusing Entries

It's easy to accept entries or turn them down. To accept an entry item, select and drag it from your **New Entries** folder to your **Entries you've accepted** folder. To refuse an entry, select and drag it from your **New Entries** folder into the **Entries you've refused** folder. Calendar updates your changes automatically on your computer and on the Calendar server.

MAKING ENTRIES

Chances are, you'll also have some entries of your own to make in your calendar. Calendar helps you schedule meetings and the use of office resources, as well as enabling you to let coworkers know when you're available.

You can make the following types of entries:

- **Agenda:** Specific tasks and events that appear as items on your agenda. To display items on your agenda, click the **Open Agenda** toolbar button. To make a new agenda entry, click the **New Agenda** toolbar button.
- **Task:** Ongoing projects that appear as items on your task list. Your task list appears next to your daily agenda. Or you can click the **Open Task** button to display a separate task list. To create a new task entry, click the **New Task** toolbar button.
- **Day Event:** Special events that take an entire day. To enter a new day event, click the **New Day Event** toolbar button.
- **Daily Note:** Daily reminders. To create a new daily reminder, click the **new Daily Note** button.

When you click one of the buttons, a window appears and prompts you for information. Since **Agenda**, **Task**, **Day Event**, and **Daily Note** windows all prompt for similar information, let's take entering a new agenda item as a typical example.

The **New Agenda Entry** window prompts you for information in the following categories:

- **General:** The **General** section in the **New Agenda Entry** window, as shown in Figure 21-5, prompts you for the following information:

FIGURE *New Agenda Entry General window.*
21.5

- **Title:** Enter a name for your new entry in the **Title:** text field. You can also select the **Tentative** checkbox if the item is tentative.
- **Date, Start Time, Duration, and End Time:** You can enter a date, start time (when the meeting or event begins), duration (number of hours and minutes that the meeting or event will last), and end time (when the meeting or event ends) by entering the appropriate dates and times in the text fields or by clicking the up or down buttons. If you select a start time and an end time, the **Duration:** field fills in automatically.
- **People and resources:** You can then enter the names of people you want to attend and the resources you want to use (such as meeting rooms) by clicking the **Directory Search** button (with the magnifying glass) and the **Select a Group** button. When the **Directory Search** or **Select a Group** dialog box appears, you can search for

items and select them. When you select items, they appear on the list below the **Add:** text field. To delete an individual, resource, or group from your list, select the item and click the **Delete** button.

- **Check Conflicts:** Click the **Check Conflicts** button to search the server for possible conflicts, such as people who have other items on their agenda or resources scheduled for use during your specified time slot.

- **Suggest Date/Time:** If conflicts are found, click the **Suggest Date/Time** button to search the server for a better time.

- **Create:** When you're finished choosing options, click the **Create** button to create your new entry. You can also click the **Cancel** button to cancel the entry.

- **Summary:** The **Summary** window, as shown in Figure 21-6, displays the title of the entry, who initiated the event, and who was invited to

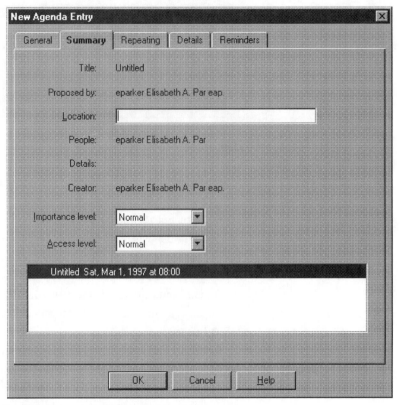

FIGURE *New Agenda Entry Summary window.*
21.6

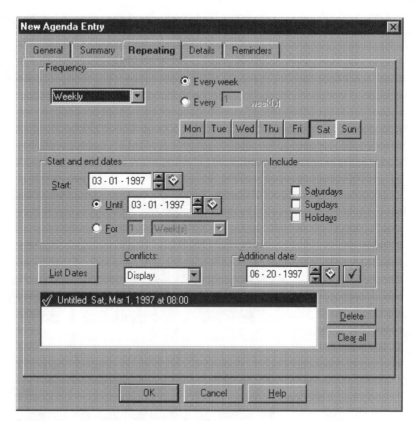

FIGURE   *New Agenda Entry Repeating window.*
21.7

attend. In addition, you can specify a location and select importance and access levels from the pulldown list.

- **Repeating:** The **Repeating** window, as shown in Figure 21-7, lets you specify options for events or meetings that recur on a regular basis. You can specify the frequency (weekly or monthly, for example) from the pulldown list, click a button for a day, and specify starting and ending dates.

- **Details:** The **Details** window, as shown in Figure 21-8, provides a **Description:** text field for entering additional information, such as a list of topics to be discussed. In addition, you can click the **Attach** button to attach a file to the entry.

- **Reminders:** The **Reminders** window, as shown in Figure 21-9, offers options for providing reminders to people who have been invited to

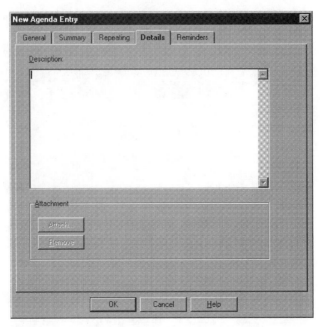

FIGURE *New Agenda Entry Details window.*
21.8

FIGURE *New Agenda Entry Reminders window.*
21.9

attend the meeting or event. To specify a reminder, click the **Set Reminder** radio button, and select a type of reminder from the **Type:** pulldown list. For example, you may want to specify that a pop-up window with a reminder message appears 15 minutes before the meeting or event so users get there on time.

When you're finished selecting options, return to the **General** window and click the **Create** button. The new agenda item automatically gets sent to the server, which automatically updates your calendar and sends entries to people's in trays.

VIEWING AND EDITING CALENDAR ENTRIES

So let's say you entered an appointment in your agenda, and now the appointment time has changed and you need to enter the new time? Or you need to view details for a mysterious entry that appears in today's agenda? No problem. You can view details for entries in your calendar and make edits to entries that you're authorized to edit by double-clicking on the item to bring up the **Edit** window. The **Edit** window displays all of the options explained in the previous section.

GIVING PEOPLE ACCESS TO YOUR CALENDAR

Sometimes, you might need to give others access to your agenda. For example, your secretary might need to set up appointments for you, or your supervisor may need to include you in a department meeting. Fortunately, it's easy to give others access to your agenda. Simply select **Access Rights** from the **Edit** menu to display the **Access Rights** window. Here, you can grant rights to other users, specify who can view your agenda and what parts of your agenda they can view, and choose designates—people who you authorize to modify entries in your calendar.

Accessing Individual and Group Agendas

In Netscape Calendar, your personal information is called your *Agenda*. If you're in charge of a project or a department, then chances are, you've been set up as a *designate* for your work group. A designate is a person who has the ability to modify agendas for individuals or groups. Even if you aren't authorized to modify other people's agendas, you might need to check up on one of your coworker's agendas before scheduling a meeting or seeing whether they're available to help with a project.

To access an individual's agenda, do the following:

1. Click the **Open an Agenda** toolbar button.
2. When the **Open an Agenda** dialog box appears, as shown in Figure 21-10, click the **Modify your own Agenda** button to view your own agenda, or select the **View the Agenda of:** radio button and enter the person's name in the text field.
3. To do a search for someone, click the **Search** (magnifying glass) icon.
4. Click the **Check** button (with the check mark) to confirm the entry
5. Click the **OK** button.

To modify another user's agenda as a designate (someone who is authorized by the user to make changes to the user's calendar), click the **Open an Agenda** toolbar button and choose the **Modify, as a designate, the Agenda of** radio button to display a list of users who have specified you as a designate.

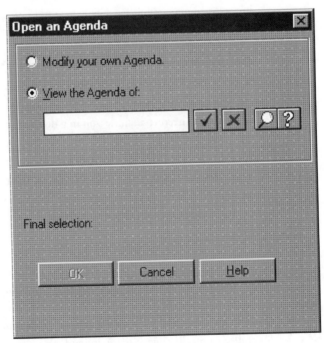

FIGURE *Open an Agenda dialog box.*
21.10

To access a group's agenda, do the following:

1. Click the **Open Group Agenda** button
2. When the **Selection Group Agenda** dialog box appears as shown in Figure 21-11, enter the name of a group and click the **Check** button (with the check mark) to display the group on the **Agenda List**.
3. To display a list of groups that you can select from, click the **Groups** icon. To search for a group, click the **Search** icon.
4. Click **OK**.

To modify another group's agenda as a designate (someone who is authorized by the group to make changes to the group's calendar), click the **Open an Agenda** toolbar button and choose the **Modify, as a designate, the Agenda of** radio button to display a list of groups who have specified you as a designate.

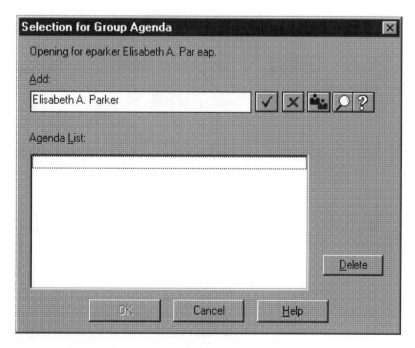

FIGURE *Selection for Group Agenda dialog box.*
21.11

WORKING WITH GROUPS

If you work in a large office, chances are you're part of some work group or another. Work groups are generally people who share something in common—for example, they're in the same department, they're working on a project together, or they're at the same management level. Since these people often get invited to the same meetings and work on the same tasks, it makes sense to set them up as groups. When agenda entries and tasks are addressed to a group, everyone in the group receives them.

There are four types of Calendar groups:

- **Public groups:** Include everyone on the Calendar server
- **Private groups:** Include only group creators
- **Administrator:** Include only those who are authorized to create and administrate groups
- **Members only:** Include only specified members

The ability to create, edit, and delete groups is determined by the network administrator.

Creating New Groups

To create a new group, do the following:

1. Select **Manage Groups** from the **Edit** menu.
2. When the **Manage Groups** dialog box appears, enter the name of the new group in the **Add Group** text field.
3. Select a group type from the pulldown menu.

Click the **Check** icon to add the new group to the **Groups** list, or click the X icon to cancel the new group.

Editing Groups

Once you create a group, you can add members and resources, delete members and resources, or edit a group's name and group type, by doing the following:

1. Select **Manage Groups** from the **Edit** menu.
2. When the **Manage Groups** dialog box appears, select the group you wish to modify from the list by clicking it.
3. When the group information displays in the **Modify Selected Group** section, you can make your changes.

4. Click the **Check** icon to save your changes, or click the X icon to cancel them.

Group members cannot have spaces in them. Instead, you must substitute a carat (^). For example, if you add someone named Lisa Smith, you'd have to enter Lisa^Smith. To enter a carat, use the Shift+6 key combination. Resources should be named in a similar manner.

CAUTION

Removing Groups

Sometimes, you may need to remove a group. For example, if your company organizes a special event, you might create a group to include people who are involved in planning the event. However, once the event is over, the group no longer has any purpose.

To remove a group, do the following:

1. Select **Manage Groups** from the **Edit** menu
2. When the **Manage Groups** dialog box appears, select the group you wish to delete from the list by clicking it.
3. When the group information displays in the **Modify Selected Group** section, click the **Delete** button.
4. Click the **Check** icon to save your changes, or click the X icon to cancel them.

Getting and Installing the Calendar Server

You can download a trial or for-purchase version of Netscape's Calendar Server from the Netscape home page (`http://home.netscape.com`). Calendar Server is available for Windows NT and UNIX users, but this chapter shows the Calendar Server running on Windows NT. Features may appear somewhat differently, depending upon the version of Calendar you download and the machine you run it on.

Each Calendar Server you run must have its own unique node-ID, and once that is chosen, it cannot be changed. Many organizations will run more than one Calendar Server, and this scheme helps them recognize each other and prevent conflicts. Each node tracks its own users and resources, as well as users and resources on remote Calendar Servers to which it is connected.

In order to use Netscape Calendar (the client) you must be running Netscape Calendar Server (or some compatible product) somewhere on your network. To install and run Calendar Server, you must have Windows NT 4.0 Service Pack 2, at least 32MB RAM, and a minimum of 15MB free disk space.

To install the Calendar server, do the following (an easy-to-use Setup Wizard takes you through the setup routine):

1. Double-click the **Calendar Server** installer icon.
2. When the Node-ID dialog box appears, enter a network-unique number between 10000 and 20000. A network-unique node ID number cannot be assigned *to any other server* on the network. Click the **Next** button.
3. When the **Node Alias** dialog box appears, enter a name for the Node ID. This should be something you can easily remember and associate with the Node ID and remember—such as Calendar Server #1. Click the **Next** button.
4. When the **Node Password** dialog box appears, create a password and enter in the **Password:** text field that consists of up to fifteen characters, then enter it again in the **Confirm:** text field to confirm the password. Click the **Next** button.
5. When the **Time Zone** dialog box appears, select the appropriate time zone—for example, I live in California so I would specify Pacific Standard Time. Click the **Next** button.
6. When the **Maximum Number of Concurrent users** dialog box appears, specify the maximum number of people that can use the Calendar server at any given time. This number depends on what your server can handle. This must be a number between 15 and 3800. Click the **Next** button.
7. When the **Mail Notification** dialog box appears, choose whether to enable or disable mail notification. Click the **Next** button.
8. When the **Netscape Mail Server Host** dialog box appears, enter the name of your Netscape mail server. Click the **Next** button.
9. When the **Calendar server configuration settings** dialog box appears, as shown in Figure 21-12, you can view your current settings. To change your settings, click the **Back** button to return to the dialog boxes and reenter settings for items you wish to correct. To confirm your configuration settings, click the **Next** button.

The Setup Wizard will configure your server for you. If you decide to remove the Calendar Server at some point, go to the Windows NT Control

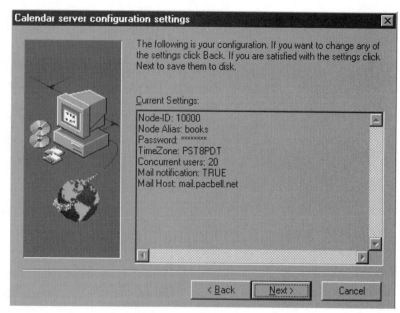

FIGURE *Calendar server configuration settings dialog box.*
21.12

Panel, use the **Add/Remove** icon, select **Netscape Calendar Server**, and click the **Add/Remove** option to display a dialog box with options.

Running the Calendar Server	Now that the initial installation is complete, you can control the server by using the Calendar Server's administration tool. You can launch the Netscape Calendar Server Administrator by selecting the **Calendar Server Administrator** from your **Start** menu. It is located in the Netscape **Calendar** folder, inside your **Programs** folder. When you launch Calendar Server Administrator, a blank window appears, as shown in Figure 21-13. The sheer emptiness of the application window may make you feel like you've done something wrong, but this really *is* how the application looks. So how do you enter settings? When you select items from the menus, dialog boxes appear.

NETSCAPE CALENDAR SERVICES

Netscape's Calendar Server runs four services that enable you to keep Calendar running smoothly. Both the Lock Manager and the Engine must be running for Netscape Calendar Server to operate.

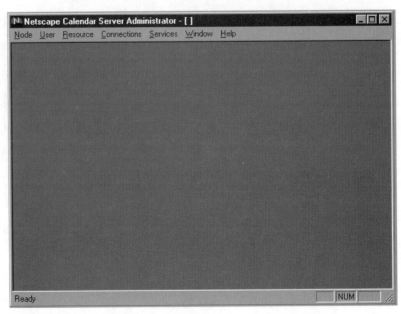

FIGURE *Netscape Calendar Server Administrator.*
21.13

- **Calendar Lock Manager:** Handles node access requests, so that authorized coworkers who log in from different servers within the organization can also view agendas and access information.
- **Calendar Engine:** Serves as the database engine for Calendar Server. As mentioned earlier in this chapter, Calendar works like a giant database and each coworker's agenda functions as part of the database.
- **Calendar Synchronous Network Connection:** Connection maintains open connections to other nodes on the network simultaneously to keep track of people's agendas, resources, and other data.
- **Calendar Corporate Wide Services:** Allows users on different nodes to exchange information.

In addition, Netscape Calendar Server comes with several command-line utilities that enable you to perform a variety of tasks. They are:

- **unicpinu:** Copies a user's agenda from a file into the server
- **unicpoutu:** Copies a user's agenda from the server to a file
- **unicpinr:** Copies a resource from a file into the server
- **unicpoutr:** Copies a resource from the server to a file

- **unirmold:** Deletes old events and tasks from the database
- **unidbfix:** Checks, repairs and defragments a server node
- **unilckd:** Controls the calendar Lock Manager service
- **uniengd:** Controls the Calendar Engine service
- **unisncd:** Controls the Calendar Synchronous Network Connection service
- **unicwsd:** Controls the Calendar Corporate Wide service

By using these command-line utilities you can import and export users and resources, delete out-dated events and tasks, and manage your four services.

STARTING AND STOPPING SERVICES

One of the first things you should know about is how to start and stop Calendar Server services. This often becomes necessary when you need to do routine maintenance on the server or deal with problems when they occur. In these situations, it is better to keep people from using the server until you finish performing tasks.

To start or stop Calendar services, do the following:

1. Select the **Sign-In** option from the **Node** menu so you can access the server.
2. When the **Sign-In** dialog box appears, enter the administrator password, node ID, and computer name in the appropriate text fields, then click **OK**.
3. Select **Properties** from the **Node** menu.
4. When the **Services** dialog box appears, as shown in Figure 21-14, choose a service from the list and click the **Start** or **Stop** button. You can also choose the **Refresh** button to ensure that you are viewing the most recent information.
5. Click the **Close** button when you finish.

Remember that in order for the server to work, the Calendar Lock Manager and the Calendar Engine must be running. When you choose to start up one of them, the other one starts up automatically.

CREATING AND EDITING USERS

In order for your coworkers to use the server, you need to give them access by creating new users. When you create new users, you assign them pass-

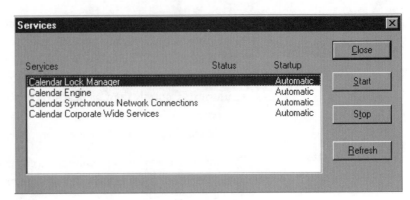

FIGURE *Starting and stopping Calendar services.*
21.14

words and also enter contact information so you can keep track of them better. The first step in creating users is to sign into a node. A node is actually a database containing all the information about users, resources, and other components of Calendar. After signing in to a node, you can start entering, editing, and deleting data about users and resources.

To sign in, select **Sign-In** from the **Node** menu, enter the administrator's password, enter the computer name and the node ID, and then click **OK**.

To begin creating a new user, do the following:

1. Select **New User** from the **User** menu.
2. When the **New User** window appears with the **User** tab displayed, as shown in Figure 21-15, enter their last name, first name, initials, password, and other contact information in the appropriate text field. You will also have to enter the password twice (once in the **Password** text field and once in the **Confirm Password** text field)
3. Click the **X400 Address** tab to display the X400 address options, as shown in Figure 21-16. Here, you can assign the user to organizational units in the **Org Unit** text field by entering the names of any groups you want the user to be part of. You can also enter the user's organization name and country code, as well as specify private and administrative domains for them. The user will have access to resources in accordance with the properties assigned to the groups you specify for the user.

When you're finished entering new user information, click **OK**.

FIGURE
21.15
The New User window, with User tab selected.

FIGURE
21.16
New User window with X400 Address tab selected.

You cannot view the X400 Address options until you enter at least the last and first name for a user.

CAUTION

EDITING USER INFORMATION

Once you create your users, you may need to modify their information and server access capabilities (as defined by the groups you assign them to) from time to time. For example, if a user gets promoted, you may want to assign that user to groups that allow him or her higher levels of access.

To edit users, do the following:

1. Select **Properties** from the **User** menu, then choose **Search**.
2. When the **Search** window appears (it displays similar options as the **New User** dialog box), as shown in Figure 21-17, make sure the **Users** tab is selected (you can also edit resources by clicking the **Resources** tab).

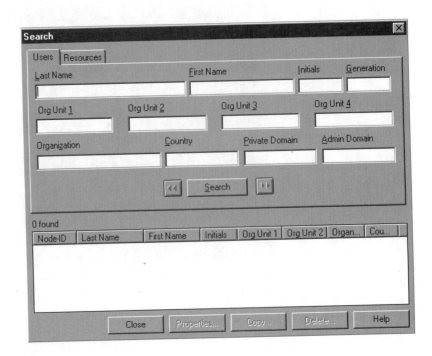

FIGURE *Search window.*

21.17

3. Enter information in any of the text fields and click the **Search** button to find the user you want to edit.
4. When the user's information displays on the list in the text area at the bottom of the window, select the user name.
5. Click the **Properties** button.
6. When the user information appears, you can change user information.

To edit information, make your changes in the appropriate data field and click **OK** to return to the **Search** window. When you're finished editing users, click the **Close** button.

DELETING USERS

To delete a user, do the following:

1. Select **Properties** from the **User** menu, then choose **Search**.
2. When the **Search** window appears, enter information in any of the text fields and click the **Search** button to find the user you want to edit.
3. When the user's information displays on the list in the text area at the bottom of the window select the user name.
4. Click the **Delete** button.

When you're finished editing or deleting users, click the **Close** button.

CREATING AND EDITING RESOURCES

Resources, unlike people, are things such as conference rooms and A/V equipment that are shared within your organization. Remember the days when each division would have its own conference room and equipment? Not any more. Nowadays we all share, and unsurprisingly, it's more cost-effective. But it also means we need a method for reserving the rooms and equipment. Netscape Calendar offers that ability by treating these things much like people, with schedules and meeting times.

To create a resource, select **New Resource** from the **Resource** menu. When the **New Resource** dialog box appears, as shown in Figure 21-18, enter the following information:

- **Resource Name:** Assign a name to the resource, such as "color printer" or "2nd floor meeting room."
- **Resource Number:** Assign a number to the resource.

FIGURE *New Resource window.*
21.18

- **Password:** Assign a password required for accessing or reserving the resource.
- **Capacity:** Enter the maximum number of users who can access this resource at once.
- **Contact's Last Name and Contact's Given Name:** Enter the administrative contact's last name and first name. This should be the person in charge of the specified resource.
- **Phone number, Extension, and Fax:** Enter a telephone number, extension, and fax number where the contact can be reached.
- **Password and Confirm Password:** Create a password for accessing or reserving the resource in the **Password:** text field, then confirm the password by entering it again in the **Confirm Password:** text field.

Click **OK** when you're finished making changes.

EDITING RESOURCES

Once you create resources, you may need to edit them. For example, the contact name or location may change. Editing resources works similarly to editing users.

To edit resources, do the following:

1. Select **Properties** from the **User** menu, then choose **Search**.
2. When the **Search** window appears, select the **Resources** tab.
3. Enter information in any of the text fields and click the **Search** button to find the resource you want to edit.
4. When the resource's information displays on the list in the text area at the bottom of the window, select the resource name.
5. Click the **Properties** button.
6. When the resource information, you can change resource information.

To edit information, make your changes in the appropriate data field and click **OK** to return to the **Search** window. When you're finished editing users, click the **Close** button.

ADMINISTRATING NODES

As mentioned earlier in this chapter, Calendar is actually a database. And each of these databases is a node. If you work for a large organization, your users probably access Calendar from multiple nodes. In most cases, these nodes are on different servers. If the nodes are not properly connected, then users who connect to the network through different servers will not be able to communicate with each other via Calendar. In order to properly manage your Calendar Server(s), you'll need to frequently create and edit nodes. The following sections talk about creating, editing, deleting, and connecting nodes. In addition, you'll learn how to grant users administration rights so they can create and manage user groups.

Creating New Nodes

You can create additional nodes to handle more people or work groups when you need to. In most cases, additional nodes are created on different computers, but you can also create them on the same computer for ease of administration. This can prove useful in certain situations—for example, if you want to put nodes in two different time zones, or if you plan on eventually moving a particular node off to another computer.

To create an additional node, do the following:

1. Select **New Local Node** from the **Node** menu.
2. When the **New Local Node** dialog box appears, as shown in Figure 21-19, enter the node ID, alias, time zone, and region from the appropriate text fields and lists.
3. Click **OK**.

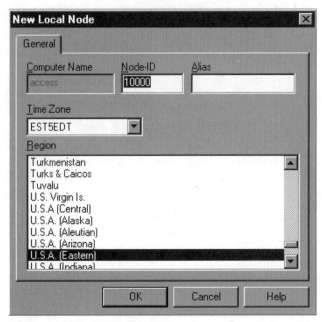

FIGURE   *New Local Node dialog box.*
21.19

Remember to enter a brand new alias and node ID for the new node.

Deleting Nodes

To delete a node, do the following:

1. Select **Properties** from the **Local Services** menu and stop all of your Calendar Server network services as explained earlier in this chapter.
2. Go to the command line and delete the directory `\users\unison\db\nodes\name of node`.
3. Delete the corresponding node section in `\users\unison\misc\unison.ini` (but don't delete the `unison.ini` file itself!).

Connecting Nodes

If you work in a very small organization you might only have one node. It is not uncommon to have quite a few nodes, however. In this case, you need to connect all of the nodes in your organization to enable people in your organization to access each other's agendas and to receive each other's entries.

To connect nodes on your Calendar Server, do the following:

1. Select **New Node Connection** from the **Connections** menu.
2. When the **Node Properties** window box appears (it displays the same information as the **New Node** dialog box), enter the name of the computer where the other node resides, and then the node ID of the other node.
3. Your next step is to determine how many total connections you want between the two. The default is 2. Just make your best estimate of the number of simultaneous connections you need. This depends on how frequently your users schedule entries with users on the other node.
4. The **Connection Retry Time/Max Retry** default value is 64 minutes. The sequence of retries is a geometric progression starting at 2 minutes and ending at 64 minutes, after which all retries are spaced 64 minutes apart. You can change this value, but the smaller the value, the higher load will be placed on your system when it is in retry mode.

Click **OK** to create the new connection. You will also need to repeat this procedure from the other server to enable it to connect to the current server.

Assigning Administration Rights for Nodes

Remember how we talked about managing groups earlier in this chapter? Unless you grant some of your coworkers administration rights, nobody will be able to create or manage groups and resources, or even declare office holidays (and you *do* want to take some holidays off, don't you?).

To assign administration rights to authorized users, do the following:

1. Select **Node Properties** from the **Node** menu.
2. When the **Node Properties** window appears, click the **Security** tab.
3. When the **Security** options appear, as shown in Figure 21-20, you can select users from the **Grant To** list and assign them the following rights from the **Rights to administer** checkboxes:
   - **Holidays:** Has the right to announce company holidays
   - **Resources:** Has the right to administer resources
   - **Public Groups—Owned by administrator:** Has the right to administer groups created by administrators and managers
   - **Public Groups—Owned by user:** Has the right to administer groups created by users.

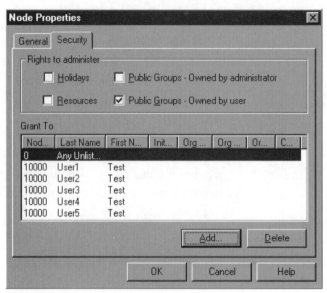

FIGURE *Node Properties window with Security tab selected.*
21.20

4. When you've selected the appropriate checkboxes for your users, click the **Add** button. To remove a user who has received administration rights, click the **Delete** button.

Click OK when you're done assigning administration rights to users.

Moving Nodes

Depending upon how fast your network requirements grow, you may have to move nodes right away, or perhaps never at all. Chances are, though, moving nodes will be a fairly common occurrence.

CAUTION

You can move nodes between NT servers or between UNIX servers, but never mix and match. It just won't work.

There are basically four steps involved in moving a node:

- **Shutting down services:** Select **Properties** from the **Local Services** menu and stop all of your Calendar Server network services as explained in the "Stopping and Starting Services" section earlier in this chapter.

- **Deleting existing node connections:** Use the process described in the "Deleting Nodes" section earlier in this chapter.
- **Copying the file from one system to the other:** Copy the `\users\unison\db\nodes\name of node` file from the originating system over to the new system, then remove the file from the old system.
- **Changing the** `unison.ini` **files:** Edit the `unison.ini` file on each computer to reflect the modifications you've made.

Your last step is to connect each node using the Calendar Server Administrator utility and modify the computer name of the node that was moved.

ROUTINE MAINTENANCE

Running a server efficiently requires routine maintenance. You should check the following on a regular basis—for large organizations, this should be at least once a day. For smaller organizations, once a week may suffice:

- **Check that all services are operational:** Select **Properties** from the **Services** menu. Started services are indicated with a flag and no entry indicates that the service is stopped.
- Verify that you have sufficient disk space available for a normal day's processing and that the previous night's backup has run.
- **Check your log file:** Log files tell you what is going on with your computer. The `dbv.log` file records problems that occur with your Calendar server. You can open the log file in a text editor like NotePad or WordPad. It is located at: `\users\unison\log\dbv.log` file.

You need to shut the server down before performing backups.

TIP

In addition, each month, the following maintenance procedures should be performed:

- Verify the consistency of the Calendar Server database
- Archive the log files
- Produce a database statistics report

CONFIGURING SERVER SETTINGS MANUALLY

Before we go, I'd like to touch on the configuration files and how you can use them manually if you wish. Ordinarily you probably won't need to use them, but it's nice to know they're there. When you enter settings with Calendar Server's Setup Wizard and menu item dialog boxes, these settings are stored in *configuration files*. Configuration files have the .ini file name extension. This section lists the configuration (.ini) files and tells you what they mean so you can familiarize yourself with them and work with them manually if you need to.

The configuration files available are:

- **unison.ini**: Contains the Calendar server parameters
- **user.ini**: Contains the default user parameters
- **resource.ini**: Contains the default resource parameters
- **timezone.ini**: Contains the timezones (DO NOT ALTER)

They are all located in the \users\unison\misc folder and are text files that you can view and edit with a text editor like WordPad or NotePad. There are mandatory and optional parameters you can set.

Configuration files include a section name (the type of setting being configured) and a list of setting names and values:

```
[SECTION NAME]
KEY_1 = VALUE_1
KEY_2 = VALUE_2
KEY_3 = VALUE_3
```

You can make changes by replacing current values with acceptable values in a text editor. For example, user settings are stored in the user.ini file. Names, addresses, organizational data, and such are included. You can specify additional configurations by adding new section names. You can even copy entire sections and simply enter new values. For example, if you want to add a configuration especially for upper managers that gives them access to everyone's events and tasks, you might add the following to the user.ini file:

```
[UPPER]
Info = Upper Managers
OU1 = Upper Managers
PersonalGroup = Upper Managers
ViewNormalEvent = Yes
ViewPersonalEvent = Yes
ViewConfidentialEvent = Yes
ViewSecretEvent = Yes
CanBookMe = FALSE
ViewNormalTask = Yes
ViewPersonalTask = Yes
```

```
ViewConfidentialTask = Yes
ViewSecretTask = Yes
CanAssign = TRUE
```

CAUTION

Do not alter the file `timezone.ini`. *It will return errors and connections will be refused.*

Configuration File Parameters

This sidebar provides tables with the `unison.ini`, `user.ini`, and `resource.ini` configuration files with a brief explanation of the configuration file parameters. Configuration file parameters consist of names paired up with values that fall within an acceptable range (such as yes or no, true or false). Name and value pairs are separated by = signs, as in: name=value.

Mandatory Parameters for `\users\unison\misc\unison.ini`

Mandatory `unison.ini` settings contain basic server settings that must have values specified.

[ENG] section	[LCK] section	[DB] section	[CWS] section
activity (**true/false**): Enables logging of sign-on/sign-offs. Default=False	lck_users (**value**): Maximum number of concurrent users (set as low as possible): Default=100	taf_max_retry (**value**): Maximum number of database locking retries: Default=100	enable (**true/false**): Starts unicwsd (the Corporate Wide services): Default=True.
max_userlogons (**value**): Limits the number of concurrent sessions per user. Default=0 (no limit)			nomail (**true/false**): No longer utilized.
max_addrlogons (**true/false**): Limits the number of "unnamed" sessions per client. Default=0 (no limit)			noreqsleep (**time_in_seconds**): Number of seconds CWS service will "sleep" before checking for requests: Default=60 seconds.
passwords (**case/ignorecase**): Specifies case-sensitivity of passwords.			startupsleep (**time-in-seconds**): Number of seconds CWS will "sleep" before checking for requests at startup: Default=15 seconds.
stats (**true/false**): Enables logging user session stats (user wait times, etc.) Default=False (no logging)			requestmaxage (**time-in-minutes**): Number of minutes CWS will wait until an unanswered request is assumed "lost": Default=2 days.

Optional Parameters for \users\unison\misc\unison.ini

Optional `unison.ini` files are basic server settings that don't have to be specified.

[CWS] section

maxmailsleep (**time-in-seconds**): Number of seconds CWS will wait before trying to connect to the mail server again.

sendmailpath (**the path**): The path to sendmail (UNIX mail program).

sncbusysleep (**time-in-seconds**): Number of seconds to wait before retrying a TCP/IP connection.

snctries (**value**): Number of retries CWS will attempt before failure is declared.

warninggap (**time-in-seconds**): Number of seconds between warning messages to Calendar Server Administrator when TCP/IP connection fails.

trace (**true/false**). Debugging/Testing mode for log entries

[LIMITS] section

autocontrol (**number_of_minutes**): Number of minutes before the client will check for new entries on the server.

mincharsearch (**characters**): Minimum number of search characters required when searching for users or resources.

mail (**true/false**): Enables mail notification.

settimezone (**true/false**): Enables the user to change timezone from the client.

resourceconflicts (**true/false**): If set to true, allows resource conflicts (double-bookings).

maxrecur (**value of max_recurs**): Defines the number of times a recurring meeting can be repeated: Default=60.

[LIMITS] section (cont'd)

.maxmaildistr (**value**): Size of the mail distribution.

maxremleadtime (**number-of-days**): Maximum lead time (in days) for a displayed reminder: Default=21 days

maxsearchresult (**value**): Sets the size of the result set from a search (number of users or resources listed).

remotewait (**value**): Seconds the client will wait before trying to make a server connection again.

allowattachments (**true/false**): Enables attachments to events or tasks.

maxattachment size (**value-in-bytes**): If attachments are allowed, specifies the maximum size.

maxwinopen (**value**): Defines the number of windows or views a user can open: Default=6 windows.

groupviewmax (**value**): Number of columns in group view: Default=30.

maxpasswordage (**number_in_days**): Number of days before users must change their password.

[SNC] section

enable (**true/false**): Starts the Calendar Synchronous Network Connection service.

[TIMEZONE] section

timezone (**timezone**): Sets the timezone.

checksum (**checksum_value**): Preset, do not alter.

[YOURNODEID] section

aliases (**names**): Aliases for the various nodes on a server, separated by commas.

localnodes (**node-IDs**): Node-IDs for the various nodes on a server, separated by commas.

User Parameters for \users\unison\misc\user.ini

Contains information about users and groups. Each user or group is specified within a section.

[DISPLAY] section	[DISPLAY] section cont'd	Default Viewing Rights section	Administrative Rights section	X.400 Address Information section
ShowSunday (**true\false**): Either shows or doesn't show Sunday.	EndDay (**00:00 to 24:00**): Sets the end time for the day.	ViewNormalEvent (**Yes, No, Time**). Sets the default Security parameter given to other users for viewing events.	CreatePublicGroups (**true\false**). Allows creation of Public Groups.	OU1 (**name**): Name of Organizational Unit 1.
ShowMonday (**true\false**): Either shows or doesn't show Monday.	TimeInc (**5, 10, 15, 20, 30, 60**): Minutes for each increment of the day.	ViewPersonalEvent (**Yes, No, Time**). Similar to above.	ManageAdmGroups (**true\false**). Allows creation of Admin Groups.	OU2 (**name**): See above. OU3 (**name**): See above.
ShowTuesday (**true\false**): Either shows or doesn't show Tuesday.	For the Refresh, Notification, and Reminders section they are:	ViewConfidentialEvent (**Yes, No, Time**). Similar to above.	ManageResources (**true\false**). Allows creation of Resources.	OU4 (**name**): See above.
ShowWednesday (**true\false**): Either shows or doesn't show Wednesday.	RefreshFrequency (**value**): Minutes between refreshes of the client.	ViewSecretEvent (**Yes, No, Time**). Similar to above.	ManageHolidays (**true\false**). Allows creation of Holidays.	O (**name**): Organization name. C (**name**): Country.
ShowThursday (**true\false**): Either shows or doesn't show Thursday.	MailNotification (**true/false**): Enables the user to receive mail notification.	CanBookMe (**true\false**). Allows others to book the user to events.		A (**name**): Administrative Domain.
ShowFriday (**true\false**): Either shows or doesn't show Friday.	DefaultReminder (**0 or 1**): 0 is disabled, 1 is enabled: Controls Pop-Up reminders.	ViewNormalTask (**Yes, No**). Similar to ViewNormalEvent, except for tasks.		P (**name**): Private Domain.
ShowSaturday (**true\false**): Either shows or doesn't show Saturday.	TimeBeforeReminder (**0, 2, 5, 10, 60, 120, 240**): Minutes between reminders: Can also use 12, 24, 48, and 96 hours, and 7, 14 and 31 days.	ViewPersonalTask (**Yes, No**). Similar to above.		
ShowLabels (**true\false**): Either shows or doesn't show labels.		ViewConfidentialTask (**Yes, No**) Similar to above.		
TimeFormat (**1 or 2**): 1 displays a 24 hour clock, 2 displays AM/PM.		ViewSecretTask (**Yes, No**): Similar to above.		
StartDay (**00:00 to 24:00**): Sets the start time for the day.		CanAssign (**true\false**): Allows others to assign user to events.		

Time Zone section	[GROUP] section	[DESIGNATE]
TimeZone (**timezone**): Defines user time zone.	Group0... Group9 (**name**): Administrative group name.	Designate0... Designate9 (**name**): Defines Designates for the user.

Resource Parameters for \users\unison\misc\resource.ini

Contains information about resources. Each resource is specified within its own section.

[DISPLAY] section	Refresh, Notification and Reminders section	Default Viewing Rights section
ShowSunday (**true\false**): Either shows or doesn't show Sunday.	RefreshFrequency (**value**): Minutes between refreshes of the client.	ViewNormalEvent (**Yes, No, Time**): Sets the default Security parameter given to other users for viewing events.
ShowMonday (**true\false**): Either shows or doesn't show Monday.	MailNotification (**true/false**): Enables the user to receive mail notification.	ViewPersonalEvent (**Yes, No, Time**): Similar to above.
ShowTuesday (**true\false**): Either shows or doesn't show Tuesday.	DefaultReminder (**0 or 1**): 0 is disabled, 1 is enabled: Controls Pop-Up reminders.	ViewConfidentialEvent (**Yes, No, Time**): Similar to above.
ShowWednesday (**true\false**): Either shows or doesn't show Wednesday.	TimeBeforeReminder (**0, 2, 5, 10, 60, 120, 240**): Minutes between reminders: Can also use 12, 24, 48, and 96 hours, and 7, 14, and 31 days.	ViewSecretEvent (**Yes, No, Time**): Similar to above.
ShowThursday (**true\false**): Either shows or doesn't show Thursday.		CanBookMe (**true\false**): Allows others to book the user to events.
ShowFriday (**true\false**): Either shows or doesn't show Friday.		ViewNormalTask (**Yes, No**): Similar to ViewNormalEvent, except for tasks.
ShowSaturday (**true\false**): Either shows or doesn't show Saturday.		ViewPersonalTask (**Yes, No**): Similar to above.
ShowLabels (**true\false**): Either shows or doesn't show labels.		ViewConfidentialTask (**Yes, No**) Similar to above.
TimeFormat (**1 or 2**): 1 displays a 24 hour clock, 2 displays AM/PM.		ViewSecretTask (**Yes, No**): Similar to above.
StartDay (**00:00 to 24:00**): Sets the start time for the day.		CanAssign (**true\false**): Allows others to assign user to events.
EndDay (**00:00 to 24:00**): Sets the end time for the day.		
TimeInc (**5, 10, 15, 20, 30, 60**): Minutes for each increment of the day.		

Time Zone section	[GROUP] section	[DESIGNATE] section:
TimeZone (**timezone**): Defines user time zone.	PersonalGroup (**name**): Administrative group name. Group0... Group9 (**name**): Adds resource to specified admin group.	Designate0... Designate9 (**name**): Defines Designates for the user.

Index

About the
CD-ROM

The CD-ROM included with this book provides users with THREE FREE software programs. All three run on Windows and Macintosh machines.

THE HTML TEMPLATEMASTER CD
by Erica Sadun

This award-winning product teaches you HTML through ready-to-use templates and clip-art. You'll learn how to create effective home pages, design fill-out forms, and code HTML.

Features:
- Step-by-step tutorials and templates allow you to create your own web pages
- Compatible with the latest versions of most browsers including Netscape Navigator and Microsoft Internet Explorer.
- Includes a full range of clip-art and icons, e.g. sports, flowers, animals, cartoons, etc.

System Requirements:
PC running Windows 3.1 or 95 or a Mac running System 7 or later. Both systems require at least 4MB RAM (8MB recommended); hard disk drive, CD-ROM drive, web browser, and a word processing program (Microsoft Word recommended).

- Some templates and tutorials may not work with the latest version of your browser.

Installation:
1. Insert CD into CD drive
2. Open your web browser
3. From the Web Browser choose the FILE menu
4. Then select "OPEN FILE…" or "OPEN LOCAL" option
5. Open the file "start.htm" (PC) or "start.html" (MAC)

THE JAVASCRIPT CD COOKBOOK
by Erica Sadun

Make your web pages come alive with the templates and recipes included in this program. You'll learn everything you need to know about JavaScript with the complete reference and tutorials provided.

Features:
- Add excitement to your existing web pages including blinking and colorized frames, pop-up messages, and more.
- Includes over 100 templates including JavaScript games, cookies, colorizing tips, status bar tricks, and strings
- Complete section on JavaScript data structures with a discussion of the object model, creating and using arrays, pointers and trees.

System Requirements:
PC running Windows 3.1 or 95 or a Mac running System 7 or later. Both systems require at least 4MB RAM (8MB recommended); hard disk drive, CD-ROM drive, web browser (if using Netscape Navigator, you must have version 2.0 or higher), and a word processing program (Microsoft Word recommended).

- Some templates and features may not work with the latest version of your browser.

Installation:
1. Insert the CD into the CD drive
2. Run your browser
3. From your browser, choose the FILE menu
4. Then select the "OPEN FILE" option
5. Open file to: MAC: start.html, PC: START.HTM, UNIX: START .HTM

THE INTERNET WATCHDOG
Developed by Algorithm, Inc.

This innovative program is a monitoring device that records all computer activity. Instead of trying to block sites that change daily, it allows parents, teachers, and employers to monitor their students or employees' activities.

- Helps you monitor all Internet activity including WWW, using email, FTP, Gopher, or Internet Relay Chat (IRC).
- Complements existing blocking software by taking intermittent "snapshots" of computer activity and Internet sites visited
- Tamper-evident feature(with password protection) monitors and records any attempt to disable or elude the program.
- Locates graphics files by scanning your hard disk to find suscpicious graphic files, whether they are hidden or not

A guided tour is included to ensure that you know exactly how to use Watch-Dog!

System Requirements:
PC running Windows 3.1 or 95 or a Mac running System 7.0 or higher. Both require a least 4MB RAM and a hard disk drive.

Installation:
Windows 3.1
1. Insert CD into CD drive
2. Choose RUN from the Program Manager file
3. Type a:install and press Enter
4. Choose hard disk letter and click install button
5. Double-click on the Internet WatchDog icon

For Windows 95
1. Click on Internet WatchDog folder
2. Click on the Install icon and follow the instructions.

For Macintosh
1. Insert CD into CD drive
2. Select the WatchDog folder
3. Double-click on the "installer" icon
4. Follow the prompts and re-boot your computer

Note: After installation: Pre-system 7.5 users may need to drag AppleGuide and AppleScript icons (located in "WatchDog" folder) into their system folders.

You may also refer to the electronic version of the manual included in the folder called Manual.